ORACLE®

Oracle Press™

Oracle Self-Service Applications

Melanie Anjele Cameron

New York   Chicago   San Francisco
Lisbon   London   Madrid   Mexico City   Milan
New Delhi   San Juan   Seoul   Singapore   Sydney   Toronto

The McGraw·Hill Companies

Library of Congress Cataloging-in-Publication Data

Cameron, Melanie Anjele.
  Oracle self-service applications / Melanie Anjele Cameron.
    p. cm.
  ISBN 978-0-07-171330-6 (pbk.)
  1. Oracle E-business suite. 2. Accounting—Data processing. 3. Electronic commerce—Computer programs. I. Title.
  HF5548.323.O73C366   2010
  005.75'65—dc22   2010004366

Oracle Self-Service Applications

1 2 3 4 5 6 7 8 9 0   WFR WFR   1 0 9 8 7 6 5 4 3 2 1 0

ISBN   978-0-07-171330-6
MHID   0-07-171330-1

Sponsoring Editor Lisa McClain	**Acquisitions Coordinator** Meghan Riley	**Indexer** Claire Splan	**Art Director, Cover** Jeff Weeks
Editorial Supervisor Janet Walden	**Technical Editor** Colin Terry	**Production Supervisor** Jean Bodeaux	**Cover Designer** Pattie Lee
Project Manager Vastavikta Sharma, Glyph International	**Copy Editor** Robert Campbell	**Composition** Glyph International	
	Proofreader Claire Splan	**Illustration** Glyph International	

*For Josie and Yuki, sleeping at my feet during
the long nights spent writing this book.*

About the Author

Melanie Anjele Cameron has dedicated her career to improving business processes and business systems, especially in the areas of finance and accounting. Always strongly believing in sharing her knowledge about computer systems and how to use them, she has been the chairperson for the AZOAUG, the Phoenix geographical Oracle applications users group, for the past eight years, participating not only in scheduling the events, but also as a lecturer. Her career has taken her from being a transaction processing clerk to an executive during an IPO, as well as co-owner of her husband's business, leaving her knowledge of business well rounded and in depth, from detailed transactions to their broader impact on the business itself. Melanie works for an alternative energy company, Southwest Windpower, Inc., as the International Controller, managing their Oracle applications.

While participating in the high-tech world of business, Melanie keeps her feet firmly planted in the low-tech world of needlework, spending most of her non-working hours knitting and creating pieces of art with a needle, including needlepoint and Japanese embroidery. This, combined with a love for good food and cooking, helps to keep the pressures of our high-tech society at bay. Melanie lives in Phoenix, Arizona, with her husband, Bill, and two dogs, Josie and Yuki.

About the Technical Editor

Colin Terry is a Chartered Management Accountant who works as an independent consultant in the ERP software and associated applications arena. Relying on his accounting background, his primary area of expertise is financial applications, and most of his experience has involved Oracle E-Business Suite. He has a strong understanding of much of the Oracle E-Business Suite product set and has had exposure to a number of other software applications, both COTS and proprietary.

Since originally transferring from the Accounting function to Information Systems & Technology some fifteen years ago, Colin has taken on roles encompassing business process design, applications configuration, training, test execution and management, data migration, and support. He has been engaged to work for companies in a wide range of industry sectors, including Aerospace and Defense, Software Publishing and Distribution, and Public Transport. Colin is an active volunteer for the UK Oracle User Group and is currently chairman of the Financials Special Interest Group.

Contents at a Glance

Contents

Acknowledgments

Writing a book is a very personal goal—not only to share in your thoughts and knowledge, but also to leave something lasting that will make an impact on other people. While manuals are not often thought of as having large impact on a particular person or organization, my sincerest hope is that this book will help someone be more successful in their position, and a company more productive.

Every technical author has two groups of people assisting to get the concept to market. The first is the editors at their publisher, and Lisa McClain and her staff have been about as helpful and patient as any author can ask for. From late-night panic e-mails to re-explaining the formatting requirements yet again, these saints all deserve halos. Second are their technical editors. Colin Terry took the time to review and ensure that this book not only brought you accurate information, but complete information and in a logical order. While all these people worked hard to ensure that there are no mistakes in this book, any mistakes that were overlooked are fully my responsibility, and no reflection on their diligent efforts.

Introduction

From being a user to an implementer, an executive to a clerk, I am a firm believer in utilizing business systems to achieve the wealth of information required to run businesses today. The systems that support corporations today are not the columnar ledgers of our ancestors. They are robust and provide in-depth insight into an organization—that is, if you can figure out what they do and how to do it. As a user of Oracle E-Business Suite, I was often frustrated by the lack of information surrounding specific functionality or fields. I have spent hours or, in a few cases, years, acquiring the information I needed to incorporate a specific functionality into my company's processes so that we could improve not only the information, but the time frame the information was available in. Another frustration is seeing products that are purchased and paid for become shelfware. This happens for many reasons, from lack of resources to implement the software, to lack of understanding as to how the software can save an organization not only money, but also time, to changing business needs. The intent of this book is to help organizations, at the executive, technical, and the user levels, understand the benefits of the self-service modules, to decide whether they can benefit your company, and to understand what it takes to implement them.

This book offers insight into what each self-service module can do for an organization, and the steps required to achieve the benefits. Since every company has different needs, the modules will not be implemented in the same way—some organizations will spend months using 100 percent of the functionality and rolling it out to hundreds of users, while others will spend less then a week rolling it out to a few key users. Companies of both sorts will achieve greater insight into the information available to them, and reduce their employee's workload, saving both time and money. But this cannot be achieved without understanding what the modules can do, and what it will take to make them do it. And that is where this book comes into play.

Each chapter is designed to enable you to understand what a module can do, and how the desired functionality can be achieved. There are a few hidden features discussed as well, that can be incorporated into your current production environment, such as Approvals Management, Bill Presentment Architecture to customize your invoices, and OA Framework to get you started on customizing the look of the self-service modules. These features can be used even without implementing any of the self-service modules.

CHAPTER
1

Role of Self-Service Modules in an Organization

ll organizations have processes that require forms to be filled out, approvals to be obtained, and then the information to be processed by other "service" departments within the organization, such as Human Resources or Accounting. These processes can be time intensive when the same data has to be rekeyed by multiple employees. A good example is expense reimbursement. Employees complete expense reports, often spreadsheet based, which are manually routed to managers for approval, and then to accounting for policy compliance and ultimate payment.

Adding corporate credit cards can increase the workload, where employees will have two different processes, one for submitting cash transactions and another for approving credit card transactions for payment. Companies report the cost of processing just one expense report is as high as $25. Reducing the amount of time related to processing these transactions can be achieved by reducing the number of duplicate and manual steps involved within the processes. This is exactly what Oracle's Self-Service modules are designed to do.

iProcurement

iProcurement was developed to automate both the requesting and approval of purchases within an organization. It allows employees to "go shopping" from their desktops from lists of approved items to purchase, and it automates the approval of the requisitions. By definition, *requisitions* are internal requests to purchase an item, while *purchase orders* are external agreements with third-party suppliers to purchase an item. The creation and approval of a requisition does not replace the purchasing function, as these requisitions, once approved, are then routed to the purchasing department, where they are combined for reduced shipping costs and to take advantage of volume discounts and supplier specials and routed to the suppliers for fulfillment. This last step is part of Oracle's core Purchasing module, and not iProcurement.

iProcurement reduces the time it takes for employees to request the items they need to do their jobs in three different ways. First, it requires data entry only one time for requisitions, where the approvers and buyers utilize the same information already entered by the requestor. Second, approvals are completed online, allowing rejections, changes, and tracking during the approval process by not only the requestors and approvers, but also the buyers. Third, providing a catalog of items and approved suppliers the requestors can shop from controls the costs of the items most commonly purchased.

iProcurement provides a web-based interface where employees can shop for items, either from an internal catalog or by using a secure punchout to a third-party web site. These purchases are assigned General Ledger account numbers, based on predefined rules, and submitted for approval. Oracle has several options for approval hierarchies and uses e-mail to route the requests for approval. Approvers have the ability to update accounting information. The approved request is then sent to purchasing, which can group requisitions from multiple employees together to take advantage of volume discounts, as well as change or assign the supplier to the order. When the item is received, the requestor can use iProcurement to receive the item and allow matching between the purchase orders, receipts, and payables invoices. Notifications are sent to the requestors for items that are not received in a specific time period.

iProcurement also offers the ability to associate Purchasing Cards, or P-Cards, to the request, which gets associated with the approved purchase order and sent to the supplier, who will charge the card when the items are shipped. An interface also exists to reconcile these P-Card purchases with the actual credit card settlement and payment in Payables.

iExpense

Expense reimbursement is one of the most labor-intensive tasks for not only accounting, but also the employees completing the expense reports. Add in the need to charge different General Ledger accounts depending on the person incurring the expense as well as the purpose of the expense, and the process can become time consuming. iExpense, at the most basic level, reduces the repetitiveness of entering, approving, and auditing expense reports by creating the accounting based on different aspects of the expenses submitted, assigning rules for the amounts the employees are allowed to submit (such as per diems or mileage reimbursement), automating management approvals based on flexible rules, providing an audit feature for accounting, and interfacing directly into Oracle Payables.

At the higher end, iExpense also allows integration with credit card companies, allowing the employees to approve and submit both cash and credit expense reports with the same integrated tool.

Taking Self-Service Outside Your Company's Walls

Enabling employees from other companies, as well as your own company, to reduce your cost to process both your payables and receivables is becoming more and more popular as companies look to trim costs wherever they can. While Self-Service modules tend not to reduce the number of questions asked, they do reduce the time your employees spend answering them.

iSupplier

iSupplier allows your suppliers to access information directly in your system, reducing phone calls while actually providing better service by allowing them 24/7 access to the data. This is especially useful in today's globalized economy where suppliers and customers can span multiple time zones. Suppliers can have access to purchase orders, and to any changes or cancellations to them, receiving transactions, agreements, and financial information, such as invoices and their payment status, all dependent on the access you give them. This information is not only useful to the supplier, but also to employees of your own organization. Buyers and planners will benefit from both the purchasing and payables information, while your payables processors can see purchase orders. This information is presented in a cleaner format than that of the traditional inquiry forms within Oracle.

iReceivables

Like iSupplier, iReceivables allows your customers to have access to data in your system, allowing them to view as well as request changes to their billing information, including address changes, and to request credit memos. Payments can be accepted via iReceivables with both credit cards and bank transfers. Invoices, aging information, and summaries are also available for the customers, providing the information the customers need to make timely payments. Giving customer service and sales people access to iReceivables allows them a better view of the company's financial relationship with a customer, enabling them to make more informed decisions and faster responses when working with a customer.

Order Management Portal

Oracle provides an inquiry-only basis for viewing and tracking orders and their delivery status. While not actually a module, it is part of Order Management and can be granted to both internal and external users for a global view of a specific customer's order.

iAssets

While not part of the scope of this book, iAssets is worth mentioning as a module that can enable internal employees and greatly reduce the paperwork involved with transferring assets within Oracle's Asset module. Tracking who owns or which department receives the depreciation expense associated with an asset is a time-consuming process to keep up to date, especially for large organizations. Enabling employees to request most types of asset transfers online will reduce the paperwork involved with this task, as well as the time it takes for the requests to reach the asset accounting.

All of these modules are designed to remove the data entry and to provide information outside of the accounting department, placing it in the hands of the end users, not only decreasing processing time, but also decreasing the time to receive payments and procure items needed to make your business run smoothly.

CHAPTER
2

Common Implementation
Considerations

hen implementing a Self-Service application, there are some key implementation considerations that apply to all the modules. What do you want users to be able to *do*? What will they be able to *see*? How much hand-holding will they need to achieve their goal?

What Do You Want Users to Be Able to Do?

The features available on internal views for iSupplier and iReceivables as well as iProcurement and iExpense are pretty much controlled by the *setups*. For example, if you do not use the credit card processing feature in iExpense, the credit card features will not appear for users to select when the system is not set up to load and process them. And in iProcurement, if you are not going to use a punchout, there will be no punchout store available to shop from.

The options available on externally facing responsibilities, on the other hand, are controlled by the *functions* that are assigned to the responsibility. Functions determine what buttons and navigation paths are available for the users to select. When working in iReceivables, the Dispute button will appear even if you have not set up the Credit Memo Request process, allowing the users to attempt to dispute an item. Unfortunately, the request will error out in the Workflow process if this feature is not set up. Control of whether users can even see the Dispute button is via a function on the menu associated with the responsibility, which is then assigned to the user. Functions can be removed either by creating a new menu or by excluding the function on the responsibility itself. All of this work is done in the System Administrator responsibility.

Menus

Menus are a grouping of *submenus* and *functions*. Submenus group other menus and functions together, while functions control access to an individual feature. It is a tree-like structure, where you need to find the lowest level where the function exists, modify that, and then rebuild the tree to the highest level. Oracle comes seeded with a large number of menus. While these are often used as the building blocks to create the tree structure, in general, they are not modified, and custom menus are created for any modifications. Since the seeded menus are updated with patches from time to time to include new functions and features, and if you were to modify the seeded ones, your modifications may be overwritten. The opposite holds true for custom menus: any changes to a seeded menu introduced with a patch for new functionality will have to be made manually to your custom menus (for example, if a function name changes or new functions are added).

To modify a menu, first find the top-level menu. This is most easily done by looking at what menu is assigned to the responsibility you want to modify (System Administrator | Security | Responsibility | Define). Query up the responsibility and note the MENU associated with it. This is the top level of the tree and will call all the submenus. For example, the menu associated with the responsibility called iSupplier Portal Full Access is called the iSupplier Portal New Application Menu.

Next, query up the menu and find the submenus that are assigned to it (see Figure 2-1). You can see that the only function is the home page, and you will need to review the next menu, the iSP HOMEPAGE Menu, to find additional functions available in iSupplier. This menu also calls multiple other menus, which align with the tabs available in iSupplier. One of the submenus, Account, is where you can create invoices. Here you can see that the function Create Invoices is being called under Prompt Create Invoices (see Figure 2-2). In this case, you would need to create

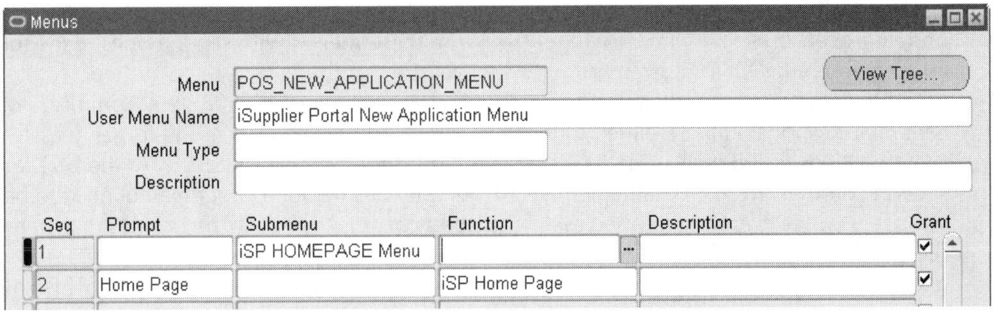

System Administrator I Application I Menu

FIGURE 2-1. *Submenus and functions assigned to a menu*

a new menu that does not have the FUNCTIONS associated with the PROMPT Create Invoices. Since this is two layers down on the tree structure, you need to create new menus for the next two levels as well. In other words, you would need a new menu to replace the iSupplier Portal New Application Menu, and one for the iSP HOMEPAGE Menu.

When creating new menus, a good rule of thumb is to uniquely identify the menu as custom with the name assigned in the MENU field. This is a unique, internal code for the menu and should contain no spaces. Usually, a naming convention is established where the menu will begin with

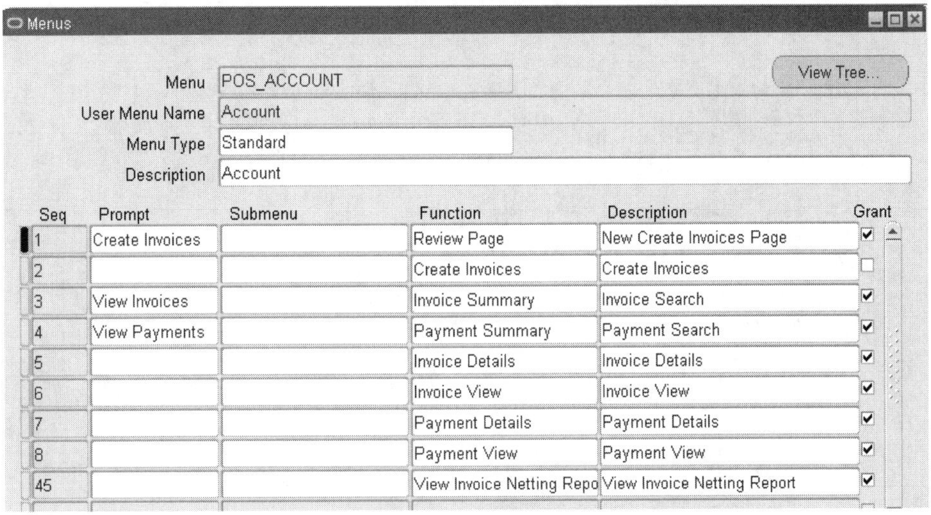

System Administrator I Application I Menu

FIGURE 2-2. *Function for creating invoices in iSupplier*

XX and two or three letters that identifies your company. For example, if your company name is Cannon Fighting Systems, you would use XXCFS. This not only makes the custom menus easy to find, it also ensures that Oracle will not overwrite these menus with seeded ones in the future, as they are reserving XX for customer modifications.

The menu then needs to be associated with a new responsibility (System Administrator | Security | Responsibility | Define). Once the responsibility is defined, don't forget to assign the profile options to it before using it (System Administrator | Profile | System). At the very least, the securing profiles (MO: Operating Unit, MO: Security Profile, GL Ledger Name) need to be set. If you are working on an established system, a good cheat is to review the profiles that were set for the existing responsibility that is being used. When querying up the profiles, *select* RESPONSIBILITY and the name from the list of values, then *unselect* SITE and PROFILES WITH NO VALUES. This will show you only the profiles that are populated for a specific responsibility.

Adding an Exclusion to a Responsibility

Without creating a custom menu, you can also exclude specific menu functions and submenus from a specific responsibility (see Figure 2-3). Since multiple responsibilities can call the same menu, this would limit the number of menus that are needed. You will still need to look at the menu and drill down into it to find out what function or submenu you need to exclude.

I have used both these options equally over the years and have found pros and cons to both methods. First, custom menus can be reused multiple times in different menu trees and responsibilities. While the same is true with associating menus with a responsibility, you have to

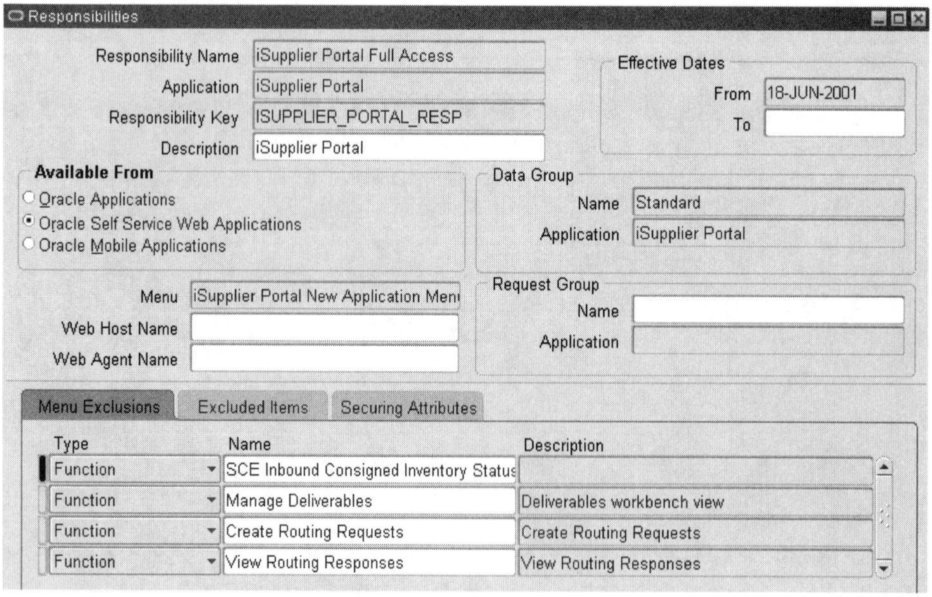

System Administrator | Security | Responsibility | Define

FIGURE 2-3. *Adding exclusions to a responsibility*

make the exclusions with each individual responsibility, and if you have multiple operating units, this can be more work than creating one menu that can be reused with each responsibility. The other consideration is that responsibility exclusions are not always selected by the audit scripts commonly used today during Sarbanes-Oxley audits to check access and segregation of duties, and they can take some explaining.

Common Functions for Self-Service Exclusion

Table 2-1 shows the common functions that you will want to review during your implementation.

Module	Function	Purpose
iReceivables	iReceivables Apply Credits Cm Flow Starting Page	Apply credit memos
iReceivables	iReceivables Apply Credits Inv Flow Starting Page	Apply credit memos
iReceivables	iReceivables Apply Credits Open Invoices Confirmation Page	Apply credit memos
iReceivables	iReceivables Manage Customer Access	Request additional access
iReceivables	iReceivables Print Requests Page	Print transactions
iReceivables	iReceivables Self-Registration Access	Registration
iReceivables	Pay Invoices	Process invoice payment
iSupplier	Acknowledge Purchase Order	Acknowledge purchase order
iSupplier	Cancel ASN	Cancel a loaded ASN
iSupplier	Cancel Purchase Order	Cancel purchase orders
iSupplier	Change Purchase Order	Request a change to a purchase order
iSupplier	Create Advance Shipment Billing Notice	Load or create ASBNs
iSupplier	Create Invoices	Create invoices
iSupplier	Create Work Confirmations	Allows creation of work confirmations
iSupplier	Creating Routing Requests	Allows routing requests to be made
iSupplier	Maintain Purchase Orders	Update and cancel purchase orders
iSupplier	Maintain Work Orders	Update work order deliveries
iSupplier	Manage Bank Account Assignments	Update banking information on the supplier
iSupplier	Manage Contract Deliverables	Update contract deliverables

TABLE 2-1. *Functions That Perform Actions in iReceivables and iSupplier* (continued)

Module	Function	Purpose
iSupplier	Manage Deliverables for POS	Allows updates to deliverables
iSupplier	Order Modifiers	Update order modifiers
iSupplier	PO Edit Agreement Submenu (this is a submenu—remove the entire submenu to remove this feature)	Allows global agreements to be edited
iSupplier	Requisition Creation (for Vendor Managed Inventory only)	Create requisitions
iSupplier	Review Page	Review invoice creation
iSupplier	Sign Purchase Order	e-Signature for PO acknowledgments
iSupplier	Supplier New/Edit Bank Account	Update banking information on the supplier
iSupplier	Supplier View: Surveys	Removes the Survey tab
iSupplier	Supplier: Supplier View: Add/Update Contact	Update contact information
iSupplier	Supplier: Supplier View: Create/Update Address	Update supplier address
iSupplier	Update Capacity	Update capacity information
iSupplier	View-Create ASN	Load or create ASNs

TABLE 2-1. *Functions That Perform Actions in iReceivables and iSupplier* (continued)

A similar review may be desired of the ability to view data, removing what the supplier or customer will not need access to and eliminating user confusion. My experience is if they can click it, they will, and if it returns an error or nothing, they will ask.

What Will Users Be Able to See?

Most times, when I ask this question, the immediate response I get is Invoices, Orders, etc. That is actually part of the first question, what do you want users to be able to do? This question has more to do with the data in your system, and its consistency and integrity. For example, if you are rolling out iSupplier, do you have problems with duplicate invoices being entered into Oracle? Are duplicate suppliers or customers being created and used? Are purchase orders closed in a timely basis? Are invoices paid on time according to the supplier's terms? For iReceivables, were on account payments entered as credit memos during your conversion? Are a large number of zero-dollar invoices being created from Order Management?

All of these things can confuse a supplier or customer, and perhaps have them lose confidence in the data in your system as well as your ability to do business with them. While for the vast majority of companies this is not an issue, there are enough out there with problems that this needs to be mentioned. Often times, the decision to use iSupplier or iReceivables is not a decision made by the finance department, but by the sales or purchasing teams, who are not familiar with the data in Receivables or Payables, and its accuracy. The main purpose of these self-service modules is to reduce questions and increase collaboration, not only for payment, but for delivery of products as well, and providing inaccurate or questionable data can reverse these benefits and have the opposite effect.

Ensuring you have tight accounting controls in place will help to eliminate these problems. These controls include (but are not limited to) Customer and Supplier creation procedures that ensure duplicates are not created, as well as a review process to merge duplicates when they do happen. To prevent duplicate invoices, add invoice entry procedures for Payables to ensure invoices are not entered with modifications to the invoice number, such as a period or letter at the end, as well as to ensure invoices are entered only from original documents and never from statements.

If you are new to Oracle, ensure you clean up both your transactional and master data prior to converting to Oracle. This includes reviewing master data (items, customers, suppliers) for relevance in terms of historical and future usage, and applying open transactions, such as prepayments and credit or debit memos, to their corresponding transactions, as well as cleaning up old transactions that may not be relevant, prior to converting to Oracle. If you are a long-time Oracle user, then do the cleanup prior to rolling out the self-service applications to your customers and suppliers. Decide if any zero-dollar invoices from Order Management are still relevant to both the customer and receivables, and update the setups in Order Management to no longer generate these, if this is appropriate. And most important, ensure old sales orders, work orders, and purchase orders are closed in a timely basis, either by setting the proper tolerance levels or by reviewing them on a regular basis for relevance.

While these controls reach out and touch many modules and departments within an organization, it is usually accounting that has a vested interest in ensuring they are followed, because not following them makes collections, supplier payments, and the financial data that is generated from them inaccurate and difficult to manage. Outside the accounting department, the controls will also ensure your purchasing is accurate as well as your manufacturing processes, driving demand and scheduling. For these reasons, it is a good idea to ensure they are implemented even when the self-service modules are not being rolled out at your company.

Rolling out the self-service modules internally first can help with the cleanup, allowing purchasing agents and salespersons to see the data and work with the customers to clean up the outstanding transactions, as well as see what types of questions may come up.

How Much Hand-Holding Will Users Need to Achieve Your Goal?

This is a usability question. And it applies to *all* self-service modules, not just externally facing ones. If an employee needs assistance entering an expense report in iExpense every time, but that employee is able to submit a paper form without assistance, then the time savings expected may not be achieved. Creating custom menus can help, and creating your setups with the end user in mind can also be of assistance. For example, the way you set up your templates in iExpense can directly affect the user experience when entering expense reports. But these can only go so far.

A good example of a seeded Oracle process that is not straightforward is submitting an invoice in iSupplier that is not associated with a purchase order. This requires that a Requestor Email, First name, or Last name be entered, and that it must match a user record in Oracle (and the search is case sensitive). This field is not explained in any way, nor marked as required. Most first-time users will not be able to get past this page. And a casual user will probably need to be assisted every time. Using Oracle's OA (Oracle Application) Framework Personalization features allows you to add tips and company branding, as well as make fields required or hide fields. The next section is not intended to be a comprehensive guide to everything you can do with OA Framework, but a basic introduction to get you started with the most commonly used features.

Using OA Framework to Add a Tip

To access the personalization's page, you must enable the profiles FND: Personalization Region Link Enabled and Personalize Self-Service Defn. Usually, these are enabled at the User level for yourself only. This will make the Personalize "Home Page . . ." links available in any framework page. EBS presents information either in a form or using OA Framework. Forms will open up three windows when you sign in to Oracle, and the work area is contained within the final window, while Framework uses Internet Explorer, Netscape, or Firefox to display the data. Currently, Oracle is moving toward the OA Framework pages and beginning to doing away with the forms-based pages. The personalization link is shown in Figure 2-4.

Each link will show the content that it controls, allowing you not only to change the order in which the data appears but also to add a personalization. In this example, we are going to add a Tip to the top of the page in iSupplier Portal. First, click the personalization link. (I selected Personalize "Home Page Right Column." The links are hierarchical, and this will display only this region. If I selected Personalize "Home Page Top Container," I could still get to the same section by moving down in the hierarchy.) The window shown in Figure 2-5 will open. This will display the content for the region. To add a Tip, you are going to use the Create Item link. Select the one next to the area where you want the personalization to exist. So to add a Tip in the right column of the page, select Create Item in the row Flow Layout: Home Page Right Column.

Next, select the Item Style called Tip, and add an ID, the only required field. Select Apply. This will make the Tip appear at the very bottom of the section and it can be updated with the actual tip by selecting Update Item (see Figure 2-6). Now you can add the actual text of the Tip in the Text field. As shown in Figure 2-6, the Tip was added at the bottom of the section and will need to be re-ordered to display on the top of the page. Use the Reorder link to do this. Again, this is a hierarchical tree, and you need to reorder at the level your Tip was associated with, which is the Flow Layout: Home Page Right Column. Figure 2-7 shows how the content on the page can be reordered, and Figure 2-8 shows the Tip as the user will see it.

FIGURE 2-4. *OA Framework personalization link*

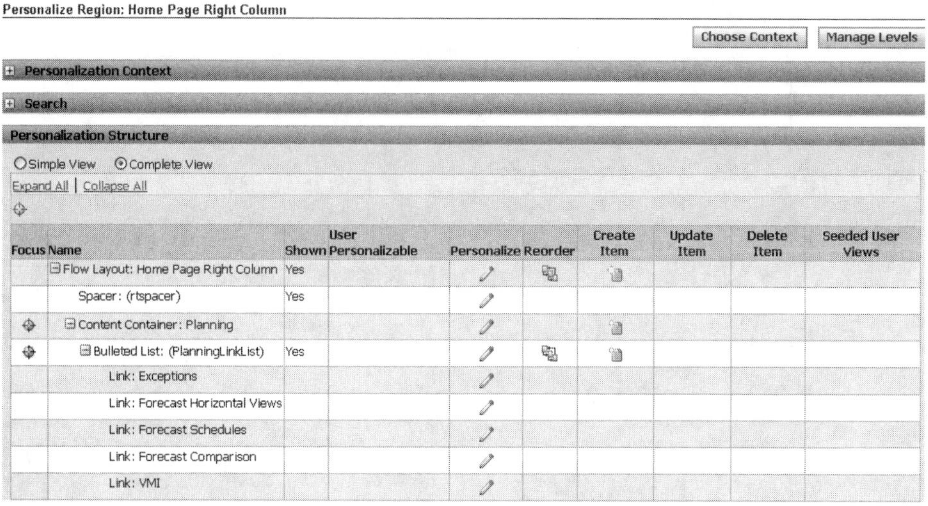

Personalize Region: Home Page Right Column

					Choose Context		Manage Levels	

⊞ **Personalization Context**

⊞ **Search**

Personalization Structure

○ Simple View   ◉ Complete View

Expand All | Collapse All

⊕

Focus	Name	Shown	User Personalizable	Personalize	Reorder	Create Item	Update Item	Delete Item	Seeded User Views
	⊟ Flow Layout: Home Page Right Column	Yes		✎	▥	🗑			
	Spacer: (rtspacer)	Yes		✎					
⊕	⊟ Content Container: Planning			✎		🗑			
⊕	⊟ Bulleted List: (PlanningLinkList)	Yes		✎	▥	🗑			
	Link: Exceptions			✎					
	Link: Forecast Horizontal Views			✎					
	Link: Forecast Schedules			✎					
	Link: Forecast Comparison			✎					
	Link: VMI			✎					

FIGURE 2-5.   *Personalization region*

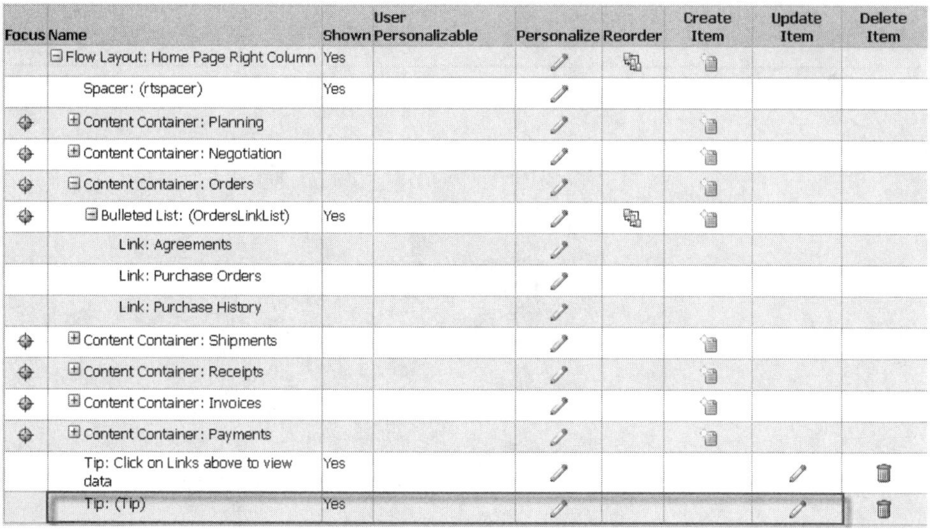

Focus	Name	Shown	User Personalizable	Personalize	Reorder	Create Item	Update Item	Delete Item
	⊟ Flow Layout: Home Page Right Column	Yes		✎	▥	🗑		
	Spacer: (rtspacer)	Yes		✎				
⊕	⊞ Content Container: Planning			✎		🗑		
⊕	⊞ Content Container: Negotiation			✎		🗑		
⊕	⊟ Content Container: Orders			✎		🗑		
⊕	⊟ Bulleted List: (OrdersLinkList)	Yes		✎	▥	🗑		
	Link: Agreements			✎				
	Link: Purchase Orders			✎				
	Link: Purchase History			✎				
⊕	⊞ Content Container: Shipments			✎		🗑		
⊕	⊞ Content Container: Receipts			✎		🗑		
⊕	⊞ Content Container: Invoices			✎		🗑		
⊕	⊞ Content Container: Payments			✎		🗑		
	Tip: Click on Links above to view data	Yes		✎			✎	🗑
	Tip: (Tip)	Yes		✎			✎	🗑

FIGURE 2-6.   *Finding the Tip to add the content*

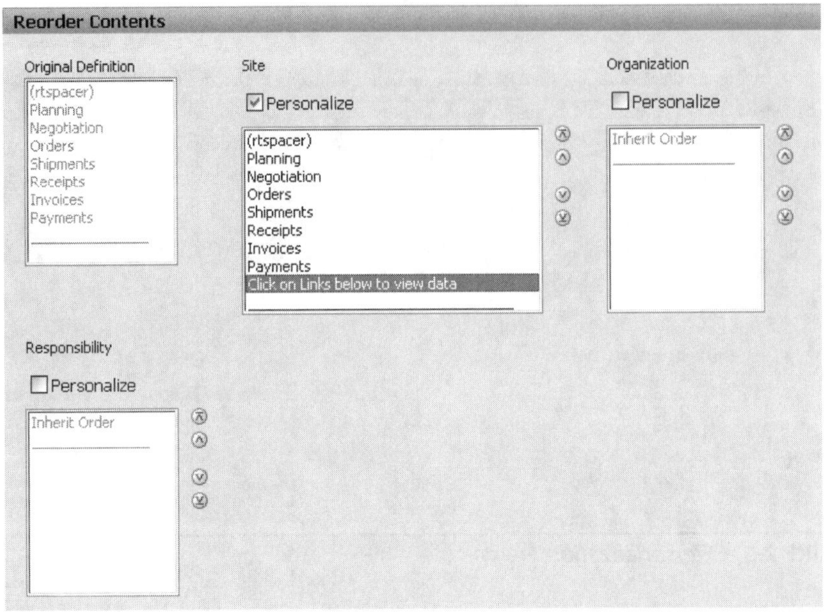

FIGURE 2-7. *Reordering content on a page*

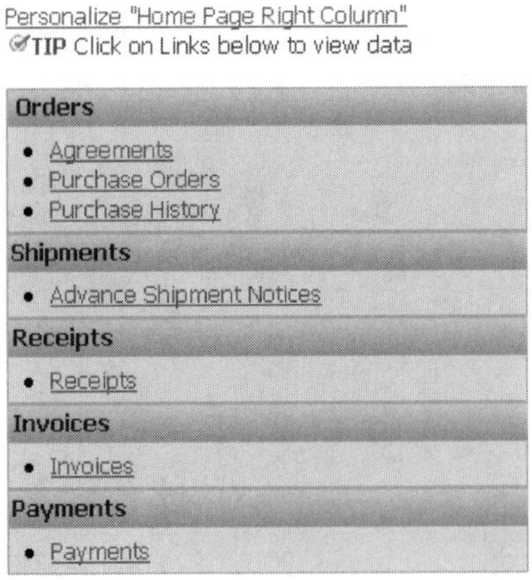

FIGURE 2-8. *Tip added to iSupplier*

Making a Field Required

Another common change is to make a field required. In general, you will only do this for fields where data is entered and not for check boxes. For example, in iProcurement, the field I NEED A PURCHASE ORDER NUMBER IMMEDIATELY defaults the value to N, so making the field required does not change the functionality of the form, since a default value already exists.

Using the Personalize Table Layout link for the region where the information you want to update resides, select the Personalize pencil next to the field you want to make required. For example, when entering a non-catalog request in iProcurement (iProcurement | Shop | Non-Catalog Request), SUPPLIER NAME is not a required field. To update the field and make it required, first select Personalize Table Layout: (InfoTableLayout). Then select the Personalize link next to Message LOV Input: Supplier Name. This level of the tree may be hidden, in which case you can use the plus sign next to Cell Format: (SupplierInfoCell) to display it. Referring to Figure 2-9, note that fields can be updated at the Site, Organization, or Responsibility level. These levels work the same as system profiles, where Oracle will look for the setting first at the Responsibility, then the Organization, and finally the Site. It will look for the first level that is personalized and take that setting. This allows you to create different personalizations for different organizations or responsibilities that are specific to a group of users.

There are several settings for each field, and Oracle displays the default value that will be used unless a personalization exists. Find the setting for Required at the bottom of the window, and change the value at the appropriate level from Inherit to Yes. Notice that all the fields are set to Inherit, which basically means use the default value. The list next to each setting gives a list of the valid values you can set to override the default. Once applied, the field will be required when completing a non-catalog request, and it will have an asterisk (*) next to it to indicate it is required.

Any personalization can be deleted with the Clear Personalization link at either the top or the bottom of the Personalization page. Select the level you want to remove the personalization from, and then Go.

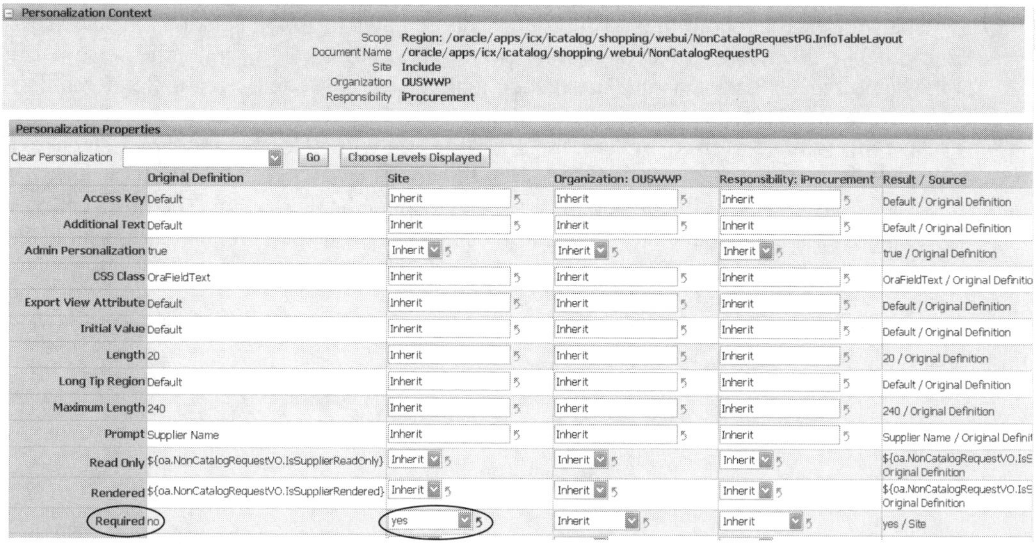

	Original Definition	Site	Organization: OUSWWP	Responsibility: iProcurement	Result / Source
Access Key	Default	Inherit ⌄5	Inherit ⌄5	Inherit ⌄5	Default / Original Definition
Additional Text	Default	Inherit ⌄5	Inherit ⌄5	Inherit ⌄5	Default / Original Definition
Admin Personalization	true	Inherit ⌄5	Inherit ⌄5	Inherit ⌄5	true / Original Definition
CSS Class	OraFieldText	Inherit ⌄5	Inherit ⌄5	Inherit ⌄5	OraFieldText / Original Definitio
Export View Attribute	Default	Inherit ⌄5	Inherit ⌄5	Inherit ⌄5	Default / Original Definition
Initial Value	Default	Inherit ⌄5	Inherit ⌄5	Inherit ⌄5	Default / Original Definition
Length	20	Inherit ⌄5	Inherit ⌄5	Inherit ⌄5	20 / Original Definition
Long Tip Region	Default	Inherit ⌄5	Inherit ⌄5	Inherit ⌄5	Default / Original Definition
Maximum Length	240	Inherit ⌄5	Inherit ⌄5	Inherit ⌄5	240 / Original Definition
Prompt	Supplier Name	Inherit ⌄5	Inherit ⌄5	Inherit ⌄5	Supplier Name / Original Defini
Read Only	${oa.NonCatalogRequestVO.IsSupplierReadOnly}	Inherit ⌄5	Inherit ⌄5	Inherit ⌄5	${oa.NonCatalogRequestVO.IsS Original Definition
Rendered	${oa.NonCatalogRequestVO.IsSupplierRendered}	Inherit ⌄5	Inherit ⌄5	Inherit ⌄5	${oa.NonCatalogRequestVO.IsS Original Definition
Required	no	yes ⌄5	Inherit ⌄5	Inherit ⌄5	yes / Site

Personalization Context

Scope **Region:** /oracle/apps/icx/icatalog/shopping/webui/NonCatalogRequestPG.InfoTableLayout
Document Name /oracle/apps/icx/icatalog/shopping/webui/NonCatalogRequestPG
Site **Include**
Organization **OUSWWP**
Responsibility **iProcurement**

Personalization Properties

Clear Personalization [⌄] [Go] [Choose Levels Displayed]

FIGURE 2-9. *Making a field required in OA Framework*

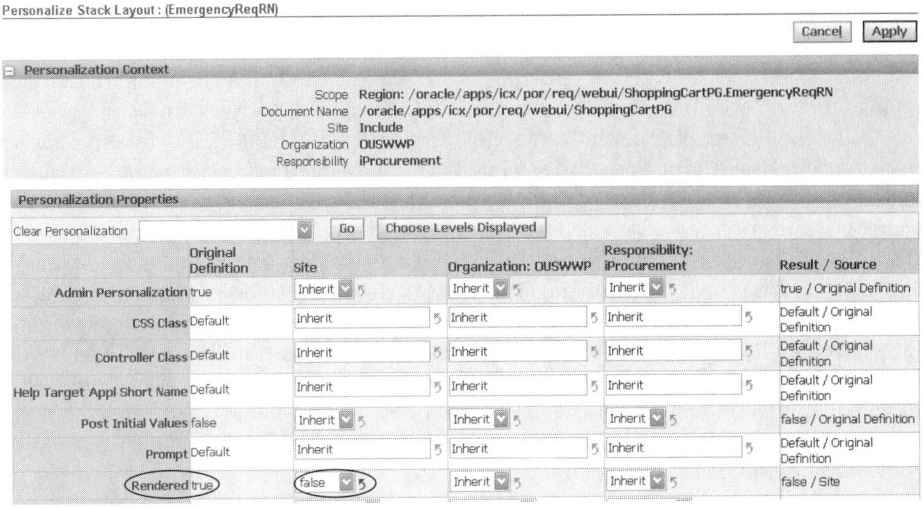

Personalize Stack Layout : (EmergencyReqRN)

Cancel Apply

Personalization Context

Scope Region: /oracle/apps/icx/por/req/webui/ShoppingCartPG.EmergencyReqRN
Document Name /oracle/apps/icx/por/req/webui/ShoppingCartPG
Site Include
Organization OUSWWP
Responsibility iProcurement

Personalization Properties

Clear Personalization [ ] Go Choose Levels Displayed

	Original Definition	Site	Organization: OUSWWP	Responsibility: iProcurement	Result / Source
Admin Personalization	true	Inherit 5	Inherit 5	Inherit 5	true / Original Definition
CSS Class	Default	Inherit 5	Inherit 5	Inherit 5	Default / Original Definition
Controller Class	Default	Inherit 5	Inherit 5	Inherit 5	Default / Original Definition
Help Target Appl Short Name	Default	Inherit 5	Inherit 5	Inherit 5	Default / Original Definition
Post Initial Values	false	Inherit 5	Inherit 5	Inherit 5	false / Original Definition
Prompt	Default	Inherit 5	Inherit 5	Inherit 5	Default / Original Definition
Rendered	true	false 5	Inherit 5	Inherit 5	false / Site

FIGURE 2-10. *Hiding a field using OA Framework*

Hiding a Field

While adding or removing functions from a responsibility can control what features are available, this control is not at the field level, and there are times when you want a specific field to be hidden while leaving the rest of the function available. For example, the field outlined in the preceding section, I NEED A PURCHASE ORDER NUMBER IMMEDIATELY, is not related to a specific function, so in order to remove it, you will need to do an OA Framework personalization.

Following the directions in the preceding section, navigate to the Personalize Stack Layout: (EmergencyReqRN) personalization window in the shopping cart. This time, the personalization is at the highest level, Stack Layout: (EmergencyReqRN). To hide a field, set the Rendered flag to False (see Figure 2-10).

After this setting has been applied, the entire section will no longer appear when checking out, as shown in Figure 2-11. This includes the link to get to the personalization, making it no longer possible to remove the personalization and display the field again. The next section will describe how to back out any personalization using the Functional Administrator responsibility.

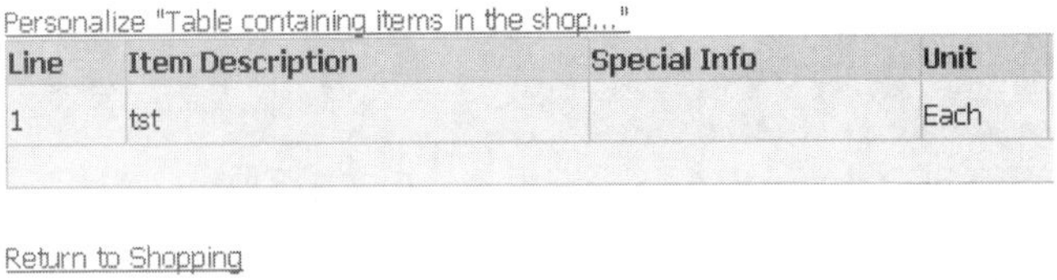

Personalize "Table containing items in the shop..."

Line	Item Description	Special Info	Unit
1	tst		Each

Return to Shopping

FIGURE 2-11. *The entire section to request a PO number is no longer visible.*

The personalizations described here are not the only features available with the OA Framework but are some of the basics to get you started. Other options include modifying lists of values that are not lookups in the applications, adding your company's branding (also called Browser Look-And-Feel or BLAF), Customizing Look-and-Feel (CLAF), and adding icons.

Backing Out an OA Framework Personalization

When adding OA Frameworks personalizations, there will come a time when you make a mistake, and the page no longer displays at all, or you need to restore a section that is no longer displayed. It is easy to get lost on these pages and make an unintended mistake. Since the page no longer displays, the personalization link is not available to back out the offending setting. Luckily, someone at Oracle must have had the same experience and added a safety net in Functional Administrator to remove the settings. On the Personalization | Application Catalog window, select either the DOCUMENT PATH or APPLICATION the personalization exists for.

When using the document path, you must use the exact path and cannot include wild cards; because of this, the application the personalization belongs to is usually easier to find than the window you are looking for. Select the application that is associated with a seeded responsibility (for example, use iProcurement instead of a custom responsibility) and see what APPLICATION it is associated with (System Administrator | Security | Responsibility | Define). Check the PERSONALIZED check box to limit the returned data to only windows that include personalizations, and optionally add LAST UPDATED date. This will return all the personalizations that exist for the application and, if added, updated during specific dates. Select the Manage Personalizations link, select the ones you want to delete, and click Delete Personalizations (see Figure 2-12).

Migrating Personalizations Between Environments

Recognizing the dangers in using OA Framework Personalizations, Oracle provides a way to migrate the changes from instance to instance. In order to use this feature, the profile option FND: Personalization Document Root Path needs to be filled in on both instances. Add the path where personalizations will be imported to in the receiving database and exported from in the instance that is sending the data. Once set, it is a three-step process to export the data from one instance, move the actual files, and then import it into another.

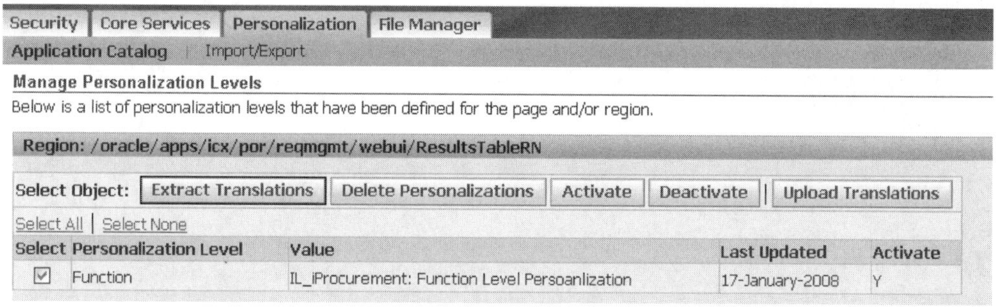

Functional Administrator | Personalization | Application Catalog

FIGURE 2-12. *Deleting personalizations using Functional Administrator*

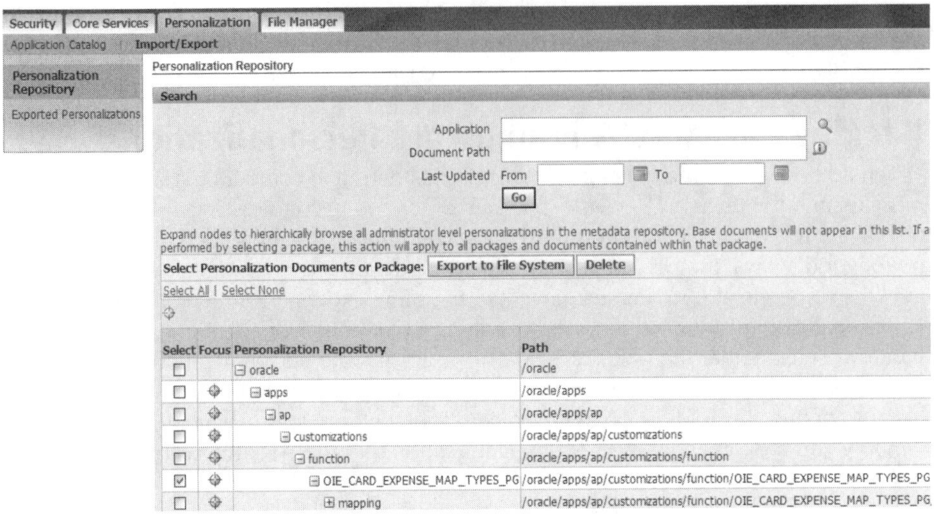

Functional Administrator | Personalization | Import/Export

FIGURE 2-13. *Moving Personalizations from one instance to another*

Using Functional Administrator again, navigate to the Personalization | Import/Export window. The Personalization Repository window is where you export the files by selecting the personalization and then Export To File System. See Figure 2-13. Oracle will save the files in the directory specified in FND: Personalization Document Root Path. Now the DBA can copy the file into another instance, again, placing it in the directory specified in FND: Personalization Document Root Path. The Import From File System button on the Exported Personalizations window is used to import the files after selecting the ones you want to import.

While taking the time to personalize the self-service modules will add to the implementation time, it will also decrease the support calls after the go live, making the time well spent.

CHAPTER
3

iProcurement Setup

etups for iProcurement can be separated into three categories: required setups outside of iProcurement, required setups specific to iProcurement, and optional setups.

Required Setups Outside of iProcurement

iProcurement is not traditionally used as a stand-alone module because of its tight integration with Oracle Purchasing and Payable. There are required setups within these areas for iProcurement to work. All of these setups, listed in Table 3-1, are outlined in detail in my *Oracle Procure-to-Pay Guide* or *Oracle General Ledger Guide* (both McGraw-Hill Professional, 2009), as well as in Oracle's application documentation.

Setup Step	Owning Module	Purpose
Define Accounting Key Flexfield	General Ledger	Determines the segments and format for the General Ledger account number.
General Ledger I Setup I Financials I Flexfields I Key I Segments		
Setup Calendars	General Ledger	Controls the dates associated with each accounting period.
General Ledger I Setup I Financials I Calendars I Accounting		
Setup Currencies	General Ledger	Determines the currencies that transactions can be entered in as well as their associated conversion rates to the Ledger's functional currency. Many currencies come seeded with EBS.
To define a currency: General Ledger I Setup I Currencies I Define *To define the conversion rate:* General Ledger I Setup I Currencies I Rates I Daily		
Setup Ledgers	General Ledger	Assigns Legal Entity– and Ledger-specific setups.
General Ledger I Setup I Financials I Accounting Setup Manager I Accounting Setups		
Define Human Resource Key Flexfields	General Ledger or Human Resources	Sets up the Job and Position Key Flexfields, which can be used for approval hierarchies within Purchasing and iProcurement.

TABLE 3-1. *Required Setups Not Related Directly to iProcurement*

Setup Step	Owning Module	Purpose
General Ledger	Setup	Financials	Flexfields	Key	Segments		
Define Locations	Purchasing	Creates both Ship-To and Bill-To locations that can be assigned to employees and used on purchase orders and requisitions as delivery information.
Purchasing	Setup	Organizations	Locations		
Define Organizations	Purchasing	Groups data and provides security for viewing and creating transactions in Purchasing, Payables, and iProcurement, as well as other modules. There are different types of organizations that can be set up, including Business Group, Legal Entity, Operating Unit, and Inventory Organization.
Purchasing	Setup	Organizations	Organizations		
Define Inventory Key Flexfields	General Ledger or Inventory	Sets up the format for item numbers. Items can be used even when inventory is not, and can have specific purchasing-related default information assigned to them.
General Ledger	Setup	Financials	Flexfields	Key	Segments		
Define Units of Measure	Purchasing or Inventory	Sets up the units of measure an item can be purchased and received in. To purchase and receive in different units of measure, conversions will also need to be defined.
Define Units of Measure: Purchasing	Setup	Units of Measure	Units of Measure *Define Conversions:* Purchasing	Setup	Units of Measure	Conversions		
Define Financial Options	Purchasing or Payables	Determines default information, including supplier-related defaults for purchase orders, for a specific operating unit.

TABLE 3-1.   *Required Setups Not Related Directly to iProcurement* (continued)

Setup Step	Owning Module	Purpose
Purchasing | Setup | Organizations | Financial Options		
Define Employees	Purchasing if Human Resources is not installed, or Human Resources when it is fully installed	Employees can be set up with base information when Human Resources is not fully installed. This step is required to use Purchasing and iProcurement.
Purchasing | Setup | Personnel | Employees		
Define Employees and Buyers	Purchasing	Defines employees as buyers in the system, which gives them rights to create and manage purchase orders, while employees who create or approve requisitions will need to be set up as employees.
Purchasing | Setup | Personnel | Buyers		
Define Purchasing Options	Purchasing or Payables	Assigns defaults and controls for the creation of documents in purchasing, including requisition numbers.
Purchasing | Setup | Organizations | Purchasing Options		
Define Receiving Options	Purchasing or Payables	Assigns receiving and accounting information related to purchase order receipts.
Purchasing | Setup | Organizations | Receiving Options		
Define Approval Groups and Assignments, or set up Oracle Approval Management	Purchasing or AME	Creates approval hierarchies and rules for approving purchasing documents.

To use approval groups and assignments: Purchasing \| Setup \| Approvals \| Approval Assignments or Approval Groups
To set up AME: Approval Management responsibility (refer to the Appendix)

TABLE 3-1. *Required Setups Not Related Directly to iProcurement* (continued)

Setups Specific to iProcurement

So here is the good news. Once the required setups referenced in Table 3-1 are complete, no additional setups are needed to make the base functionality of iProcurement work. But some of the previously mentioned setups require more discussion to understand their specific impact on iProcurement.

Requisition Approval Options and Setups

Oracle provides many options for the path all purchasing documents follow for approvals. Two of the options come as part of the standard Purchasing functionality, and the rest utilize Oracle Approvals Management. Standard functionality includes routing documents for approval based on a strict employee-supervisor hierarchy, or based on a position hierarchy. Which of these routes is followed is determined by the setting of the check box in the Financial Options called USE APPROVAL HIERARCHIES, as shown in Figure 3-1. When this box is selected, documents are routed based on the hierarchy of the position that is assigned to the employee, and approval limits are assigned to the position. When it is not selected, documents are routed according to the supervisor of the employee, and the job assigned to the approver is used to determine the approval limits.

Supervisor approvals will follow the supervisor hierarchy that is built off the employee record. For example, when John Smith creates a requisition in iProcurement, it will look at the supervisor associated with John Smith's employee record. Referring to the following illustration, that means the approver would be Jane Doe. If Jane Doe does not have the proper approval limits to approve the requisition, Oracle looks to see who Jane Doe's supervisor is, and checks what that person's approval limit is. And so on until it finds the person in the hierarchy with the proper authority. On the other hand, when EBS was set up to use a position hierarchy, it will look to see what position the requestor holds, and based on the position hierarchy set up in EBS, it will route the requisition for approval as follows: John Smith holds an Accountant position. The Accountant position reports to the Controller, while John Smith's supervisor is the Accounting Manager. Because the

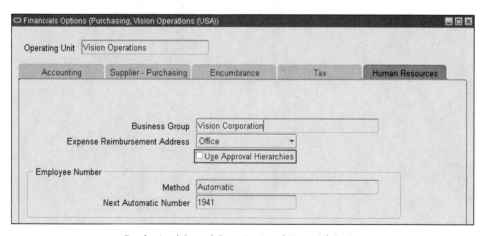

Purchasing | Setup | Organizations | Financial Options

FIGURE 3-1. *Determining if positions or jobs are used to route documents in purchasing for approval*

Accounting Manager is not in the position hierarchy for John Smith, the person holding this position will never see the requisition.

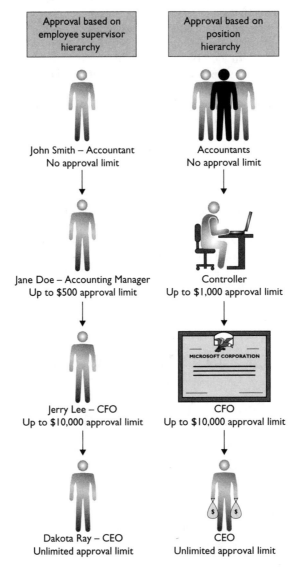

Approvals Management (AME), a separate module in Oracle that comes with your EBS license, allows more flexibility in setting up approval limits and does not adhere to strict hierarchies. While the position and supervisor hierarchies can be utilized by AME, additional conditions can be added. These options can be as simple as this: If the Category on the order equals Computer Equipment, send it to the CIO for approval. Or they can be as complicated as routing computer equipment purchases first to the person's supervisor, then to the IT Computer Specialist for configuration approval, and then to the CIO for final approval.

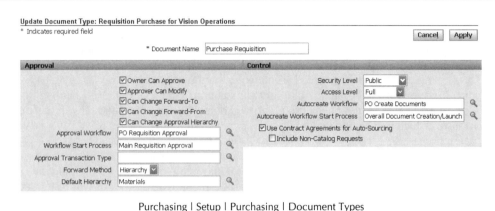

Purchasing | Setup | Purchasing | Document Types

FIGURE 3-2. *Determining if Approvals Management is used for approving purchasing documents*

Determining If Approvals Management Is Used

Setting up Purchasing and iProcurement to use AME versus either a position or supervisor hierarchy needs to be completed for each individual document type. This allows different documents to use different paths for approvals. As shown in Figure 3-2, update the Document Type called Requisition Purchase to determine what approval options are used.

The Approval section defines the rules for approving this document. Selecting OWNER CAN APPROVE will start the approval process by looking at the approval limits of the person creating the document. If you have the proper authority, then you can approve your own request. When this option is not checked, EBS will go to the next person in the approval chain to start the process. APPROVER CAN MODIFY determines if the person approving the document (when this is not the document owner) can make modifications to it, such as updating a distribution account number. CAN CHANGE FORWARD-TO and CAN CHANGE APPROVAL HIERARCHY both determine if the person submitting the document for approval can change the path the approval will follow. The Forward To person is the first person EBS selects to approve a document, based upon the hierarchy. The hierarchy will follow either the person-supervisor hierarchy, the position hierarchy, or the custom-designed hierarchy set up with Approvals Management.

APPROVAL WORKFLOW determines the workflow name that will be used to process the approval. This setting allows any changes to the workflow to be saved to a custom workflow, leaving the seeded workflow intact for future reference or troubleshooting, and removing the risk of the customizations being overwritten during patching. This workflow is called only when either supervisor or position hierarchies are being followed, and AME is not being used. WORKFLOW START PROCESS is the process in the workflow where the approvals will begin.

APPROVAL TRANSACTION TYPE, on the other hand, is populated with the transaction type that was set up in AME for this specific document approval. When this field is populated, AME is used, as opposed to the position and supervisor hierarchy workflows. FORWARD METHOD defines how the first person in the approval hierarchy is determined. When this is set to DIRECT, EBS will send the document to the first person in the chain with the authorization limits to approve the document. HIERARCHY, on the other hand, will require all persons in the chain to approve it until it reaches the person with the authority. For example, if someone on the warehouse staff enters a requisition that can only be approved by the VP of Operations, DIRECT will require only the VP of Operations to approve the document, whereas HIERARCHY will send it to the Warehouse Manager, to the Warehouse Director, and then to the VP of Operations. Each person in the chain must approve it to advance it to the next person.

The DEFAULT HIERARCHY can only be entered when the approval method is set to HIERARCHY in the Financial Options (Purchasing | Setup | Organizations | Financial Options | Human Resource tab, Use Approval Hierarchies check box). This will default the position hierarchy in the approval window, which can be updated when a document is submitted for approval if CAN CHANGE APPROVAL HIERARCHY is checked.

Several control options exist here as well. SECURITY LEVEL determines who can access this specific document type. When set to HIERARCHY it allows the owner (or creator) and any person above that person in the hierarchy to access a document, whereas PRIVATE will restrict access to only the owner. PUBLIC will allow all users to access all the documents, while the last option of PURCHASING limits access to the purchasing owner, who is also set up as a buyer. The ACCESS LEVEL determines what access is granted to people with the proper security level, selecting from FULL, which includes create, modify, and view; MODIFY, which does not allow document creation; and VIEW only. No matter what the ACCESS LEVEL is set to, the document owner will have access to create or modify his or her own documents—the access level only relates to documents created by other users.

AUTOCREATE WORKFLOW determines how requisitions are created automatically into purchase orders using the autocreate feature. This workflow determines grouping rules for the requisitions as well as how they are routed to buyers. Again, because this workflow name can be populated here, it can be modified to meet your company's specific needs. The AUTOCREATE WORKFLOW START PROCESS determines where in the workflow it begins. Selecting USE CONTRACT AGREEMENTS FOR AUTO-SOURCING will ensure that the autosourcing logic for creating requisitions includes approved contract purchase agreements. This setting will override the profile PO: AUTOMATIC DOCUMENT SOURCING, set in System Administrator | Profile | System. The final option, INCLUDE NON-CATALOG REQUESTS, can be left unchecked to exclude non-catalog requests from autosourcing rules.

Setting Up Jobs

Jobs are created against a JOB GROUP, which was defined when Purchasing or Human Resources was set up. When the form opens up, click New, and the Job form shown in Figure 3-3 is seen.

From here, the NAME of the job is entered. This can either be the actual name of the job, or when EBS is not being used as the human resource system, you may want to consider using the actual approval amount as the job NAME. This will make setup and maintenance much easier. For example, instead of setting up a position for marketing manager and one for accounting manager, both of whom can approve the same dollar amounts, set up one job called "1,000 limit" that can be assigned to employees holding both jobs. Since there are usually fewer dollar amounts than there are jobs, this is less work to maintain and makes approval research easier.

Enter the DATES this job will be effective. The begin date is required, but the end date should be left blank unless you are actually discontinuing use of this job. The APPROVAL AUTHORITY is used when AME is set up, and links the job to a specific Action Type, determining the approval limit for each person. When jobs are being set up only for approval reasons, no additional information is required here, since the rest of the fields relate to Human Resources.

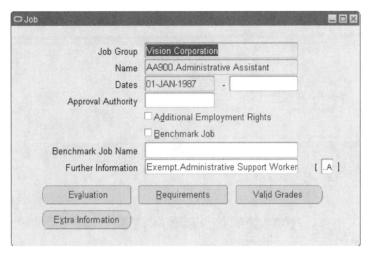

Purchasing I Setup I Personnel I Jobs

FIGURE 3-3.   *Setting up jobs*

Setting Up Positions

Positions and Jobs are very similar in EBS when Oracle Human Resources is not being used. The best description is that jobs can belong to multiple positions, but each position can only have one job. The main difference from an approval standpoint is that when the supervisor hierarchy is used for approvals, the approval limits are assigned at the job level, while using Approval Hierarchies requires the approval limits to be assigned to the position. To add a position, enter a FROM date, as shown in Figure 3-4. This is the first date this position can be used, and it can be backdated if need be to accommodate existing documents waiting for approval. The TO date should be left blank unless you want to discontinue using this position.

Enter the NAME of the position that is being added, and select the ORGANIZATION the position belongs to from the list of values. The same methodology described for jobs can be used to set up positions. Next, add the JOB that will be assigned to this position, and the default LOCATION for it. STATUS is not required, and leaving it either blank or selecting Valid will allow employees to be assigned to this position. If the STATUS is Invalid, then it cannot be assigned to any employees. The rest of the fields will default in and are not required for use with purchasing document approvals.

Selecting the Reporting To button will allow the position hierarchy to be set up, but this is easier to do in the Position Hierarchy form, described next.

Creating the Position Hierarchy

The position hierarchy only needs to be set up when USE APPROVAL HIERARCHIES is selected on the Financial Options (Purchasing I Setup I Organizations I Financial Options); it tells EBS the hierarchy to use to route approvals. To create a hierarchy, enter the NAME of the hierarchy (normally, only one hierarchy will be set up when Human Resources is not fully installed), and

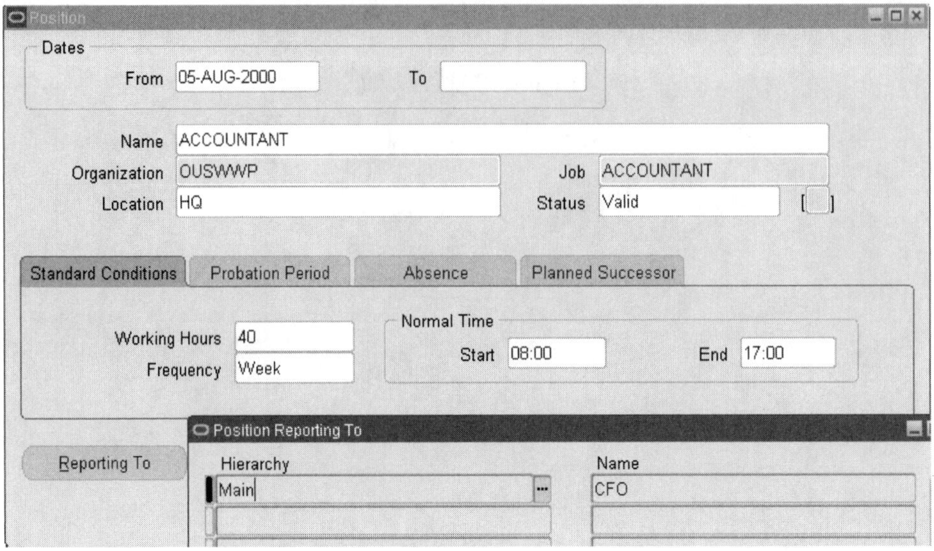

Purchasing | Setup | Personnel | Positions

FIGURE 3-4. *Setting up positions*

select it as PRIMARY, as shown in Figure 3-5. At this point, the hierarchy must be saved before you can proceed. Referring to the figure, notice that the hierarchy is version controlled. Enter **1** as the NUMBER, and select the date this version is effective. If you are making a change to the hierarchy, arrow down to add the new version, and enter the next version NUMBER. When you enter a DATE FROM on the new version, EBS will end-date the prior version, and a note will appear telling you so.

The Copy Hierarchy button can only be used when a new version or new hierarchy is being created; it copies any other hierarchy and version to the current hierarchy, allowing updates to be done to it. This prevents having to re-create the hierarchies from scratch. Again, you must save at this point prior to proceeding.

If you are not copying a hierarchy, then you must re-query your position hierarchy at this point. This will cause the actual positions set up to populate. NAME is the position name, and positions appear in alphabetical order. You can arrow down to see the next position. HOLDER will populate with the employee name that holds this position, when there is only one. If there is more than one employee, the field will read "** X Holders **," or No Holders if it is not assigned to any employee. WORKER NUMBER is only populated when one employee holds the position; it is the employee number for that person, while WORKER TYPE is the type associated with the employee record, usually Employee, Applicant, or Contingent Worker, though additional types can be set up. The NUMBER OF SUBORDINATES is again only populated when there is one HOLDER for the position;

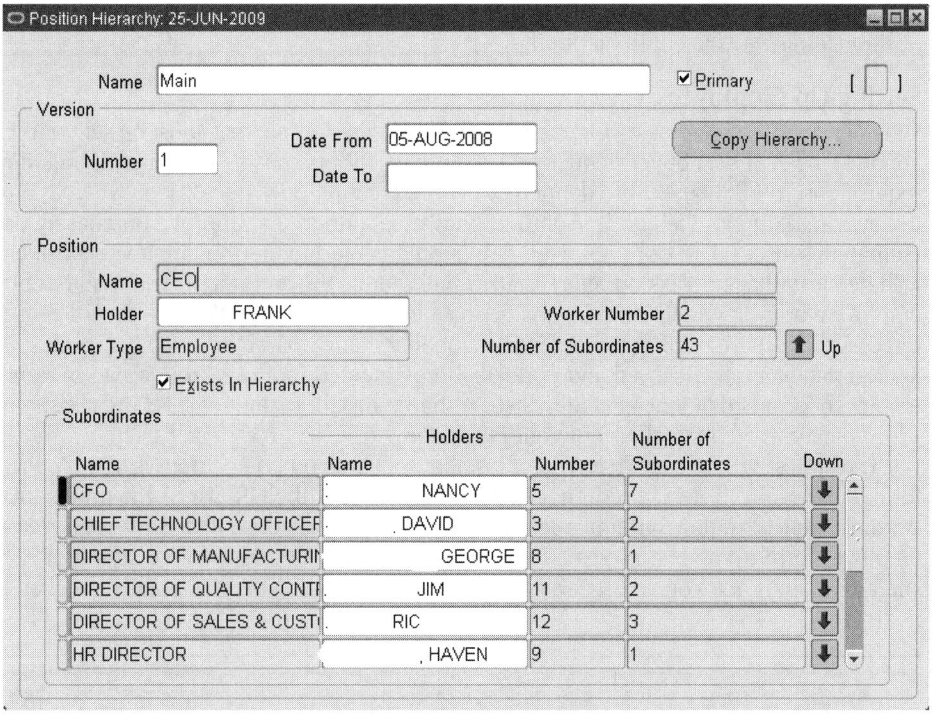

Purchasing I Setup I Personnel I Position Hierarchy

FIGURE 3-5. *Creating position hierarchies*

it reflects the total number of employees reporting to this person. This may not agree with the number of Subordinates listed, as it includes indirect reports as well as direct reports.

Clicking the up button for any position will take you to the parent of that position. For example, if the POSITION you are on is the CFO, and the CFO reports to the CEO, clicking UP will take you to the CEO record. This holds true for any position that is in the hierarchy, as identified with the check box next to EXISTS IN HIERARCHY. This box will become checked when a position is added as a subordinate to another position.

To actually build the hierarchy, you will need to add Subordinates to each Position. As this is a position hierarchy, the Subordinate NAME you are adding is a position name, and not any actual employee. The Holders section will show the employee name when it is filled by only one employee, or No Holders, or the actual number of Holders. The next two fields, NUMBER and NUMBER OF SUBORDINATES, are only populated when one employee is assigned to the position; they reflect the employee number and number of people reporting to them. Selecting the DOWN arrow will take you to the next level in the hierarchy. For example, if you click the DOWN arrow next to the CFO in Figure 3-5, it will take you to the position for CFO and display the subordinates for that position.

There is a report that can be helpful when reviewing your hierarchies, called Position Hierarchy Report. Since this report can only be run by position, ensure you run it for your top position to display the entire hierarchy.

Setting Up Employees

Whether or not you are using Oracle Human Resources, employees must be set up in EBS for anyone who will be a buyer, requestor, or approver for purchasing documents, including requisitions. In EBS, buyers are defined as people creating purchase orders, whereas a requestor is the person asking for the goods. Approvers have the authority to approve purchasing documents. Human Resources (HR) does not need to be implemented to use the Employee form. Ensuring it is a shared install as opposed to fully installed will reduce the amount of data required on the employee form. In Oracle terms, a shared install is when the module is not fully licensed with Oracle, but you are using some of the functionality that is *shared* across other modules, whereas a full install is a fully licensed and hopefully implemented module. From a system standpoint, the employee form is different for a full versus a shared install, making it less time consuming to set up employees when Oracle is not your HR system.

The easiest way to see what type of installation HR is on your system is to open the employee form (Purchasing | Setup | Personnel | Employees). Ensure the HR User Type profile (System Administrator | Profile | System) is set to HR User for the responsibility you are accessing the employee form from. If you see the form shown in Figure 3-6, then your system has HR listed as a shared install. If not, you will receive an error message stating that HR is fully installed and that

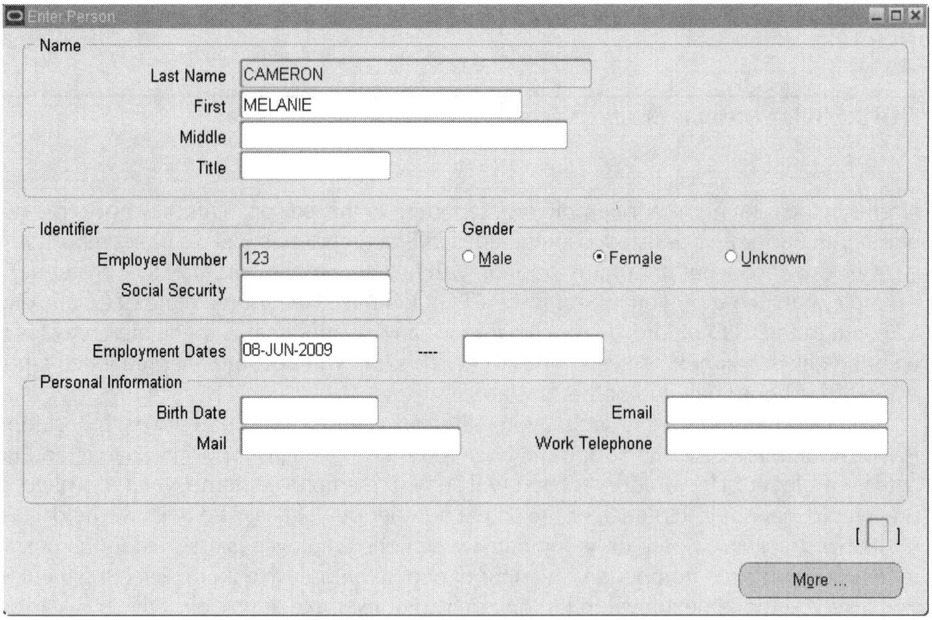

Purchasing | Setup | Personnel | Employees

FIGURE 3-6.   *Setting up employees when HR is a shared install*

you must use the Persons form instead. While there are many ways to change the out-of-the-box installation status of HR from shared to fully installed, there is only one way to change it back, and that is with SQL. Work with your DBA to run the following script, ensuring you run it in a test environment first:

```
update fnd_product_installations
set status = 'S'
where application_id = 800
```

Here on the modified employee form, you can set up the employee-supervisor relationships, as well as the Ledger the employee is assigned to, plus a default expense account that can be used in the Purchasing and Requisition Account Generators on the assignments page.

When creating an employee for use only in Purchasing, the employee LAST NAME and FIRST need to be entered, and an EMPLOYMENT begin DATE. If you are using the Workflow Mailer to send out notifications from Oracle, you will want to add the EMAIL address as well. No other information is needed on the first page. After saving the record, click More and then the Assignment tab, shown in Figure 3-7. Either a JOB or a POSITION will need to be entered, selecting from the list of values. Jobs are entered when the supervisor hierarchy is being used, while both the JOB and POSITION can be entered when the Approval Hierarchies are used. SUPERVISOR is only required when the supervisor hierarchy is selected. ORGANIZATION will need to be populated with the HR Organization that was set up when Purchasing was set up.

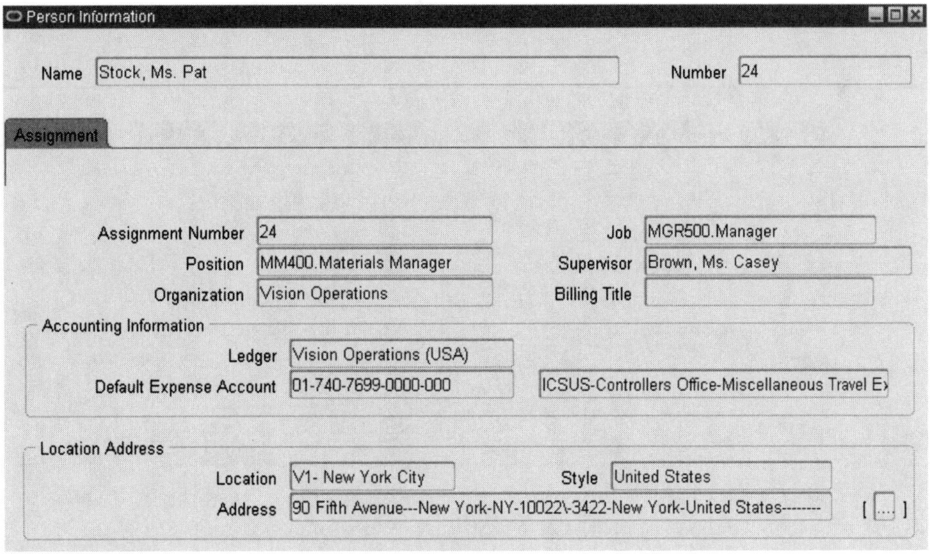

Purchasing I Setup I Personnel I Employees I More button I Assignments tab

FIGURE 3-7. *Setting up employees when HR is a shared install*

The ACCOUNTING INFORMATION and LOCATION ADDRESS sections are important default information for iProcurement. Assigning a LEDGER determines the ledger the requisition will be associated with, while the DEFAULT EXPENSE ACCOUNT can be used as part of the requisition account generator to determine the default account number that will be assigned to non-inventory requisitions in iProcurement.

The LOCATION ADDRESS entered here will become the default ship-to location for the requisition. While this information becomes the default for the employee, employees will also have the option of updating some of their information in iProcurement, explained in the section "iProcurement Preferences."

Locations

Locations in EBS are really just a listing of addresses that can be reused multiple times. Locations are associated with employees and will default onto their iProcurement preferences, where the employee can update them, becoming the deliver-to address that appears on the purchase orders. To set up a Location, refer to Figure 3-8. Scope determines whether this location is related to a specific business unit or group, or it crosses business groups. Selecting LOCAL will restrict this location to the current business group that is associated with the responsibility (set as a profile in System Administrator | Profile | System | HR: Business Group), while GLOBAL allows this location to be accessed by all business group. Next, add the NAME of the location, remembering that this is what the users will see most on forms, so it should be descriptive. Add a DESCRIPTION, which will appear only when selecting the location from a list of values. The INACTIVE DATE can be added when this location is no longer used. The LEGAL ADDRESS check box cannot be selected by the user and will be populated by the system for any location that was set up in association with a Legal Entity (Legal Entity Manager | Legal Entity Configurator | Legal Entities | Establishments); it can only be updated from the Registrations window where it was defined.

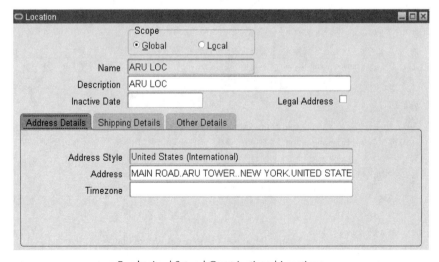

Purchasing | Setup | Organizations | Locations

FIGURE 3-8.   *Setting up locations*

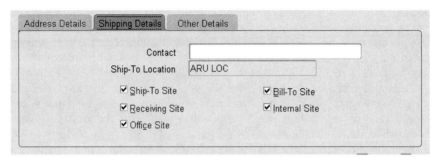

FIGURE 3-9. *Shipping details on locations*

Under the Address Details tab, add the physical address of the location. This is the address that will appear on a requisition using this location. The Shipping Details tab, shown in Figure 3-9, can be used to add a default CONTACT for this location, as well as the default SHIP-TO LOCATION, allowing the system to have one bill-to address associated with a different ship-to address. This location is then identified for different uses:

- **Ship-To Site** Determines if this location can be used as a ship-to address on both purchase orders and requisitions.
- **Receiving Site** Determines if this location can be used when receiving a purchase order.
- **Office Site** An identifier in the system that denotes if this location is an office. This designation does not have any functionality in EBS and is for information only.
- **Bill-To Site** Determines if this location can be selected as a Bill-To address on requisitions and purchase orders.
- **Internal Site** Used only with Internal Requisitions, allows this location to be selected on Internal Requisitions.

Items and Categories, and How They Are Used in iProcurement

There are two ways a shopper can request what he or she wants to purchase in iProcurement: Items and Categories. While selecting an item will default in the category associated with it, categories can also be used alone without an item. Both classifications (Items and Categories) allow accounting information to be defaulted in on the requisition, as well as assist with analysis of purchasing trends and expenses.

Items

Items are most commonly thought of in conjunction with manufacturing, but in reality, they can play a powerful role in purchasing as well. While setting up and maintaining items in EBS does take a certain amount of time and effort, it will reduce the time users spend shopping in iProcurement and make the purchases consistent for analysis as well as reducing costs by providing a list of approved items and associated suppliers.

Oracle recommends that items be set up in a master inventory organization that is not associated with any transactions, and then assigned to additional organizations where the transactions, such as purchasing and receiving, take place. Purchasing does validate that items exist in the inventory organization set up in Order Management as the Item Validation Organization, and this should be set to your master organization (Order Management | Setup | System Parameters | Values | Parameter = Item Validation Organization). Each of the controllable features of an item can be set at either the master or the organization level, depending on how it is defined in the Attribute Controls form (Purchasing | Setup | Items | Attribute Controls). Any attribute that is controlled at the master level will default to the organization level and cannot be updated, while attributes controlled at the organization level can be updated to a different value for each inventory organization. It is the organization level settings that will determine how an item behaves in a specific organization, while the master level controls are shared for all organizations.

There is a field on the Financial Options (Purchasing | Setup | Organizations | Financial Options | Supplier-Purchasing tab) that determines which inventory organization is used in iProcurement for a specific operating unit. The INVENTORY ORGANIZATION assigned here will determine which items can be purchased and received in iProcurement.

When setting up an item, as shown in Figure 3-10, you have two fields that can affect the accounting of a purchase order. When purchasing an item, it can either be delivered to inventory, in which case the account numbers associated with the subinventory will be used (Inventory | Setup | Organizations | Subinventory), or to expense, which then uses the EXPENSE ACCOUNT on the Purchasing tab of the item to generate the account number.

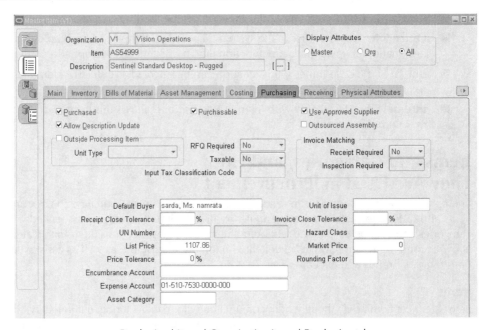

Purchasing | Items | Organization Items | Purchasing tab

FIGURE 3-10.   *Purchasing controls on items*

Purchasing I Items I Master Items I Tools I Categories

FIGURE 3-11. *Adding categories to items*

All items are then associated with one or more categories. Categories are really just a way of grouping items for reporting and searching purposes. While the system has predefined types of categories, such as Inventory or Purchasing, additional categories can be set up for reporting. These are assigned to an item from the Tools menu, shown in Figure 3-11. From here, select the CATEGORY SET of Purchasing. (See the section "Creating a Value Set for the Purchasing Category" for more information on category sets.)

Categories

While categories are assigned to an item, they can also be used without an item, allowing reporting and analysis to be performed on purchases without having to set up items. Categories are required when creating a non-catalog request, or a request for something that is not set up as an item, as well as being associated with purchases from a third-party shopping site, or punchout. At least one default category is required in EBS, but any reporting benefits are lost by not setting up additional categories. Categories can also be assigned to account numbers, which can then be used to generate the accounting on a requisition. Categories are key flexfields and therefore have a different number of segments and group of values in every system. As with all key flexfields, once the segments of the category have been defined, Oracle does not support changing the length or number of segments.

Defining the Category Key Flexfield To set up your category flexfield, first you query the seeded category flexfield by using the flashlight on your toolbar and selecting Inventory for the APPLICATION and Item Categories for the FLEXFIELD TITLE. Refer to Figure 3-12.

From here, scroll down till you find PO_ITEM_CATEGORY in the CODE field. Usually, it is the PO item category that is used for classifying purchases and requisitions, but any item category flexfield can be defined and used as the Default category set, whose setups are described later in this chapter, under "Setting the Default Category Set." At the bottom of the form, additional features can be selected for this flexfield. FREEZE FLEXFIELD DEFINITION needs to be checked for the flexfield to be active, but it must remain unchecked when you are setting it up or making changes. Once you are using EBS for production transactions, unfreezing key flexfields when users or processes are using the flexfield can cause data integrity problems, so maintenance to any key flexfield is always recommended during scheduled system down times. ENABLED allows

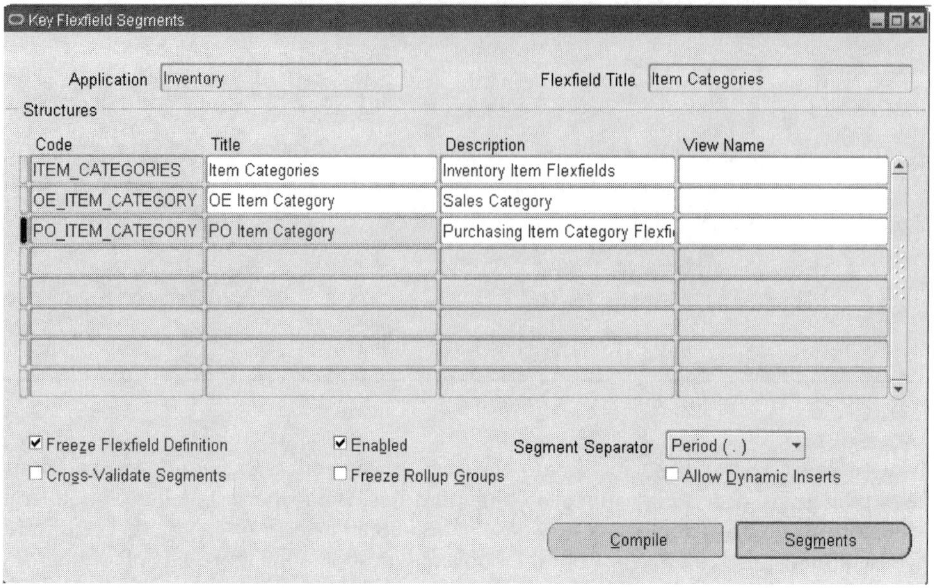

Purchasing | Setup | Flexfields | Key | Segments

FIGURE 3-12.   *Defining the purchasing category flexfield*

the structure to be used in the application and should only be unchecked when the flexfield is not in use.

The last field used for item categories is the SEGMENT SEPARATOR, which determines what character will separate your segments when there are more than one, and is used when keying combinations or printing on reports. EBS comes with Period, Dash, and Pipe installed and allows you to add additional custom characters. Remember to think about how people will do data entry when deciding on your segment separator—selecting a tilde, on the left side of many keyboards, will slow down data entry for numbers, which are still often done with a keypad. The other options on this page cannot be used with item category flexfields and should remain unchecked.

Adding Segments to the Category Flexfield   Next, click SEGMENTS to create each segment, shown in Figure 3-13. The NUMBER is the order in which your segments will appear on reports and in EBS forms. Leave no gaps in the numbering to prevent processing problems. NAME is the name of the segment, while PROMPT is what appears on data entry screens. Making the NAME and PROMPT consistent will help eliminate confusion when creating custom reports.

A good rule when setting up data in EBS is to use a convention for case—either all upper or mixed. When querying with the Enter Query function and sorting data, note that EBS is case sensitive and can have some strange results for different cases. I like to use all UPPER case for internal names, and Mixed Case for data the user sees—this makes programming easier, which uses the internal name, but the users see mixed case, which is easier to read. COLUMN denotes the column in the tables where this segment will appear—it is traditional to make the NUMBER

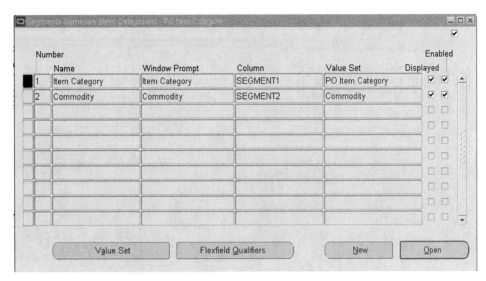

Purchasing I Setup I Flexfields I Key I Segments I Segments button

FIGURE 3-13. *Adding segments to the category flexfield*

correspond with the COLUMN number, mostly to help eliminate confusion. If you are on segment NUMBER 1, make this segment SEGMENT1.

You can identify up to 20 segments in your PO category flexfield, with each segment having 240 characters. Ensure you make it as detailed as required to track purchasing and allow searching in iProcurement, remembering that it should still be usable by the shoppers who will need to select the category when it is not assigned to an item.

Creating a Value Set for the Purchasing Category A VALUE SET needs to be set up for each segment in your category and is used to store the valid values for the PO item category (refer to Figure 3-14). The VALUE SET NAME is the name of the segment, usually prefixed with a unique code that identifies your company, often preceded with "XX" to ensure it is not a code that will be used by Oracle in future releases. Beginning most of the setup data with a code that identifies your organization is a good way of tracking custom setups in EBS. Usually, three or four characters are used at the most. As EBS grows in size, functionality, and acquisitions, we have been seeing more and more two- and three-letter combinations being used by EBS itself. To help eliminate confusion, not only today but in the future, it is now recommended that XX be added in front of this code, as Oracle has proposed this as a letter combination they will never use. For example, one of Oracle's profiled customers, Korea Telecom FreeTel, uses KTF as its corporate abbreviation. Adding XXKTF in front of all the Names in EBS will identify this as added data by KTF, and they will never need to worry about Oracle adding a module and calling it KTF.

To see where an existing value set is used in Concurrent Program Parameters, Descriptive Flexfield Segments, or Key Flexfield Segments, click on the Usages button. DESCRIPTION is a more detailed description of what this value set is used for. The LIST TYPE for the PO item category should

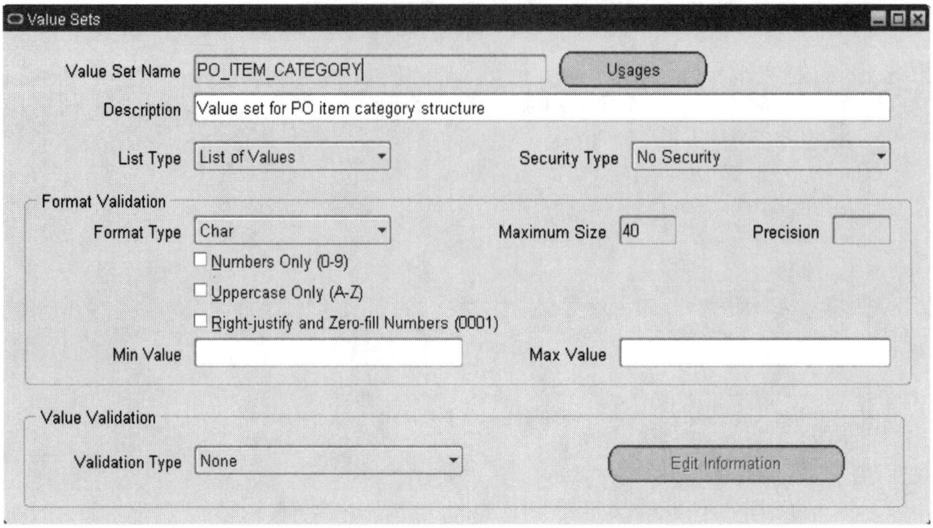

Purchasing | Setup | Flexfields | Key | Segments | Segments button | Value Set button

FIGURE 3-14. *Creating a value set*

always be LIST OF VALUES, meaning that the user must enter (or select from a drop-down box) a value that is set up and active in this value set. Security can be added to the PO item category, which will use Oracle's Security features to control the segments that can be used by a specific responsibility. This is particularly useful because PO item category can be shared across different inventories and operating units. SECURITY TYPE can be set to No Security, which allows all segment values to be used at all times, Hierarchical Security, which uses the flexfield's Parent-Child relationships to ensure that the child values follow the same security rules as the parent, and Non-Hierarchical Security, which requires that security be added independently for both the parent and child values. Security rules are set up under Purchasing | Setup | Flexfields | Key | Security | Define.

FORMAT TYPE is often set to CHAR, which allows alphanumeric characters. Forcing the value set to use UPPERCASE ONLY helps ensure consistency, whereas RIGHT-JUSTIFY and ZERO-FILL will automatically zero-fill any numbers entered during data entry for values that are numeric. MAXIMUM SIZE is the number of characters in the segment, and usually no MINIMUM VALUES or MAXIMUM VALUES are assigned for category segments, which would restrict the range of valid values that can be set up. Since each value needs to be set up, usually access to the setups is restricted but the values that can be used are not, allowing for future growth.

VALIDATION TYPE for a PO item category flexfield can only be DEPENDENT, INDEPENDENT, or TABLE VALIDATION (the other options are not valid for the category flexfield's value sets). INDEPENDENT will validate against the predefined values but has no restriction on their use. DEPENDENT means that the value of this segment is dependent on the value in another segment, where a subset of values are identified as valid for the previous segment. TABLE VALIDATION allows the data to be validated against a custom table in the database.

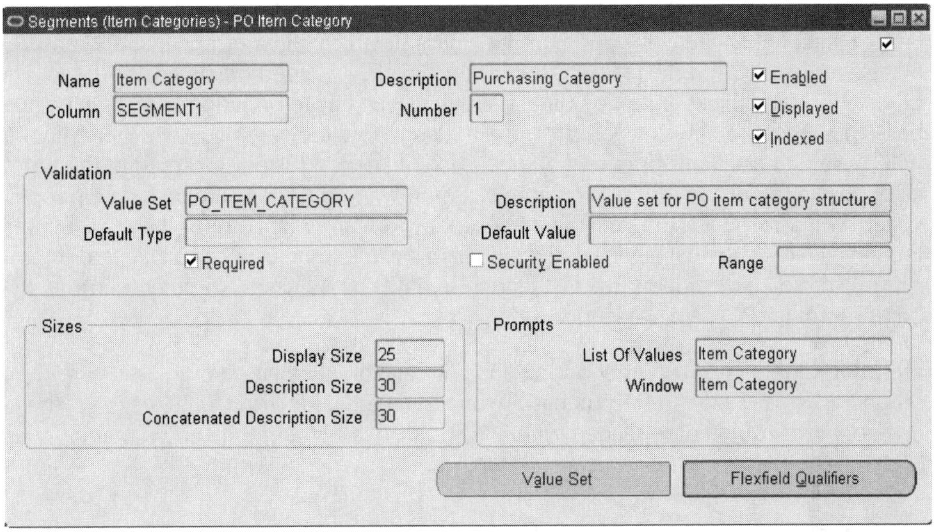

Purchasing | Setup | Flexfields | Key | Segments | Segments button | Value Set button | Open button

FIGURE 3-15.   *Additional segment information*

Once the value set is saved, it can be added back on the Segments form in the VALUE SET field, and also ensure all segments of your PO item category flexfield are ENABLED and displayed. Select Open to complete the setups for each segment, shown in Figure 3-15. The NAME, DESCRIPTION, COLUMN, and NUMBER will default from the previous page. Ensure ENABLED and DISPLAYED are still checked as well. The VALUE SET and DESCRIPTION will default in from the previous page as well.

Adding a DEFAULT TYPE and a DEFAULT VALUE will cause all items to default these values into the PO item category. REQUIRED needs to be checked for all segments of the category. The SECURITY ENABLED feature is not allowed with the PO item category flexfield. The DISPLAY SIZE will default from the value set, whereas the DESCRIPTION SIZE will determine how much of the value's description will appear on the forms and can be modified. CONCATENATED DESCRIPTION SIZE is used on reports when this segment is concatenated with the other segments, allowing a smaller portion of each segment's description to appear on the report—this is really for space saving on the report, especially descriptions that are not written in XML using Oracle's BI Publisher. PROMPTS are what the users will see in both the LIST OF VALUES and WINDOW in EBS.

Adding Values to the Value Set   Now that the value set and key flexfields are set up, you can add the valid values that the users can use. When you enter the form, the Find Key Flexfield Segment box appears. Enter the following information:

- **Application** = Inventory
- **Title** = Item Categories
- **Structure** = PO Item Category
- **Segment** = either leave blank to query up all segments, or select a specific segment from the list of values

Referring to Figure 3-16, enter the VALUE you want the user to see, which will also populate the TRANSLATED VALUE field. This field is used when EBS is installed to use multiple languages, called NLS or National Language Support, and is not updatable. Add a DESCRIPTION, and ensure that ENABLED is checked. While a FROM date is not required, it is good practice to add one, ensuring it is on or prior to the first transaction date that will utilize this information. Adding a begin date can be helpful because new categories can be added before they are needed, where the FROM date will prevent transactions prior to that date. Also, it keeps a historical record of the first date this category was available for use. Sometimes, if you want to use a value on a date prior to today, the system will assume it is only effective from today forward when a FROM date is not entered. Entering a FROM date that is backdated allows this value to be used for backdated transactions. Adding a TO date determines the last date this value can be used. No other information is needed on this form for PO Item Categories.

Defining Category Sets   After setting up your category flexfields, you must first set up a category set and assign a default to the purchasing functional area. Referring to Figure 3-17, the Purchasing category set should come seeded with EBS, but if it is not there, it can be manually added.

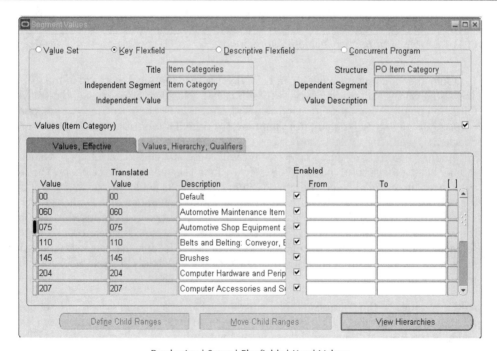

Purchasing | Setup | Flexfields | Key | Values

FIGURE 3-16.   *Entering values for the Categories Key flexfield*

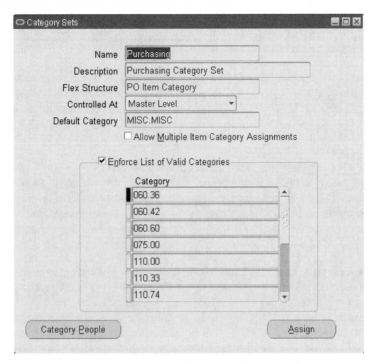

Purchasing | Setup | Items | Categories | Category Sets

FIGURE 3-17. *Defining category sets*

Enter the NAME as Purchasing, and add a DESCRIPTION. The FLEX STRUCTURE must be the same structure you just set up in the previous step. Determine if the categories assigned to an item will be assigned at the master level for all organizations this item is assigned to, or at the organization level, allowing each organization to have a different purchasing category, by selecting the proper value in the CONTROLLED AT field. Then enter a DEFAULT CATEGORY, which will default in when creating items.

Selecting ALLOW MULTIPLE ITEM CATEGORY ASSIGNMENTS determines if an item can only be assigned to one category for a set, or multiple. When selected, it allows an item to have more than one purchasing category, such as belonging to both the Electronics and Computer categories. When ENFORCE LIST OF VALID CATEGORIES is selected, any category value that is *not* assigned to the category set will not appear on the list of values for the users to select from. The main advantage to using this feature is that it allows the same value set to be assigned to multiple categories but restricts the valid values within a specific category to only those assigned to the category set. This not only reduces data entry when different categories have overlapping values, it also ensures consistency across the different categories where values are shared.

An example of how this works is if both the Inventory and Purchasing item categories use the same value set called Category. This set contains the values Computers, Monitors, Mice, and Complete Computers. While items that are part of inventory can be computers, monitors, or mice, Purchasable items can be assigned to these categories, as well as the category Complete Computers.

Under the CATEGORY section, add the valid categories for this category set. Selecting the Assign button will allow you to assign this category to specific items. This feature is only available when a default category has been set up. Clicking the Category People button allows specific ITEM CATEGORIES to be assigned to a ROLE and a person or group. This feature will then restrict access to the sales report for this role, person, and category.

Setting the Default Category Set   At this point, the category flexfield, which was assigned to a category set, needs to be set as the Default Category for the Purchasing functional area. It is this category that will appear in Oracle iProcurement for the purchase of both items and non-catalog requests. Referring to Figure 3-18, select the FUNCTIONAL AREA of Purchasing, and enter the CATEGORY SET you just defined in the previous step. Values defined in this category set will then become available to search on in iProcurement.

Setting the Category Profile   There is one profile that will affect the way categories appear in iProcurement. It is called POR: Autocreate Shopping Category and Mapping. This is set in System Administrator | Profile | System. By default, this is set to No, which means the categories will have to be manually mapped in iProcurement for users to search for them using the shopping category. A second setup on a content zone, including items without shopping categories, allows items to be displayed in iProcurement when they are not mapped to a shopping category, but the item will not show up the same in the searches. Setting it to Yes will create the mapping automatically, where the category code description, defined in the next step, becomes the shopping category. While setting this profile to No will cause additional steps to be performed before it can be used in iProcurement, it does allow multiple purchasing categories to be assigned to the same shopping category, which aids the users during the shopping process. How you set these will depend on how items and categories are being used as well as how users will be shopping for items. The profile can be changed, and the mappings can also be overridden in iProcurement.

When deciding how to set this profile, it is important to know that any category assigned to an item before the purchasing-to-shopping mapping is complete will not appear in iProcurement, even after the mapping is set up. There are two ways to fix this problem. One is on an item-by-item basis, and the other will correct multiple items at the same time.

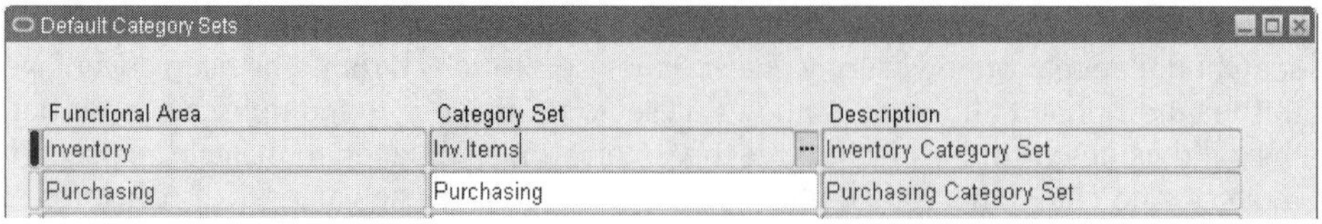

Functional Area	Category Set	Description
Inventory	Inv. Items	Inventory Category Set
Purchasing	Purchasing	Purchasing Category Set

Purchasing | Setup | Items | Categories | Default Category Sets

FIGURE 3-18.   *Setting the default category set for the Purchasing functional area*

To fix a single item, query up the item, and change the category assigned to the Purchasing category set. (Purchasing | Items | Master or Organization Item | Tools | Categories). After saving the record, change the category back to the category, which has now been mapped properly. The reason this works is that the category mappings are not updated for a specific item after the mapping is created, leaving the mtl_categories_kfv.ip_category_id = –2, which tells iProcurement to ignore this item. Changing the category and then changing it back will trigger the category ID to be updated correctly, based on the new mapping, and the item will appear in iProcurement.

If there are a large number of items not appearing in iProcurement due to this problem, there are scripts that can be used to update the category ID associated with the items. The current script is called ICX_CAT_POPULATE_MI_PVT.upgradeR12MIs, and directions can be found on My Oracle Support under document ID 454694.1. As always, run this script in a test instance to ensure you get the proper results prior to running it in production.

Creating Category Codes   Category codes are used to create valid combinations of the individual values entered for each category segment, and assign the combination to a specific structure. Referring to Figure 3-19, select the STRUCTURE NAME of PO item category, and select the CATEGORY from the list of values. Add a DESCRIPTION, which will be used as the Shopping Category in iProcurement when the profile POR: Autocreate Shopping Category and Mapping is set to Yes. Ensure ENABLED is checked for this category combination to be usable in both the category set as well as on an item. Adding an INACTIVE ON date will ensure this category is not used on or after this date. If you are using iSupplier, checking VIEWABLE BY SUPPLIER will allow suppliers to see this category when they sign in.

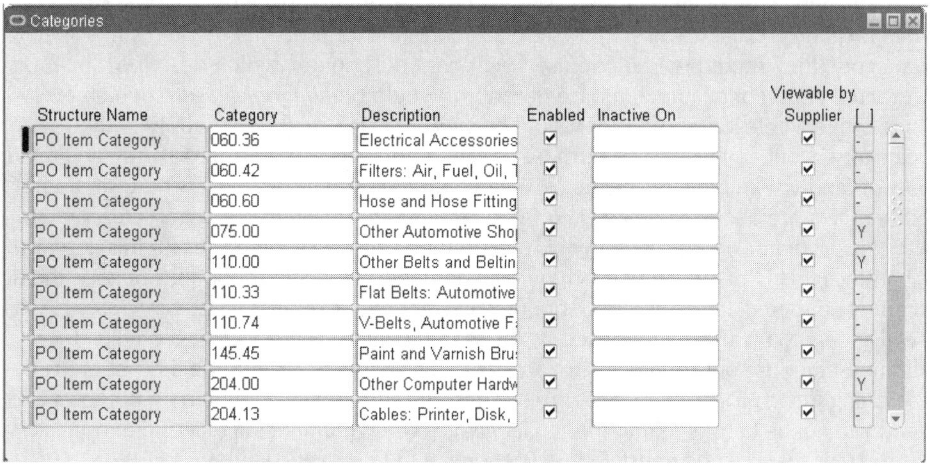

Structure Name	Category	Description	Enabled	Inactive On	Viewable by Supplier	
PO Item Category	060.36	Electrical Accessories	✔		✔	-
PO Item Category	060.42	Filters: Air, Fuel, Oil, 1	✔		✔	-
PO Item Category	060.60	Hose and Hose Fitting	✔		✔	-
PO Item Category	075.00	Other Automotive Sho|	✔		✔	Y
PO Item Category	110.00	Other Belts and Beltin	✔		✔	Y
PO Item Category	110.33	Flat Belts: Automotive	✔		✔	-
PO Item Category	110.74	V-Belts, Automotive F:	✔		✔	-
PO Item Category	145.45	Paint and Varnish Bru:	✔		✔	-
PO Item Category	204.00	Other Computer Hardw	✔		✔	Y
PO Item Category	204.13	Cables: Printer, Disk,	✔		✔	-

Purchasing | Setup | Items | Categories | Category Codes

FIGURE 3-19.   *Adding category codes*

| Agreements | Stores | Schema | Configuration |
| Upload | Base Descriptors | **Item Categories** | Category Hierarchy | Categ |

Schema: Item Categories >

Create Item Category

* Indicates required field   Cancel   Apply

* Category Key   RM
                  Unique internal identifier. This value can be
                  the same as the name.

* Category Name   Raw Materials

Description   Used for all Raw
              Materials
              purchasing

iProcurement Catalog Administration I Schema I Item Categories I
Create Category button

FIGURE 3-20.   *Creating shopping categories*

Creating Shopping Categories   Unlike the purchasing and inventory categories described
earlier in this chapter, shopping categories are not key flexfields, and are created and maintained
in a different way. Using the iProcurement Catalog Administration responsibility, go to Schema I
Item Categories, and select the Create Category button. Figure 3-20 shows that only a CATEGORY KEY
and CATEGORY NAME are required (the asterisk denotes a required field in the web windows). The
key is the internal name for this category, while the name appears on the search screens. An
optional DESCRIPTION can also be added.

Once the shopping category is saved, it can be queried back up, and the category descriptors
can be added. Category descriptors are attributes that describe all the items in a specific shopping
category; they should not be confused with base descriptors, which describe all items within
iProcurement. For example, a base descriptor would be *Unit of Measure,* which every purchase
has, while a category descriptor would be *Wood,* which might only apply to the shopping
category Wooden Desks. The purpose of setting up category descriptors is to facilitate more
user-friendly searching. Shoppers can search and find items by keys that are set up in Oracle, and
descriptors are one of these keys. Refer to Figure 3-21 to set up a category descriptor.

First, assign a DESCRIPTOR KEY, which is a unique code the system uses for this descriptor. Note
that since this is a unique code, and it is set up under a specific shopping category, the descriptors
cannot be shared across multiple shopping categories. Next, add the DESCRIPTOR NAME, which is what
will appear to the users and is used by the search engine. The DESCRIPTION, on the other hand, is for
administrator use only and does not appear to the shoppers. Determine the TYPE of the descriptor,
selecting from TEXT, NUMBER, or TRANSLATABLE TEXT. TEXT descriptors can be both numbers and characters
and will not be translated into foreign languages when multiple languages are installed, whereas
TRANSLATABLE TEXT can be translated. NUMBER only allows numeric values.

SEQUENCE determines where this descriptor will display in the search results screen for the
shoppers. Note that these descriptors will only display when you browse by category or use an
advanced search, and not during other types of searches. When a SEQUENCE is not added, then the
category descriptors will appear after the base descriptors for this item. The next three fields
determine how this category descriptor will interact with the shoppers. Selecting Yes for

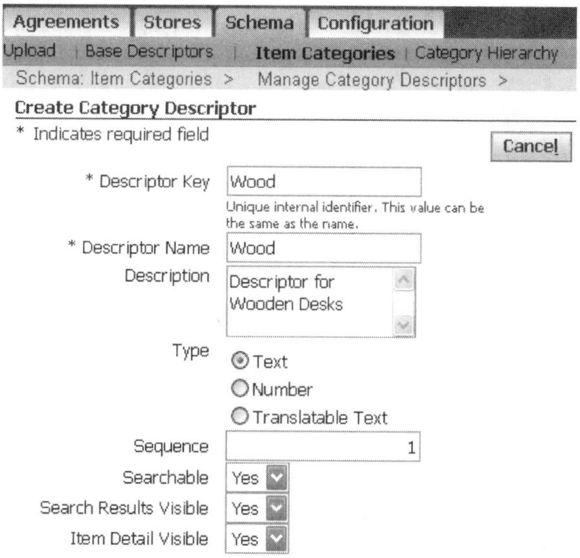

iProcurement Catalog Administration | Schema | Item Categories | query up a category, select Manage Category Descriptors

FIGURE 3-21. *Adding category descriptors to shopping categories*

SEARCHABLE is what will make this descriptor available for the shoppers to search on. When this is not selected, then it is really just additional information about the category the shoppers can see after they have found an item, but does not assist with actually finding the items they want to buy. SEARCH RESULTS VISIBLE determines if the shoppers can see this descriptor after they have found an item associated with it in the search results screen. The last option, ITEM DETAIL VISIBLE, determines if the shoppers can see this descriptor when they click the item link.

Mapping Purchasing Categories to Shopping Categories If the profile POR: Autocreate Shopping Category and Mapping is set to Yes, the purchasing and shopping categories will be already mapped when they are added to an item (see Figure 3-22). Note that while a shopping category can be mapped to multiple purchasing categories, each purchasing category can only be mapped once, to a single Shopping category. Also notice that you can search or create mappings by purchasing category or by shopping category, depending on which tab you select.

When a category is not mapped, click Map after finding the item, noting in Figure 3-23 that more than one purchasing category can be selected to be mapped at the same time. After clicking Map, select the shopping category you want to map them to and save. Use the Remove Mapping button to unmap purchasing and shopping categories.

Tying It All Together The setup steps given previously are in the order they have to happen for a new implementation of Purchasing and iProcurement, but they are a little confusing for a system that is already implemented when you are adding new items and categories during the

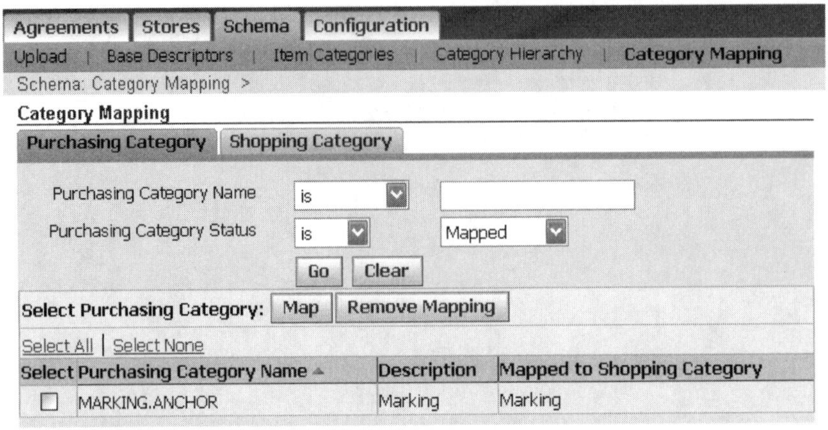

Agreements	Stores	Schema	Configuration

Upload | Base Descriptors | Item Categories | Category Hierarchy | **Category Mapping**

Schema: Category Mapping >

Category Mapping

Purchasing Category	Shopping Category

Purchasing Category Name	is [▾]	[ ]
Purchasing Category Status	is [▾]	Mapped [▾]

Go   **Clear**

Select Purchasing Category: **Map**   **Remove Mapping**

Select All | Select None

Select	Purchasing Category Name ▲	Description	Mapped to Shopping Category
☐	MARKING.ANCHOR	Marking	Marking

iProcurement Catalog Administration | Schema | Category Mapping

FIGURE 3-22.   *Purchasing category already mapped to a shopping category*

Agreements	Stores	Schema	Configuration

Upload | Base Descriptors | Item Categories | Category Hierarchy | **Category Mapping**

Schema: Category Mapping >

Category Mapping

Purchasing Category	Shopping Category

Purchasing Category Name	is [▾]	[ ]
Purchasing Category Status	is [▾]	Not Mapped [▾]

Go   **Clear**

Select Purchasing Category: **Map**   **Remove Mapping**   ⊙ Previous   1-10 [▾]   Next 10 ⊙

Select All | Select None

Select	Purchasing Category Name ▲	Description	Mapped to Shopping Category
☐	DEFAULT.DEFAULT	Default	
☑	BULK RAW MATL.ANGLE STOCK	Bulk Raw Materials	
☑	BULK RAW MATL.FLAT STOCK	BULK RAW MATL.FLAT STOCK	
☑	BULK RAW MATL.H STOCK	BULK RAW MATL.H STOCK	
☑	BULK RAW MATL.ROUND BAR STOCK	BULK RAW MATL.ROUND BAR STOCK	
☑	BULK RAW MATL.ROUND TUBING	BULK RAW MATL.ROUND TUBING	
☑	BULK RAW MATL.SQ/RECT TUBING	BULK RAW MATL.SQ/RECT TUBING	
☐	CD.DEFAULT	CD.DEFAULT	
☐	DEMO PRODUCT.STAND	DEMO PRODUCT.STAND	

iProcurement Catalog Administration | Schema | Category Mapping

FIGURE 3-23.   *Selecting items to map the purchasing to the shopping category*

course of normal maintenance. The following illustration shows the steps to add a new category and item, and have them appear in iProcurement. Notice that the Purchasing to Shopping mapping takes place *prior* to a category being assigned to an item.

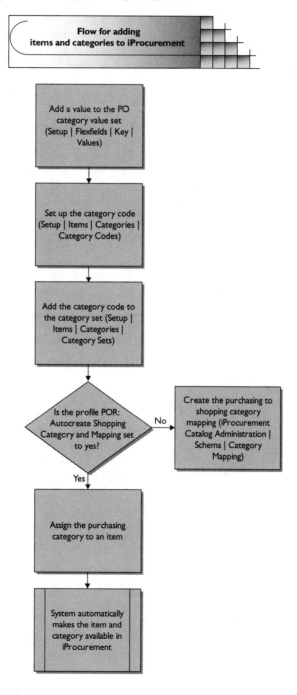

Setting Up and Using Expense Account Rules

Rules can be set up for generating account numbers associated with a requisition *without* actually modifying the PO Requisition Account Generator (POWFRQAG). This account generator determines what General Ledger account number is associated with each line of a requisition, and is usually modified by each organization to meet its specific accounting needs. Out of the box, it will default items being delivered into inventory to the receiving account for the inventory organization, and expense items based on the default expense account assigned first to the item, then to an employee's default expense account, or when neither is populated, the shoppers Primary Favorite account set in their Preferences (see the later section "iProcurement Preferences").

Note that the account generator workflow *must* be modified to use project information to generate an account number based on project information. Expense Accounts Rules come into play when the employee expense account is used by the workflow to generate the expense account, allowing defaults to override specific segments on the account number, based on the category associated with the requisition line. There is a profile, POR: Apply Expense Account Rules to Favorite Charge Accounts, that will also call these rules when shoppers do not have an expense account associated with their employee records, and the Primary Favorite Charge Account is selected by the workflow as the default expense account. This is only called when the favorite account is defaulted in, and not when the shopper selects a favorite account manually.

Table 3-2 explains the different conditions for defaulting an account number, and where the default comes from. While reviewing it, keep in mind that the new feature in R12 called Subledger Accounting, or SLA, does not replace the account generators in EBS. It can use the values assigned by the account generator, or use other defining attributes on a transaction, to generate the final account number used to create the journal entry for a transaction.

To set up an Expense Account Rule, refer to Figure 3-24. The rules must be set up not only for each purchasing category you want it to apply to, but also for each individual account segment in your chart of accounts that you want to default. When rules are not set up for all segments, the undefined segments will default from either the expense account assigned to the shopper, or the primary favorite account in the shopper's preferences.

ACCOUNT RULE TYPE will default to ITEM CATEGORY, and there are no other selections. ACCOUNT RULE VALUE is where the purchasing category is entered. When the shopper either selects an expense item associated with this category or enters this category on a non-catalog request, then this rule will be used. SEGMENT NAME is the segment in the chart of accounts you are setting this rule for; again, if you want to default all the segments in your account number for this category, you must create a rule for each segment separately. SEGMENT VALUE is the actual value you want to use for the account number.

Optional Setups

There are a number of additional setups that can now be added to increase functionality and usability within iProcurement.

Setting Up the Main Store

The Main Store is the area where all the items set up in Purchasing can be purchased. Employees can search for these items using a search option, or by drilling down into the store. This drill-down feature uses category hierarchies, which associate browsing hierarchies with shopping categories.

Condition	Default Account	Navigation or Comments
Delivered to Inventory	Receiving Account	Purchasing | Setup | Organizations | Receiving Options | Receiving Inventory Account
Delivered to Expense	Expense Account on the Item	Purchasing | Items | Organization Items | Purchasing tab
	Employee Expense Account	Purchasing | Setup | Personnel | Employees | Assignment tab| Default Expense Account
	Primary Favorite	iProcurement | Preferences | iProcurement Preferences | Favorite Charge Account set as Primary
Delivered to Expense and Expense Account Rules are set up and the employee has a default expense account	Expense Account Rules for the defined segments, the rest of the segments from the Employee Expense Account.	Purchasing | Setup | Financials | Accounting | Expense Account Rules
Delivered to Expense and Expense Account Rules are set up and the employee does *not* have a default expense account	Expense Account Rules for the defined segments, the rest of the segments from the Primary Favorite Account for the shopper.	Profile POR: Apply Expense Account Rules to Favorite Charge Account must be set to Yes
No Account defaults on the requisition	This occurs when an item is delivered to an expense location (not inventory) and there is no default expense account on the employee, and no primary favorites account.	

TABLE 3-2. *General Ledger Account Number Defaults for Requisitions*

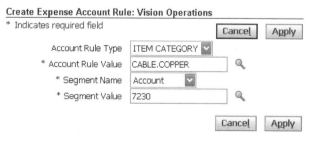

Purchasing | Setup | Financials | Accounting | Expense Account Rules

FIGURE 3-24. *Creating expense account rules*

As outlined previously in this chapter, the shopping hierarchies are associated with purchasing categories, which are then assigned to items, whereas a browsing category is a collection of shopping categories used for drilling down in a store. It is important to understand this relationship, because if the hierarchies and mappings are not set up correctly, the shoppers will not be able to drill down to items. The following illustration shows this relationship, along with the navigation path to set up each part of the hierarchy.

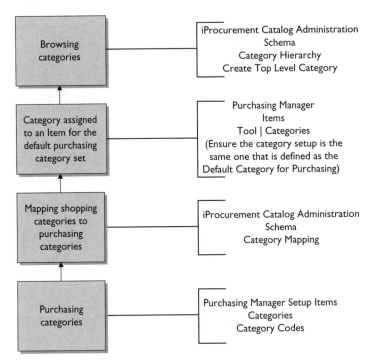

Purchasing Categories is explained in the section "Creating Category Codes," while the mapping of purchasing categories to shopping categories is defined in the section "Mapping Purchasing Categories to Shopping Categories." Refer to the section "Items" of this chapter to assign a category to an item from the default purchasing category set.

Notice the order of these setups: the hierarchy has to be built from the bottom up, with the browsing categories and hierarchy being the last setup to be completed. The way the hierarchy works is when you click the Main Store, the Browsing Categories appear. Drill down into one of the Browsing Categories, and the Shopping Categories associated with it appear. From here, drilling down one more level, the Purchasing Categories associated with the Shopping Category show, and the final level will show all the items assigned to this Purchasing Category. Refer to Figure 3-25 to see how the setups are linked in iProcurement Catalog Administration.

To set up your category hierarchy for browsing, click the Create Top-Level Category and add the CATEGORY KEY, or short name, for this browsing category. The CATEGORY NAME is what the shoppers will see in iProcurement, while the DESCRIPTION does not appear. Clicking Apply will save the category, assigning it a TYPE of Browsing. Next, the category type of item is associated with it and can either be added from an existing shopping category by selecting Insert Existing Child, or by selecting Create Child to create a new one. Creating a child has the exact same fields (CATEGORY KEY,

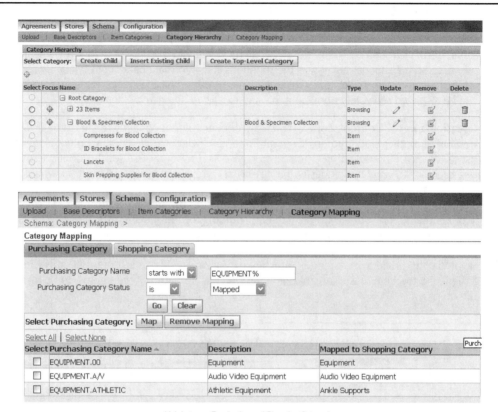

Link between Purchasing and Shopping Categories

iProcurement Catalog Administration I Schema I Category Hierarchy

FIGURE 3-25. *Linking the browsing and shopping categories to purchasing categories to create the shopping hierarchy*

CATEGORY NAME, and DESCRIPTION) as creating a top-level category, but the type will be Item instead of Browsing when it is saved. When a category is created this way, it is not mapped to any purchasing categories and will therefore have no items underneath it until it is mapped.

Adding Content Zones for Security

Content zones replaced Realms in prior releases of iProcurement; they allow security to be added based on the supplier associated with an item or specific shopping and browsing categories (the restrictions cannot be done at the purchasing category level). Not only do content zones restrict access, they also are required to grant access to items for shopping. By default, the local content zone is accessible to the Main Store.

There are four different types of content zones that can be created: Local, Punchout, Transparent Punchout, and Informational. Local content consists of all items and their associated categories defined in Oracle Purchasing. Punchout and Transparent Punchout both are supplier-maintained items that can be accessed and purchased via iProcurement, but where the items are maintained on a supplier's web site. The main difference between the two is that when using a Punchout, you access the supplier's web site directly to shop, while a Transparent Punchout accesses the supplier's site in the background and returns matched items directly to iProcurement for browsing and purchase, so the shopper never sees the supplier's site. Informational content, or *smart forms,* are additional information fields added to specific items or purchasing categories, and access to them can be restricted separately from the items and categories they are associated to.

Creating a Local Content Zone   To create a local content zone, navigate to the iProcurement Catalog Administration | Stores | Content Zone, and select Create Local Content Zone from the list of values, before selecting Go (refer to Figure 3-26). Add a NAME for this content zone, and a DESCRIPTION as to what it includes, what it restricts, who should be assigned it, or what store it pertains to.

Local content zones can restrict or include specific suppliers. These suppliers are either the supplier the item is sourced from in Oracle Sourcing, or the specific supplier associated with an item on the Approved Supplier List (Purchasing | Supply Base | Approved Supplier List). When you select INCLUDE or EXCLUDE ITEMS FROM SPECIFIC SUPPLIERS, you must also identify the suppliers you want to either include or exclude. Selecting INCLUDE ITEMS WITHOUT SUPPLIERS will allow items only assigned to the item master organization, as well as internally sourced items, to be displayed in iProcurement.

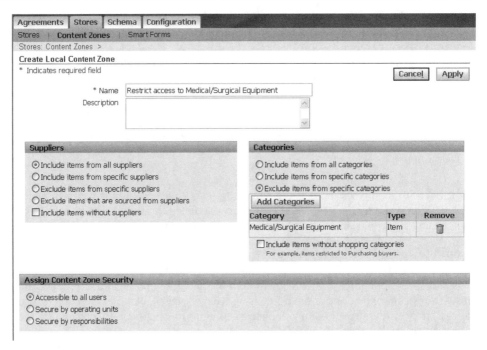

iProcurement Catalog Administration | Stores | Content Zones

FIGURE 3-26.   *Creating a local content zone*

Shopping and browsing categories can also be included or excluded, which restricts or grants access to items associated with that category via the purchasing and shopping category mappings. Select the category to include or exclude from the list of values (which appears once INCLUDE or EXCLUDE ITEMS FROM SPECIFIC CATEGORIES is selected). Checking INCLUDE ITEMS WITHOUT SHOPPING CATEGORIES will allow items set up in Oracle Purchasing that are assigned to purchasing categories that are not mapped to a specific shopping category to appear.

Once the categories and suppliers are defined for a specific local content zone, security can be added to make it available to all users, or to secure it to a specific operating unit or responsibility. Restrictions can only be made at the operating unit or responsibility levels.

Creating an Informational Content Zone   Figure 3-27 shows an informational content zone that will take the user to a third-party site to make travel arrangements. This is different than both a punchout and an information template. *Punchouts* allow users to shop for items found at a third party's web site, such as Dell or Staples, either by using their web site to browse and select items (direct punchout) or by returning matches within iProcurement during a search (transparent punchout). *Information templates* (Purchasing | Setup | Information Templates) allow additional information to be required when purchasing an item. An example of this would be adding the fields required when requesting business cards. Informational content added via the content zone works similar to a punchout in that you are directed to a supplier site, with one major difference: the items are not returned to iProcurement to create a requisition. These are really links to where you want the users to make the actual purchases.

To create an informational content zone, add the NAME and DESCRIPTION the shoppers will see in iProcurement. An IMAGE can be added by using the URL (Uniform Resource Locator) where the image resides, or the web address. Images can also be loaded into a location on the server, identified with the profile option POR: Hosted Images Directory. In this case, only the name of the image file would need to be entered here and not the actual location. KEYWORDS can be added to ensure this informational content appears during searches. When KEYWORDS are not added, then this content would only appear when a shopper searched on either the name or one of the words in the description. Add the URL where you are directing the shoppers to make their purchases, and then assign who will have access to this informational content zone and click Apply to save.

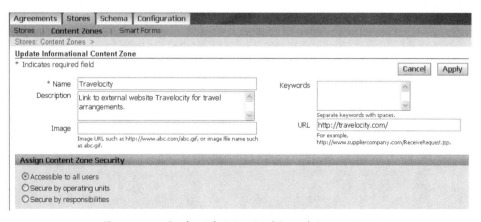

iProcurement Catalog Administration | Stores | Content Zones

FIGURE 3-27.   *Creating an informational content zone*

Creating Transparent Punchouts and Direct Punchouts As mentioned previously, the difference between a direct punchout and a transparent punchout is where the shopper actually does the shopping. When using a direct punchout, the shopper is taken to a supplier's web site, usually one set up specifically for your company that limits the items available and includes your company's specific pricing. Searching for items and creating a shopping cart happens on the supplier's web site; upon checkout, the items are returned to iProcurement for finalization and approval. These items that are available on the supplier's site will not come up during a search in iProcurement. But a transparent punchout is the exact opposite: shoppers are not redirected to the supplier's web site, but instead items that are available for purchase are displayed in iProcurement during searches and browsing. Both are set up as content zones, and there is only one difference in the setup, which will be noted.

Figure 3-28 shows a direct punchout. Add the NAME and DESCRIPTION that will appear for the shoppers, and optionally add a URL for an IMAGE, either referencing a web address or a file on the Oracle server located where the POR: Hosted Images Directory is set to.

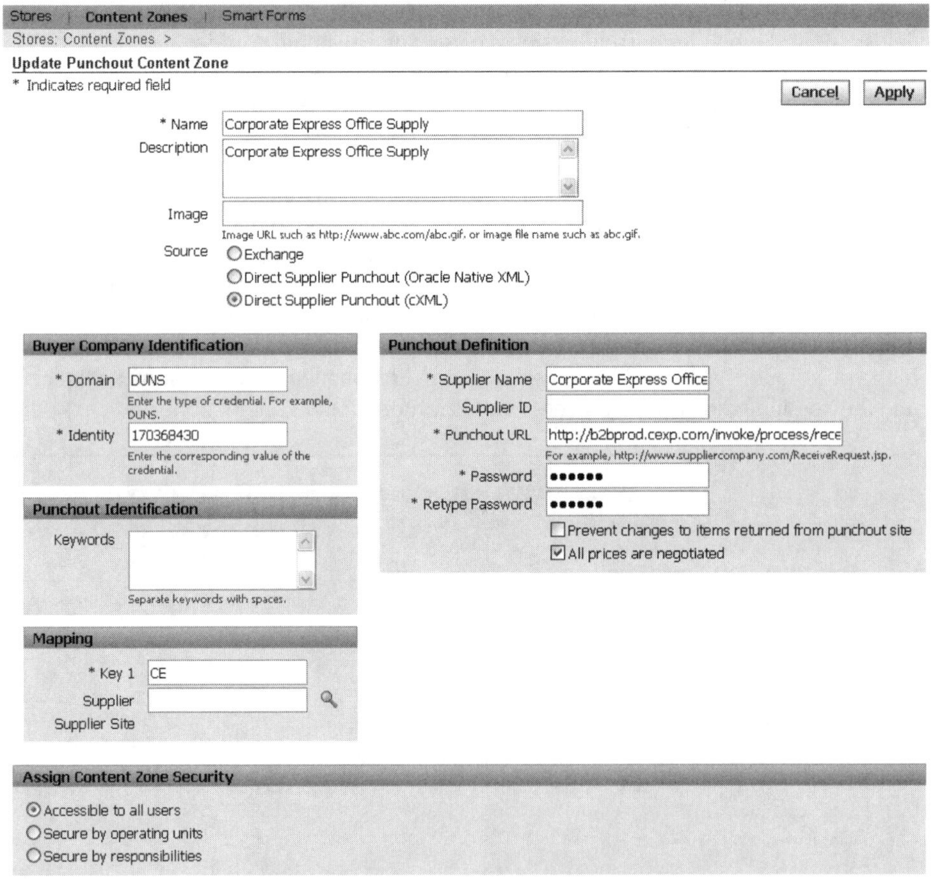

iProcurement Catalog Administration | Stores | Content Zones

FIGURE 3-28. *Creating a punchout content zone*

Source	Available With	Description
Direct Supplier Punchout (cXML)	Punchout	Punching out directly to a supplier site for shopping using cXML (commerce eXtensible Markup Language). While this does appear as a list in R12, it is no longer supported.
Direct Supplier Punchout (Oracle Native XML)	Punchout	Punching out directly to a supplier site for shopping using Oracle's native XML.
Exchange	Punchout and Transparent Punchout	Exchange (https://Exchange.Oracle.com for production or https://TestExchange.Oracle.com for the test site) is a web service providing B2B (business-to-business) free service that allows buyers to hook up with sellers to purchase items via iProcurement. This option can be used when the supplier does not have the abilities to have a customer punch directly into their web site, or when an authentication service is required. When this option is selected, Oracle Exchange acts as the host to the punchout, facilitating the communication between the buyer and the seller.
Supplier	Transparent Punchout	Directly access data directly hosted by the supplier, allowing searches in the main store to return data from the supplier site directly in iProcurement. This differs from regular punchouts where the shopper accesses the seller's web site directly to do searches, select items, and then returns back to iProcurement for requisition submission.

TABLE 3-3. *Punchout Source Options*

SOURCE is the only area that is different between a direct and transparent punchout. Direct punchouts have the option of EXCHANGE, DIRECT SUPPLIER PUNCHOUT (ORACLE NATIVE XML), or DIRECT SUPPLIER PUNCHOUT (cXML), while transparent punchouts allow either EXCHANGE or SUPPLIER. Refer to Table 3-3 for an explanation of each SOURCE.

To complete setting up a Punchout via Exchange or Direct Supplier Punchout (Oracle Native XML), add the Buyer Company Information by entering the COMPANY NAME that you will be using to identify yourself with to the supplier. The COMPANY ID is a unique identifier that can be passed to identify your company to the supplier. When working with your supplier in setting up the punchout, this is the information that will be passed in the field called companyDUNS that is sent as part of the login request. These fields are not available when setting up a Direct Supplier Punchout (cXML), which requires a DOMAIN and IDENTITY instead. Punchout Identification KEYWORDS can be added to ensure that searches always include these words during a punchout. KEY 1 under the Mapping sections should be populated with Exchange when the Source selected was

Exchange, or to the supplier name for other options. When the Source was *not* Exchange, a SUPPLIER and a SUPPLIER SITE can be selected from the list of values, which will populate on the requisition. When these fields are not populated, then Oracle derives the supplier and site from the information passed back from the punchout.

To complete the Punchout Definition, add the PUNCHOUT URL, which is the URL of the supplier site where you are punching into, along with the program name that will be receiving the login request. Note that this is not the same URL you would use to access the site from a web browser for testing, as it requires the login information to be passed along with the actual address. Next enter the USER NAME if the Source is Exchange, and add the password in both the PASSWORD and RETYPE PASSWORD fields. Since this field is hidden so that you cannot see your typing, ensure that you save the password someplace outside of Oracle, and that people know where it is.

The encoding method, used with a Source of Direct Supplier Punchout, determines what encoding standard is used for the login request. While other methods are supported, Oracle recommends that UTF-8 is used. Selecting PREVENT CHANGES TO ITEMS RETURNED FROM PUNCHOUT SITE will prevent the shoppers from making any changes to the quantities that were returned from the supplier site. This option is needed when the supplier is processing information in their system based on quantities entered on their site. SEND OPTIONAL USER AND COMPANY INFORMATION TO PUNCHOUT SUPPLIER SITE is only available when setting up a Direct Supplier Punchout; it will send additional information to the supplier site during the login request.

Selecting EXTEND USER'S IDLE SESSION TIMEOUT DURING PUNCHOUT, available for both Exchange and Native XML setups only, will extend the timeout for inactivity, as set with the profile ICX: Session Timeout, ensuring that Oracle does not time out the shoppers' sessions while they are working on the supplier site and outside of Oracle. If you select this option, you will need to ensure that the supplier's web site is accessing the iProcurement servers every time a web page is opened, which will keep the session active. When this is not selected and set up, then Oracle will time out the shoppers after the time set with the session timeout profile is reached. The final option, ALL PRICES ARE NEGOTIATED, determines how this supplier is handled in Daily Business Intelligence for reporting.

The last section, Assign Content Zone Security, determines if this content zone is accessible to all users or secured by operating units or by responsibilities.

When performing a transparent punchout, the same fields apply when the Source is Exchange, but there are a few differences when the Source is Supplier. First, under Transparent Punchout Definitions, you will need to add a SUPPLIER NAME and a SUPPLIER ID. The supplier name is required and refers to the name of the supplier whose site you are accessing. If the Source was Exchange, then the name will be Exchange. The SUPPLIER ID is optional and is not required when you assigned a SUPPLIER and SUPPLIER SITE. The SUPPLIER ID field is then passed back with the shopping cart from the supplier and is used to map to an internal supplier. The only other difference is the ability to add Supplemental Information when the Source is Supplier. This information (NAME and VALUE) is then passed during the punchout and can be used by the supplier's site to adjust the information being passed back to iProcurement (such as special pricing for certain divisions.)

Once the content zones are set up, they are then assigned to specific stores in iProcurement.

Using Smart Forms

"Smart forms" is really just another term for non-catalog requests. As previously mentioned, you have the option of shopping for items either from a supplier web site or from the items set up in Purchasing, or else you can create a non-catalog request for purchase of items that are not available from the first two sources. A smart form is a predefined non-catalog request for a specific item,

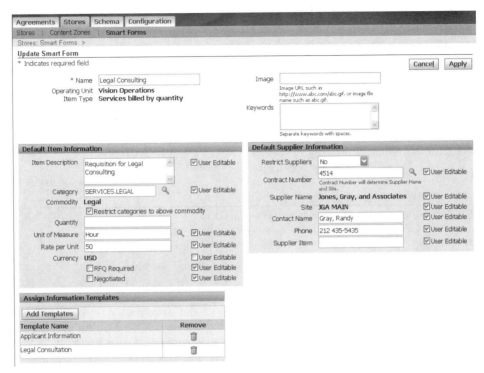

iProcurement Catalog Administration I Stores I Smart Forms

FIGURE 3-29. *Setting up smart forms for non-catalog requests*

where some of the fields are predefined for the users. A default non-catalog request smart form is delivered by Oracle, and additional smart forms can be set up to reduce the data entered by a shopper as well as ensure required data for this purchase is provided.

Refer to Figure 3-29 to set up a smart form. Assign a NAME to the form, which the shoppers will see when they sign in to a store containing this smart form. Select the OPERATING UNIT that will have access to this form, or leave it blank to make it available for all operating units. Note that if you want to have a smart form with different information, such as currency, for multiple operating units, you must create one smart form for each operating unit.

The ITEM TYPE can be set to Goods Billed By Quantity, Goods or Services Billed By Amount, or Services Billed By Quantity. Select these options carefully, as they will affect how the requisition becomes a purchase order as well as how the payables invoice is matched to the purchase order. Goods Billed By Quantity and Services Billed By Quantity work very similarly in that they require a quantity, a unit of measure, and a unit price (or price per unit, in the case of services) to calculate the actual price. Services Billed By Amount, on the other hand, will end up defaulting the quantity to 1, allowing an amount to be entered. The main difference is how these are then subsequently received and matched. This last choice, Services Billed By Amount, makes it very confusing to receive or invoice less than the full amount and is therefore usually used for fixed-price services. In R12, these

Item Type	Profile	Default Calculation
Goods billed by quantity	POR: Goods Line Type	Goods *Calculation:* Quantity times Unit Price
Goods or services billed by amount	POR: Amount-Based Services Line Type	Fixed Price Services *Calculation:* Amount only (quantity equals 1)
Services billed by quantity	POR: Rate-Based Services Line Type	Svcs – Qty *Calculation:* Quantity times Rate per Unit

TABLE 3-4.   *Setting Calculations for Item Types*

ITEM TYPES can be associated with different line types set up in Purchasing (Setup | Purchasing | Line Types) via profile options. The association between the item type, the line type, and their default settings is outlined in Table 3-4.

An IMAGE can be added to the store to display on the home page next to the store; it is either the path where the image exists (ensuring that all shoppers will have access to that path) or a filename, where the file is loaded into the directory identified with the profile POR: Hosted Images Directory. KEYWORDS can be added for searching as well. Notice that only the NAME is a required field on a smart form; all additional information can be left blank so that the shoppers enter the information themselves.

Under both the Default Item Information and Default Supplier Information sections, each field has the option of being USER EDITABLE, allowing the shoppers to make updates to the defaults. When this field is not checked, the shoppers cannot update the information in the field.

Default Item Information includes an ITEM DESCRIPTION, which is the description of what is being purchased. Even though these fields are called Item Information, they are not related to items set up in Purchasing. A default for the CATEGORY can also be entered; these categories are the purchasing categories, not the shopping or browsing categories. The COMMODITY will populate with the commodity associated with the CATEGORY selected and cannot be updated (Purchasing | Setup | Items | Commodities | Commodities). Selecting RESTRICT CATEGORIES TO ABOVE COMMODITY will restrict the categories a shopper can select to the commodity assigned to the category on the smart form; this setting has functionality only when USER EDITABLE is selected for the CATEGORY field.

The next few fields change, depending on the ITEM TYPE selected for this smart form. When Goods Billed By Quantity was selected, then the QUANTITY, UNIT OF MEASURE, and UNIT PRICE can be entered (all fields are not required when defining the smart form, though they are for shoppers when adding this purchase to the shopping cart). If Services Billed By Quantity was selected, then the fields change to QUANTITY, UNIT OF MEASURE, and RATE PER UNIT, but they mean the same things. Goods or Services Billed By Amount only allows an AMOUNT to be entered. Next select the CURRENCY for this request. When the currency is not entered, it will default to the currency assigned to the operating unit assigned to the responsibility. Selecting RFQ REQUIRED will alert the buyer that this requisition should go out for a request for quote prior to procuring. The last option in this section, NEGOTIATED, works with Daily Business Intelligence for reporting.

In the Default Supplier Information, this smart form can be restricted to a specific operating unit only, by setting RESTRICT SUPPLIERS to No. When this field is set to Category ASL, then the list of available suppliers is restricted to the approved supplier list, or ASL, for the selected category (Purchasing | Supply Base | Approved Supplier List). Note that the purchasing category is called COMMODITY on the ASL form. When all items purchased with this smart form are related to a specific contract purchase agreement or global contract in purchasing, the contract number can be entered. This will default the SUPPLIER NAME and SITE, and the shopper *cannot* update this information, even when USER EDITABLE is selected. SUPPLIER NAME and SITE can be entered without a CONTRACT NUMBER as well, including the CONTACT NAME at the supplier and their PHONE number. For reference on the purchase order, the SUPPLIER ITEM number can also be included.

Once the Default Item and Supplier Information is completed, an information template can be added to the smart form. Informational templates are used to provide additional fields for the shoppers to complete when making a request. The section Business Card Info seen in Figure 3-30 displays how an information template will appear on a smart form.

To create an information template, refer to Figure 3-31. Assign a name to the TEMPLATE, which is the name that will appear at the beginning of the section in iProcurement to the shoppers. Selecting AVAILABLE IN ALL ORGANIZATIONS will allow this template to be used on smart forms in more than one operating unit. Selecting an ATTACHMENT CATEGORY of To Supplier will allow this template to be an

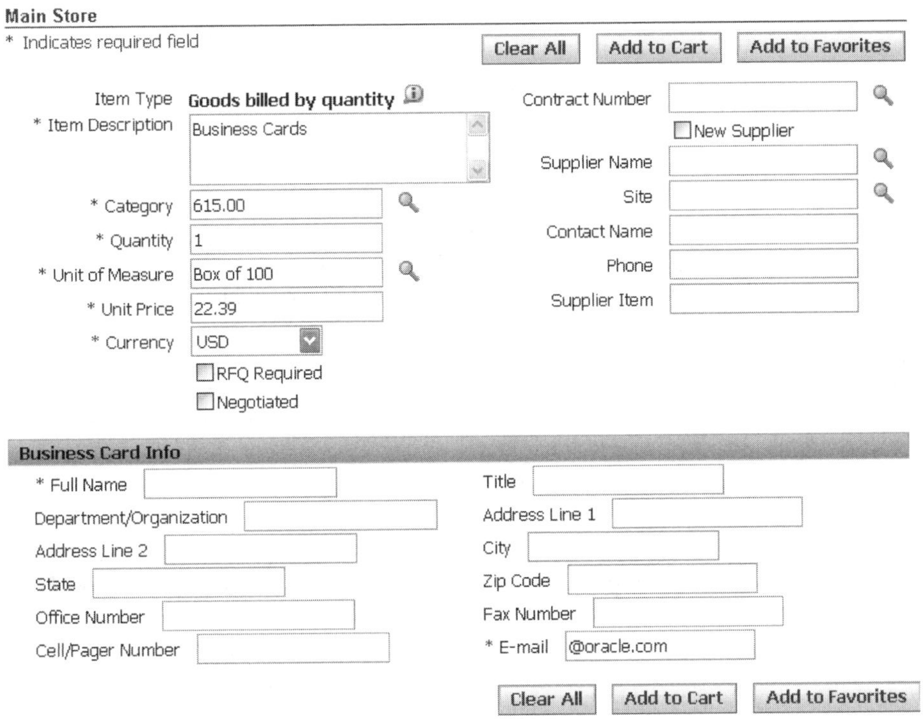

Main Store
* Indicates required field   [Clear All] [Add to Cart] [Add to Favorites]

Item Type	Goods billed by quantity
* Item Description	Business Cards
* Category	615.00
* Quantity	1
* Unit of Measure	Box of 100
* Unit Price	22.39
* Currency	USD
	☐ RFQ Required
	☐ Negotiated

Contract Number	
	☐ New Supplier
Supplier Name	
Site	
Contact Name	
Phone	
Supplier Item	

Business Card Info

* Full Name		Title	
Department/Organization		Address Line 1	
Address Line 2		City	
State		Zip Code	
Office Number		Fax Number	
Cell/Pager Number		* E-mail	@oracle.com

[Clear All] [Add to Cart] [Add to Favorites]

FIGURE 3-30. *Using information templates with a smart form*

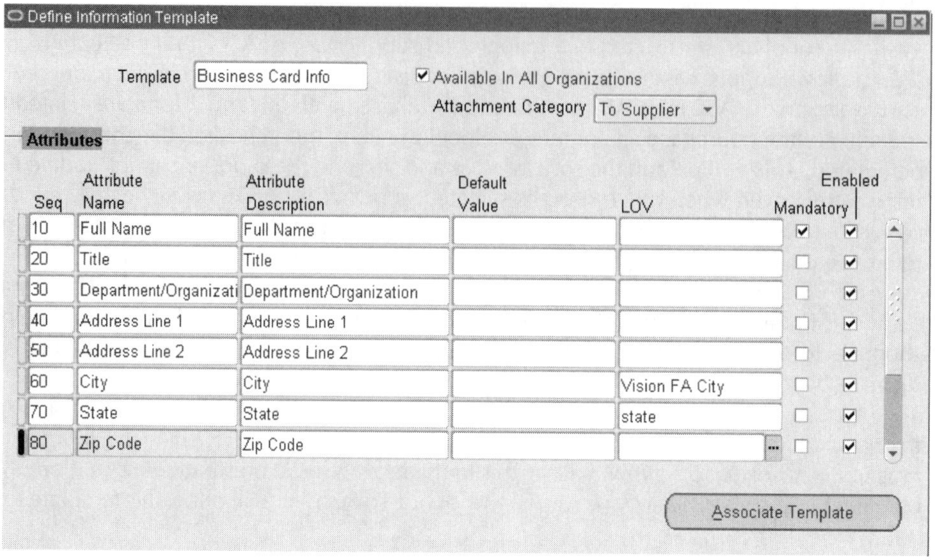

Purchasing | Setup | Information Template

FIGURE 3-31. *Creating an information template to use with a smart form*

attachment to the purchase order for the supplier, while To Buyer makes it available to the buyers when they are creating the purchase order. The SEQ is the order in which this information will appear to the shoppers, along with the ATTRIBUTE DESCRIPTION. The ATTRIBUTE NAME is an internal name for this field, and making the name and description consistent can eliminate confusion. A DEFAULT VALUE can be assigned to this attribute, which the shopper can then override if necessary.

Entering an LOV, or list of values, provides a list the shopper can select from for this attribute. While EBS comes seeded with a large number of lists of values, additional lists can be set up (Purchasing | Setup | Flexfields | Validation | Sets, and Validation | Values to add the actual values. Refer to the section "Creating a Value Set for the Purchasing Category" for more information on adding a list of values.) Select MANDATORY if this is a required field, and ENABLED must be selected for this attribute to appear in iProcurement. Click the Associate Template button to associate this template to a specific item or category. This will cause this information template to be displayed in iProcurement not only when using the smart form, but when purchasing any items or categories that are associated with it.

Creating Stores and Adding Content Zones and Smart Forms

At this point, you are ready to start defining a *store,* which the shoppers will see when they sign in to iProcurement. Oracle comes with a Main Store and a Non-Catalog Request subtab already set up, but additional stores can be added for easier browsing, security, and for punchouts. To create a store, refer to Figure 3-32. Assign a NAME to the store, along with a DESCRIPTION. Both of these will appear on the iProcurement page for the shoppers to select from. An image can appear next to the name either by entering the URL where the image resides, ensuring all iProcurement

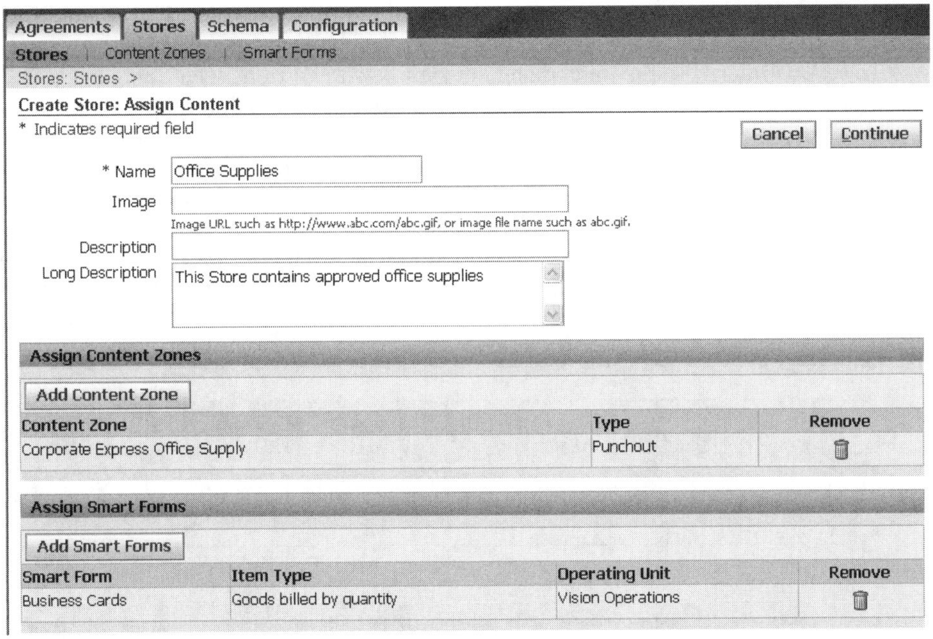

iProcurement Catalog Administration I Stores I Stores

FIGURE 3-32. *Creating a store*

users have access to this location, or by entering the filename and ensuring the file resides in the
location entered for the profile POR: Hosted Images Directory. A long description can also be
added to provide a more detailed explanation of what this store is used for. Once the store is set
up, content zones and smart forms can be added to it. Click either the Add Content Zone or Add
Smart Forms button and select from the list of values. Note that when smart forms are operating
unit specific, a separate smart form would need to be set up for each operating unit.

   Once this is saved, a sequence can be added to the content of the store, which will determine
the order in which items appear on the window, and the option to ALWAYS SHOW AS MATCH can be
selected. This will ensure that this content will always match a search, even if the keywords do
not. The store that is set as SEQUENCE 1 will default in on the Search screen if a user has not set a
My Favorite Store under that user's preferences.

Enabling Shipment Tracking for Requisitions

Oracle not only allows you to view requisitions, receipts, and purchase orders in iProcurement,
but also shipping information relating to orders. This feature works only when Advance Shipment
Notices, or ASNs, are received from the supplier when an item is shipped, and are loaded into
Oracle. A supplier can send your company an ASN one of two ways—either the ASN can be sent
electronically and imported directly into Oracle using the Receiving Open Interface, or manually
loaded into the iSupplier Portal, which allows the supplier to enter the ASN (see Chapters 5
and 6, "iSupplier Setups" and "Using iSupplier"). The ASN is required to include information

on the shipment, such as shipment number, shipment date, and expected receipt date, but it can optionally include freight carriers and waybill or airbill numbers. It is when this additional information is included that users can track their shipments.

To set up Oracle's shipment tracking integration with carriers, refer to Figure 3-33. In order to track shipments for a particular carrier, it must first be created in Purchasing (Setup | Purchasing | Freight Carriers). Once setup, then it can be selected from the list of values for the CARRIER NAME, and the CARRIER SHORT NAME will default in from the Freight Carrier setups. The TRACKING LEVEL should be set to Shipment Tracking, which allows each shipment that an ASN was received for to be tracked. Next, you will need to determine the REQUEST METHOD for obtaining the information from the carrier's web site. The two methods supported here are Get and Post. The main difference is that Get will display the requested information as part of the URL, while Post will not. Which you

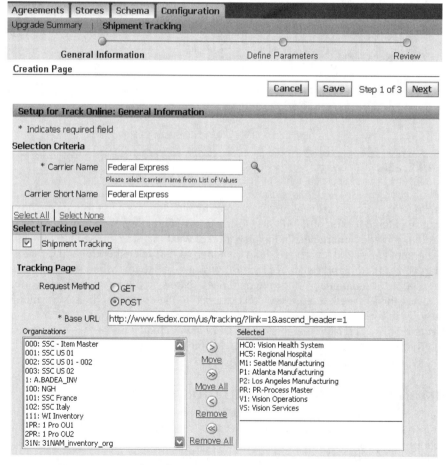

FIGURE 3-33. *Setting up shipment tracking*

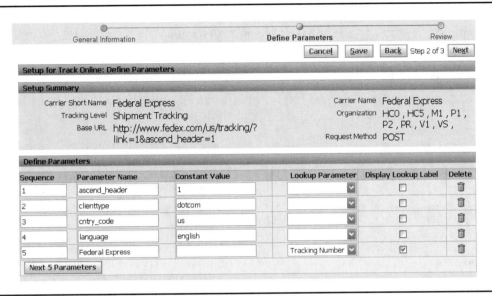

FIGURE 3-34. *Defining online tracking parameters*

select is actually determined by the carrier's web site. The BASE URL is entered and is the URL that Oracle will use to get the tracking information for the shipment.

Each carrier set up for tracking shipments can be restricted to the organizations that can see the data—only the organizations that appear on the SELECTED section can track shipments from this carrier.

Define Parameters are added on the next page. In the example in Figure 3-34, you can see that a country code (cntry_code) and the language are passed as constants to the web site, but the Tracking Number is a variable based on the tracking number associated with the shipment. These parameters will be unique for each carrier, depending on the information required by their web site to return tracking information. Selecting DISPLAY LOOKUP LABEL will display this parameter on the delivery tracking page in iProcurement. A summary page will display before you can finish the setups.

The process called Receiving Transaction Processor needs to be set to run on a scheduled basis to populate the shipment information with incoming ASNs. This is run as a concurrent request in Purchasing.

Profile Options

There are a large number of profile options that control the way iProcurement processes transactions, defaults information, and looks. Profiles can be set at different levels. At the highest level, site, profiles will affect all applications installed. The application level pertains to only a specific application, such as Purchasing or Payables. Responsibility will restrict this setting to a specific responsibility only, whereas server will restrict the control of the settings to a specific EBS server. Organization is used for anything for a specific organization, and finally, user is valid only for that user. The hierarchy of these levels always goes from user at the top, then organization, server, responsibility, application, and site at the bottom. Review Table 3-5 for a listing of the profiles, their default settings, and a description of what they control.

Name	Default Setting	Description
HR: Cross Business Group	No	When set to Yes, allows —buyers to be assigned to the same requisition when they are in different business groups. —approvers to exist in a different business group than the requestor. —buyers to select a request from outside the person creating the requisition's business group. This profile is most often needed when HR is installed and more than one business group has been defined.
ICX: Date Format Mask		When set, overrides the default date format of DD-MMM-YYYY.
ICX: Default Requisitions Template		Determines the requisition template (Purchasing | Setup | Purchasing | Requisition Templates) that will become the default.
ICX: Media directory	Default	Identifies the location where the media files are stored. Is usually the same as the OA_MEDIA location.
ICX: Numeric characters	Null will result in 1,000.00	Determines the display format for currency.
MRP: Default Sourcing Assignment Set		Determines which sourcing rules are used by iProcurement to select a supplier. (Purchasing | Supply Base | Assign Sourcing Rules)
PA: Allow Override of PA Distributions in AP/PO		Setting to Yes will allows the shopper to update the distribution account associated with a project.
PO: Allow Requisition Approval Forward Action	Yes	Determines if approvers can Forward or Approve and Forward a requisition. When set to No, approvers can only Approve and Reject requisitions.
PO: Enable Services Procurement	No	Should be set to Yes when Services Procurement is licensed and being used. Will allow Contractor Requests tab to appear in iProcurement.
PO: Legal Requisition Type		Determines the source for requisitions, selecting from Internal, Purchase (i.e., Supplier), or Both, based on the sourcing rules. This also affects searching for items. When this is set to Internal, only internally sourced items will be returned during a search.

TABLE 3-5. *iProcurement-Related Profiles*

Name	Default Setting	Description
PO: Notification Lines Display Limit	20	Sets the maximum number of lines that can be displayed on an approval notification.
PO: Validate Need-by Time for Requisition Submit		When set to Yes, a time stamp will be validated on the requisition. This profile works with POR: Default Need By Time, allowing it to return a time stamp for today's date that is prior to the system time stamp (e.g., if the system date and time is 01-JAN-2009 14:00, and the requisition date and time stamp is 01-JAN-2009 00:00, dates prior to 01-JAN-2009 are still not allowed).
PO: Workflow Processing Mode		Selecting Online starts the approval process immediately, while Background will start the process when the Workflow Background Process is next run. You must schedule the workflow Background Process in System Administrator if Background is selected.
POR: Allow Manual Selection of Source	No	When set to Yes, and PO: Legal Requisition Type is set to Internal or Both, allows the shopper to see the Stocked Internally field under Selected Source.
POR: Allow P-card Use with Encumbrance		Yes will allow a purchasing card (either a supplier or an employee card) to be associated with a requisition when encumbrances are turned on.
POR: Amount Based Services Line Type		Setting this determines the line type for non-catalog requests. This option sets how quantities, units of measure, and unit price are entered.
POR: Apply Expense Account Rules to Favorite Charge Accounts	No	Enforces expense account rules for a requestor's favorite charge account when set to Yes.
POR: Auto Load Category Descriptors	No	When this is set to Yes, category descriptors are created automatically from upload files, if one exists.
POR: Auto Load Root Descriptors	No	Root Descriptors is another name for Base Descriptors. Selecting Yes here will create the base descriptor if it does not exist during the bulk load process.
POR: Auto Load Shopping Categories	No	When set to Yes, Shopping Categories will be created if they do not exist during a bulk load.

TABLE 3-5.   *iProcurement-Related Profiles* (continued)

Name	Default Setting	Description
POR: Autocreate Shopping Category and Mapping	No	When set to Yes, will create a shopping category and mapping to the purchasing category as soon as a purchasing category is saved. When set to No, the shopping categories and mapping will have to be manually created.
POR: CA Certification File Name		When using punchouts and transparent punchouts, the certificate for secure sites will need to be stored, usually on the middle tier, and its location is entered here.
POR: Change Catalog Language	No	Allows searches to be done in a different language than the session language. Controls this by controlling if the field Change Catalog Language field is visible.
POR: Context value for Requisition distribution descriptive flexfield		Unlike forms, Context Sensitive DFF, or flexfields that appear or are required based on data stored in the applications, such as Organization Id, because this data lives in the forms, not the window. The data required for a specific value can be added to this profile for the requisition distribution.
POR: Context value for Requisition header descriptive flexfield		Unlike forms, Context Sensitive DFF, or flexfields that appear or are required based on data stored in the applications, such as Organization Id, because this data lives in the forms, not the window. The data required for a specific value can be added to this profile for the requisition header.
POR: Context value for Requisition line descriptive flexfield		Unlike forms, Context Sensitive DFF, or flexfields that appear or are required based on data stored in the applications, such as Organization Id, because this data lives in the forms, not the window. The data required for a specific value can be added to this profile for the requisition lines.
POR: Contractor Expense Line Type		Determines the line type associated with contract expenses (when using Services Procurement).
POR: Days Needed By	2	Determines the number of days added to the system date when populating the Need By date.
POR: Default Currency Conversion Rate Type		Default rate for non-catalog requests, uploaded items, punchout items, and contractor assignments when no rate is supplied.

TABLE 3-5. *iProcurement-Related Profiles* (continued)

Name	Default Setting	Description
POR: Default Need-by Time		Selecting Yes will default the time next to the date in the Need By field.
POR: Display Graphical Approval List	Yes	Determines if a graphical representation of the approvers on a requisition is displayed.
POR: Enable Advanced Search and Category Browse	Null, which enables the search	Controls if the users can see the Advanced Search field and browsing categories.
POR: Enable Automatic Debit Memo Creation for Returns	No	Setting this to Yes will create Debit Memos in Payables when an item is returned to a supplier using the return feature (as opposed to a correction).
POR: Generate and Display Account at Checkout	No	Determines if the charge account is displayed in the Billing region of the checkout page. When this is not set to Yes, the shopper will not see the charge account unless they edit the lines prior to checking out.
POR: Goods Line Type	Goods	Determines the default line type for both uploaded items and quantity-based non-catalog requests.
POR: Hosted Images Directory		Location where image files are stored, usually associated with the /OA_MEDIA/ Directory.
POR: One Time Location		Assigns a location code to any single-use, or one-time, delivery addresses added when checking out.
POR: Override Location Flag(1)	Yes	When set to Yes, allows the default location to be updated by the shopper when checking out.
POR: Override Requester	No	Allows the shopper to update the requestor's name associated with a requisition. Options include By All, which allows the user or shopper to select any requestor, or Within Organization, which will only allow a person assigned to the same business group to be selected.
POR: Preferences – Deliver to Location		Determines the default Deliver To location for iProcurement users.
POR: Preferences – Requester		Determines the default Requestor. When not set, the requestor will default to the employee associated with the user creating the requisition.
POR: Preferences – Selected Items Default to Inventory		Indicates if the Deliver To Subinventory box is checked on a user's iProcurement Preferences.

TABLE 3-5. *iProcurement-Related Profiles* (continued)

Name	Default Setting	Description
POR: Preferences – SubInventory		Provides a default subinventory for inventory requisitions when POR: Preferences: Selected Items Default to Inventory is set to Yes.
POR: Preferences for project-related fields		System defaults can be set for the following Oracle Projects–related fields: Award Expenditure Item Date Offset Expenditure Org Expenditure Type Project Task
POR: Proxy Server Name		When using punchouts and iProcurement is set up with a Proxy Server, this is the name of the server. Ensure you reboot the Internet Application Server if you make a change to this setting.
POR: Proxy Server Port		When using punchouts, determines the port used by the proxy server. Ensure you reboot the Internet Application Server if you make a change to this setting.
POR: Purchasing News Location		When iProcurement is implemented in a multi-org, allows the region of the window called Purchasing News to be specific per each operating unit. Normally, this is set to a directory in OA_HTML/ where the purchasing news file, PORPNEWS.htm, is stored.
POR: Rate Based Services Line Type		Determines the default line type for rate-based non-catalog requests.
POR: Require Blind Receiving	No	Blind receiving will not populate the quantity outstanding or quantity ordered to be visible during the receiving process, requiring the shopper to enter the numbers.
POR: Select Internal Requisition for Confirm Receipt	Yes	Allows internal requisitions to send out confirm receipt notifications.
POR: Select Internal Requisition for Confirm Receipt	Yes	Determines if internal requisitions are included in the confirm receipts notifications, reminding the shopper to receive the items.

TABLE 3-5. *iProcurement-Related Profiles* (continued)

Name	Default Setting	Description
POR: Select Inventory Replenishment Lines for Confirm Receipts	Yes	Selecting Yes will send out confirm receipts notifications for both inventory and expense requisitions. No will only send out reminders for expense requisitions.
POR: Support Review for Express Receive	Yes	The default of Yes will show a Review and Submit screen prior to processing an express receipt. No bypasses this review page.
POR: System Approvers are Mandatory	Yes	When set to Yes, the shopper cannot remove the approvers who are determined by the system, based on the approval setups.
POR: Transparent Punchout Timeout Limit	60	Set in seconds, determines the time period where a transparent punchout does not respond, and the user is informed that the web page is not available.
POR: Use Sequence for Requisition Numbering	No	When set to No, iProcurement requisitions will use the same numbering as requisitions created within purchasing. When set to Yes, iProcurement uses a different sequence, and the numbers are shared across operating units. Yes may also improve iProcurement performance, depending on your environment.

TABLE 3-5. *iProcurement-Related Profiles* (continued)

Shopper Preferences

Just as profiles affect the way the system works and sets default settings, each shopper has preferences they can set to increase the speed of shopping and checking out. There are two types of preferences: General Display preferences and iProcurement preferences. General display preferences determine how all self-service applications (iExpense, iProcurement, iSupplier, and iReceivables) display specific data, while iProcurement preferences are specific to shopping and checking out. Many of these settings are defaulted and controlled with other setups and are noted in this section.

General Display Preferences

General display preferences control language, date, and currency formats, as well as allowing users to update passwords, as shown in Figure 3-35.

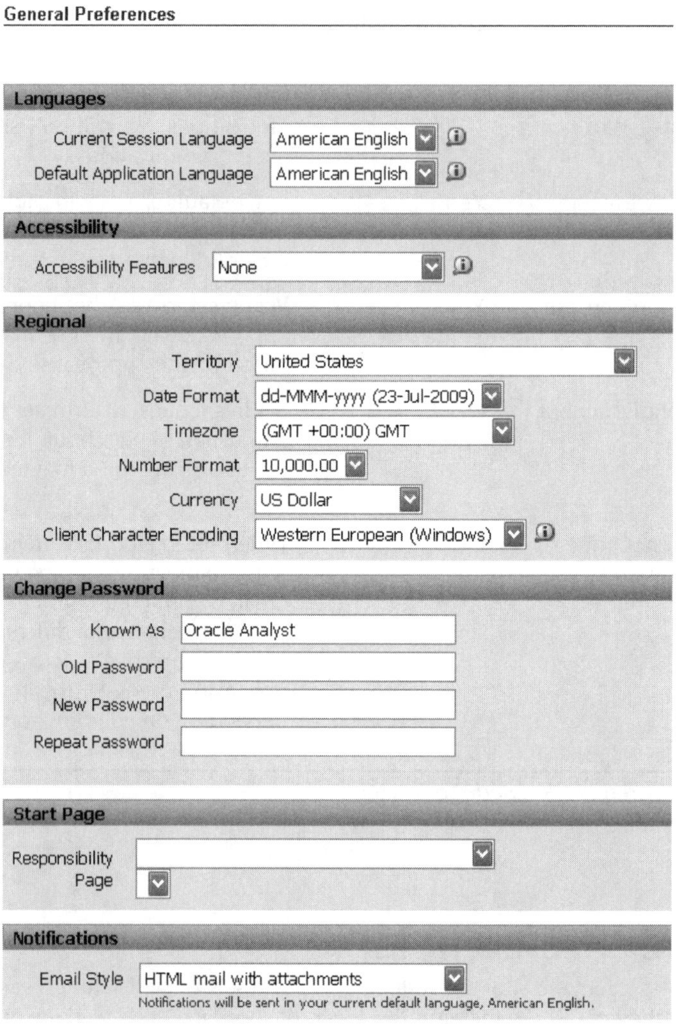

General Preferences

Languages

Current Session Language	American English ⌄ ⓘ
Default Application Language	American English ⌄ ⓘ

Accessibility

Accessibility Features	None ⌄ ⓘ

Regional

Territory	United States ⌄
Date Format	dd-MMM-yyyy (23-Jul-2009) ⌄
Timezone	(GMT +00:00) GMT ⌄
Number Format	10,000.00 ⌄
Currency	US Dollar ⌄
Client Character Encoding	Western European (Windows) ⌄ ⓘ

Change Password

Known As	Oracle Analyst
Old Password	
New Password	
Repeat Password	

Start Page

Responsibility	⌄
Page	⌄

Notifications

Email Style	HTML mail with attachments ⌄
	Notifications will be sent in your current default language, American English.

iProcurement | Preferences | Display Preferences

FIGURE 3-35. *General display preferences*

Languages

Oracle provides National Language Support, or NLS, and when implemented, will default both a general language preference and a preference for the current session only. DEFAULT APPLICATION LANGUAGE is controlled by the profile ICX: Language and determines not only the default language for the users, but all the languages that e-mails and notifications are received in. Users have the option of overriding the system default and setting a default for themselves. CURRENT SESSION

LANGUAGE, on the other hand, controls the language for only the current session, allowing users to see the application in a different language for this session only.

Accessibility

This feature is available for users who have vision problems. None is the setting that should be used for ACCESSIBILITY FEATURES for general users, while Standard Accessibility provides the pages in a format accessible for users who are using assistive technology, such as screen magnifiers. The final setting, Screen Reader Optimized, optimizes the page for users who are using screen readers by moving the content around and adding extra tags for the screen readers.

Regional

Regional settings allow the formatting of the date and number to be changed, among other things. TERRITORY is the default country for this user and can control the formatting of addresses. This will default to the country populated in the profile ICX: Territory. Remember that all profiles can be set at different levels: site, application, organization, responsibility, and user. Site, application, organization, and responsibility become default settings, looking for a value first at the lowest level, responsibility, and then up to organization, application, and finally site. User is even lower, and updating data in the preferences will also update the information stored at the user-level profile, and vice versa. DATE FORMAT will default to Oracle's standard, which is dd-MMM-yyyy. Select from the list of values to update the format to one that is more familiar to the users. This relates to the ICX: Date Format Mask profile. TIMEZONE can be set for each user and will determine what time stamp is added according to his or her time zone; it relates to the Client Timezone profile. Additional setups are required to use multiple time zones in your system.

Both NUMBER FORMAT and CURRENCY can be selected from the list of values. The format of the numbers does not affect the actual currency—that is set at the Ledger. CURRENCY, however, will default the user currency in on transactions, and should be set when the user does most of their transactions in currencies other than the base currency assigned to the Ledger. NUMBER FORMAT is stored in the profile ICX: Numeric Characters, while the CURRENCY updates two profiles for the user: ICX: Preferred Currency and TF_PROFILE_DEFAULT_CURRENCY.

The final option to set under Regional is CLIENT CHARACTER ENCODING, which relates to the profile FND: Native Client Encoding. This option is used when uploading and downloading data files from an Oracle web-based form, like iProcurement, to your desktop or network. Most commonly, this will affect XML, which requires it to be set to UTF-8, or Unicode Transformation Format-8.

Change Password

Each user's account controls when that user is forced to change his or her password (System Administrator | Security | User | Define | Password Expiration), but the user has the option to change it at any time, both in the web applications and the form applications. From the forms, this is done under Edit | Preferences | Change Password, which is controlled by a function called Applications Change User Password and must be included in one of the menus assigned to the responsibility. In both places, form and web applications, you are required to enter your current password, and a new password twice, adding security to this feature so that someone cannot come by and change a user's password without knowing the current password. Passwords cannot be seen in any form in EBS and are stored encrypted in the database.

The KNOWN AS field will populate from the description associated with the user (System Administrator | Security | User | Define, Description field).

Start Page

Any responsibility and page can be selected as your default start page, and you will be logged in directly to this page after entering your user name and password instead of selected from a responsibility and page every time you log in. For example, if I select my RESPONSIBILITY as iExpense, and my PAGE as OIE OTL Home, then after I enter my user name and password, Oracle will open up the home page of iExpense. This will populate the profile Applications Start Page for the user.

Notifications

The E-MAIL STYLE is the one setting that I see cause the most problems for users with receiving notifications. A user will inadvertently change this profile and no longer receive e-mails for notifications. The default for this is setting is actually in Workflow Administrator (Workflow Administrator Web (New) | Administrator Workflow | Administration | Workflow Configuration | Global Preferences, Notification Style). Table 3-6 shows the different options and their effects on receiving notifications via e-mail. Note that this setting does not affect whether notifications are generated for the user and visible in Oracle, but only if the notifications are e-mailed to the user when the workflow mailer is turned on.

iProcurement Preferences

iProcurement preferences control how someone goes shopping and default delivery and billing information. These settings are specific to iProcurement, unlike the General Display Preferences described earlier, which will affect any web-based application.

E-Mail Notification Style	Meaning
Disabled	This option is set by the system when the e-mail address on file for the user is not valid.
Do not send me mail	Does not send any e-mails for notifications.
HTML Mail	Sends notification in HTML without any attachments, except a custom attachment that has been defined.
HTML Mail with Attachments	Sends the notification in HTML with an attached link to the Notifications Detail page.
HTML Summary Mail	Sends only a HTML summary of all the open notifications the user has, and the user will have to sign in to Oracle to respond.
Plain Text Mail	Sends notifications in text without any attachments, except a custom attachment that has been defined.
Plain Text Mail with HTML Attachments	Sends the notification in plain text with an attached link to the Notifications Detail page.
Plain Text Summary Mail	Sends only a text summary of all the open notifications the user has, and the user will have to sign in to Oracle to respond.

TABLE 3-6. *Notification E-Mail Style Options*

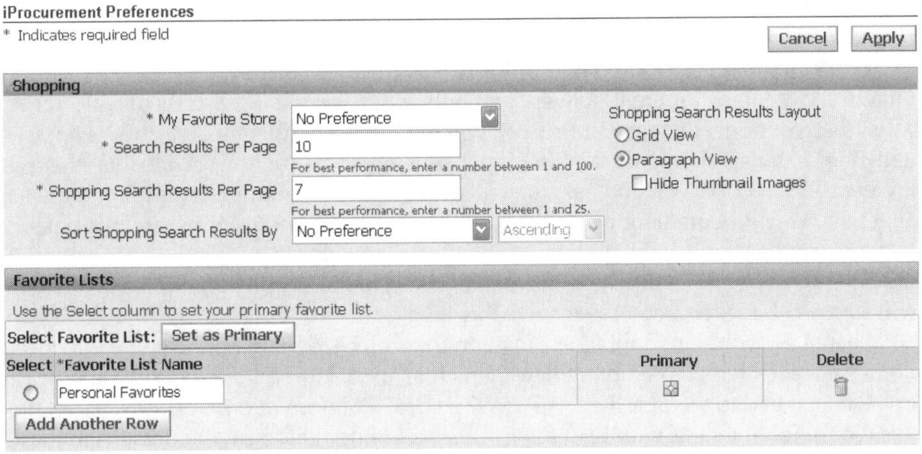

FIGURE 3-36. *iProcurement preferences, shopping, and favorite lists*

Shopping and Favorites Lists

The Shopping and Favorites region of the window, shown in Figure 3-36, allows the user to set up some specifics about how information is displayed on their page when shopping. MY FAVORITE STORE will determine the default store for searching. When this is set to No Preference, then the search store will default to the first store in the sequence (iProcurement Catalog Administration | Stores | Stores). This setting is stored in the profile POR: My Favorite Store.

The next two options determine how receipts, requisitions, and searches will return data. SEARCH RESULTS PER PAGE controls the number of records returned when looking for both receipts and requisitions, while SHOPPING SEARCH RESULTS PER PAGE determines the number of items returned when searching a store. Again, these values are both stored in a profile. SEARCH RESULTS PER PAGE will populate POR: Result Set Size at the user level, while SHOPPING SEARCH RESULTS PER PAGE is stored in POR: Catalog Results Set Size.

SORT SHOPPING SEARCH RESULTS BY determines the way Oracle will return items during a search; it is stored in the profile POR: Default Shopping Sort. The option selected here determines how Oracle's sort and relevance algorithm scores the results and displays them to the shopper. Most of the options are based on one of the item's base or category descriptors, such as Price or Source. The one that is a little more vague is Relevance. Selecting this sort option looks at the search word, comparing it to both the item's description and keywords, as well as any of the descriptors associated with the item. Based on this, the item is ranked and returned. After deciding how to sort the results, the user can select the results to be returned in either Ascending or Descending order. (This is stored in the profile POR: Default Shopping Sort Order.)

The final options affect the way items are displayed on the page, changing not only the layout but how fast the search results are returned (images take longer to display than searches without images). GRID VIEW and PARAGRAPH VIEW both control the way search results are displayed. GRID VIEW returns the results in a spreadsheet-like format, with a row and multiple columns for each item that meets the search, while PARAGRAPH VIEW returns the data in a more narrative format, including a long description for each item. The last option, HIDE THUMBNAIL IMAGES, determines if images can be seen during searching; selecting this option will return the search results faster.

Delivery, Billing, and Charge Accounts

Oracle allows many different delivery and billing options to be preset as defaults for the shoppers. All of these options, seen in Figure 3-37, will default from different areas of the application, allowing each user to update them for that user's specific situation. While the other settings in Preferences affect the way the user interacts with iProcurement, the settings in these sections affect the way iProcurement will default information in on requisitions, and the defaults have a larger effect than for just the individual shopper. For example, NEED BY DATE OFFSET will determine the need-by date on the purchase order that is sent to the supplier, as well as when the shopper will start receiving reminders to receive this item.

Charge accounts and billing information for projects determine the general ledger account numbers associated with different lines, which again default onto the purchase order and then the invoice matched to the purchase order. When project information is added, it also affects the way this requisition interacts with Oracle Projects. It is important to set the defaults in these areas correctly, and ensure the shoppers know how updating this information interacts with the rest of the Oracle system.

Delivery information will default onto the requisition during the checkout process. NEED BY DATE OFFSET is the number of days added to today's date to become the Need By date on the purchase order. Setting this too low may result in having expedited charges from a supplier who uses this date to determine the shipping method, while setting it too high may result in the item being delivered later than when it was needed, but also may cause a delay of payment when using three-way matching; since this date drives when the first reminder goes out the user to receive a requisition,

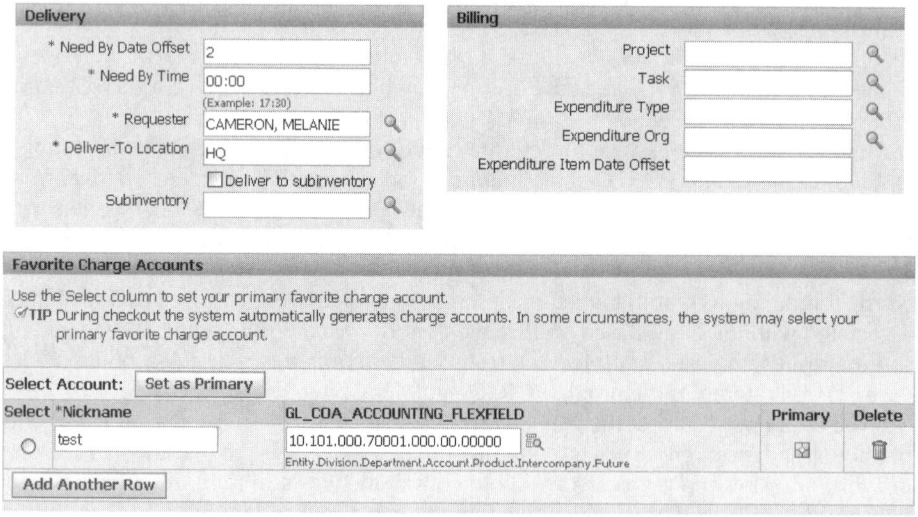

FIGURE 3-37.   *iProcurement Preferences: delivery, billing, and charge accounts*

the user may delay receiving it, leaving the invoice on hold and potentially losing out on a discount. This setting is stored in the profile POR: Days Needed By. NEED BY TIME is the default time that will appear on the requisitions during checkout. Note that this is a required field, and Oracle does not allow you to leave it blank and let the system default the time to the system time.

Setting the profile POR: Validated Need By Time for Requisition Submission will allow this time to be prior to the current time in the system when the need-by date is today. Oracle does not allow requisitions to be created in the past, and when the time is validated, then it also will give a warning to the shoppers when the time is in the past. Notice that the format for this field is HH:MM, but when you check out, it will display as HH:MM:SS. This inconsistency can be confusing, because the default time format will not allow seconds.

REQUESTOR is the default person who will appear as the requestor for any requisition. This will default in from the employee associated with the user account and can only be updated when the profile POR: Override Requestor is set to either Within Organization, limiting the options to employees in the same business group, or By All, allowing any employee set up in Oracle to be selected. When the requestor field is updated, it will populate the profile POR: Preferences – Requestor. When these fields have never been updated, the associated profiles will not be set at the user level; only after it has been changed, even if it is changed back to the employee associated with the user, will a value populate here.

DELIVER TO LOCATION, again, populates from the location associated with the employee on the user and can be updated to any location in the system. Once updated, the profile POR: Preferences – Deliver to Location will be set. When the location is associated with an inventory organization, the organization will appear in parentheses in the profile value, but not in the user Preferences. When the location selected is associated with an inventory, the user can select DELIVER TO SUBINVENTORY (which populates the profile POR: Preferences – Selected Items Default to Inventory) and enter a default SUBINVENTORY location, causing the profile POR: Preferences – Subinventory to be populated. This will default the subinventory on any requisition where an inventory item is purchased (as opposed to an item that is expensed), as determined by the item settings (Purchasing | Items | Organization Items | Inventory tab).

The Billing region relates specifically to project-related information. This information can be added when Oracle Projects Costing and Billing is implemented, and requisitions need to be associated to a specific PROJECT, TASK, EXPENDITURE TYPE, and EXPENDITURE ORG. The final field, EXPENDITURE ITEM DATE OFFSET, is the number of days added to the system date. The expenditure item date is used by Oracle Projects in several areas not only to determine if the project is valid during that time period, but to associate burden schedules to the cost.

The final section allows users to set up default charge accounts that are used on a regular basis. Because of the way Oracle determines the charge account for a requisition, the user may or may not be allowed to use these on a given requisition. Oracle uses a workflow to generate account numbers, and without modifications, it will use the account number by first determining if it is an inventory or expense item (when an item is selected). Oracle uses the inventory account numbers associated with the organization or subinventory the item is being delivered to, while expense account numbers are built one of three ways: If an item is associated to the requisition, Oracle uses the expense account number associated with the item. When a project is assigned to the line, then the account number is built from the project setups, and when there is no item or project, then Oracle uses the default account associated with the employee who is the requestor. The only override to the workflow, without modifying it, is when Expense Account Rules are set up (see the prior section "Setting Up and Using Expense Account Rules").

These rules will override specific segments of the account number when a rule is set up for the category selected on the requisition. FAVORITE CHARGE ACCOUNTS come into play when the line is an expense line and the following profiles are set: PA: Allow Override of PA Distributions in AP/ PO allows the user to update the account associated with a project, while POR: Apply Expense Account Rules to Favorite Charge Account will cause the expense account rules to be applied to any charge account that is set up as a user's Primary Favorite account that defaults onto a requisition; it is not applied to Favorite accounts that are manually assigned to a requisition line.

The default account for the employee, which is on the employee record, does not appear in this section, and the user has no access to see or update this account. As long as this field is populated on the employee record, it will always override a Primary account set up in the Favorite Charge Account section. The Primary account will only default in when the expense account is not populated on the employee record. These accounts are not stored in a profile, but directly to a table in the database. They are specific to a user and a responsibility, so if a user has more than one iProcurement responsibility, that user will have to set up more than one FAVORITE CHARGE ACCOUNTS list. In R12, the number of favorite accounts has been expanded to 50 per user per responsibility.

Purchasing Cards and iProcurement

The use of credit cards has always been prevalent within organizations, allowing specific users to purchase certain items without having to use any personal cash, or get a cash advance, or a purchase order. Historically, these cards were restricted to management, or specific purchases, such as gas for your fleet. Today, their use has expanded greatly within companies, as has Oracle's features to assist with the use of the cards.

Oracle supports two main types of purchasing cards, or P-cards, in iProcurement: Employee and Supplier cards. Employee cards are credit cards where each employee will have his or her own number and physical card assigned, which can either be used for unrestricted purchases or be restricted to making specific types of purchases, such as office supplies or hotel reservations. (The main difference between a credit card and a purchasing card is usually what can be bought with it. Credit cards by nature have no restrictions, while P-cards have smart chips embedded in them, restricting items that can be purchased with them.) Suppliers can also provide credit cards that can be used by all employees purchasing from a given supplier. This would be comparable to a Staples or Dell credit card. The usage of both types of cards in iProcurement does not bypass the approval rules in Oracle, allowing employees to go on a shopping spree, but it does allow the settlement of the approved items to use a P-card as opposed to the traditional invoicing process in Payables.

The way this works is that once the requisition is approved and turned into a purchase order, which in turn also has to be approved, the P-card information will appear on the purchase order when it is communicated to the supplier, allowing that supplier to charge the card for the items shipped as opposed to sending an invoice for payment. To close the loop on this process, Oracle also provides a P-card reconciliation process, which reconciles the P-card statement received from the bank to the P-card transactions that were approved in Purchasing, allowing faster and easier settlement and reconciliation of the P-card statement.

P-card transactions can also be imported from the credit card company into Payables for payment in the scenario where requisitions were not used. This process is not part of the iProcurement functionality and is not described here (though many of the setups are the same as the credit card setups listed next).

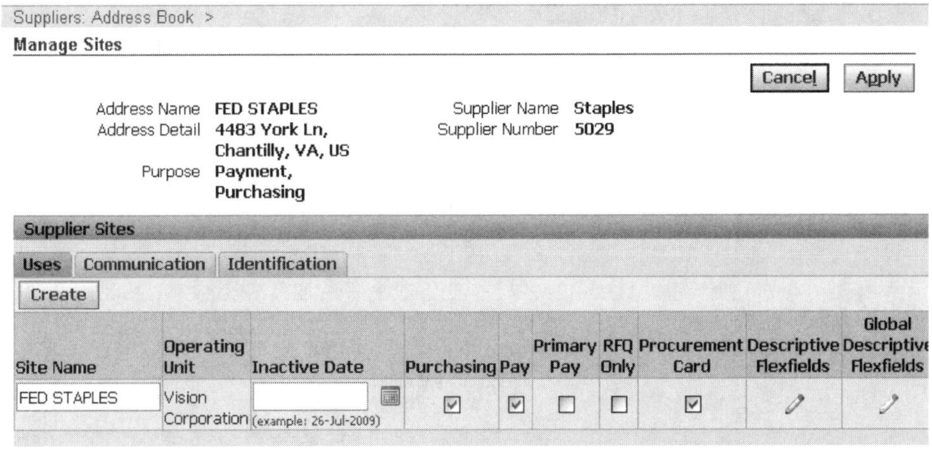

Purchasing | Supply Base | Suppliers | Address Book | Manage Sites

FIGURE 3-38. *Setting a supplier site to accept credit cards*

Supplier Setups

Before using either a supplier or employee P-card, the supplier who will be accepting it will need to be identified in Oracle. This is done on the supplier site, as seen in Figure 3-38. After querying up the supplier, click Address Book and then Manage Sites for the address you want to use credit cards with, and then check Procurement Card. If all transactions for this supplier address are not going to be credit card related, you may want to set up two sites—one setup to accept credit cards and the other without the box checked.

Setting Up Procurement Cards

The setup steps are comparable for both employee and supplier P-cards, with the main difference being how specific fields are completed. The first step is to create a code set for the card. *Code sets* allow you to map credit card transaction code classifications, such as SIC (Standard Industrial Classification) or MCC (Merchant Category Code), to your general ledger natural account segment of your chart of accounts (refer to Figure 3-39). After selecting the Operating Unit, add a Code Set Name that identifies the card this will be used with, and optionally a Description. Sometimes a code being provided by the credit card company encompasses more than one type of transaction, or grouping. In this case, check Blocking Group, which will inform Oracle that this has more than one group included in it and that it should not be mapped. Note that when you select this item, a default, or Account mapping, cannot be added. Enter the Value from your credit card provider, such as the SIC value, a Description, and the general ledger natural Account you want to map it to. Add an Inactive On date only when this mapping is no longer valid.

While this information may not be required for reconciling a credit card using the features described earlier in this chapter, this is still a required setup. These mappings do play a large part in the general ledger coding when importing credit card transactions directly into Payables.

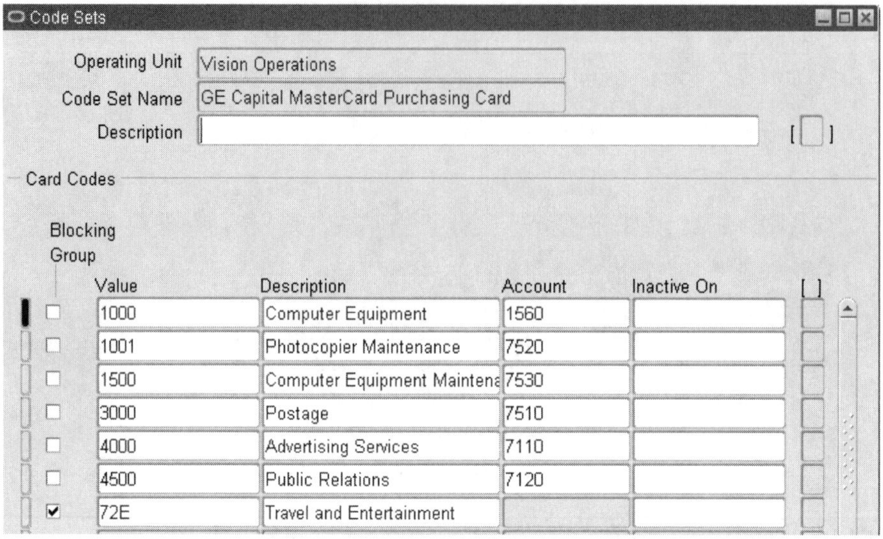

Purchasing | Setup | Credit Cards | Credit Card Code Sets

FIGURE 3-39. *Adding credit card code sets*

You can add a credit card code set that contains a bogus mapping, but remember that you will need to go back and update the information if you decided to expand your Oracle credit card functionality (for example, you may want to start importing Travel and Entertainment expenses into iExpenses).

Once the credit card code set is set up, the card program can be defined. (The credit card code set is a required field on this setup, which is why it needs to be set up even if credit card information is not going to be imported and mapped to your general ledger.) The card programs can be seen in Figure 3-40. After selecting the OPERATING UNIT, assign the CARD PROGRAM NAME, which will be used to identify this credit card to Oracle. Select the card brand from American Express, Diner's Club, Master Card, or Visa; most of the supplier cards will fall under one of these programs these days, or at least follow the format. A DESCRIPTION can be added, and then the CARD TYPE. There are three card types to select from: Procurement, Supplier, and Travel. Travel is used with Internet Expenses only and will be covered in depth in Chapter 7, "iExpense Setups"; it refers to corporate credit cards as opposed to purchasing cards. Supplier is only usable with iProcurement. Procurement is usable either for iProcurement or as a direct import into Payables.

The CARD ISSUER needs to be added; it refers not only to the bank that issued the card but the supplier set up in Oracle in the prior section. This represents the supplier to whom the check will be cut to settle the credit card invoice. Also, the CARD ISSUER SITE, or supplier site that is set up to accept procurement cards, needs to be populated. From the list of values, select the CARD CODE SET you created in the previous step. The rest of the fields are used when importing credit cards into iExpenses for approval and processing; they will be described in Chapter 7, "iExpense Setups."

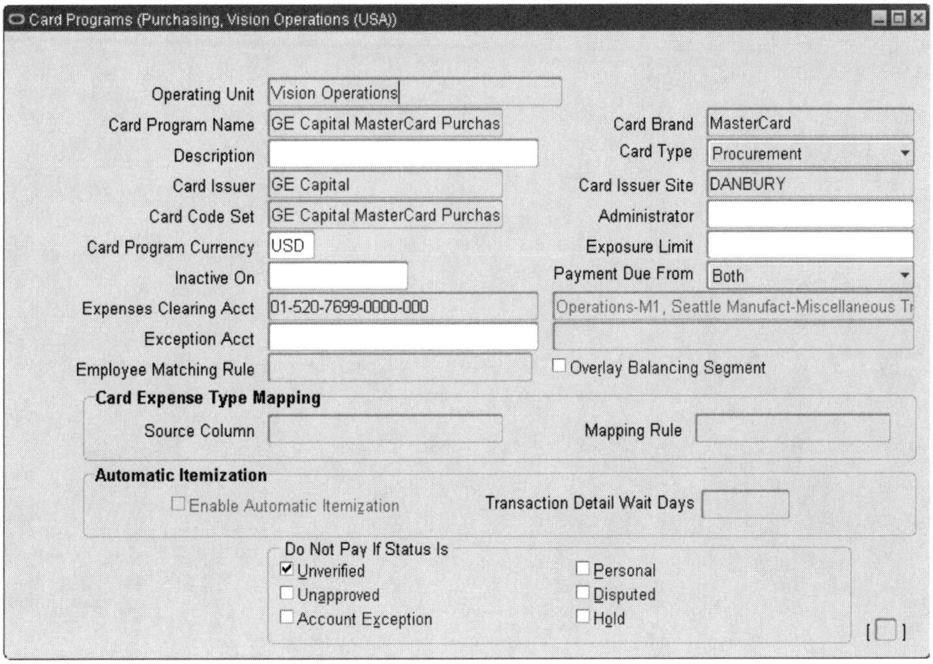

Purchasing | Setup | Credit Cards | Credit Card Programs

FIGURE 3-40. *Creating card programs*

Reconciling Your P-Card Transactions to Requisitions

There are two options for reconciling your P-card transactions to the requisitions in Oracle, and they mainly surround what system is used for the reconciliation process. The first option is to utilize Oracle Payables to perform this reconciliation. How this works is that a feed from your P-card holder is received, which will need to include the purchase order number and amount, as well as coding information in the form of the GL Account Number or based on codes set up and mapped in your credit card code sets, which can then be loaded and imported directly into Payables using the Payables Open Interface. Since the purchase order number is loaded in here, the invoice can be matched directly against the purchase order.

The second method is by utilizing a system outside Oracle, usually a reconciliation tool provided by your card issuer. You can then run a concurrent request in Purchasing called Purchase Order History Feed for P-Card Reconciliations, which will save the file to the location identified as the UTL_FILE_DIR in the init.ora file. This setting will determine what directory the output is stored in and allow it to be either automatically or manually uploaded to the reconciliation site. Once reconciled, the invoice can be imported into Payables using the Payables Open Interface, or else it can be manually entered into AP.

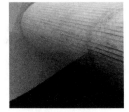

CHAPTER
4

Using iProcurement

Procurement serves several functions in the purchasing process for an organization: employees can go shopping and place requests for goods and services, requestors can monitor the status of their requisitions, while approvers can review, modify, and approve requests routed to them. Receipts for approved requests can also be made, with notifications going out to remind employees about expected deliveries. This chapter will walk through each of these areas step-by-step.

Shopping

Let's face it—who doesn't like going shopping and getting new things, especially when it is with someone else's money? Controlling the items and suppliers an employee has access to purchase can help keep expenses under control. iProcurement also allows these items to be organized for easier shopping. To look at how this works, let's first understand the types of purchases employees typically make. They request items that are defined in Oracle Purchasing by shopping in the Main Store; shop at a web site linked to iProcurement with a punchout; use a shopping list; ask for specific, undefined purchases using a non-catalog request; or request contract labor. Each of these scenarios will be described in detail next.

Shopping the Main Store for Internal Items and Items Available via a Transparent Punchout

When you sign into iProcurement, it will open up to the home page, as seen in Figure 4-1. This page gives a quick overview of past purchases, pending notifications, as well as the stores available for shopping. Note that every company's Shop, or home, page for iProcurement will appear different, depending on the stores that are set up.

The Main Store contains items set up in Oracle Purchasing or Inventory that are included in the content zones assigned to either the responsibility or a specific operating unit the shopper is associated with. Oracle documentation refers to these as *local items*. There are two types of local items you can shop for: *internally sourced* items, which are purchased from one of the inventory organizations setup within Oracle, or *supplier-sourced* items, which are purchased from a source external to Oracle, such as Staples. You can shop the Main Stores by using a simple search, shown at the top of most iProcurement windows, using an advanced search, or drilling down into the Main Store itself.

To drill down, click the Main Store link. This will bring up the Browsing categories. Remembering back to the setups (see the illustration in Chapter 3 under "Setting Up the Main Store" for a visual picture), these Browsing categories are then associated with Shopping categories, which is the next layer down. The Shopping categories are directly mapped to Purchasing categories, which are in turn assigned to specific items. As you drill down in the Main Store, you are drilling down through each of these layers.

Simple searches are done from any window in iProcurement and only require that a single word or phrase be entered. A wildcard (% or * are both supported) can be used in any part of the search word. A wildcard is a replacement for a character or space in the search, and using one can result in more items being returned. An example of the use of a wildcard is to search on "pen%," which will return both pens and pencils. Without the wildcard, only items that begin with "pen" would be returned. EBS will search any local content, as well as content available

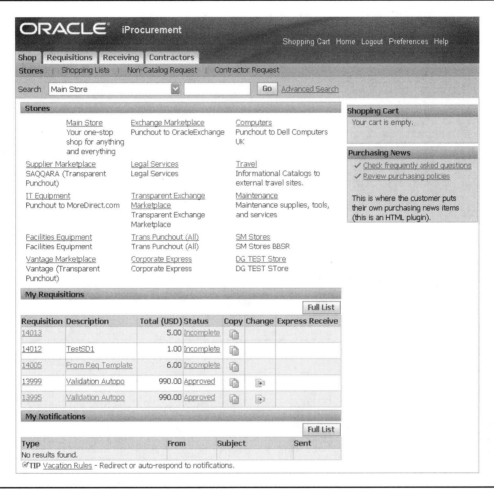

FIGURE 4-1. *iProcurement home page*

from a transparent punchout, matching on any field in iProcurement (such as item, description, and category). The content is controlled with the Content Zones that are associated with the stores, operating unit, or responsibility. Figure 4-2 shows the results of a simple search.

Once items are returned from the search, shoppers can click the item name, such as Roll-N-Rack Printer, to get additional information on the item. The Search results can be sorted by several different options to assist in finding what you are looking for. In the SORT BY field, select one of the values, outlined in Table 4-1.

Also notice that additional suggestions for searches became available under the Related Links section of the window after performing a search. These are shopping categories and shopping lists that meet the search criteria, allowing the shopper to browse them.

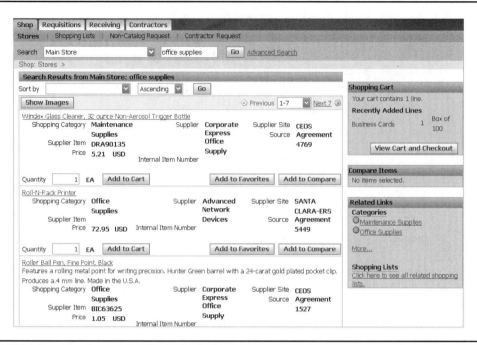

FIGURE 4-2. *Simple searches in the Main Store*

Sort by Value	Meaning
Currency	Sorts alphabetically on the currency associated with the item.
Description	Based on the short description of the item.
Functional Currency Price	Sorts by converting the price to the functional currency of the Ledger associated with iProcurement's operating unit.
Internal Item Number	Based on the Purchasing item number.
Long Description	Uses the long description to sort.
Price	Based on the actual price of the item, and disregards currency.
Relevance	This will rank the results based on keyword matches and match to the item's description.
Shopping Category	Based on the shopping category mapped to the item.
Source	Any agreement or other source that is associated with the item based on a Sourcing Rule (Purchasing I Supply Base I Sourcing Rules and Assign Sourcing Rules).
Supplier Item	Supplier Item number from a transparent punchout or associated with an internal item.
Supplier Site	Supplier site name.
Unit	Based on the unit of measure associated with the item.

TABLE 4-1. *Sorting Options for Search Results*

Once an item is found, additional options include adding this item to your personal favorite's lists with the Add To Favorites button. This option is good for repeat purchases, allowing the shopper faster access to it without performing a search, and is unique for each shopper. The Add To Compare feature allows multiple items to be compared for all the item attributes, including price, and if a price break is available, giving the shopper the information needed to make more informed purchasing decisions. To use this feature, click the Add To Compare button for each item you want to compare, which will add them to a Compare Items region on the right of the window. Once more than one item is added, click Compare to see a side-by-side comparison. Click Clear to remove the items from the compare region.

To add an item to your shopping cart, update the QUANTITY to the desired amount and click Add To Cart.

Advanced Searches work the same as simple searches, with the exception that you have more fields to search on, narrowing down the results (see Figure 4-3). iProcurement displays STORE, DESCRIPTION, SUPPLIER ITEM, and SUPPLIER as default fields, but additional fields are also available. In the ADD ANOTHER field, select additional fields and click Add. Table 4-2 explains the meaning of each search field. Since each implementation of Oracle is a little different and not every company uses the fields the same way, these search fields may or may not make sense for your company. As you can see from the Meanings, many of the fields are associated with items

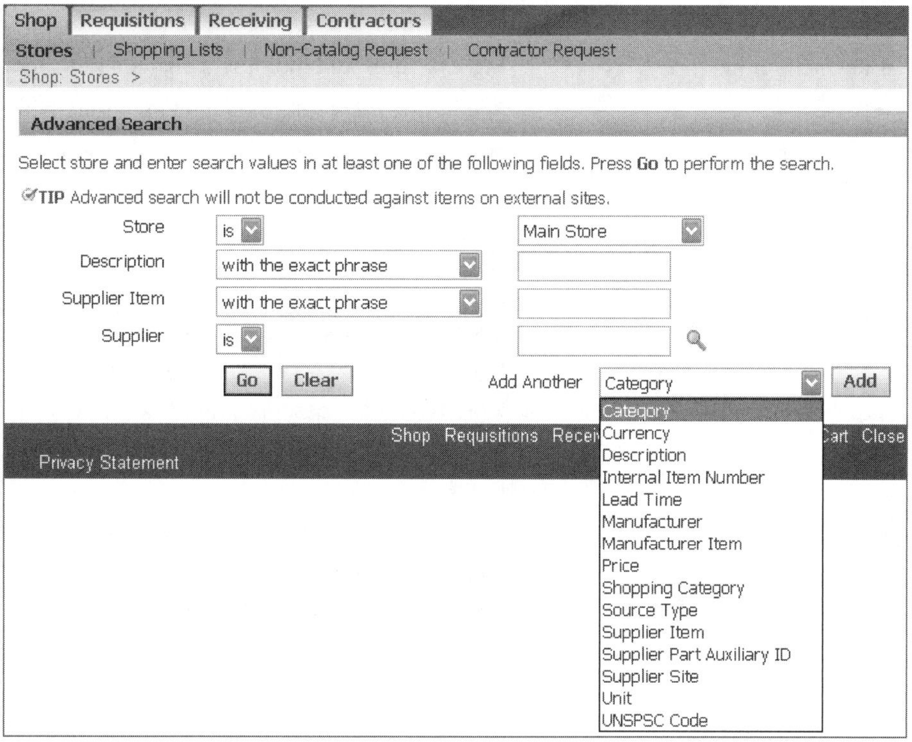

FIGURE 4-3. *Advanced searches*

Field	Meaning
Store	Local stores available to the shopper. Advanced searches cannot be done on a store that is a punchout.
Description	Description associated with an item in Purchasing.
Supplier Item	Supplier Item Number associated with an item in Purchasing.
Supplier	Supplier associated with an item with Sourcing Rules.
Category	Purchasing Category associated with an item in Purchasing.
Currency	Refers to the Functional Currency for the item.
Description	Description on the item.
Internal Item Number	This is the actual item number, internal referring to internal to Oracle.
Lead Time	Number of days lead time it take to manufacture or purchase an item.
Manufacturer	Manufacturer associated with the item.
Manufacturer Item	Manufactures item number assigned to the item.
Price	Purchasing price set up on the Purchasing tab on an item.
Shopping Category	Shopping category associated with the purchasing category assigned to an item.
Source Type	Limits selections to item associated with an Agreement, a Quotation, the Item Master, or a Requisition Template.
Supplier Item	Supplier item number associated with an item. This is not the same as the manufacturer's item number, especially when an item is purchased from a distributor.
Supplier Part Auxiliary ID	Stored as a base descriptor in iProcurement.
Supplier Site	Supplier site associated with this item in the Sourcing Rules.
Unit	Unit of measure associated with an item.
UNSPSC Code	United Nations Standard Products and Services Code, stored as a base descriptor in iProcurement.

TABLE 4-2. *Advanced Search Fields*

and are not required fields, and all organizations do not always populate or maintain them. Advanced searches can only be done if the profile POR: Enable Advanced Search is set to Yes. This is usually set to No when there is no local content in iProcurement and it is being used for punchouts only.

Shopping Using a Punchout

When you shop a store that is a direct punchout, clicking the store name will take you directly to the web site of the supplier. From here, you can shop as you would on any other Internet site, with one major exception. When you check out with your shopping cart, you are returned to iProcurement, where you can continue with the normal checkout process and create a requisition within Oracle.

Creating and Using Shopping Lists

There are two types of shopping lists: personal favorites and public, or corporate, lists. Personal favorites are private lists that each shopper creates, and are private in that no one can see them except the shopper that created them. Public lists are shared across all users, and the only security available is based on the operating unit the public list was created under. Both lists are really just groupings of commonly purchased items, making shopping faster for these items.

Creating a Personal Favorites Shopping List

Personal Favorites are created when a shopper clicks the Add To Favorites button when shopping. This button is available on all items and windows in iProcurement *except* when shopping in the Personal Favorites list.

Creating a Public Shopping List

A public list that can be accessed by all iProcurement users is created in Purchasing using the Requisition Template form. To create a Requisition Template, refer to Figure 4-4. After selecting the OPERATING UNIT this template will be used in, assign it a TEMPLATE name and a DESCRIPTION. The operating unit that you have access to is controlled with Oracle's MOAC, or Multi Org Access Control, using the profiles MO: Operating Unit and MO: Security Profile. These can only be set in the System Administrator responsibility (Profile | System). The INACTIVE DATE is added to represent the date it can no longer be used; it can be left blank or set to the current or a future date. Next, use the TYPE field to determine if the template will be used for Internal Requisitions or only Purchase Requisitions sourced outside of EBS. To assign a requisition a RESERVE PO NUMBER when it is created, select Yes, while Optional will allow the creator to decided. No prevents the user from reserving a purchase order number. By default, reserving the purchase order number will make the supplier field required.

When a PO number is reserved as part of the requisition process, the requisition cannot be combined with any other requisitions or split into multiple orders when a purchase order is created from it, and the purchase order number will be lost if the requisition is eventually canceled. While requisition templates can be used to create requisitions both in Purchasing and in iProcurement, the feature to reserve a PO number is available only when the requisitions are created in iProcurement.

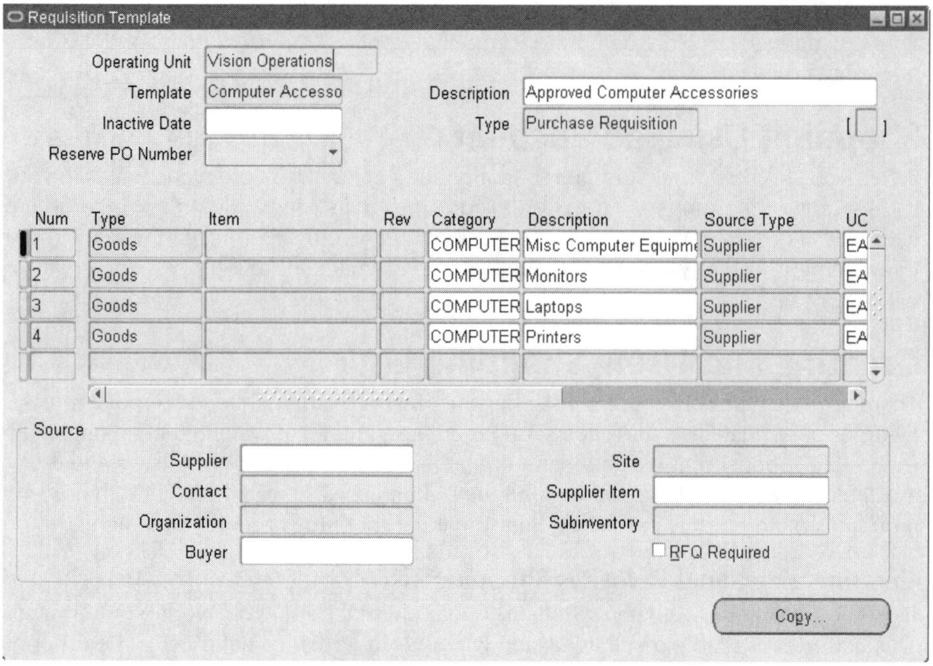

Purchasing | Setup | Purchasing | Requisition Templates

FIGURE 4-4. *Creating requisition templates for a public shopping list*

Next, enter the specific items associated with this template. Select the line TYPE that will default in when this item is selected, and either an ITEM number or a CATEGORY name. Category is required and will default from the item, if one is entered, while the item number is optional. The DESCRIPTION will default in from the item when entered, or category when an item is not used, and SOURCE TYPE determines if the item is purchased from a supplier or internally sourced from an internal location. A SUGGESTED QUANTITY can be added, which will default in when the template is used to create a line, and can then be updated by the user. This is especially beneficial when the item has price breaks associated with it. Depending on the line TYPE, enter either PRICE or AMOUNT to default on the order. Again, the requestor can update this information. Selecting NEGOTIATED SOURCE will identify this price as being created from a negotiation.

When the Source section is completed for a specific line, it will populate this information on the requisition. Available fields include SUPPLIER and SITE, which must be active in EBS, and a supplier CONTACT. The SUPPLIER ITEM number can also be added; it will appear on the purchase order for the supplier to reference. ORGANIZATION and SUBINVENTORY are only available for purchasing items that are set up as inventory items (Purchasing | Items | Master Items | Inventory tab | Inventory Item is checked) and will determine the inventory location and subinventory the item will be received in. Adding a BUYER to the template will default in on the requisition as well. Selecting RFQ REQUIRED alerts the buyer that this item should go out for a quote prior to purchasing.

The Copy button allows you to create the requisition template lines directly from an existing purchase order or requisition. After clicking Copy, select the TYPE of Purchase Order or Requisition, depending on which you want to copy. Then enter the document NUMBER and click OK. The lines of that document will default in as lines on the requisition template, which can then be updated as needed.

Once this is saved, it is available for shoppers in iProcurement.

Shopping Using a Shopping List

Once items are added to a personal favorites list or a requisition template as a public list, the shoppers can browse the lists for faster shopping. Referring to Figure 4-5, choose the list from the options available in SELECT LIST and click Go. The same sorting options are available as when browsing in the main store. To purchase an item, ensure the quantity is correct and click Add To Cart.

Shopping from Non-Catalog Requests and Other Smart Forms

Non-catalog requests and smart forms are used to make purchases that are not set up as items in Oracle. They require only a category and do not allow item numbers, using the description instead to tell the buyer what is being purchased. While these can be used to make any purchase, creating items for repeat purchases allows analysis on price, frequency, and items the shoppers are buying to be done, while using non-catalog requests makes this more difficult due to inconsistency in most fields except category.

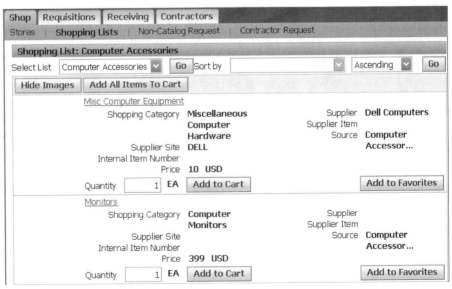

FIGURE 4-5.   *Shopping from a shopping list*

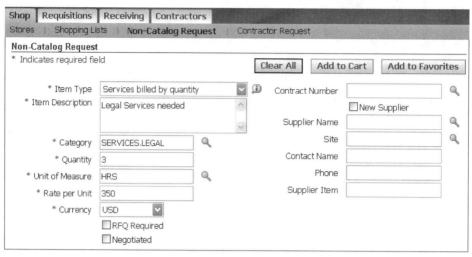

FIGURE 4-6. *Shopping using a non-catalog request*

Non-Catalog Requests

iProcurement comes with one smart form called a non-catalog request. This allows shoppers to create a requisition for items that do not exist either as purchasing items or in a supplier's catalog (made available via a punchout). To create a non-catalog request, refer to Figure 4-6. The ITEM TYPE will determine how the amounts and quantities are entered on the requisition; you should select one that corresponds to how the supplier will be invoicing, as this will impact the way the invoice is matched to the purchase order. In R12, these options can be associated with specific line types set up in Purchasing (Purchasing | Setup | Purchasing | Line Types) via profile options explained next.

Table 4-3 shows the item type, the profile that controls it, and the default setting and calculation. By creating new Line Types and associating them with the profile, you can control how each item type is calculated, ensuring that the matching of invoices to the purchase orders is accurate.

Item Type	Profile	Default Calculation
Goods billed by quantity	POR: Goods Line Type	Goods *Calculation:* Quantity times Unit Price
Goods or services billed by amount	POR: Amount Based Services Line Type	Fixed Price Services *Calculation:* Amount only (quantity equals 1)
Services billed by quantity	POR: Rate Based Services Line Type	Svcs – Qty *Calculation:* Quantity times Rate per Unit

TABLE 4-3. *Setting Calculations for Item Types*

An ITEM DESCRIPTION will need to be added, describing what the requestor is asking to be purchased. The shopper then selects a CATEGORY from the list of values, which is a listing of purchasing categories. QUANTITY, UNIT OF MEASURE, and RATE PER UNIT PRICE (or UNIT PRICE), fields will change based on the ITEM TYPE selected, and will determine the quantity and price for this request. CURRENCY will default to the base currency assigned to this operating unit, and can be changed if need be to any currency activated in Oracle. If a foreign currency is entered, then an EXCHANGE RATE TYPE and EXCHANGE RATE DATE will be needed. When the type is set to User, the EXCHANGE RATE field is displayed, and requires the user to enter the rate for the transaction.

Selecting RFQ REQUIRED informs the buyer that a quote will be needed from the suppliers prior to purchase, while NEGOTIATED provides additional reporting in Daily Business Intelligence. Additional information can also be added for this request, such as CONTRACT NUMBER. The shopper can select the contract number from a list of contract purchase or global contract agreements that are set up in Purchasing (these are purchase orders created with the type of Contract Purchase Agreement). When a CONTRACT NUMBER is entered, the SUPPLIER NAME and SITE will default from the contract and cannot be updated. When a CONTRACT NUMBER is not entered, the shopper has the option to select a SUPPLIER NAME from a supplier that is already set up and active as a purchasing supplier in Oracle, or to check the NEW SUPPLIER option for supplier information that is not in EBS. The way this feature works is that the supplier information will appear on the requisition to the buyer, who then has the option of changing the supplier to a different one, or to create a new supplier by the person who has the proper access prior to creating the purchase order (Sarbanes-Oxley and segregation of duties requirements will sometimes prevent purchasing agents from creating suppliers themselves). Additional supplier information, such as CONTACT NAME, PHONE, and SUPPLIER ITEM number can also be added. Notice that most of the fields just described do not have an asterisk (*) next to the field names. This means that they are not required fields. Once all the information is completed, the shopper clicks Add To Cart.

Smart Forms

Additional smart forms do not appear as tabs in iProcurement, as the non-catalog request does, but as stores. When looking at the stores in iProcurement, you cannot tell which store contains items set up in purchasing, items from a punchout, or a smart form. Smart forms behave like other content for purchase and will appear when you search or drill down in a store. Each smart form will contain the same fields as a non-catalog request, along with any additional fields that were set up as an information template (Purchasing | Setup | Information Templates) and associated with the smart form. Each organization can set up its own smart forms and information templates, so this will look different at each company. See Figure 4-7 for an example of a custom smart form.

Contractor Requests

Contractor requests uses a smart form that comes seeded with Oracle and integrates with what is called Oracle Services Procurement. While licensed separately, this is not actually a separate module, but an integrated feature that works with iProcurement, Purchasing, iExpense, and Oracle Time and Labor to allow companies to track not only the need for a contract laborer, but also the laborer's progress and expenses. Additional setups are also required to use Oracle Services Procurement, which are outside the scope of this book. What is in scope is using iProcurement to request a contract laborer.

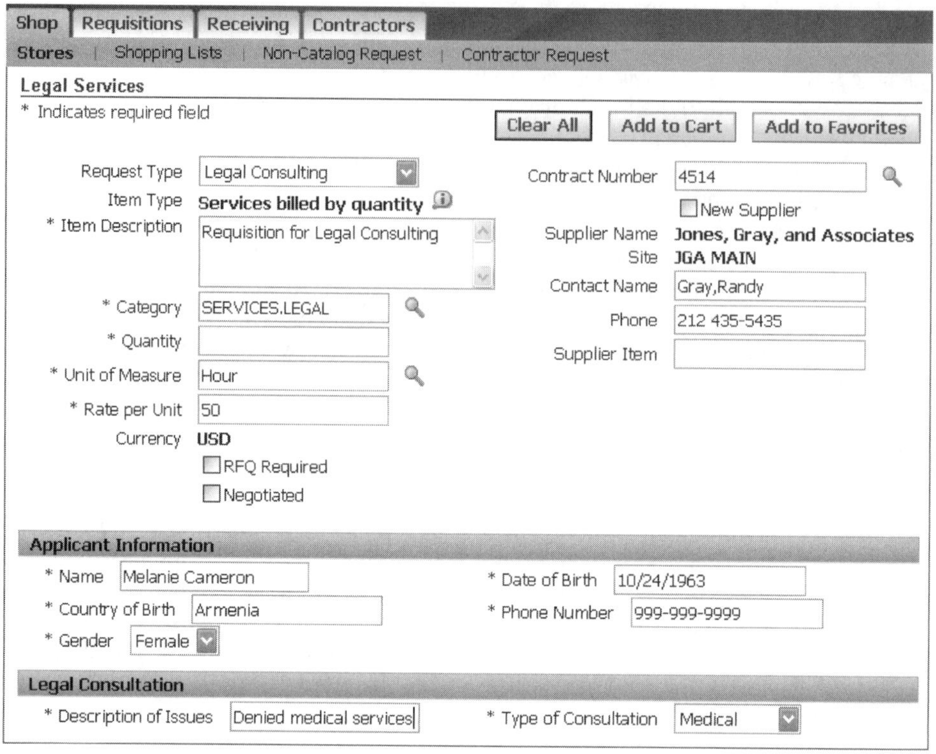

FIGURE 4-7. *Example of a smart form with two associated information templates*

Referring to Figure 4-8, first select the TYPE of labor you are requesting from either Wage-Based Temporary Labor or Fixed Price Temporary Labor. Jobs can be set up within Oracle to define the type of position and skills you are looking for, and then selected when requesting temporary labor. Once a job is entered, additional information may be required for that specific job, providing skill requirements. When REQUIRE CANDIDATE SCREENING is selected, it informs purchasing or human resources to screen all candidates prior to sending them to you for review. START DATE and END DATE define the time period you are looking for the contractor, and a REQUESTOR and the LOCATION the contractor will be reporting to is added. The location will default to the location associated to the requestor, and can be updated to another location or to a one-time address not in Oracle.

Additional JOB DETAILS are added to ensure the qualifications for this position are met, and specific CONTACT INFORMATION can be added, usually a phone number, an e-mail address, or possibly a different person than the requestor, such as a shift supervisor.

The next page, shown in Figure 4-9, will provide information about the supplier used to get the labor as well as budget information for this position. Oracle can be set up with a preferred supplier where your company does repeat business, or a specific supplier can be recommended. Either way, you have the option to add a contractor name if there is someone you have used before. Once the LABOR and EXPENSE AMOUNTS are added, you can add this request to your cart and check out.

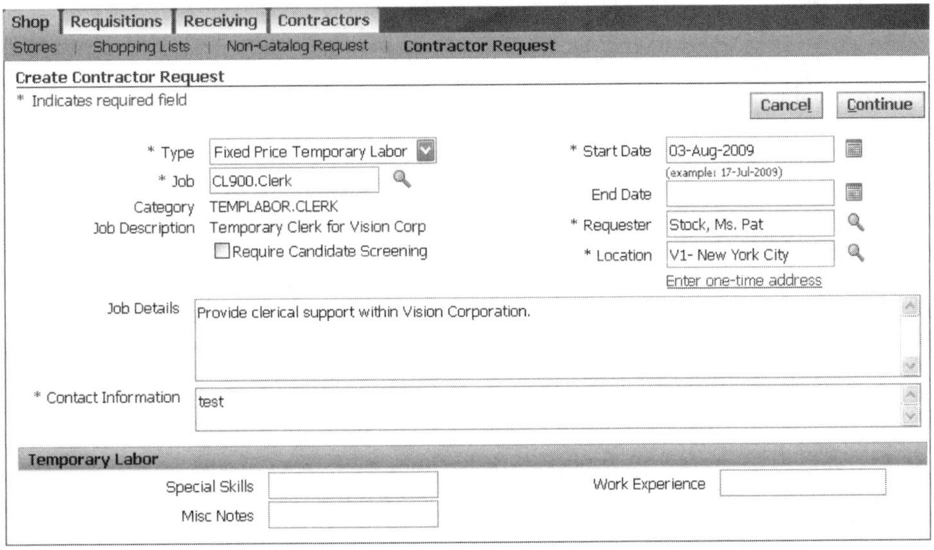

iProcurement | Shop | Contractor Request

FIGURE 4-8. *Requesting contractors in iProcurement*

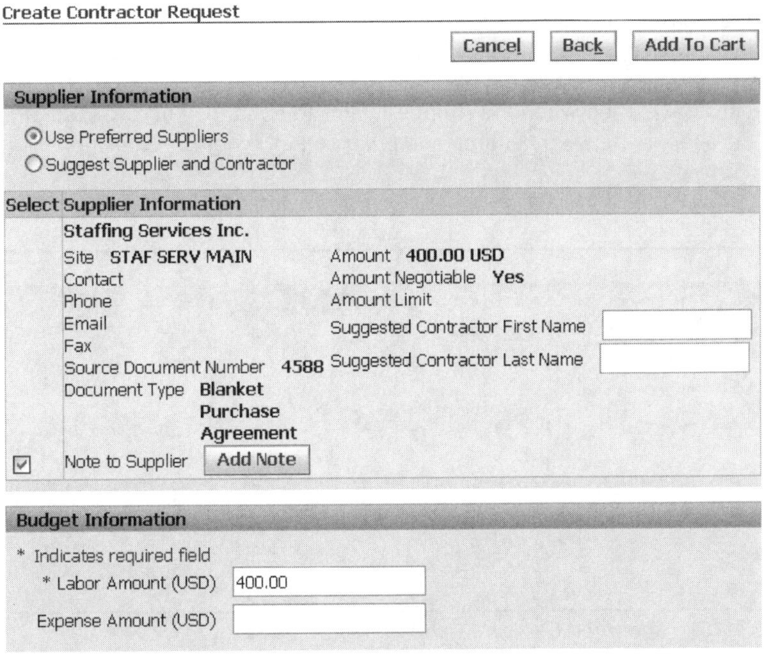

FIGURE 4-9. *Page 2 of requesting a contractor*

Checking Out and Creating Requisitions

Once a shopper is finished adding items to her cart, she can view the items and continue on with checking out. The act of checking out will submit the requisition for approval, based on the approval rules set up in Purchasing for requisitions, and send it to the Autocreate feature in Purchasing, which will allow buyers to request changes, combine requisitions to take advantage of price breaks, adjust the suppliers, and create purchase orders (Purchasing | AutoCreate). Until the shopper checks out, the items in the shopping cart are not visible from Purchasing. Once the checkout is complete, the request will appear in Purchasing as a Requisition (Purchasing | Requisitions | Requisition Summary).

Your shopping cart is visible from the home page, as shown in Figure 4-10. Click View Cart and Checkout to start the process. At this point, the Shopping Cart window will appear, seen in Figure 4-11. QUANTITIES can be updated here, or an item removed with the DELETE icon, but new items can only be added by selecting the RETURN TO SHOPPING link at the lower-left side of the page. This leaves the items in the cart for a future checkout. Any item that was added to the cart that had an Information Template associated with it will have a link populated in the Special Info section, which can be clicked to update the information.

If the shopper selects I NEED A PURCHASE ORDER IMMEDIATELY, Oracle will assign a purchase order number from Purchasing and associate it with this requisition. There are a few implications to using this feature. This feature is usually selected when the requestor requires a purchase order number to purchase or order something from a supplier. If there are company policies surrounding whether an employee who is not part of purchasing can procure items, this may be a violation of the policy. Also, assigning a purchase order immediately will prevent the buyers from combining this requisition with any other requisitions when creating the purchase order document, possibly missing out on volume discounts or lower prices. The last issue with using this is that it might allow a requestor to place an order prior to approvals being completed. If this requisition is eventually canceled, the purchase order number assigned to it will not be reused and is never visible from Oracle Purchasing.

Selecting Save, used when the shopper wants to continue checking out at a later time, will prompt the shopper to assign a name and create an incomplete requisition. This will appear in

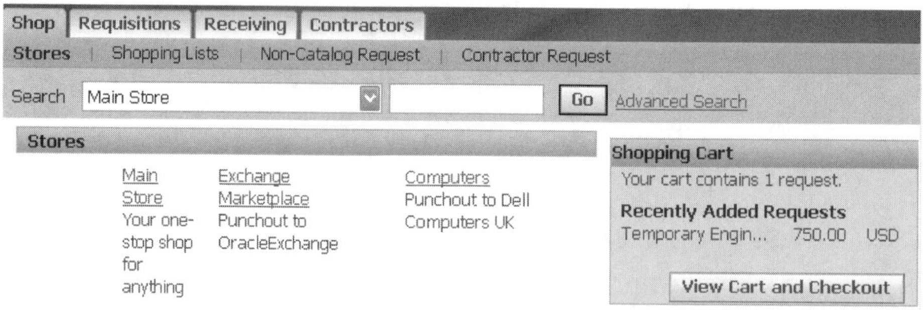

FIGURE 4-10. *Shopping Cart on the home page*

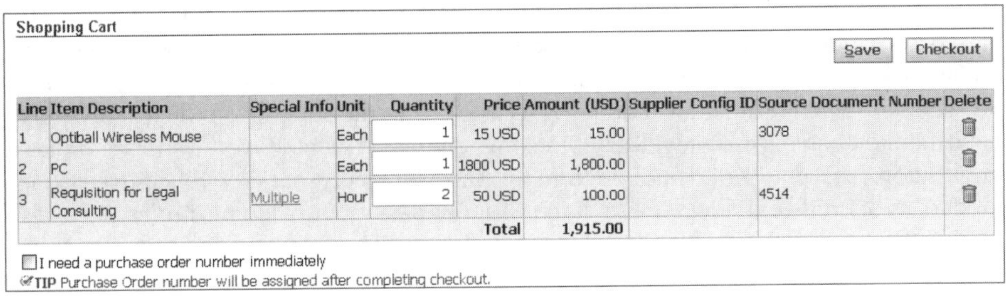

FIGURE 4-11. *Shopping Cart during checkout*

the middle of the shopper's home page under My Requisitions, freeing up the cart for other purchases and allowing the shopper to delete it, combine it with other items, or complete at a later time. Selecting Checkout will start the checkout process.

During the checkout process, much of the information will default in based on the system setups and preferences, but it is important that you understand what information can be updated and where it defaults from, especially the fields that are not displayed during the normal checkout steps. The first page will show Delivery and Billing information, seen in Figure 4-12. The REQUISITION DESCRIPTION will default from the description of the first line in the cart and can be updated. The main purpose of this is to allow not only the shopper but also the buyers to easily identify what this requisition is for. The life of a requisition does not end for your company with the shopper checking out, as it would for other web shopping sites, such as Amazon.com. The requisition still needs to be routed for approval, turned into a purchase order, received, and matched to an invoice. (Each of these options will depend on how Oracle Purchasing and Payables is set up and may or may not be required, and they may also be automated.)

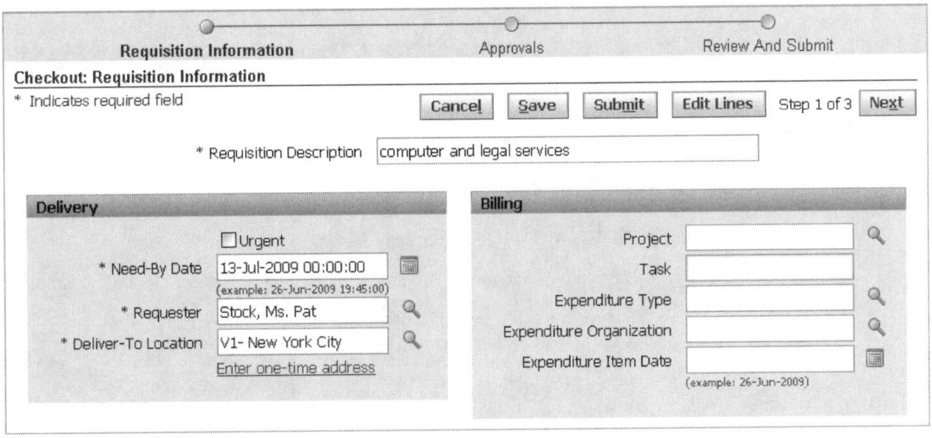

FIGURE 4-12. *Checking out a cart*

In the Delivery section of the page, the shopper can check URGENT. While this will not change the steps required to purchase this shopping cart, it will alert the buyer that the requisition, once approved, is required and should be processed as soon as possible. The NEED-BY DATE will populate in for the requisition and serves two purposes. First, it will print on the purchase order, alerting the supplier when this item is required. Depending on the supplier's policies, this may result in an expedite charge. Also, it will tell Oracle when to start reminding the shopper to receive this requisition. This date will default in from the shopper's personal Preferences (see Chapter 3, under "iProcurement Preferences"). If the shopper has not updated his preferences, it will populate based on the profile POR: Days Needed By. The REQUESTER will populate to the employee associated with the user name the shopper is signed in as, or if based on his preferences, if it has been updated. The shopper can update this field if the profile POR: Override Requestor is set to Yes. DELIVER-TO LOCATION will again default in from the shopper's preferences, which comes in turn from the employee record. There is a system profile that controls if the shopper can update the default location: POR: Override Location Flag. When this is set to Yes, shoppers will have the option of changing the DELIVER-TO LOCATION. The shopper can select a new deliver-to location from the list of values, which displays all the addresses that are set up as locations in Purchasing (Setup | Organizations | Locations), or add an address that does not exist in Oracle by clicking ENTER ONE-TIME ADDRESS. Using the one-time address feature does not automatically create a location in Purchasing, and the address is not available for reuse with other requisitions.

Billing information is used to tie this requisition to a specific project when Oracle Project Costing and Billing is implemented, as well as purchasing card information. P-CARD, available only when they are set up in Purchasing, allows you to select a purchasing card that is associated with either you or the supplier. When a P-card is entered, this requisition will be settled using the credit card as opposed to having the supplier bill your company. Enter the PROJECT, TASK, EXPENDITURE TYPE, EXPENDITURE ORGANIZATION, and EXPENDITURE ITEM DATE. This information will then default on the purchase order, and the Payables invoice that is matched to it, where it will be sent over to Projects. At this point, the requisition can be submitted for approval without any additional information, but there is a lot of additional information that has defaulted in.

Click Edit Lines to see line-specific information, shown in Figure 4-13. Under the Delivery tab, the shopper can take the defaults from the last page and update each individual line with

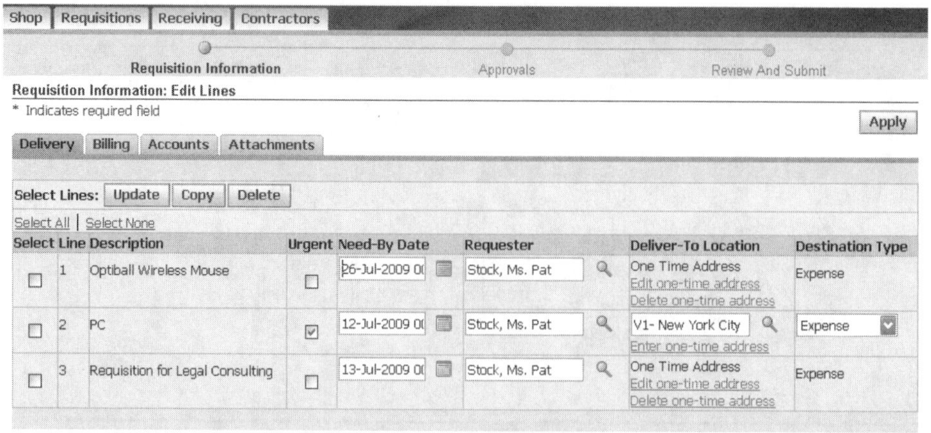

FIGURE 4-13. *Editing line information on a requisition during checkout*

different information for URGENT, NEED-BY DATE, and REQUESTOR. The DELIVER-TO LOCATION as well as the DESTINATION TYPE can be updated here. One-time addresses will always default to a DESTINATION TYPE of Expense, while items that are set up as inventory items will default to Inventory; items can also be updated to Shop Floor, which will cause the items to be received directly into work in process, usually used with outside services.

Checking the box next to a line and then selecting Update gives a comprehensive view of the item, supplier, delivery, and billing information, allowing information specific to the checkout process to be updated (such as quantity or need-by date). A line can also be deleted or copied in the shopping cart. What is not available here is the ability to add a new item to this checkout.

The next tab, Billing, allows the project information to be updated for each line. The ability to split one line between multiple projects, tasks, or expenditure types or organizations also exists. Click the Split icon, where a percent, quantity, or amount can be assigned separately to each project coding. When splitting the billing information, the total percent for each line must still equal 100 percent.

The Accounts tab allows the account number assigned to each line to be updated. Oracle uses account generators to build account numbers assigned to requisitions. A common misperception is that in R12, account generators were all replaced with Subledger Accounting (SLA), but this is not true. There is a distinct difference between what the two processes do. Account generators are used to build account combinations, which are added to such documents as purchase requisitions and purchase orders. SLA will generate the accounting entries, either using the accounts generated by the account generator or from additional setup or transaction information. Note that additional SLA transactions for what are typically considered purchasing transactions are actually owned by cost management and are found in the SLA setups there, including Receiving and Delivery accounting entries, Period End Accruals, and Price Adjustments on Purchase Orders. While SLA can utilize the accounts generated by the account generator, it does not have to.

The account generator for the expense account on requisitions is a seeded Oracle workflow that can be modified by companies to meet their specific needs. Without modifications, EBS will build the inventory account from the inventory setups, and expense accounts from either the expense account associated with an item or, when no item is used, the PO Expense Account associated with the requestor.

Expense Account rules (Purchasing I Setup I Financials I Accounting I Expense Account Rules) can also be set up to override a particular segment in the account combination for a particular category. This will override that segment for every item associated with this category. The profile POR: Apply Expense Account Rules to Favorite Charge Accounts will need to be set to Yes if you want this expense account rule to apply even when a favorite charge account was chosen for this line.

Again, clicking the Split icon will allow you to split the percentage, quantity, and amounts associated with each account. As a shopper, you can either key the account combination into the OPERATIONS ACCOUNTING FLEX field, use the list of values icon found to the right of the account number field to select the segments from a list of values, or select a saved account combination from your preferences. To select a saved combination, use the NICKNAME field and select a name from the list of values. These combinations are saved with a nickname in the shopper's personal favorites.

There is a profile option that will affect the way the account combinations are displayed in iProcurement: POR: Display Legacy Accounting Flex UI. By default, this is set to No and will display the account combination as a string of numbers. When it is set to Yes, the account combination will appear as individual segments, providing a list of values for each segment individually.

The final option is to determine if you want the charge accounts to be applied to all the lines on this requisition with the same destination type. When you select APPLY THIS COST ALLOCATION INFORMATION TO ALL APPLICABLE REQUISITION LINES, it will take the account combinations and percentages and apply the account to all the lines with the same DESTINATION TYPE.

Attachments is the last tab available under edit lines; it allows the shopper to attach additional information, such as a spec, to the requisition line. This attachment will be routed to the buyer, who can opt to include it on the purchase order for the supplier. Figure 4-14 shows the window for adding attachments. Attachments can consist of a file that resides outside of Oracle, text, a specific URL, or a document from Oracle's Document Catalog. In the ADD field, select if you want to add a Desktop File / Text / URL or From Document Catalog. Oracle has the ability to save any document to its document catalog, making it available for viewing from other screens, as well as attach to more than one document.

When adding a file, text, or URL, you can supply information about the attachment in the Attachment Summary Information section of the window. Give the attachment a TITLE, add a DESCRIPTION, and select a CATEGORY. Categories are described in Table 4-4.

Select the TYPE of attachment. FILE allows you to browse to a file that you have access to, such as on your desktop or a network drive, which becomes a file attached to the requisition. URL allows you to enter a URL for future reference, while TEXT allows a message, such as a reason for needing to use a specific supplier, to be attached. The text is typed directly into the form.

When you add something from the document catalog, a search screen will come up to search for a document to add. The Document Catalog consists of saved documents to the Oracle database,

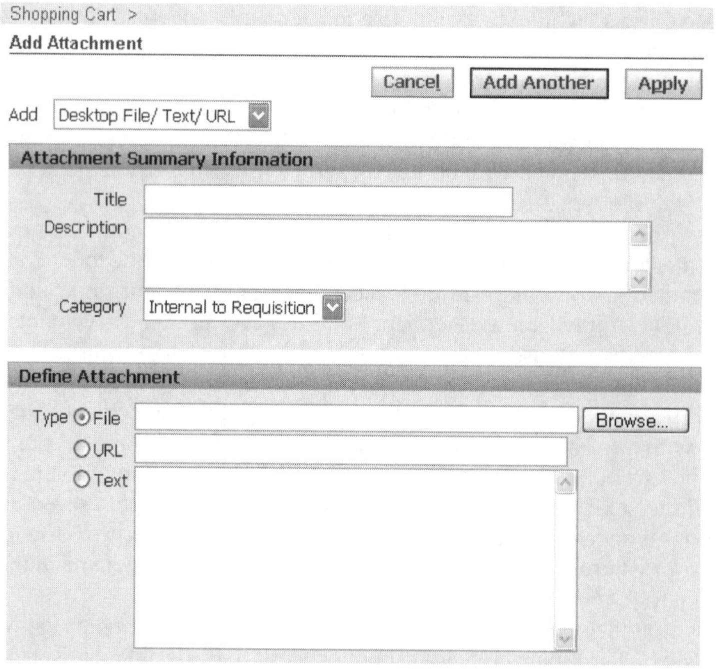

FIGURE 4-14.   *Adding attachments to lines of a requisition in the shopping cart*

Category	Meaning
Internal to Requisition	Keeps the attachment on the requisition for future references, but the attachment is not visible on any related documents
Miscellaneous	A general type of attachment that is viewable from many places within Oracle but is not routed outside the system, such as to a supplier
To Approver	Displays for the approvers when they receive notification to approve this requisition
To Buyer	Displays for the buyer to see when creating a purchase order from this requisition
To Receiver	Displays for the receiver, when it is a person different than the requestor, when performing a receipt
To Supplier	Becomes an attachment on the purchase order when the purchase order is transmitted electronically via EDI (Electronic Data Interchange), e-mail or XML (Extended Markup Language)

TABLE 4-4. *Attachment Categories*

which are populated in this catalog when added to any transaction, such as a purchase order, and the user selects Publish to Catalog. This document then becomes available to attach to other documents in Purchasing. The search screen allows you to search on TITLE, or by clicking the Show More Search Options link, by DESCRIPTION, CATEGORY, LAST UPDATED BY, LAST UPDATED DATE, TYPE, or USAGE. These fields would have been populated when the document was added to the catalog, or updated.

Once you are done editing line information, click Apply to return to the checkout.

Click Next to view information on Approvers, add Notes, and add an attachment that is not line specific. Requisitions need to be approved before the documents are final and ready for the next step in the process. An approval process can range from something as simple as any shopper approving her own purchases, to a supervisor hierarchy approval process with limits based on an employee's position, or a complicated process where approvals are based on the item being purchased and the dollar amount of the document. There are two options for creating these approval rules: the purchasing hierarchies, which have the limitation of a straight supervisor- or position-based hierarchical approval path, and Oracle Approvals Management (AME). AME allows more complicated rules, such as that all requisitions with the category of Computer Equipment must go to the CIO for approval (see the Appendix for information on setting up AME). Purchasing approvals will default to the supervisor hierarchy unless the Use Approval Hierarchy box is checked in the financial options (Purchasing Superuser | Setup | Organizations | Financial Options | Supplier-Purchasing tab). AME will be used when the Approval Transaction Type is populated on the document type selected on the requisition (Purchasing | Setup | Purchasing | Document Types).

The Approvals section, shown in Figure 4-15, will show the default approvals for this requisition, based on the system setups and hierarchies. The graphical representation shown of the approval list is controlled by the system profile POR: Display Graphical Approval List and appears when the setting is Yes. Clicking Manage Approvals will allow the shopper to change the approvers or add additional approvers into the hierarchy. No matter who the approvers are changed to, only

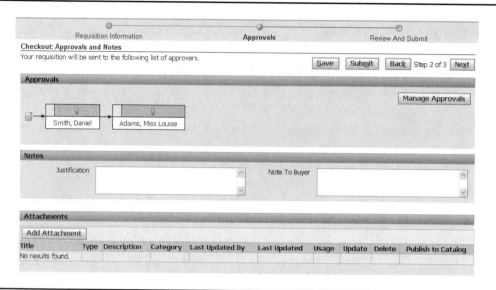

FIGURE 4-15. *Approvals, notes, and attachments to the cart*

approvers with the proper authority can approve a requisition, based on the amount, account number, item category, item, and location. While this is a useful feature, companies may want to restrict who has access to modify the default approvers on a requisition, which can be done by restricting access to specific functions on a responsibility (System Administrator | Security | Responsibility | Define, and adding an Exclusion) or by creating a new menu without access to these functions (System Administrator | Application | Menu). The functions and the access they control are listed in Table 4-5. The Action refers to the option on the Manage Approvals window.

Function Name	Controlled Access
Add Approver Action: Insert Approver	Allows shoppers to change the requisition approval routing by adding a new approver.
Change First Approver Action: Change Managerial Approver	Allows the shopper to add a new first approver, which may in turn change the routing.
Delete Approver Action: Delete Approver	Allows the shopper to delete an approver that is not mandatory from the approval route. Mandatory approvers can not be deleted (based on how the approvals are set up in Purchasing).
User Default Approver List Action: Reset Approval List	Defaults the approval list in based on the system setups, no matter if any changes are made by the shopper.

TABLE 4-5. *Functions That Control Access to the Approval Routing*

When Managing Approvals, you can either insert an approver, change the managerial approver, delete an approver, or reset the approval list. Select INSERT APPROVER to add a new approver to the hierarchy, and determine the ADD TO LOCATION where this person should be inserted into the hierarchy. CHANGE MANAGERIAL APPROVER allows the shopper to select a NEW MANAGERIAL APPROVAL, which will start the approval hierarchy from that person instead of the requestor. DELETE APPROVER will display the current non-critical approvers, allowing the shopper to check specific approvers to be deleted, and RESET APPROVAL LIST returns the list to the initial hierarchy when the Submit button is selected.

Notes can be added either as a JUSTIFICATION, which the approver can see, or as a NOTE TO BUYER, which appears for the buyers when they are creating a purchase order from this requisition.

Attachments can also be added here, and are related to the entire document as opposed to a specific line. The attachment options here are the same as the attachments added to a line, described earlier in this section.

After selecting Next, you can see an overview of the requisition for review prior to the shopper's clicking Submit. The option to create a printable page is also available for his records, but since these requisitions are always available online for future reference, this may be an unnecessary step. The shopper is informed of the requisition number, and the process is complete

Managing Requisitions

Once requisitions are submitted for approval, they can be monitored for progress. The processing includes approval, creation into orders, cancellation, change requests, or completion of requisitions that were saved without submitting. While many of these items can be handled from the home page, Figure 4-16 is from the Requisitions tab. When first navigating to the Requisitions tab, you will find all of your requisitions in numerical order with the most recent on top. Notice at the top of the page, under the Views section, you can select the VIEW you are seeing. The default is All My Requisitions, which will only include your requisitions. If you select My Group's Requisitions, you will see all the requisitions for the members of your group. This group is dictated by the SECURITY LEVEL assigned to the

Shop	Requisitions	Receiving	Contractors
Requisitions	Notifications	Approvals	

Requisitions

Search

Views

View: All My Requisitions Go

◉ Indicates requisition with a pending change request.

Select requisition:	Copy To Cart	Cancel Requisition	Change	Complete	⊙ Previous 1-10 Next 10 ⊙	
Select	Requisition	Description	Total (USD)	Creation Date ▽	Status	Order
○	14103	Misc Computer Equipment	10.00	13-Jul-2009 17:20:21	Approved	
○	14102	hager	0.00	13-Jul-2009 15:39:47	Cancelled	
○	14092	computer and legal services	1,818.20	11-Jul-2009 14:50:23	Approved ◉	Multiple
○	14091	Temporary Engineer in Vision Corp	750.00	11-Jul-2009 14:26:58	Incomplete, Not Applicable	
○	14090	testing supplier	1.00	11-Jul-2009 13:50:11	Approved	
○	14084	Test Lab OTC	89.10	10-Jul-2009 21:45:32	Approved	64005
○	14082		7,500.00	10-Jul-2009 10:52:07	Approved	5524
○	14081		0.00	10-Jul-2009 10:44:34	Incomplete	
○	14080		3,500.00	10-Jul-2009 10:43:13	Approved	5044
○	14079		5,000.00	10-Jul-2009 10:08:40	Approved	5524

FIGURE 4-16. *Requisitions tab*

document type for requisitions (Purchasing | Setup | Purchasing | Document Type, where the TYPE = Requisition Purchase). There are four options: Hierarchy defines the group as the creator of a document and any documents you have approval authority over. Private will only display your requisitions. Public will display all requisitions in the system, no matter who created them, and Purchasing, the last option, allows you to see your own requisitions only, unless you are defined as a buyer in the system (Purchasing | Setup | Personnel | Buyers), in which case you will have access to all requisitions.

Viewing Requisitions and Their Statuses

You can drill down to get more information on the requisition by clicking either the REQUISITION number or the DESCRIPTION. They both take you to the same place and provide more information about the requisition. Clicking the STATUS, on the other hand, will show you who this requisition was submitted to for approval, and their actions, if any. Requisition Statuses are described in Table 4-6, and Actions are described in Table 4-7.

When the ORDER number is populated, this requisition has been created into a purchase order (if it reads Multiple, then more than one purchase order was created for a single requisition). Figure 4-17 shows a recap of the purchase order this requisition created, which can be seen by clicking the ORDER number. A few things are of note on this window. First, the SUPPLIER, ORDER DATE, and STATUS of the order can be seen. This STATUS refers to the internal purchase order document status; it does not mean that the supplier has received the purchase order or accepted the terms on the order. On the right side of the window, a Summary of the order can be seen, showing the purchase order TOTAL, the amount RECEIVED, and the amount INVOICED, as well as a PAYMENT STATUS. Clicking any of the amounts will show the details of the numbers, such as individual receipts and invoices.

Status	Meaning
Approved	Requisition has been approved.
In Process	Requisition has been submitted for approval and is still pending a response from the approver.
Incomplete	Requisition has been saved but not yet submitted for approval.
Pre-Approved	Approver with the proper authority has approved the requisition, but also forwarded it to another approver for additional approvals.
Requires Reapproval	Changes were made to a requisition that was already approved, requiring it to be re-approved.
Reserved	Budgetary funds are reserved for this requisition. This status is only valid for systems using budgetary controls, or encumbrances.
Returned	An approved requisition is returned to the requestor by the buyer. Since requisitions in this status are still considered by MRP (Materials Requirement Planning), companies running MRP will want to control requisitions in a Returned status.

TABLE 4-6. *Requisition Statuses*

Action	Meaning
Accept	A change request against this requisition was accepted.
Adjust	The reserve amount was adjusted when using budgetary controls.
Answer	Response to a question an approver made.
Approve	Requisition is approved.
Approve and Forward	Requisition has been approved, but the approver forwarded it for additional approvals.
Approve and Reserve	Requisition has been approved and funds reserved when using budgetary controls.
Buyer Rejected	Requisition was approved, but the buyer is rejecting it.
Check Funds	Requisition was submitted to check available funds when using budgetary controls, but the funds were not reserved.
Delegate	Approval authority for this document was delegated to another person, as set in the approver's vacation rule.
Forward	Document has been forwarded by the system to another employee. The employee it was forwarded to will appear on the next line.
No Action	No action has been taken by the person, and the workflow controlling the action has reached a time out.
Pending	Oracle is waiting for a response from this person.
Question	The approver has forwarded the requisition to another person with a question, and is waiting for a response.
Reject	Requisition was rejected by the approver.
Reserve	Funds have been reserved, and is used with budgetary controls.
Respond	Buyer's response to a Change Request against an approved requisition.
Return	Buyer has returned an approved requisition to the requestor.
Submit	Requisition has been submitted and is starting the approval process.
Submit Change	A change is being requested against an approved requisition.
Supplier Rejected	This document was sent to a supplier for approval, and they rejected it.
Unreserve	Funds were released for this document when using budgetary controls.
Withdraw	A requisition is withdrawn from the approval and purchasing process.

TABLE 4-7. *Requisition Actions*

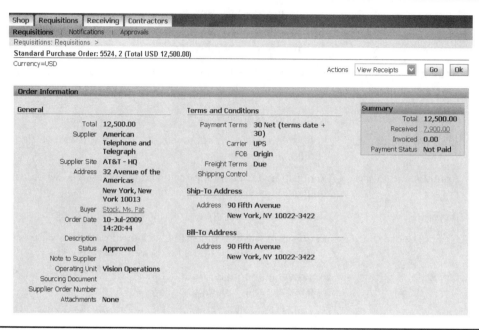

FIGURE 4-17. *Order information and available actions*

This will take you to the same place as the ACTIONS just above it. In the ACTIONS, you have available View Receipts, View Invoices, and View Payments. The final option cannot be accessed except through this option; it is called View Shipments. If you have an agreement with your supplier to send Advance Shipment Notices (ASNs) to you via XML or another electronic interchange or iSupplier, then you can see if the supplier has shipped the product and it is in transit.

Basic Requisition Flow

This is a good point to stop and review the basic flow and integration of requisitions within Purchasing and Payables. Once the requisition is entered and submitted by the shopper, Oracle will check on the approval rules and route it for approval, or in the case where the shopper has the proper approval authority and Oracle is set up to allow the person creating the document to approve it, the document will be approved without further routings. Once approved, it moves to the autocreate queue for buyers to turn it into a purchase order. The relationship between requisitions and purchase orders is many to many, where each requisition can create multiple purchase orders, and each purchase order can be created from many requisitions. The purchase orders are then submitted for approval, but most companies who have the approval level at the requisition level usually set up buyers to have unlimited approval for purchase orders created from a requisition.

The next step performed after the purchase order is approved and the items have been delivered is for the shopper to receive the order in the system. This can be done either from the iProcurement Receiving tab or from the notification that is sent out on the expected delivery date (based on the need-by or promised date on the purchase order). Payables can enter an invoice and match it to the purchase order at any time after it is approved, or match it to a receipt any time after the receipt has been performed. Note that if the receipt is not made, and the purchase order was set up to match to receipt, the invoice cannot be entered against the receipt until the receipt is actually made. Invoices that are entered and matched to the purchase order, on the other hand, can be entered any time after the order is approved, and as long as the order was set up for 3-way matching and matching tolerances are defined properly in the system, the invoice will go on a system hold and be released by the system after the receipt is made.

Notice in this process that after the requisition is approved and turned into a purchase order, all the future actions (receipt and invoice) are against the purchase order and not the requisition.

Other Requisition Actions

Other actions you can take on requisitions include copying the information on a requisitions to your cart to create a new requisition, leaving the old one active, canceling a requisition, changing information on a requisition, or completing a requisition that is incomplete. All of these actions can be done from the main window under Requisitions.

Copying an Existing Requisition to Your Shopping Cart

Any requisition you have access to can be copied to your cart to create a new requisition. Once in your cart, you can remove lines, add it to additional lines, and change the quantities and billing information when checking out. Creating a copy is just that—a copy. It does not change the information or the status of the original requisition.

Canceling a Requisition

A requisition may need to be canceled for multiple reasons. It may no longer be needed, be a duplicate, or be returned from a buyer, among other business reasons. When canceling a requisition, you have the option to cancel a specific line, or the entire requisition. Canceling the only line on a requisition will inherently cancel the entire requisition.

When the requisition or its lines are either incomplete, returned, in process for approval, or approved and not yet associated with a purchase order, it can be canceled at any time. Any notifications an approver has received that is pending action will be canceled at this time. This will also remove the approved requisitions from the buyer's Queue (Autocreate) to create into purchase orders. When the requisition line has already been turned into a purchase order, the buyer must approve the cancellation request. Lines that are not yet associated with a purchase order can be canceled without the buyer's approval. This is because the purchase order, a legally binding document when accepted by both the buyer and the seller, may not be able to be canceled without penalties or legal consequences. Once the buyer approves the cancellation, the status on the requisition or its line will update to canceled.

The status of the requisition will show a round circle next to the Status, as seen back on Figure 4-16 for requisition number 14092. If you click the status, a button will appear to View Change History, allowing you to see the changes that are pending. (Buyers will see the change request in the Pending Purchase Order Change form, and can approve them—Purchasing | Purchase Orders | Pending Purchase Order Changes.)

Changing a Requisition

Creating changes to a requisition has the same limitations as any requisition that is already part of a shopping cart. You can modify the quantity, along with the delivery, billing, and line information.

Other changes, such as to the item requested, will need to have the line canceled and a new line added to either the existing cart or a new cart.

Changes will cancel any approval notifications that are waiting for actions, and also remove an approved requisition from the Autocreate screen so that the buyers cannot create a purchase order out of it. The requisition will be re-routed for approval when it is submitted after the changes. However, if a purchase order already exists, the buyer will have to approve the changes that were requested before they are processed.

Additional Features Under the Requisitions Tab

There are two additional subtabs under the Requisitions tab. First is the ability to view your notifications. Notifications in Oracle may be informational in nature or denote items that you must act on. These notifications are generated by Oracle Workflow when it reaches a specific stage in any workflow. Oracle comes seeded with many notifications, and companies can not only select which ones they want to send out, they can also modify the notifications with the information that is important to their company. Workflow notifications can be set up to send out e-mails or used without the e-mail integration. Either way, a user notification can always be seen in iProcurement under Requisitions | Notifications. One thing to remember is that canceled notifications will disappear from the user's notification list, while she will receive a cancellation e-mail, informing her that a previously received notification is now canceled. This sometimes causes confusions when a user, usually an approver, has a notification in her inbox but cannot approve it, and the notification no longer appears on her open notifications list.

The general notifications for iProcurement are listed in Table 4-8.

General Functions	Explanation
Approval Workflow Item Type: PO Requisition Approval	Approvers receive notifications to approve requisitions, as well as reminders.
Confirm Receipts Workflow Item Type: PO Confirm Receipt	Requestors are sent reminders to receive requisitions that are approved requisitions and are set up for 3- or 4-way matching. These are set to send out one day after the need-by date on the purchase order or if an invoice is matched to the purchase order and the system applied a Quantity or Amount Received hold. Reminders can also be sent out after the initial request.
Requisition Status Workflow Item Type: PO Order Status	Requestors can be informed when a requisition is approved, rejected, returned, or turned into a purchase order.
Supplier Notifications Workflow Item Type: PO Send Notifications for Purchasing Documents	Suppliers can also receive notifications directly out of Oracle for Contractor requests, including notice that a request has been made, that a request has been canceled, or that one is approved.

TABLE 4-8. *Notifications Generated by iProcurement*

Approvals

Approvers have the option of approving requisitions either from iProcurement or from an e-mail notification they receive. Notifications will appear both on the iProcurement home page under My Notifications and on the Requisitions I Approvals window. Figure 4-18 shows a receiving notification.

The approver has several options when an approval notification is received. The buttons along the top allow you to respond to this requisition by clicking either Approve, which will then route this requisition to the buyers to create a purchase order, or Approve And Forward, sending it to another person for an additional approval. When using the Approve and Forward feature on a requisition you have the authority to approve, the requisition status will change to Pre-Approved, and will then be routed to the Forward person for additional approvals prior to routing it to purchasing. Forward will send this requisition to another person without approving it, and it will still require someone with the proper approval authority to approve it. When using either the Approve And Forward or Forward buttons, you must select the person you are forwarding this requisition to. Any requisition you do not have the proper authority to approve will continue up the approval chain until it finds the person who does. When you select a forward to someone who was not in the approval chain, then Oracle will not allow this requisition to be approved, and the approval workflow will fail with Approver Not Found. This prevents someone from forwarding a requisition outside the proper approval channel to commit fraud.

Reject will return the requisition to the shopper or requestor, if they were not the same, as rejected, requiring her to either resubmit it for approval or cancel the requisition. Reassign allows you to either DELEGATE YOUR RESPONSE or TRANSFER NOTIFICATION OWNERSHIP to another person. When you DELEGATE YOUR RESPONSE, you are giving the person you forward this requisition to the authority

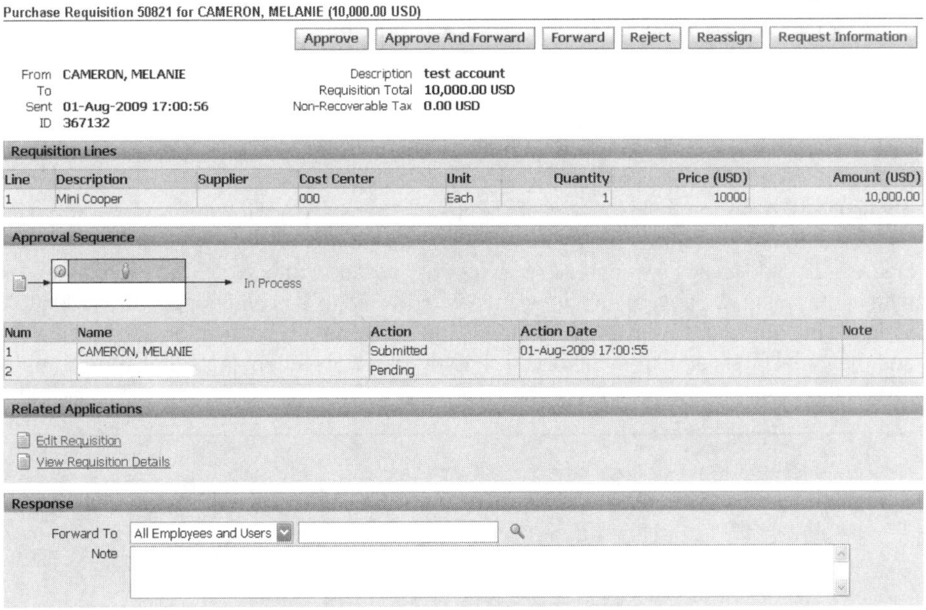

FIGURE 4-18. *Approval notification*

to respond on your behalf. This means that the person will have the same approval authority as you do for approving this requisition, and the notification is still owned by you. One of the things this also does is list your name as the approver if the person you delegated this to approves it—they approved it on your behalf and under your authority, which is comparable to you approving it. This is also done so that the person who you delegated your authority to does not appear as the approver, when they did not have the proper approval authority. While logical, this can cause an auditing catch-22 and sometimes needs some explaining during an audit.

When you TRANSFER NOTIFICATION OWNERSHIP, you are reassigning this entire notification to another person, and it is his approval authority that will be evaluated when the approval is made. These two options are controlled by a profile called WF: Notification Reassign Mode. This can be set to Transfer, which only allows users to Transfer Notification Ownership, or Delegate, which allows them to Delegate their Response, or Reassign, which allows the approver to select either option.

The Request Information button allows you to send a notification within Oracle to either the requestor or any other Oracle user about this requisition. The requisition is still pending your approval while you wait for the additional information.

Two links lower on the page allow you to edit the requisition or view additional details on this requisition. EDIT REQUISITION is only available if the check box APPROVER CAN MODIFY is selected on the Document Type for Purchase Requisition (Purchasing | Setup | Purchasing | Document Type). VIEW REQUISITION DETAILS will take you to the same form that you see when you view a requisition.

The final section allows the approver to add a response when approving or rejecting the requisition. Add your response in the NOTE section, and it will appear on the notification the requestor receives about the response.

Vacation Rules

When talking about approvals, people being on leave (such as for vacation, family emergency, or illness) always comes up. How will approvals sent to you, either on purpose or in error, be responded to while you are out? Oracle provides Vacation Rules to handle this situation. From your iProcurement home page, there is a link for Vacation Rules at the very bottom of the page under My Notifications (see Figure 4-19).

The next window will show any rules that you currently have set up, and it allows you to create a new rule by clicking Create Rule. Rules can be set up for a specific type of notification, or for all notifications, based on the ITEM TYPE selected next. After selecting the items you want to create a rule for, you come to the same screen you saw if you reassigned an approval notification, shown in Figure 4-20. Add a START DATE and END DATE for your vacation rule. Note that even if you select today's date as the START DATE, any notifications already delivered to you will not get forwarded to the person assigned in your rule. Add a MESSAGE that will appear with each notification for the person you select, and then select the name from the box next to the REASSIGN section. Note that you can only select a person that is set up as an employee in Oracle.

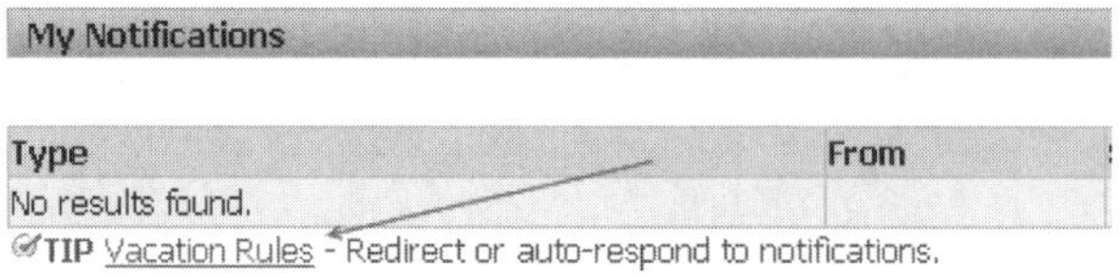

FIGURE 4-19. *Vacation Rules link*

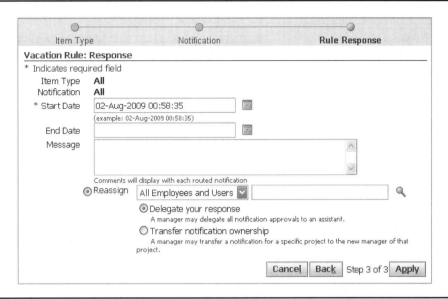

FIGURE 4-20. *Vacation rules*

The same options are available as when reassigning an approval, and they are controlled by the same profile. Select Apply to save the rule, and it goes into effect on the date and time assigned on the START DATE, and stays in effect till the date and time on the END DATE, or until it is removed if there is no END DATE. This Vacation Rule link is specific to the user who is signed into Oracle, and general users cannot create a Vacation Rule for other users, but the workflow administrator can (set up under Workflow Administrator Web Applications | Administration | Vacation Rules). This is useful when someone is out unexpectedly and is a key approver in the system.

Receiving Requisitions

Shoppers can receive items directly in iProcurement, as well as from an e-mail notification. Empowering the shoppers with these receiving processes better enables 3-way matching in Payables, where invoices are matched to the purchase orders and only paid after the receipt has been processed.

Receiving from an E-Mail Notification

Oracle can be set up to send out notifications for requestors to receive an approved requisition that is attached to an approved purchase order. These notifications are both a reminder to the shopper to receive the goods and a method for actually creating the receipt. Notifications can either be sent out via e-mail or viewed directly within Oracle in many places, including the iProcurement home page. Sending out notifications requires that the Confirm Receipts Workflow Select Orders concurrent request be run on a scheduled basis, while receiving the notification via an e-mail requires that the Oracle Workflow Mailer be set up and running. Each user has the ability to control his preferences for notifications, and if this is set to Disable or Do Not Send Me Mail, e-mails will not be received (iProcurement | Preferences link | Display Preferences | Notifications region).

Notifications are sent out on the need-by date that is on the purchase order, which will default in from the requisition. This date on the requisition is controlled by the NEED-BY DATE OFFSET on the user's preferences (iProcurement I Preferences link I iProcurement Preferences I under the Deliver region of the window). While users can update this field for the requisitions they enter, it will default from the value set in the POR: Days Needed By profile option when a user is first set up.

Once the notification is received, shoppers have the option of receiving the entire order, partially receiving the order, reassigning this notification to another user to perform the receipt, or informing Oracle that the item has not yet been received, in which case Oracle will send out a new notification in a set number of days, depending on how you set up this workflow (REQAPPRV).

Basic Receiving

Receiving can also be performed directly from the Receiving tab in iProcurement, as seen in Figure 4-21. From this window, you can perform a new receipt, correct or return a previously made receipt, view any requisitions that are waiting for receipts, and view a previously made receipt.

There are actually multiple ways you can get to the receiving screen from here, but they will all take you to the same screen. You can use the Search feature at the top of the window, where you can find a requisition to receive by requisition number, by order number (PO Number), or by supplier. You can click any requisitions that are listed under the Requisitions to Receive region of the page, or you can click either of the Receive Items links, under Receiving and Receiving Process.

These last two links will actually allow you to search for and find any requisition that is waiting for a receipt, no matter who is the requestor on the order. This is helpful, as it allows one person to request an item and another to perform the receipt. For example, if an administrative assistant created an order for suppliers for the department, he may be on vacation when the order comes in. This will allow another person to perform the receipt in his absence. This search screen is seen in Figure 4-22. To find a requisition to perform a receipt against, some or all of the fields will need to be completed. The REQUESTER will default to your name, but you can leave it blank or

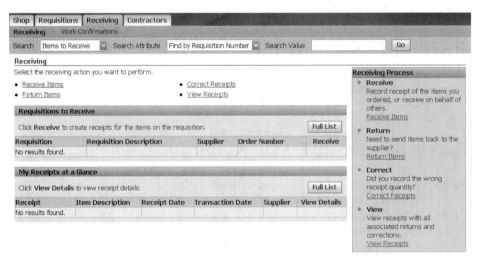

iProcurement I Receiving I Receiving

FIGURE 4-21. *Receiving in iProcurement*

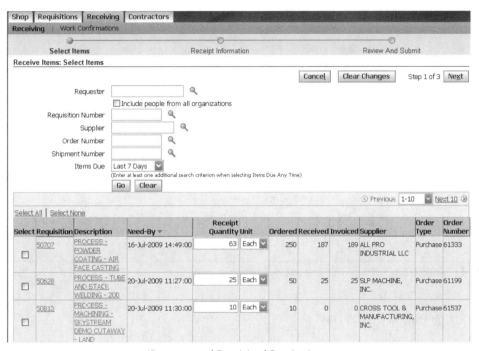

FIGURE 4-22. *Finding orders to receive*

put in another employee's name instead. When INCLUDE PEOPLE FROM ALL ORGANIZATIONS is selected, the limitation to see only requesters within your own organization is removed, giving you access to other organizations. A specific REQUISITION NUMBER can be entered. This will only accept a requisition number that is in a state to receive, which means the requisition is approved, it is turned into a purchase order, and the purchase order is approved. The NEED-BY date on the requisition can be in the future to receive against it. SUPPLIER can also be entered to search by. ORDER NUMBER refers to the purchase order number, while SHIPMENT NUMBER is only available for internal and inter-organization orders, or for any supplier order where an Advance Shipment Notice (ASN) has been received in Oracle. ITEMS DUE looks at the need-by date and determines which requisitions to return. Options here include Last 7, 30, or 60 Days, which looks for any requisition that was due in the past; Future 30 or 60 days, which looks at requisitions that have need-by dates in the future; Today; or Anytime. When selecting Anytime, you do need to add at least one other selection criterion before performing a search.

Once the requisitions are found, a requisition can be selected and the RECEIPT QUANTITY and UNIT updated before clicking Next. From here, the RECEIPT DATE will default to today's date. While this date can be updated, Purchasing, General Ledger, and Inventory periods for items being delivered into inventory must all be open. In most systems, that will usually restrict the receipt date to the current accounting period. As seen in Figure 4-23, a WAYBILL number, a PACKING SLIP, and a RECEIPT COMMENT can also be added but are not required. The receiver is then prompted with a review screen prior to submitting the receipt, allowing him to ensure that the information he entered was accurate.

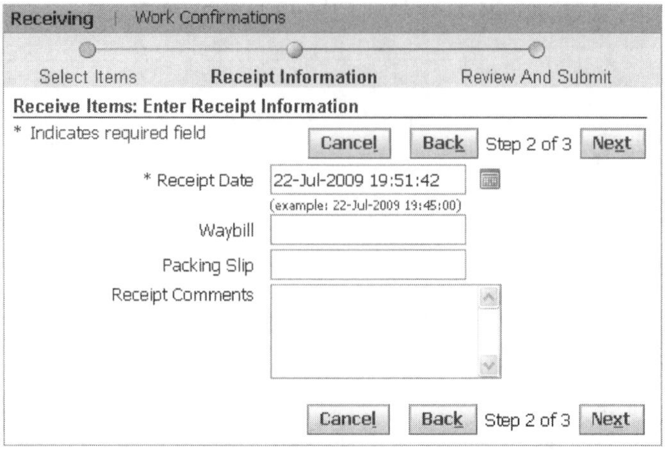

iProcurement | Receiving | Receive Items

FIGURE 4-23. *Receiving a specific requisition*

Express Receiving

Express receiving reduces the data the users can update during the receiving process, as well as the number of screens seen and mouse clicks they need to do. A normal receipt has three pages that need to be reviewed prior to completing the receipts, whereas Express Receipts will receive the item as soon as the Express Receipt button is clicked. The profile POR: Support Review for Express Receive will determine if the receiver sees a review page prior to the system committing the receipt, as seen in Figure 4-24. When this profile is not turned on, the receiver will be informed of the receipt number, seen in Figure 4-25.

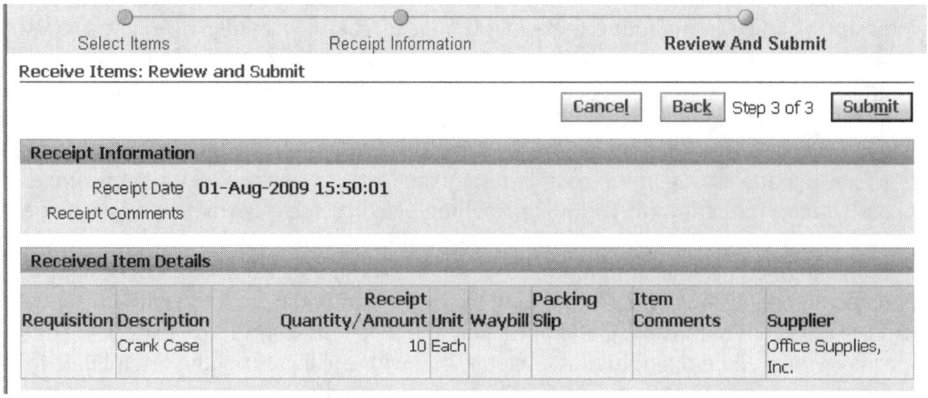

iProcurement | Receiving | Express Receive icon

FIGURE 4-24. *Express Receipt with Review*

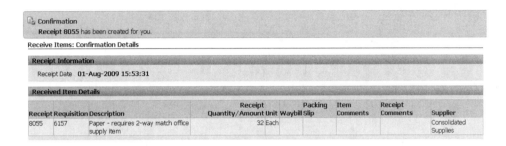

FIGURE 4-25. *Express Receipt Confirmation*

Viewing Receipts

After a requisition has been received, you can view the receipt at any time by selecting View Receipts and finding the receipt with the same search options that were available to create a receipt (see the immediately preceding section). Clicking the RECEIPT NUMBER will show details about the receipt, as seen in Figure 4-26.

Receipt Corrections

Inevitably, receiving mistakes happen, and a correction needs to be done. Selecting the Correct Receipts link from the main receiving page allows corrections to be made to the quantities received. Receipts can be found by the person who performed the receipt (RECEIPT CREATED BY), the

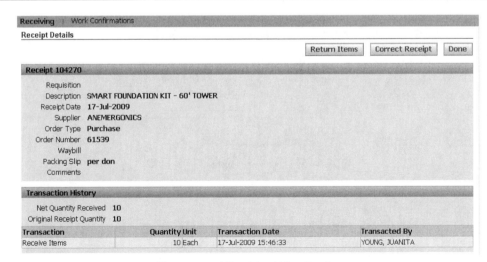

FIGURE 4-26. *Viewing receipts*

iProcurement | Receiving | Correct Receipts

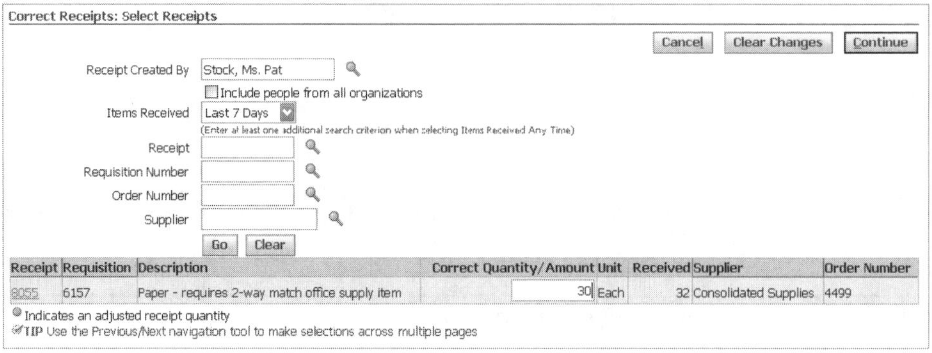

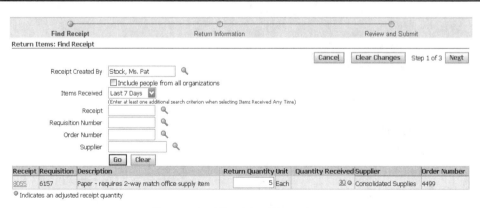

FIGURE 4-27. *Correcting receipts*

date it was received (ITEMS RECEIVED), RECEIPT number, REQUISITION, or ORDER NUMBER, or else by the SUPPLIER on the purchase order. Once the receipt is found, a CORRECT QUANTITY/AMOUNT can be entered, shown in Figure 4-27. A review page allows the receiver to see the change in receipt quantities or amounts before submitting the change.

Returning Items to Suppliers

From time to time, an item needs to be returned to the supplier, possibly because it was damaged or the wrong item was ordered. Receipt Corrections should not be confused with Returns (sometimes called RTS, or Return to Supplier). Corrections are performed to correct a mistake in the receiving transaction, whereas an RTS is performed when the item is returned, and indicates to the accounting department that a credit should be expected from the supplier.

To perform a return, use the Return Items link from the receiving home page. Referring to Figure 4-28, the RETURN QUANTITY can be entered. Notice that the QUANTITY RECEIVED in this example

iProcurement | Receiving | Return Items

FIGURE 4-28. *Returns to the supplier*

has a small circle next to it. This indicates that the receipt has a correction against it, and clicking the quantity will show both the original receipt and any corrections.

After clicking Next, the receiver can enter a REASON for the return, as well as a RETURN MATERIAL AUTHORIZATION, or RMA, if one was received from the supplier. The RMA is like a purchase order, except it is issued from the supplier and authorizes the company who ordered the product to send it back. Additional COMMENTS can also be added. Notice that the REASON field has a flashlight next to it, indicating that the user needs to select a value from a predefined list. This list is set up in Purchasing | Setup | Transaction Codes. After this information is completed, a review page appears before allowing you to submit.

Creating Debit Memos Automatically for Returns

As mentioned earlier, a return to the supplier indicates to accounting that a credit should be expected for these items. In today's automated world, every shipment will generate an invoice, and every return a credit. Oracle allows the system to automatically generate a debit memo in Payables for these items. (The only difference between a debit memo and a credit memo is who generates the transaction. Debit memos are generated internally, whereas credit memos are generated and sent from the supplier.) When the profile (System Administrator | Profile | System) called POR: Enable Automatic Debit Memo Creation for Returns is set to Yes, Oracle will automatically generate a debit memo in Payables for each return made to a supplier with the CREATE DEBIT MEMO FROM RTS TRANSACTION option selected, as shown in Figure 4-29.

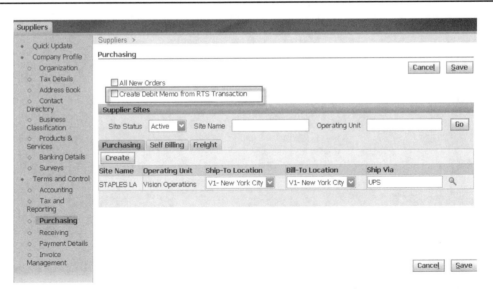

Purchasing | Supply Base | Suppliers | Reporting | Purchasing

FIGURE 4-29.   *Enabling a supplier to generate debit memos in Payables for returns*

CHAPTER
5

iSupplier Setups

Supplier Portal is designed to allow more efficient collaboration between your company and the companies that supply the goods and services you need to do business. Purchase order management, shipment notifications, and invoice and payment views are available both internally and externally. While this application was initially designed to be utilized as externally facing collaboration with suppliers, it has many internal uses as well, giving employees a global view of supplier transactions and interactions. As with most of the self-service modules in Oracle E-Business Suite, iSupplier does now work as an independent module, being tightly integrated with Purchasing and Payables.

General Required Setups

While Payables is not required for iSupplier, having Purchasing licensed and fully set up is. If you are not using Oracle Payables, the invoice and payment information will not be available for the suppliers to view, but iSupplier can still be used for the purchasing information. For complete purchasing set ups, please refer to Chapter 2 of my book *Oracle Procure-to-Pay Guide* (McGraw-Hill Professional, 2009).

iSupplier-Specific Setups

iSupplier has a number of setups that are both required and optional that determine both the data and features that the suppliers will have access to.

Securing Attributes for the Users

Securing attributes are settings added to both the responsibility and the user account setup for the supplier, and control what data is accessed. Four specific securing attributes are used in iSupplier, controlling not only the specific supplier or site that can be viewed, but also the level of detail available for the supplier to see. Securing attributes at the responsibility level, identifying that security can exist for this responsibility, work hand in hand with the securing attribute values added to the supplier user accounts, which actually controls the access. Once a securing attribute is identified at the responsibility level, shown in Figure 5-1, it looks for the associated value for that attribute on the user account. This limits the data each supplier can see in iSupplier to their own company's or location's information. Table 5-1 explains what each securing attribute controls.

Profiles

There are several profiles that affect the way iSupplier will function and appear. These profiles and what they control are listed in Table 5-2. Profiles are set using the System Administrator responsibility (Setup | Profile | System).

Supplier Setups and Management

Suppliers can request access to iSupplier, or be granted access by the administrator. How your company will be using the portal determines the best method(s) for you to use. iSupplier is implemented to allow them to inquire into their account details online, to submit transactions, such as invoices or rescheduling a delivery, or to respond to a request for quote that you have posted.

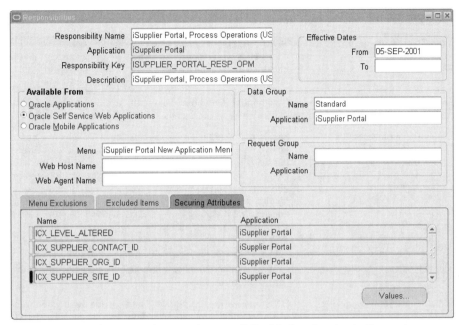

System Administrator | Security | Responsibility | Define, Securing Attributes tab

FIGURE 5-1. *Securing attributes on a responsibility*

Securing Attribute	Controls
ICX_LEVEL_ALTERED	This attribute can only be added at the responsibility and controls whether the supplier will have access to view the distribution details associated with a purchase order. (Distributions are where the internal accounting designation resides on the order.) Using the Values button, add either HEADER LINE or SHIPMENT to restrict access to these levels. Since there is no list of values, you will need to type these values in (they are case sensitive).
ICX_SUPPLIER_CONTACT_ID	Associates the user with a specific contact set up in Oracle on the supplier, and limits access to only documents that have this contact associated with it. This is identified as a security attribute on the responsibility, but the actual value is added to the user.
ICX_SUPPLIER_ORG_ID	Associates the user with a specific supplier set up in Oracle, and restricts access to this supplier's documents as well as a specific operating unit. This is identified as a security attribute on the responsibility, but the actual value is added to the user.
ICX_SUPPLIER_SITE_ID	Identifies the supplier site associated with a user, and limits access to only that site in iSupplier. This can be left blank to view all sites. This is identified as a security attribute on the responsibility, but the actual value is added to the user.

TABLE 5-1. *Security Attributes for iSupplier Portal*

.

Profile Name	Control
Application Framework Agent	Set for the responsibility called POS Supplier Guest User, it identifies the external web server the suppliers are using to access iSupplier, also identified in the profile POS: External URL profile. Setting this allows notifications for the suppliers to go to the correct server.
Business Classification Re-Certification Notification Reminder Days	Determines the number of days prior to when the business classification re-certification is due that the supplier is reminded to update their information.
Business Classification Re-Certification Period	Suppliers can add their business classification, which is required by government agencies when doing business with an organization. In the past, this was known as a SIC, or Standard Industrial Classification; it recently changed to the North American Industry Classification System, or NAICS. This option determines how many times a year (in days) that the supplier is required to update their classification. If you are using this feature, ensure the concurrent request Business Classification Recertification Notification is scheduled to run periodically.
EDR: E-Records and E-Signatures	Set to Yes to enable Oracle's E-Signature functionality.
HR: Security Profile	Gets assigned to iSupplier responsibilities to restrict or grant access to specific business groups.
POS: ASL planning attribute updates from supplier approved by	Determines who can approve changes made by suppliers to both the order modifiers (fulfillment details) and the delivery capacity. Select from Buyers, Planners, or No Approval Required. Buyers and Planners are associated with the item being modified (Purchasingfreight I Items I Organization Items I Purchasing tab for Buyer, General Planning tab for Planner).
POS: Default Promise Date while acknowledgement	When this is set to Yes, the Promise Date on an order shipment acknowledgment will default to the Need By date entered on the order.
POS: Default Responsibility for Newly Registered Supplier Users	*Required*. Assigns the responsibility name that will default in for all new suppliers requesting access to the system from the Prospective Vendor Registration window.
POS: Display AP AR Netting Information	Determines if invoice details can be seen when transactions from receivables are netted against open payables. Defaults to No.
POS: External Responsibility Flag	*Required*. Set at the Responsibility level, Yes will make a specific responsibility available to assign to suppliers in Supplier User Management.
POS: External URL	URL for the external web server for iSupplier. This is usually set for the responsibility called POS: Supplier Guest User, where a supplier completes a request to have access to the system.
POS: Internal URL	URL for the internal web service for iSupplier.
POS: Limit invoice to single PO	When set to Yes, will limit the supplier from creating an invoice in iSupplier against more than one purchase order. Default is No.
RCV: Fail All ASN Lines if One Line Fails	When set to Yes, this will fail all lines associated with an Advance Shipment Notice (ASN) or Advance Shipment Billing Notice (ASBN) when there is an error on one or more of the lines. Default is No.
Responsibility Trust Level	Needs to be set to External for the responsibility POS: Supplier Guest User.

TABLE 5-2. *Profiles That Affect iSupplier*

Usually, when a supplier is already set up in Oracle for either purchasing or payables, you would grant them access by sending an invitation or by setting them up manually. When you want to allow suppliers to respond to RFQs (requests for quote) for items that you have available for open bidding, then you can create a link on your web site to allow suppliers with whom you are not currently doing business with to request access and is called Prospective Supplier Registration.

Prospective Vendor Registration Setups

When a supplier who is not currently doing business with your organization requests access to iSupplier from your web site, it is called Prospective Vendor Registration. Suppliers would do this when they want to receive requests for quotes using iSupplier. This step needs to be performed only if you plan on allowing suppliers to request access instead of being invited.

Adding a Registration Link to Your Web Site

To use this feature, a link is added to your web site that would direct the potential suppliers to the supplier registration page, where they would need to complete required information and submit the request. This request is then routed to your iSupplier administrator, who decides if access will be granted, and begins the setups. The web site link you are going to send them to is http(s)://*server*:*port*/OA_HTML/jsp/pos/suppreg/SupplierRegister.jsp?ouid=101. The ouid=(org_id for the operating unit) part of the registration page can be used to restrict the operating unit information for each supplier (such as addresses) to only one operating unit. This is required when Organization Encryption is turned on (Purchasing | Setup | Profile Management Configuration | Organization Encryption). When you open this window, check the SELECT box next to the organization you want to secure, and an ENCRYPTION STRING is generated for you. Now the org_id (ouid) can be added to the end of the URL, securing the data. You will need to set up one registration page for each operating unit when encryption is used. Figure 5-2 shows an example of the Supplier Registration page that comes seeded. Remember, when a supplier requests access, they are creating access for the company and one user. Additional users will have to be registered separately, after the supplier is registered.

The supplier registration page comes with specific information that is requested. This information can be customized for your company in two ways. First, you can show or not show specific regions of the registration page, and second, you can use Oracle's Scripting module to add additional required information, in the form of a Survey. Both of these are controlled with the Onboarding Configuration, shown in Figure 5-3. By checking or unchecking a section, you control whether the registration page displays or hides that region of the page. Any surveys that you want to add, which create additional fields, can be added in the Survey section.

Once the supplier requests access, the request will be routed to the buyer administrator for approval. If it is approved, the supplier is created in Oracle, along with the user for the User Details submitted on the request. Access to this supplier information by the administrators is secured by the profile HR: Security Profile, which determines the operating units each responsibility can access for supplier information. These security groupings are created in Human Resources (Security | Global Profile). Ensure you run the concurrent request Security List Maintenance after setting up or maintaining a Global Profile. The Global Profile is then assigned to the profile option HR: Security Profile for the iSupplier administrator's responsibility.

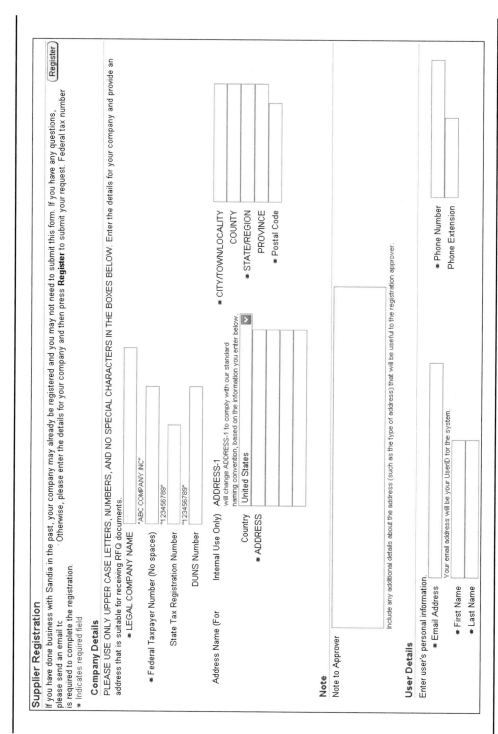

FIGURE 5-2. *iSupplier Portal Registration page*

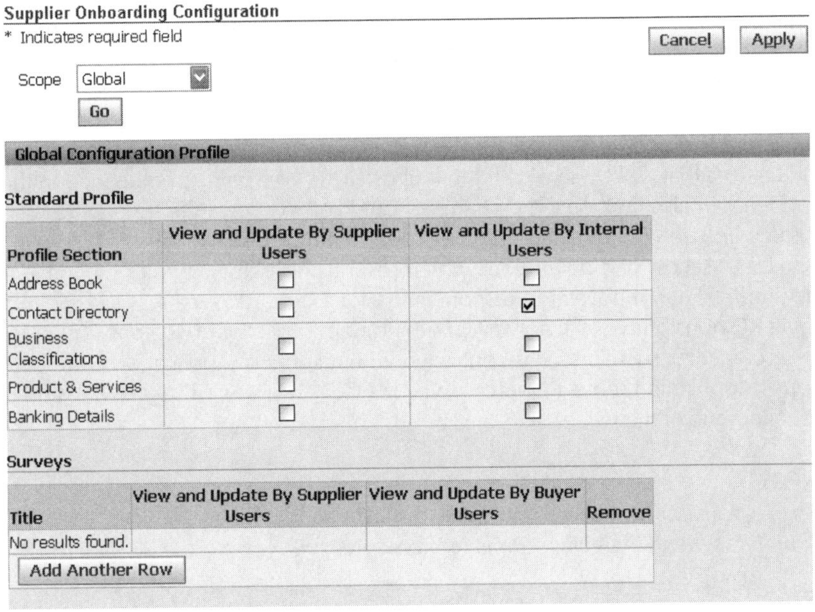

Supplier Onboarding Configuration
* Indicates required field   [Cancel] [Apply]

Scope [Global ▾]
      [Go]

Global Configuration Profile

Standard Profile

Profile Section	View and Update By Supplier Users	View and Update By Internal Users
Address Book	☐	☐
Contact Directory	☐	☑
Business Classifications	☐	☐
Product & Services	☐	☐
Banking Details	☐	☐

Surveys

Title	View and Update By Supplier Users	View and Update By Buyer Users	Remove
No results found.			

[Add Another Row]

Purchasing I Setup I Profile Management Configuration I Supplier Onboarding Configuration

FIGURE 5-3. *Controlling requested information on the Supplier registration window*

Setting the Default Responsibility

When the supplier either requests access or is invited to access iSupplier, default responsibilities can be identified. As a fast review, *suppliers* are created in Oracle, with *contacts*, either as a normal course of doing business, or from an unsolicited request that an administrator approved. *Users* are then created in Oracle for each *contact* who has been granted access to iSupplier. These users will need *responsibilities* added to their user profiles, which will determine the specific functions they will have access to. The data itself is secured by the security attributes added both to the *user* account and the *responsibility*.

To help streamline the user creation process, Oracle has three profiles that are set in the System Administrator responsibility (Profile I System). These profiles define the default responsibility that will be assigned to users for Sourcing, for Collaborative Planning, or as the default responsibility for external users (those that requested access external to your company as opposed to being invited by someone within your company). Since you associate the responsibility with the profile and control the functions and features that are granted to that responsibility, you have complete control over what access is assigned with these defaults.

The profile names used to set these default responsibilities are Sourcing Default Responsibility For External User, Collaborative Planning Responsibility, and iSP Default Responsibility For External User.

Inviting a Supplier to Join

As mentioned earlier, suppliers can either submit an unsolicited request, which is usually used for suppliers who want access to respond to RFQs, or they can be invited to access iSupplier by someone in your company. Since a supplier you are inviting already exists in Oracle, it is their user accounts and access that are being administered. Referring to Figure 5-4, select the SUPPLIER NAME using the find link or type in the SUPPLIER NUMBER. Enter the person's EMAIL ADDRESS you want to invite, and add a NOTE that will be sent with the request. This NOTE will be embedded in the e-mail that is sent, which will also include the URL they should use to access the supplier registration page. This is the same link described earlier, in the section "Adding a Registration Link to your Web Site."

The User Access part determines which responsibility the supplier will have access to, based on the profiles Sourcing Default Responsibility for External Users (SOURCING), Collaborative Planning Responsibility (COLLABORATIVE PLANNING), and iSP Default Responsibility for External Users (INTERNET SUPPLIER PORTAL). This list is controlled with a Lookup (Application Developer | Application | Lookups | Application Object Library | Type = POS_USER_ACCESS_ITEMS), and can be controlled by disabling one of the values.

NOTE
The responsibility Preferences SSWA should be assigned to all suppliers when Single Sign-On is implemented.

When the supplier receives the e-mail, they click the link and continue just as a supplier responding from a link on your web site would. The only difference is that because a supplier is already associated with the invite, it will populate in for them so that a new supplier is not created. The buyer administrator will approve the request, which creates the contact and user in Oracle. In this case, the e-mail address the invite was sent to will become the default user name.

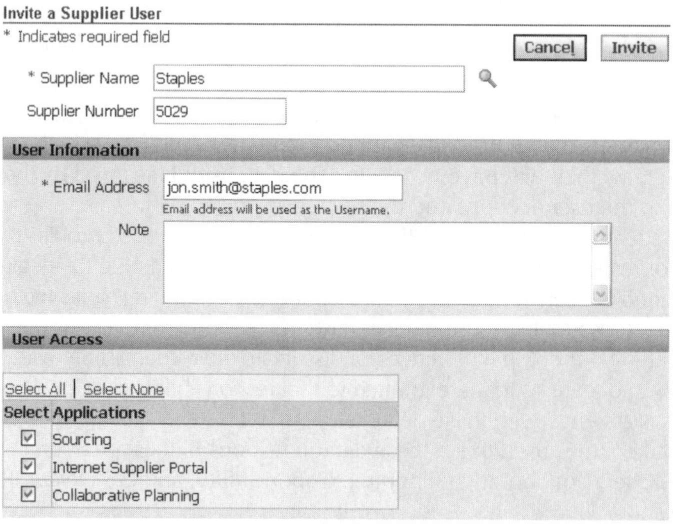

Invite a Supplier User
* Indicates required field

[Cancel] [Invite]

* Supplier Name: Staples
Supplier Number: 5029

User Information

* Email Address: jon.smith@staples.com
Email address will be used as the Username.
Note:

User Access

Select All | Select None
Select Applications
☑ Sourcing
☑ Internet Supplier Portal
☑ Collaborative Planning

Supplier User Administrator | Supplier User Creation | Invite Supplier User

FIGURE 5-4. *Inviting suppliers to access iSupplier*

Registering Users

The third way to have a supplier get access to iSupplier is for the buyer administrator to register them (see Figures 5-5 and 5-6). Again, the SUPPLIER NAME or NUMBER needs to be entered to correspond to the supplier record that already exists in Oracle. User Information is added next, which will also create a contact associated with this supplier. The only required fields are EMAIL, so the supplier is sent access information such as the URL to sign in to iSupplier and their USERNAME and LAST NAME; USERNAME will default to the e-mail address but can be updated. The e-mail provided by Oracle uses a shell notice that reads "You have registered at Default enterprise name . . .". To modify the e-mail content, you will need to modify in the notification in the workflow called Supplier User Registration Workflow Version 2 (POSREGV2). Additional User Information is not required to register the supplier. The password for this user is generated by the system, ensuring it is kept secure from the Supplier Administrator.

The User Access section of the registration page allows you to select the responsibility the user will have access to. The responsibilities that appear here will be any responsibility where the profile POS: External Responsibility Flag is set to Yes. Most often, suppliers are only given access to one responsibility with iSupplier Portal, granting them all the access they will need. Notice that this registration option is the only time you can select a specific responsibility, as opposed to the users being assigned a default responsibility.

Data available in iSupplier to any single supplier is restricted to the supplier that is associated with their user account. Figure 5-7 shows how securing attributes are added to the user account. This is done automatically when a user is created using one of the methods just described; if the user is set up manually the same way internal users are, using the User form in System Administrator (Security | User | Define), then these attributes need to be manually set. If you are manually setting them, make sure you select the attribute names that are associated to iSupplier and not iProcurement. Also notice that they use the database identification number, or a unique code that the users cannot see that is stored in the database, as opposed to the supplier or contact number. When you enter the value, you can use the list of values to select the supplier name, and Oracle will assign the identification for you.

In addition to a supplier restriction, User Access Restrictions can also be added to include only specific sites and contacts. When this section is not completed for the contact and site, then the user will have access to all documents created for a supplier. Once a contact or a site restriction is added, the user access will be limited. The Supplier restriction is available to add multiple suppliers to this user's account, allowing them to see documents for more than one supplier. Note that this feature is not available before Release 12.1.

If you are having problems with the supplier signing in after they have been given access, and they are receiving a message that they have access to more than one supplier hierarchy, go back and ensure that you have a site added under the User Access Restrictions. This error is usually because a site restriction is missing.

Adding User Access Restrictions will automatically populate the securing attributes on the user record. Adding Suppliers will create the ICX_SUPPLIER_ORG_ID entries, Contacts will populate ICX_SUPPLIER_CONTACT_ID records, and Sites will populate ICS_SUPPLIER_SITE_ID records. These attributes can also be assigned manually to the user record. The final option for creating users is found on the supplier record itself (Purchasing | Supply Base | Suppliers | Contact Directory). When creating the contact, ensure the box CREATE USER ACCOUNT FOR THIS CONTACT is selected, and you will be prompted to supply a USERNAME. Here, you can select the responsibilities they will have access to as well as restrict the sites or contacts. Oracle will create the user account and e-mail the password to the EMAIL ADDRESS that is on the contact. Once the contact is

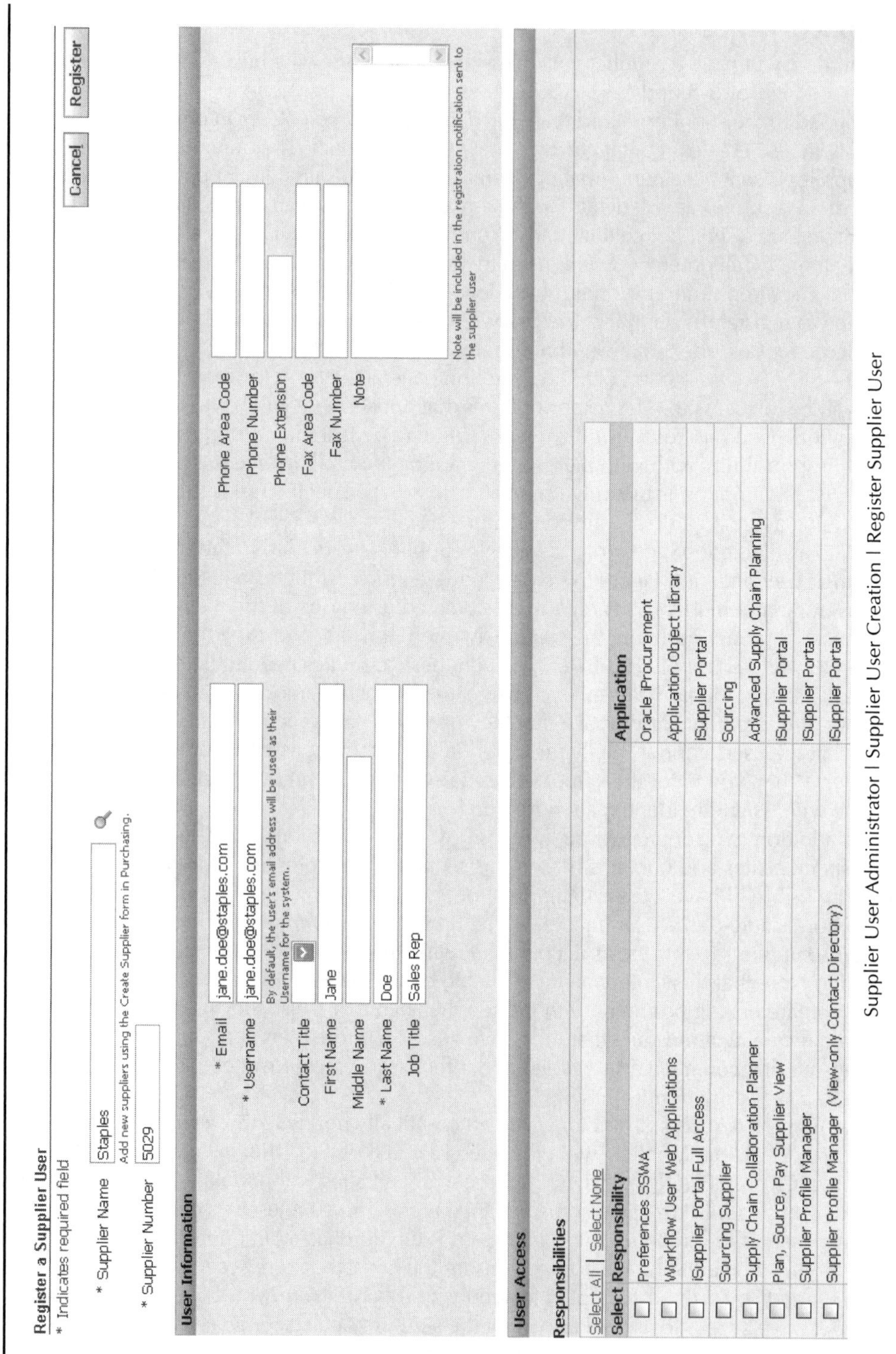

Register a Supplier User

* Indicates required field

Cancel | Register

* Supplier Name Staples

Add new suppliers using the Create Supplier form in Purchasing.

* Supplier Number 5029

User Information

* Email jane.doe@staples.com

* Username jane.doe@staples.com

By default, the user's email address will be used as their Username for the system.

Contact Title

First Name Jane

Middle Name

* Last Name Doe

Job Title Sales Rep

Phone Area Code

Phone Number

Phone Extension

Fax Area Code

Fax Number

Note

Note will be included in the registration notification sent to the supplier user

User Access

Responsibilities

Select All | Select None

Select Responsibility	Application
☐ Preferences SSWA	Oracle iProcurement
☐ Workflow User Web Applications	Application Object Library
☐ iSupplier Portal Full Access	iSupplier Portal
☐ Sourcing Supplier	Sourcing
☐ Supply Chain Collaboration Planner	Advanced Supply Chain Planning
☐ Plan, Source, Pay Supplier View	iSupplier Portal
☐ Supplier Profile Manager	iSupplier Portal
☐ Supplier Profile Manager (View-only Contact Directory)	iSupplier Portal

Supplier User Administrator I Supplier User Creation I Register Supplier User

FIGURE 5-5.　*Registering a supplier*

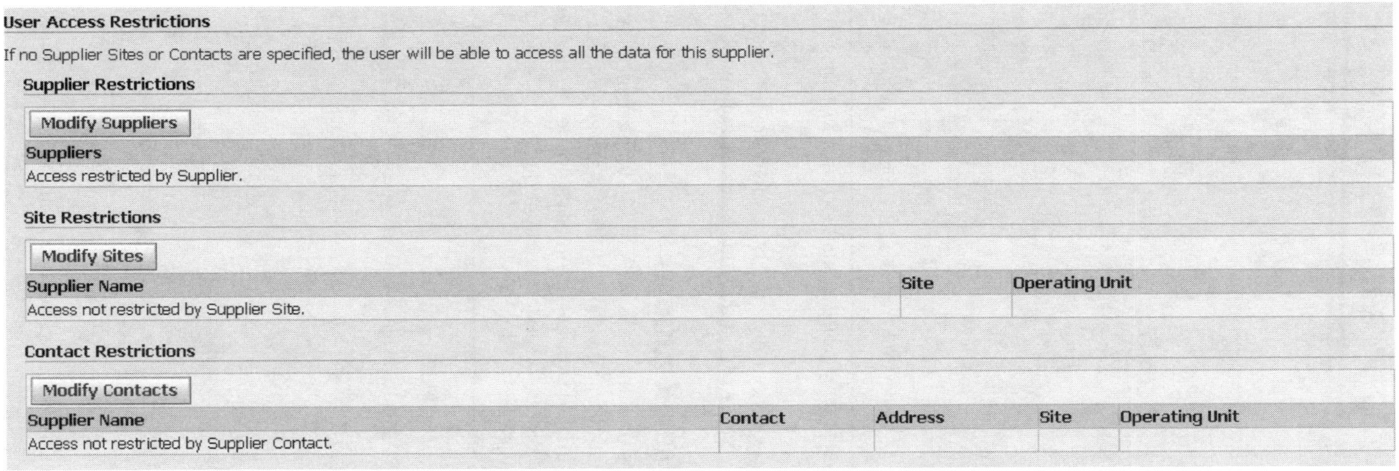

User Access Restrictions

If no Supplier Sites or Contacts are specified, the user will be able to access all the data for this supplier.

Supplier Restrictions

[Modify Suppliers]

Suppliers

Access restricted by Supplier.

Site Restrictions

[Modify Sites]

Supplier Name	Site	Operating Unit

Access not restricted by Supplier Site.

Contact Restrictions

[Modify Contacts]

Supplier Name	Contact	Address	Site	Operating Unit

Access not restricted by Supplier Contact.

Supplier User Administrator | Supplier User Creation | Register Supplier User

FIGURE 5-6. *Restricting supplier access during registration*

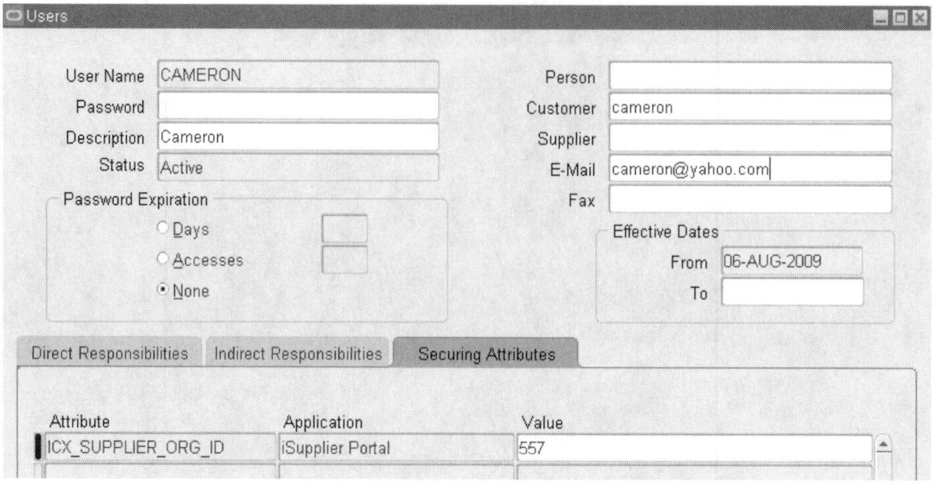

System Administrator | Security | User | Define

FIGURE 5-7. *Secured user for a supplier registered by a buyer administrator*

set up, you can also inactivate the user account, and you can choose RESET PASSWORD, where the system will generate a new password and e-mail it to the contact.

Administering User Requests

The buyer administrator has one final task, which is managing supplier requests for access. These would include both unsolicited and invited suppliers. As seen in Figure 5-8, you can see all Pending Approvals, Approved, and Invited suppliers who have not yet responded to a request. For approved requests, you can click VIEW DETAILS to see the actual request.

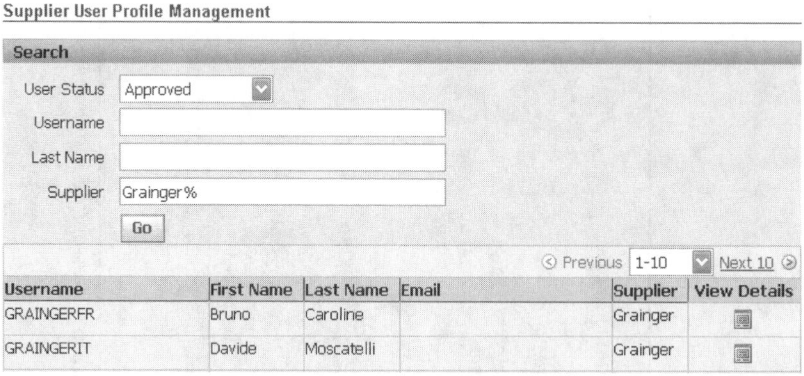

Supplier User Administrator | Supplier User Administration | Approve Users And Manage User Profiles

FIGURE 5-8. *Managing user requests*

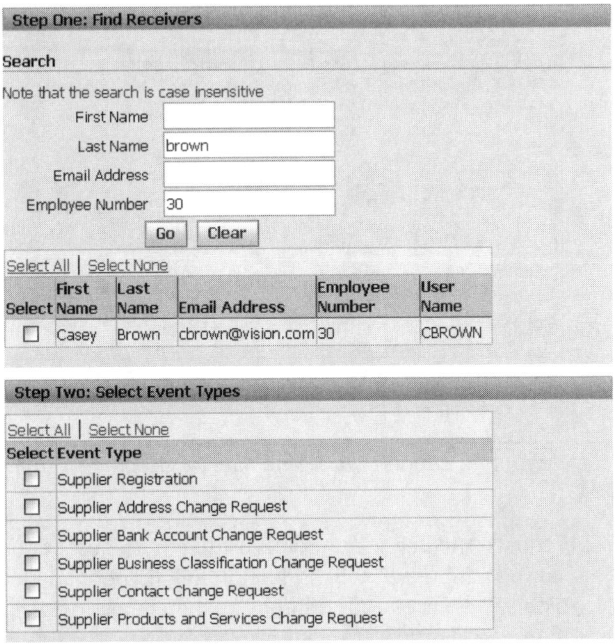

Step One: Find Receivers

Search

Note that the search is case insensitive

First Name	
Last Name	brown
Email Address	
Employee Number	30

Go   Clear

Select All | Select None

Select	First Name	Last Name	Email Address	Employee Number	User Name
☐	Casey	Brown	cbrown@vision.com	30	CBROWN

Step Two: Select Event Types

Select All | Select None

Select	Event Type
☐	Supplier Registration
☐	Supplier Address Change Request
☐	Supplier Bank Account Change Request
☐	Supplier Business Classification Change Request
☐	Supplier Contact Change Request
☐	Supplier Products and Services Change Request

Purchasing | Setup | Profile Management Configuration | Setup
Notification Subscription | Add Subscriptions button

FIGURE 5-9.   *Adding administrators to receive notifications*

Setting Up Buyer Administrators to Receive Notifications

There are several notifications that you can set up the buyer administrators to receive. The most commonly used in R12 is Supplier Registration. The other notifications, such as Supplier Address Change Requests, were more useful in prior releases, when the administrators had to approve all the supplier requests for changes to their accounts. Now, the suppliers have access to update the records in Oracle directly via the Admin window and they no longer require approval. Since some of the data that can be updated is sensitive, such as addresses or bank accounts, turning these notifications on are still an effective way to monitor the changes the suppliers are making. To add someone to receive a specific type of notification, click the Add Subscription button to bring up the screen shown in Figure 5-9. Search for the employee name that you want to assign the notification to. You can select from any Employee that is associated with a User in the system. After clicking SELECT next to the employee, determine which notifications that employee will receive by clicking the Event Type associated to it. Event Type is Oracle's name for something that happens in the system that you want to know about or have the system act upon in some way.

Additional Setups for Classifying Suppliers (Optional)

Suppliers have the ability to classify themselves when they register or maintain their account. They complete this under the Products and Services section on the supplier (iSupplier Portal Full

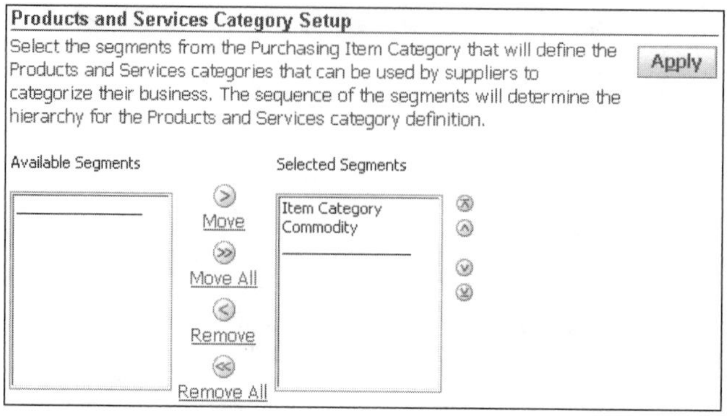

Purchasing | Setup | Profile Management Configuration | Products And
Services Setup

FIGURE 5-10. *Determining which purchasing category segments suppliers can use to classify themselves*

Access | Admin | Products And Services—you must log in as a user tied to a specific supplier, identified by the securing attribute ICX_SUPPLIER_ORG_ID populated, to get access to this page). You can control which segments of your purchasing item category the suppliers will have access to for this classification (see Figure 5-10). In this example, the category has two segments, and both are available for the supplier to select.

Suppliers can also classify their business as such things as Small Business, Minority Owned, etc. (iSupplier Portal Full Access | Admin | Products And Services—you must log in as a user tied to a specific supplier, identified by the securing attribute ICX_SUPPLIER_ORG_ID populated, to get access to this page). The list of values that appear here are a value set, POS_BUSINESS_ CLASSIFICATIONS, shown in Figure 5-11, and they can be disabled or added to.

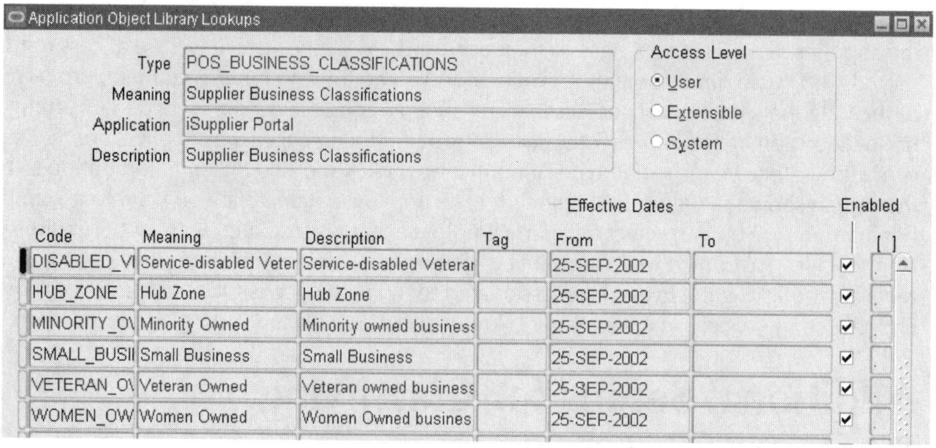

Application Developer | Application | Lookups | Application Object Library

FIGURE 5-11. *Maintaining business classifications*

CHAPTER
6

Using iSupplier

Supplier portal was designed with two main audiences in mind: external suppliers and internal users. Externally, suppliers can view a wide array of information, such as ordering information and payment details; update information about themselves and the products or services they can provide; manage inventory stock quantities; respond to notifications; as well as upload shipment notifications or invoices for payments. All of these functions are controllable at the administrative level, ensuring each individual supplier not only has access to only their specific information, but also the specific features that will meet their needs.

Internally, employees can get access to all supplier information, including purchasing, shipments and receiving functions, and invoices and payment history. This view-only data is arranged for easy viewing and can be accessed outside of your company's firewall.

iSupplier, Internal View

The seeded responsibility used to grant access to employees is iSupplier Portal Internal View. The nice thing about using this feature is that, besides assigning the responsibility to the users, there are no setups required: once it is assigned, it is usable. All of the views described here are the same views the suppliers will see on these pages, making the internally and externally viewed data exactly the same.

Home Page

The home page provides not only quick links to additional information, but a recap page of the most recent orders and any pending actions or notifications (refer to Figure 6-1). Notifications will show both notifications that are waiting for a response and information-only notifications. Orders At A Glance shows the last five orders for a specific supplier or if you are a buyer, it will show the last five that were approved. Both of these sections have a link to Full List, which will allow you to see and search for any notification or purchase order. Notice that requisitions do not appear in iSupplier. This is because they are internal to an organization, while iSupplier is an externally facing product.

The last section, Pending Change Requests, refers to change requests placed by a supplier. These occur when a supplier receives a purchase order (via iSupplier) and requests a change to the order. These changes will go back to the buyer, who can accept or reject them, and are then evaluated and routed for approval, same as any change to an approved purchase order would be.

The links at the right of the page are the same tabs and subtabs available across the top of the home page, each described next.

Orders

Internally, the Orders tab displays information about purchase orders, agreements with your suppliers, purchasing history, work confirmations, and any pending supplier changes.

Purchase Orders

On the Purchasing tab, you can perform searches for purchase order information by selecting an OPERATING UNIT, and either PO NUMBER or SUPPLIER. The operating units that appear on the list of values are controlled by the profiles MO: Operating Unit and MO: Security Profile. Additional search fields include ORDER DATE, which corresponds to the CREATED date on the purchase order;

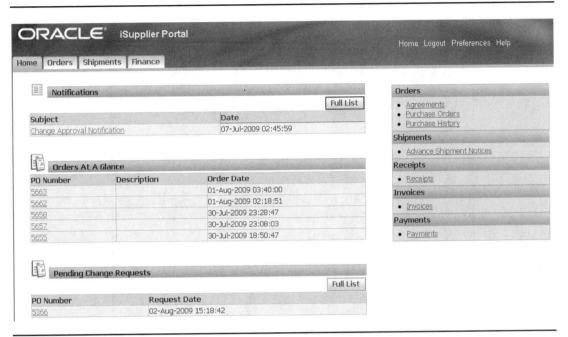

FIGURE 6-1. *Internal view: home page*

SUPPLIER SITE; BUYER; or based on a specific NOTES TO SUPPLIER. (This is the Note to Supplier field on the More tab of a purchase order.)

Remember when searching in the NOTES TO SUPPLIER (or any field in Oracle) that the % can be used as a wildcard to perform the search. A wildcard is a simple character replacement that Oracle understands to mean Provide Any Result here. For example, if you search for "Urgent", Oracle will only return notes where the exact word is "Urgent". When a wildcard is used at the beginning and end, %Urgent%, then it will find any note where the word "Urgent" is someplace in the note. This is also useful when looking for a supplier and you are not sure how to spell their name (or how it is spelled in Oracle).

Referring to Figure 6-2, notice that there is also an Export button, which can be found on most of the pages. Clicking this button will export the search results into a .csv (comma-separated values) file that can then be opened or saved. This file format is easily opened into a spreadsheet. Note that even though only 25 lines are displayed on the first page, Oracle will export all the lines that meet the search criteria.

Also available on many of the search screens is a button to perform an Advanced Search. This feature will provide additional search fields (in this case, acknowledgment status, document type, and ship-to location are available), but it also provides the option to SHOW TABLE DATA WHEN ANY CONDITION IS MET or only when *all* conditions are met. These options work with the ability to do searches on multiple fields with different search criteria on each field. You can select from the options of CONTAINS, ENDS WITH, IS, IS NOT, or STARTS WITH. Table 6-1 shows how each one of these is used in searching. Because advanced searches allow you to add specific fields for searching, you can add a field more than one time—for example, Date—and use the matching options to have begin and end dates.

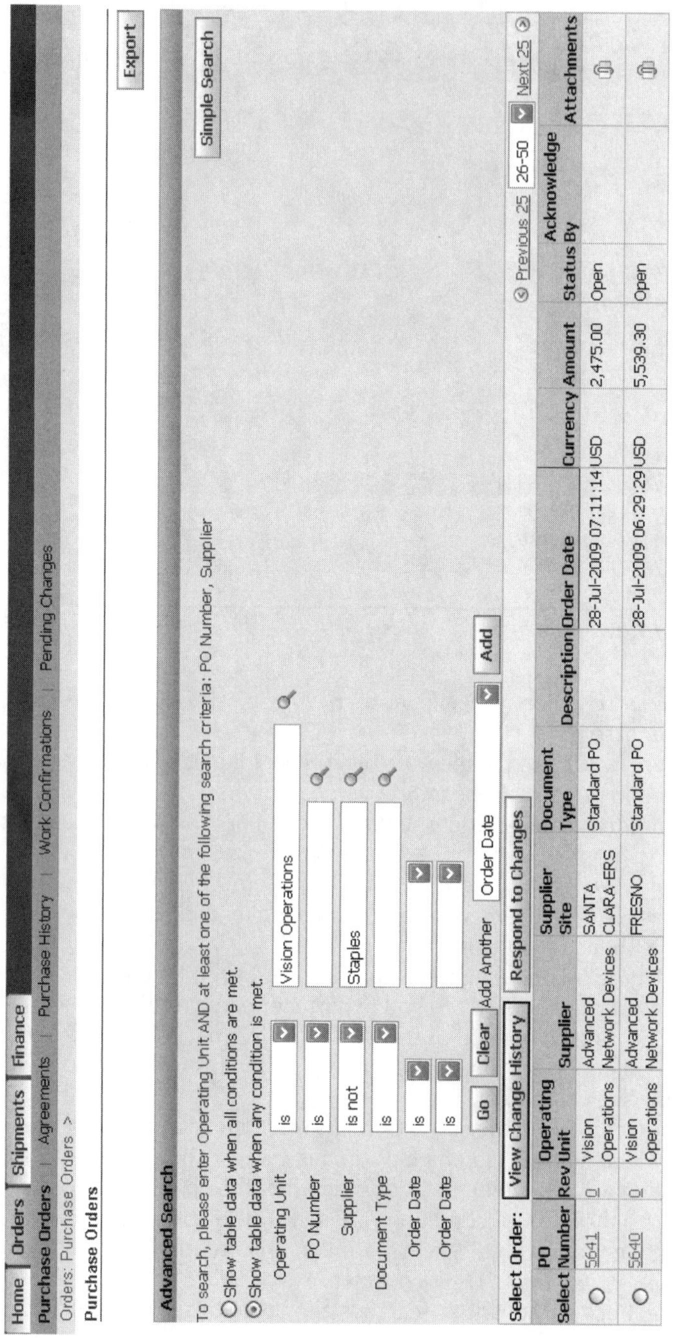

Home | Orders | Shipments | Finance

Purchase Orders | Agreements | Purchase History | Work Confirmations | Pending Changes

Orders: Purchase Orders >

Purchase Orders

Export

Advanced Search

To search, please enter Operating Unit AND at least one of the following search criteria: PO Number, Supplier

○ Show table data when all conditions are met.

● Show table data when any condition is met.

Operating Unit	is	▸	Vision Operations	🔍
PO Number	is	▸		🔍
Supplier	is not	▸	Staples	🔍
Document Type	is	▸		🔍
Order Date	is	▸	▸	
Order Date	is	▸	▸	

Go   Clear   Add Another   Order Date   ▸   Add

Select Order: | View Change History | Respond to Changes

Simple Search

Ⓧ Previous 25 | 26-50 ▸ | Next 25 Ⓧ

Select	PO Number	Rev	Operating Unit	Supplier	Supplier Site	Document Type	Description	Order Date	Currency	Amount	Acknowledge Status By	Attachments
○	5641	0	Vision Operations	Advanced Network Devices	SANTA CLARA-ERS	Standard PO		28-Jul-2009 07:11:14	USD	2,475.00	Open	📎
○	5640	0	Vision Operations	Advanced Network Devices	FRESNO	Standard PO		28-Jul-2009 06:29:29	USD	5,539.30	Open	📎

FIGURE 6-2. *Internal view: Purchase Orders*

Matching Condition	Description
After / Before	This can only be used with date fields.
Contains	Works similar to a wildcard (%) search, where the wildcard is used at the beginning and end of a word, and the results will be returned when the entered data matches any part of the field.
Ends With	Works similar to a wildcard (%) search where a wildcard is only at the beginning of the word, where information at the end of the field matches the data entered.
Greater Than / Less Than	This can only used for number fields.
Is	Performs only an exact match.
Is Not	Returns data where the entered field is Not *not* found. For example, if the supplier field is set to Is Not Staples, then the results would be all purchase orders that are not made out to Staples.
Starts With	Works similar to a wildcard (%) search where a wildcard is only at the end of the word, where information at the beginning of the field matches the data entered.

TABLE 6-1. *Searching Options*

Agreements

Agreements are blanket purchase orders created in Purchasing. The same search fields are required (OPERATING UNITS, and either a PO NUMBER or SUPPLIER), but you can also limit the search by effective dates or if the agreement is GLOBAL or not. Blanket purchase orders represent an agreement between the buying and selling companies for payment terms and negotiated prices on specific goods or services, but when the delivery dates are not yet known. Releases are then created against the agreements for specific deliveries. The effective dates on an agreement determine when these terms and prices are good, while Global determines if this agreement is for all operating units or restricted to the operating unit it was created in (Global = No). Agreements will also appear on the Purchase Order window when a search is performed, and can be identified by the document type of Global Blanket Agreement, or Blanket Agreement. Refer to Figure 6-3 for the information available on Agreements.

Purchase History

The information provided on the Purchasing History window is very similar to the Purchase Orders and Agreements windows, but it will allow the user to compare different versions, or revisions, of a document, as well as view all the purchase order changes. When researching a question for a supplier, or an issue with a purchase order in general, this is very useful information. Click the icon in the SHOW ALL PO CHANGES field to see a chronological listing of all the changes made to this purchase order, resulting in a new revision number (not all changes will result in a new version of the document, but most will). COMPARE TO ORIGINAL PO will allow you to see the revision you are on,

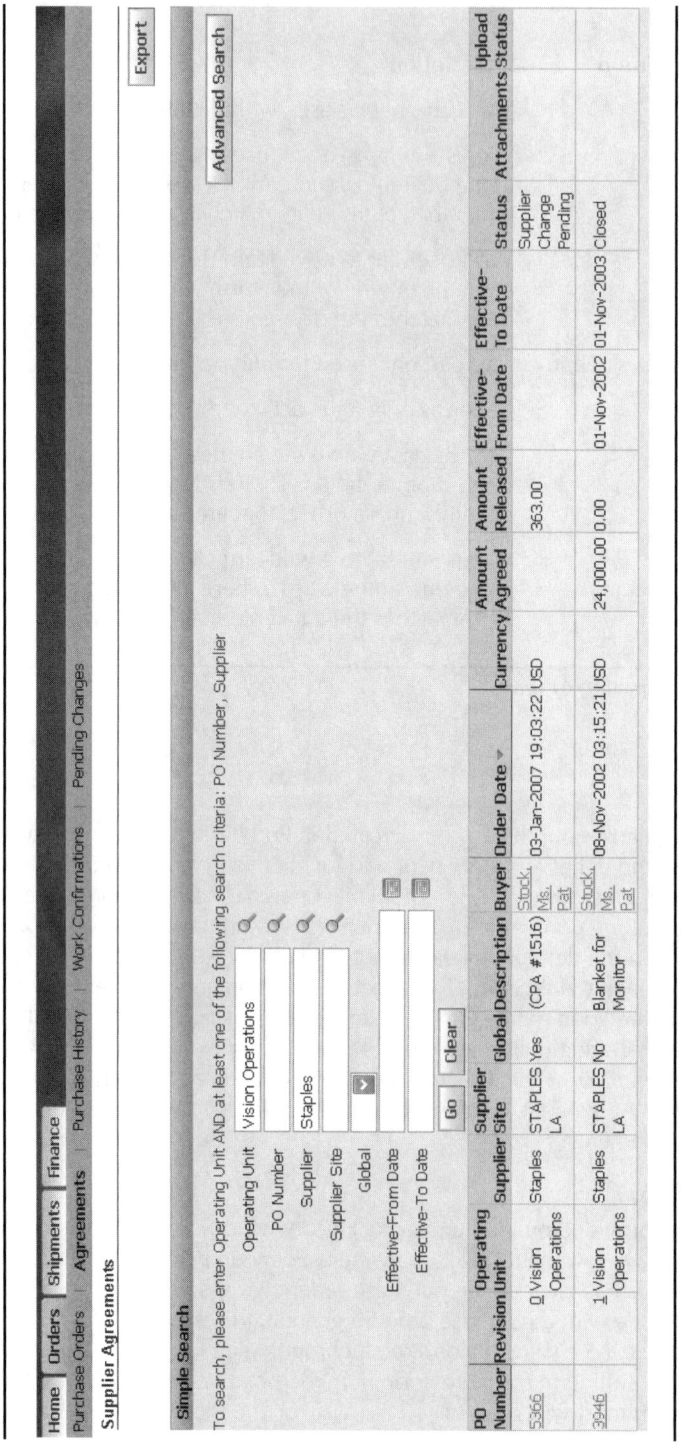

Home | Orders | Shipments | Finance
Purchase Orders | Agreements | Purchase History | Work Confirmations | Pending Changes

Supplier Agreements

Export

Simple Search

Advanced Search

To search, please enter Operating Unit AND at least one of the following search criteria: PO Number, Supplier

Operating Unit [Vision Operations]
PO Number
Supplier [Staples]
Supplier Site
Global [>]
Effective-From Date
Effective-To Date

Go   Clear

PO Number	Revision	Operating Unit	Supplier	Supplier Site	Global	Description	Buyer	Order Date	Currency	Amount Agreed	Amount Released	Effective-From Date	Effective-To Date	Status	Attachments	Upload Status
5366	0	Vision Operations	Staples	STAPLES LA	Yes	(CPA #1516)	Stock, Ms. Pat	03-Jan-2007 19:03:22	USD		363.00			Supplier Change Pending		
3946	1	Vision Operations	Staples	STAPLES LA	No	Blanket for Monitor	Stock, Ms. Pat	08-Nov-2002 03:15:21	USD	24,000.00	0.00	01-Nov-2002	01-Nov-2003	Closed		

FIGURE 6-3. *Internal view: agreements, or blanket orders*

and compare it to the original data, while COMPARE TO PREVIOUS PO will show the changes back to the prior version only. Selecting any of these icons will allow you to print any version of the purchase document.

Work Confirmations

Work Confirmations are a part of Oracle's solution for complex ordering for goods such as consulting, advertising, or research and development. While the features of complex orders are part of a separate module, they are tightly integrated with Purchasing, iProcurement, and Service Procurement, all of which must be licensed and implemented in order to use the benefits of complex orders. When all of these are implemented, you can create service-related requests that include retainage (withholding part or all of the payment until specific tasks or phases of the project are complete). iSupplier will allow the supplier to request payment for these items, using what is called a Work Confirmation. When these are submitted, the buyer can confirm that the work is completed, and approve the confirmation. This will in turn receive the line against the purchase order, opening it up for payment. Note that the invoice is not automatically created and still needs to be entered and processed by matching to the purchase order by Accounts Payable. The supplier would also have the option of uploading the invoice via iSupplier.

Pending Changes

The Pending Changes window shows all supplier changes that are waiting your approval. These will appear when a buyer signs into an internal view and a purchase order they are the buyer on has a change request from the supplier. General internal users who are not buyers will not have any information on this page.

Buyers can review and respond to the changes by selecting a change request and then Respond To Change. From here, a recap of the order information appears at the top of the page, and the requested changes below, allowing you to respond (see Figure 6-4). Notice that the Price/Rate field has a sunburst next to it, indicating that this is the requested change. Click the Show link under Details to see more information about who requested the change, and the actual change made. To respond to the change, select a RESPONSE of Accept, Reject, or None from the list of values. Above these fields is also the ability to Reject All or Accept All, which will respond to all the changes being requested at the same time for this notification. None is used when there is more than one request displayed, and you want to approve or reject only some of them; the lines you do not want to respond to at this time are given a response of None and will remain open for later action. A REASON can also be given for the response. Clicking View Change History in the show details region will allow you to see all the changes on this order and line. The final option, APPLY PRICE UPDATE TO EXISTING POS AND RELEASES, will automatically update the costs on open purchase orders and releases and resubmit them for approval.

Shipments

The Shipments tab has both Advance Shipment Notices (ASNs) and receiving information.

Shipping Notices

The Shipment Notices tab will only have information if your suppliers are uploading ASNs into your system. While there are many benefits surrounding having an ASN in Oracle, additional automation that can be achieved using this document is probably one of the biggest time-savers in iSupplier. When an ASN is uploaded, Oracle can be set up to receive the items based on the expected delivery date and automatically create an invoice in Payables. This information is all

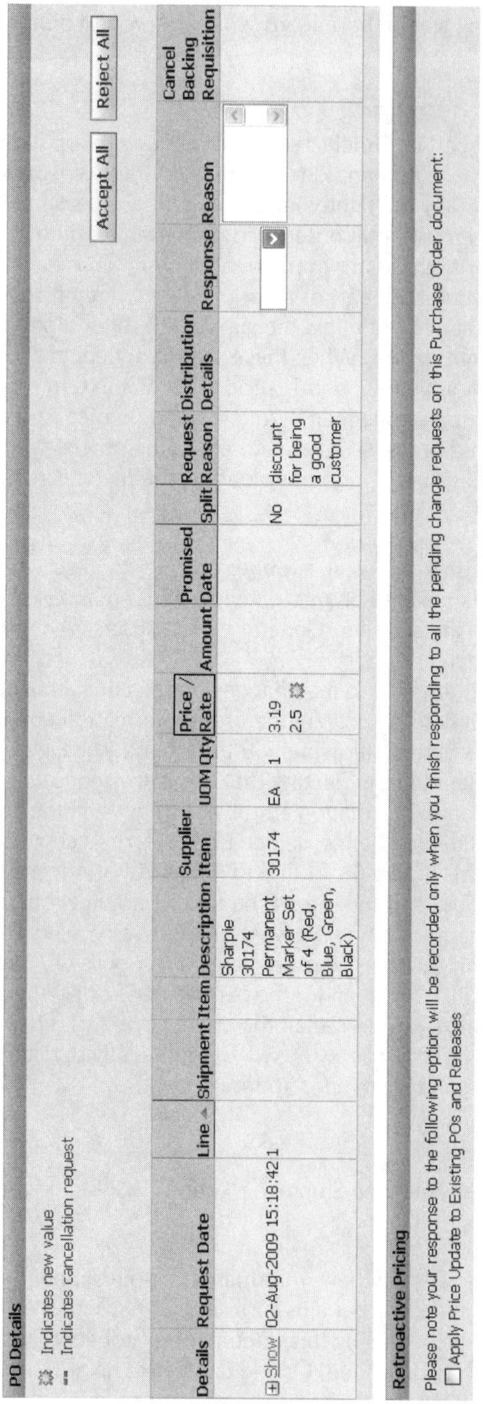

PO Details

✿ Indicates new value
·· Indicates cancellation request

Accept All   Reject All

Details	Request Date	Line ▲	Shipment	Item	Description	Supplier Item	UOM	Qty	Price / Rate	Amount	Promised Date	Split	Request Reason	Distribution Details	Response Reason	Cancel Backing Requisition
⊞ Show	02-Aug-2009 15:18:42	1			Sharpie 30174 Permanent Marker Set of 4 (Red, Blue, Green, Black)	30174	EA	1	3.19 2.5 ✿			No	discount for being a good customer		

Retroactive Pricing

Please note your response to the following option will be recorded only when you finish responding to all the pending change requests on this Purchase Order document:

☐ Apply Price Update to Existing POs and Releases

FIGURE 6-4. *Responding to a pending change request from a supplier*

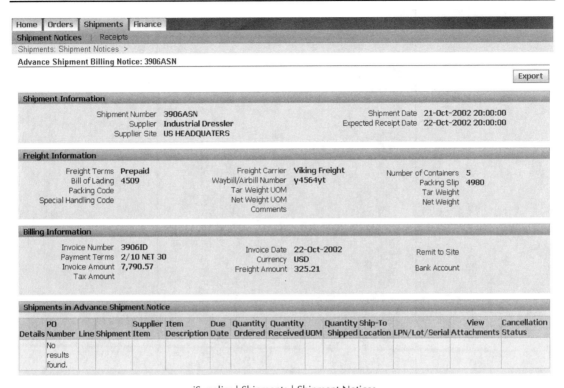

iSupplier | Shipments | Shipment Notices

FIGURE 6-5. *Viewing an Advance Shipment Notice*

processed using the receiving open interface. The Shipment Notices screen will show as much or as little information as is received from the supplier, as seen in Figure 6-5.

Receipts

Receipts can be queried up and reviewed by using either a SUPPLIER name or a RECEIPT NUMBER, in addition to other fields. Links on each receipt allow you to view additional RECEIVING, PURCHASE ORDER, or INVOICE information.

Finance

Financial information for payments and invoices is available, for both invoices matched to purchase orders as well as invoices that are not. Drilling down into either the invoice number or due date shows additional information about the invoice, such as specific line information, when and how the payments are scheduled, and any holds that may be applied to the invoice that are preventing payment. You can also drill down or query on payment information to see if a settlement has been issued, and if so, if it has been cashed yet (available when checks are cleared using Cash Management). See Figure 6-6.

Invoice	Invoice Date ▾	Type	Supplier	Supplier Site	Currency	Amount	Due	Status	On Hold	Payment Status	Due Date	Payment Number	PO Number	Receipt	Attachments
8013081241	25-Jul-2009	Standard	STAPLES BUSINESS ADVANTAGE	480	USD	274.76	274.76	Approved		Not Paid	24-AUG-2009				
8013029560	18-Jul-2009	Standard	STAPLES BUSINESS ADVANTAGE	480	USD	530.76	530.76	Approved		Not Paid	17-AUG-2009				
8012976415	11-Jul-2009	Standard	STAPLES BUSINESS ADVANTAGE	480	USD	661.60	661.60	Approved		Not Paid	10-AUG-2009				
8012910831	04-Jul-2009	Standard	STAPLES BUSINESS ADVANTAGE	480	USD	260.10	0.00	Approved		Paid	03-AUG-2009	23131			
8012812523	20-Jun-2009	Standard	STAPLES BUSINESS ADVANTAGE	480	USD	580.34	0.00	Approved		Paid	20-JUL-2009	23000			
8012759628	13-Jun-2009	Standard	STAPLES BUSINESS ADVANTAGE	480	USD	229.82	0.00	Approved		Paid	13-JUL-2009	22895			

iSupplier Portal Full Access | Finance | View Invoices

FIGURE 6-6. *Finance tab*

Of all the information available to suppliers in iSupplier Portal, I would advise that the Finance tab will require the most discussion prior to releasing the information. Part of this is because of how Oracle places holds on invoices, and how well these holds are managed. If holds are long in being resolved, or placed in error because of processing errors (not uncommon during new implementations), supplying this access may raise more supplier questions than it prevents. Additionally, if invoices are entered multiple times or payments created and canceled prior to sending them out, questions again will probably arise more often than not.

iSupplier, External View

The Suppliers view for iSupplier has many of the same screens as the internal view, except that the data is limited to information associated with the supplier who is signed in. In addition to viewing information, there are several actions a supplier can request or take, including changes to purchase orders as well as uploading invoices.

Remember that when implementing iSupplier, you can decide what functions and features the supplier has access to, described in Chapter 2. Understanding how your company uses Oracle for a specific supplier, and in general, should play a large role in deciding what access they are granted. You want to ensure you give them everything they need, and the least amount of "extras" to cause confusion and questions as possible.

Purchase Order Actions

Actions that suppliers can take on purchase orders include acknowledgments, requesting changes to blanket agreements (when iProcurement is also implemented), changes to standard purchase orders, and printing documents.

Acknowledgments

Acknowledgments are used to record that a supplier has received a purchase order and agrees to the terms and conditions, including the delivery schedule. From the Orders | Purchase Orders window, select the PO NUMBER and click the Acknowledge button. Suppliers can acknowledge only purchase orders created with specific acceptance requirements (Purchasing | Purchase Orders | Purchase Orders | Terms), such as Document, Document or Shipping, or Signature, indicating that an electronic signature is required, set up on the document. These orders will show a STATUS of Require Acknowledgment when they are pending the supplier confirmations. When acknowledging an order, the supplier can also request changes and add additional information, such as SUPPLIER ORDER NUMBER and SUPPLIER ITEM NUMBER. The PRICE, QUANTITY ORDERED, and PROMISED DATE can also be added, before taking the action of Accept, Change, or Reject for an individual line (on the far right of the line) or for the entire order. Accept should be used when there are no changes to the order, while Change indicates an update has been made. This starts a workflow (PO Supplier Change), which routes the request to the buyer to either accept or reject the changes.

When the buyer accepts the supplier changes to a purchase order, a new REV of the order is created and, if required, routed for approval. Rejecting the changes will send it back to the supplier, but no reason can be added to it, so communication will still need to happen outside of iSupplier to inform the supplier of the reason. If the supplier just acknowledges the order without requesting a change, then the buyer is notified, but no actions are required. In addition to updating the Acceptances window (Purchase Orders | Tools | Acceptances), notifications are sent to both the supplier and the buyer when any acknowledgments are requested or confirmed.

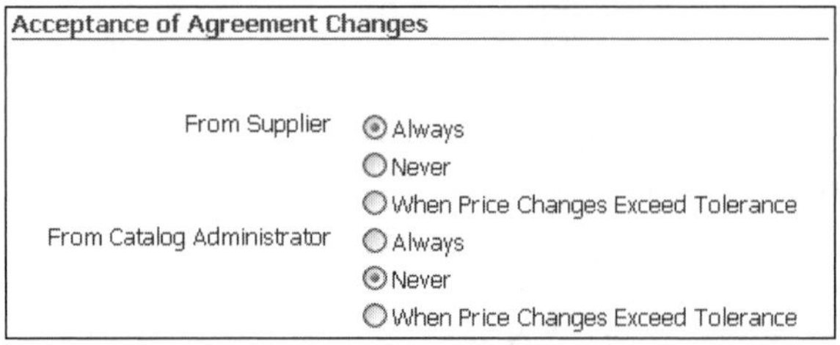

Purchasing | Setup | Tolerances And Routings | Acceptance Of
Agreement Changes

FIGURE 6-7.   *Determining if changes during supplier acceptance require buyer approval*

When changes are made during the acceptance of an agreement, you decide if these changes require approval. The options are Always, Never, or When Price Changes Exceed Tolerance. These tolerances are the Supplier Change Order tolerances (Setup | Tolerances And Routings, see Figure 6-7).

Requesting Changes

Change requests work very much like acknowledgments, where the supplier can update SUPPLIER ORDER NUMBER, SUPPLIER ITEM, PRICE, and DELIVERY SCHEDULES. These changes are routed to the buyer for approval, and if required, through the purchasing approval process. Note that the supplier adding a SUPPLIER ORDER NUMBER does not require an approval by the buyer, but all other changes do.

Tolerances can be set up to determine what changes require buyer approval, and which ones do not. For example, you can set a tolerance that if the promised date is moved forward by more than two days, it requires approval, and all delivery dates that are pushed into the future require approval. Tolerances can also be set for document amounts, both as a percentage and a hard dollar limit, unit price, and line amount. Since changes to the delivery dates and quantities may affect the requestor as well as the purchasing person, changes to the promised date, schedule quantity, or price can be routed to the requestor as well as the buyer for approval. Figure 6-8 shows the tolerances available.

Canceling Purchase Orders

Suppliers also have the option to cancel an entire order, or a specific line on an order. This will send a notification to the buyer on the purchase order, allowing them to Accept or Reject the cancellation, and no action will be taken on the actual order until the notification is responded to.

Printing Purchase Orders

Suppliers (as well as internal users) have the option to Print the PDF format of the purchase order. The format of this PO will be the template that is assigned to the document type in Purchasing (Setup | Purchasing | Document Types | Document Type Layout); it can be modified using XML Publisher.

Editing Global Blanket Agreements

A supplier can be allowed to edit, or author, a blank agreement that is already saved in Oracle based on the settings assigned when the document was created. To enable supplier authoring,

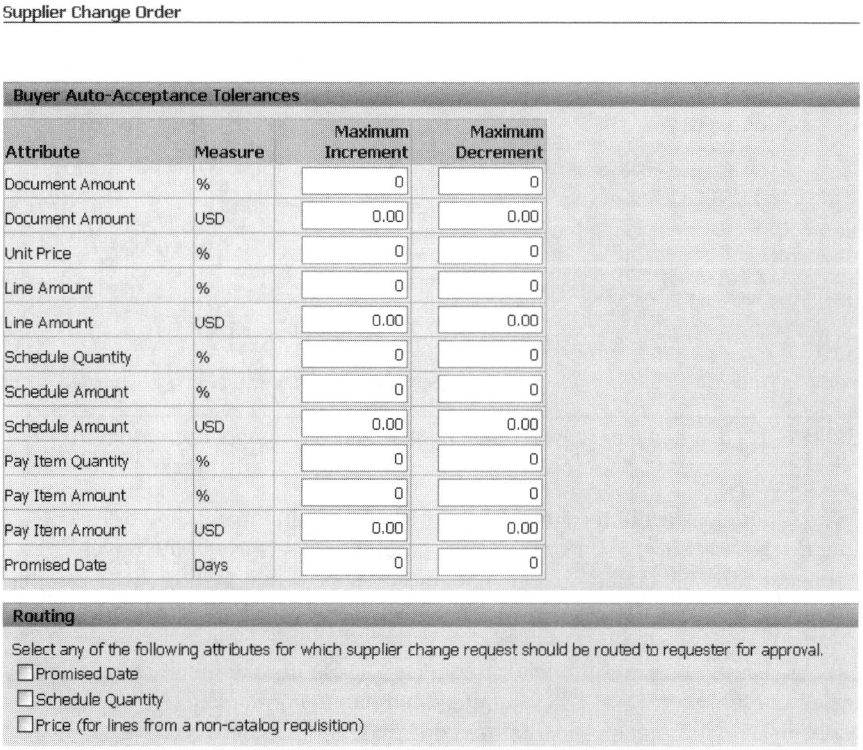

Supplier Change Order

Buyer Auto-Acceptance Tolerances			
Attribute	Measure	Maximum Increment	Maximum Decrement
Document Amount	%	0	0
Document Amount	USD	0.00	0.00
Unit Price	%	0	0
Line Amount	%	0	0
Line Amount	USD	0.00	0.00
Schedule Quantity	%	0	0
Schedule Amount	%	0	0
Schedule Amount	USD	0.00	0.00
Pay Item Quantity	%	0	0
Pay Item Amount	%	0	0
Pay Item Amount	USD	0.00	0.00
Promised Date	Days	0	0

Routing

Select any of the following attributes for which supplier change request should be routed to requester for approval.
☐ Promised Date
☐ Schedule Quantity
☐ Price (for lines from a non-catalog requisition)

Purchasing | Setup | Tolerances And Routings | Supplier Change Order

FIGURE 6-8. *Supplier change tolerances*

you must use the Buyer Work Center to create the agreement (Purchasing | Buyer Work Center | Agreements | Create). After adding at least the supplier information to the document, save the document without submitting it. This will allow you to requery it on the Agreements window (View = My Incomplete Agreements) and reopen it. Now, under the Actions section, you can select Enable Supplier Authoring, but then ensure you select Go. This option is only available after saving the record and requiring it. Now save the document again without submitting it and the supplier will be able to edit the agreement from iSupplier (see Figure 6-9).

Note that using the Buyer Work Center will create a global agreement. Global agreements are different in two ways from non-global agreements. First, you do not create releases against a global agreement; instead, you create a standard purchase order, using the Catalog button to add each line, selecting from the Negotiated Sources tab. Second, these are available across operating units. (For more information on global agreements, see my *Oracle Procure-to-Pay Guide* published by McGraw-Hill or Oracle's user's manual.) Basically, a blanket agreement is usually for specific items to be purchased where the delivery dates are unknown, whereas a global agreement is more of a catalog of agreed-upon prices.

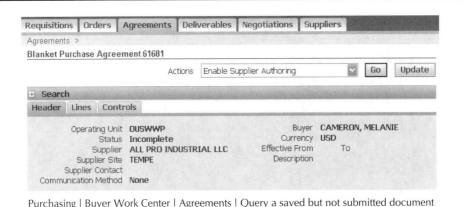

FIGURE 6-9. *Enabling a global blanket agreement for supplier authoring*

The supplier can edit the agreements either directly in the window or by uploading a file (see Figure 6-10). This is the exact same window that the buyers use in the Buyer Work Center, but the supplier can only update specific line information. When the supplier is adding lines in the window, the ITEMS and CATEGORIES and UNITS must all reside in Oracle. Descriptions can be added without an item and are not validated against any data in Oracle.

By using the Add Lines link, the suppliers can also upload their catalog directly into Oracle from a Tab-Delimited Text, XML, Catalog Interchange Format (CIF), or cXML file. These files *must* be in Oracle's predefined format in order to be processed. Suppliers can use the Download Resources button to download directions as well as data such as valid categories. When uploading their catalog, suppliers have the option of submitting it for approval immediately after the data is validated, or manually submitting it later on, using any mapping that is set up in Oracle's e-Commerce Gateway in your environment, or adding tolerances as to the number of errors that should be encountered when uploaded before the file stops. Oracle also provides an XML Converter online if the supplier is using an older version of XML, where the data will be converted to the proper version for them.

Advance Shipping and Advance Billing Notices

Supplier can upload or create directly in iSupplier both Advance Shipment Notices (ASNs) and Advance Shipment Billing Notices (ASBNs). While similar, these two notifications serve different purposes in Oracle. Both of them are standard EDI (Electronic Data Interchange) formats, where ASN uses the EDI 856 format, and ASBN uses EDI 857. Both will populate the Receiving Interface tables (rcv_headers_interface and rcv_transactions_interface), and both will allow receipt transactions to be created automatically. Where they differ is that the ASBN is utilized when your supplier is set up as Pay on Receipt in Oracle. Pay on Receipt is an agreement between your company and the supplier that invoices will be automatically created in Payables based upon the prices on the purchase order when the items are received. This process is also known as ERS, or Evaluated Receipt Settlement, or Self Billing in different Oracle documentation. To set up a supplier as Pay on Receipt, you need to update the key purchasing setups on the supplier (Purchasing | Supply Base | Suppliers | Quick Update | Key Purchasing Setups | Pay On field).

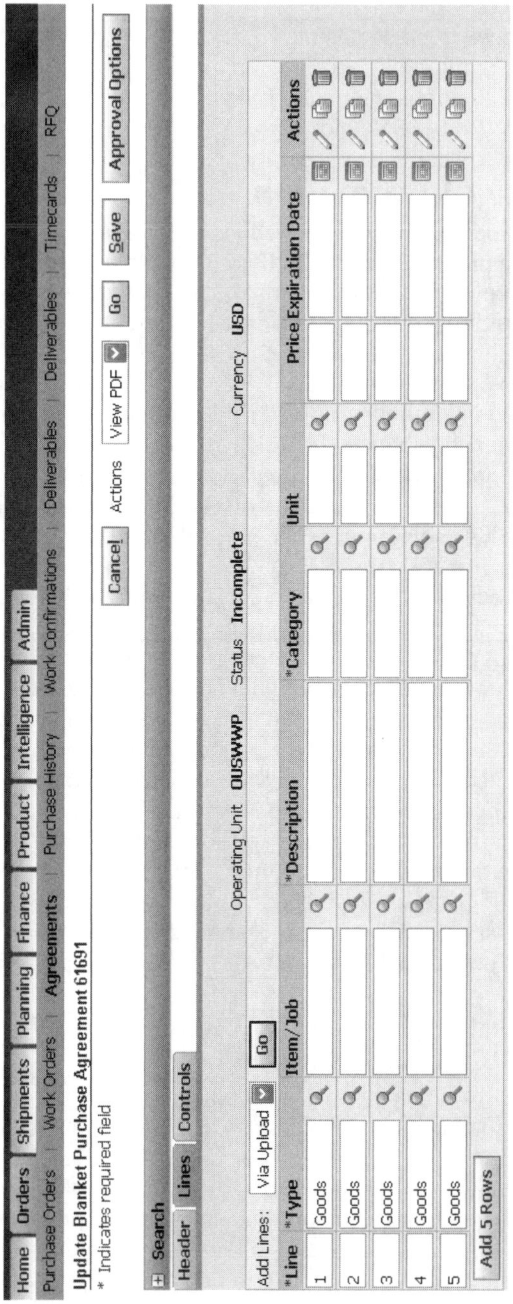

| Home | Orders | Shipments | Planning | Finance | Product | Intelligence | Admin |
| Purchase Orders | Work Orders | **Agreements** | Purchase History | Work Confirmations | Deliverables | Deliverables | Timecards | RFQ |

Update Blanket Purchase Agreement 61691

* Indicates required field

Cancel   Actions [View PDF ▾] Go   Save   Approval Options

| Search |
| Header | **Lines** | Controls |

Operating Unit **OUSWWP**   Status **Incomplete**   Currency **USD**

Add Lines: [Via Upload ▾] Go

*Line	*Type	Item/Job	*Description	*Category	Unit	Price	Expiration Date	Actions
1	Goods							
2	Goods							
3	Goods							
4	Goods							
5	Goods							

Add 5 Rows

iSupplier Portal Full Access | Orders | Agreements | Actions, Edit Agreement (only available for saved and not submitted agreements)

FIGURE 6-10.   *Adding lines to global agreements in iSupplier*

Unlike using Pay on Receipt without an ASBN, which creates the invoice based on the actual purchase order, the invoice will be created from the invoice information included in the ASBN, and invoice price variances can be created.

Suppliers have the option of uploading the advance notices from a preformatted file, manually create them directly in iSupplier, or canceling a previously entered notice. As with blanket agreements, Oracle provides format information and key data files for the supplier to download and use to create accurate ASN and ASBN uploads.

Updating Product Information

Suppliers can view and update product information. This is available for items that are associated with the suppler on an Approved Supplier List (Purchasing | Supply Base | Approved Supplier List). This enables the supplier to search by item and see all the orders associated with the item, as well as performance information such as Overdue orders, Defects, Returns, and On Time indicators for deliver.

Suppliers can also update order modifiers, which includes processing lead time, minimum order quantities, and fixed lot multiples, as well as maintaining their manufacturing capacity. Information such as the quantity that can be produced per day, an overage tolerance and the number of days advance notice the supplier needs to increase the capacity to include the overage. This is only available for items that are on Global purchase orders and included on the Approved Supplier List. This information, when populated, is used with Oracle Advances Supply Chain Planning capacity. There is a profile that controls whether these changes will require an approval from either the buyer or the planner associated with the item, or not at all. It is called POS: ASL Planning Attribute Updates From Supplier Approved By.

Suppliers can also maintain any inventory that is either vendor managed or consigned. These are two different types of inventory and should not be confused. Vendor-managed inventory (VMI) is inventory that your company owns but is managed by the vendor for replenishments. Usually, an agreement has been made with the vendor that stock will not fall below a minimum quantity and will not exceed a maximum quantity. Consigned inventory, on the other hand, is actually owned by the supplier, and ownership is not transferred until it is consumed, either during manufacturing or a sale of the product, and sometimes it will transfer ownership when the product has reached a certain age. Consigned inventory transactions, even though they are not owned by your organization, are still recorded in Oracle, so that they can be consumed during the manufacturing process. Items are set up to be managed by the vendor or consigned on the Approved Supplier List (Purchasing | Supply Base | Approved Supplier List | Attributes), on the Inventory tab.

Uploading Invoices

In addition to loading ASBN to create invoices, suppliers can also create invoices in iSupplier and route them for approval and payment. Invoices can be created both against a purchase order and without one.

To create an invoice against a purchase order, the supplier will first need to select the PO along with the lines they wish to invoice. This will default the supplier and line information onto the invoice screen, just as it would in Payables for the person entering an invoice matched to a PO. When using this feature, you will need to ensure that your purchase orders are set up to Match to Purchase Order, as opposed to Match to Receipt, as this is not supported. This setting can be found on the Purchase Order on the Shipments, using the More tab, and defaults in from the Invoice Match Option selected on the supplier record. While the buyer can control this on each individual purchase order, it will default from the Invoice Match Option in the Key Payment Setup section of the supplier record. The default for the supplier when it is created is found on the Payables System Setup (Payables | Setup | Options). Referring to Figure 6-11, the supplier can select any Bill To address that is active in Oracle as the REMIT TO ADDRESS, and that is the address that will appear on the check. They can also select that the payment be made electronically by selecting a REMIT TO BANK ACCOUNT that is associated with their supplier record. While they cannot create or change the banking information here, updates can be made on the Admin window, explained in the next section.

Specific Invoice information is then added, including the INVOICE NUMBER and INVOICE DATE. The same constraints surrounding invoice numbers being unique that exist in Oracle Payables also exist in iSupplier, and an invoice number that already exists in Oracle Payables cannot be submitted. The invoice date is used along with the terms associated with the supplier's bill-to site to determine the due date for the invoice. Note that both Invoices and Credit Memos can be created here by selecting the proper INVOICE TYPE.

Ensure you work closely with your supplier if they are using iSupplier to submit invoices and you have the supplier set up to CREATE DEBIT MEMO FROM RTS TRANSACTIONS in your system. This is set up on the supplier (Payables | Suppliers | Entry | Key Purchasing Setups) and will automatically

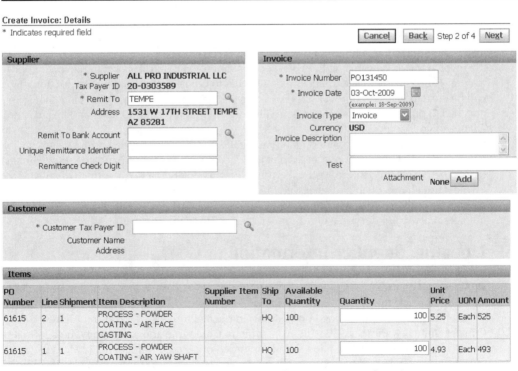

FIGURE 6-11. *Creating an invoice against a PO*

create a debit memo in Payables when you perform an RTS, or Return to Supplier, in Oracle. In this case, the supplier should not create a credit memo in iSupplier for the transaction as well. Next, they need to select the CUSTOMER TAX PAYER ID from the list. This is your company's tax identification number and is required to ensure the invoice is associated with the correct legal entity in Oracle.

The supplier can add both a description for the invoice and an attachment, which might include the actual invoice or a shipping manifest for the items they are invoicing for.

When an invoice is associated with a purchase order, where the price was agreed upon when the purchase order was accepted by the supplier, the supplier cannot update the UNIT PRICE but can modify the QUANTITY they are invoicing for. Additional charges can be added for either freight or any additional costs associated with this invoice, as well as any applicable tax information, before reviewing and submitting the invoice.

Invoices submitted without a purchase order include all the same information, but the supplier must add the items and amounts they are invoicing for manually. The only additional information is REQUESTOR EMAIL, FIRST NAME, and LAST NAME. The information entered here is the requestor within your company who will be approving the invoice, not the supplier requesting the information. These fields are required, and at least one of them must be properly populated so that Oracle can find the user record. It compares the e-mail address, first name, or last name associated with the user to the information entered on the invoice and will not allow the invoice to proceed to the next screen unless a match is found. There are two things that make this unusable for the suppliers. First, the fields are case sensitive. And second, there is no list of values for them to select from. Hopefully, Oracle will provide a better solution for this in future releases. Until then you may want to add a Tip to this page to assist the suppliers (see Chapter 2 for more information on adding a tip using OA Framework).The data entered here is used by Oracle to route the invoice for approval using Payables' normal approval chain. Having the invoice approval feature set up is prerequisite to allowing a supplier to upload an invoice; otherwise, the invoices will be created with an approval status of Rejected and cannot be processed. Note that invoices matched to purchase orders are not normally routed for approval in Oracle, and this may require a change to your approval rules.

Once the invoice is submitted, it automatically creates an unvalidated invoice in Payables. It is not necessary to run the Payables Open Interface Import program to create these invoices in R12. When using this feature, you will probably want to set up a process that will ensure these invoices are all approved and reviewed prior to processing for payment. The invoices created without a purchase order will come over with an invoice type of Standard Invoice Request, while invoices matched to purchase orders are created as Standard invoices.

Updating Supplier Information

Suppliers can view and update specific information on their supplier record using the Admin tab. With the R12 change to suppliers (they are now part of Oracle's Trading Community Architecture) suppliers now use the same supplier windows used internally when creating or maintaining a supplier to update the following information: Company Profile; Organization; Address Book; Contact Directory; Business Classification, which includes the ability to certify the information; Product and Services; and Banking Details. In order to use the Product and Services feature, you must first assign which category segments you want available for suppliers to classify their products. This is done in Purchasing | Setup | Profile Management Configuration | Products And Services Setup. This feature is usually used in conjunction with RFQs. When it is completed, the planners can review which supplier can provide a specific product and include them on the RFQ.

Suppliers can also see Payment and Invoicing information on the supplier record, but this is a limited number of fields and does not include all the data that is available on the supplier records internally. Suppliers have the ability to update PAYMENT METHOD, PAYMENT CURRENCY, INVOICE CURRENCY, and NOTIFICATION METHOD for each active site. The notification methods include e-mail, fax, print, or none, which determines how the supplier wishes to be informed of new or changed purchase orders. While the supplier can see if they are set up to hold any payments, such as Unmatched Invoices or All Payments, as well as if there is an invoice amount limit, they cannot update this information.

Surveying Suppliers

Using Oracle's Survey tool, you can create and post online surveys for the suppliers to respond to.

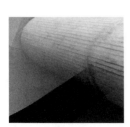

CHAPTER
7

iExpense Setups

Expense is a self-service module that integrates with Oracle Payables and streamlines the processing of both cash and credit card expense reports. This process includes submitting and approving expense reports as well as auditing for policy compliance. The settlement of these expenses is then completed in Payables. This chapter outlines the setups that control the processing of expense reports in iExpense.

Setting Up Employees

Just as with iProcurement, employees need to be set up in Oracle to process expense reports. Human Resources (HR) does not need to be implemented to use the Employee features. Ensuring HR is a shared install as opposed to fully installed will reduce the amount of data required on the employee form. In Oracle terms, a shared install is when the module is not fully licensed with Oracle, but you are using some of the functionality that is *shared* across other modules, whereas a full install is a fully licensed and implemented module. From a system standpoint, the employee form is different for a full install than for a shared one, making it less time consuming to set up employees.

The easiest way to see how HR is classified on your system is to open the employee form (Payables | Employees | Enter Employees). Ensure the HR User Type profile (System Administrator | Profile | System) is set to HR User for the responsibility you are accessing the employee form from. If you see the form shown in Figure 7-1, then your system has HR designated as a shared

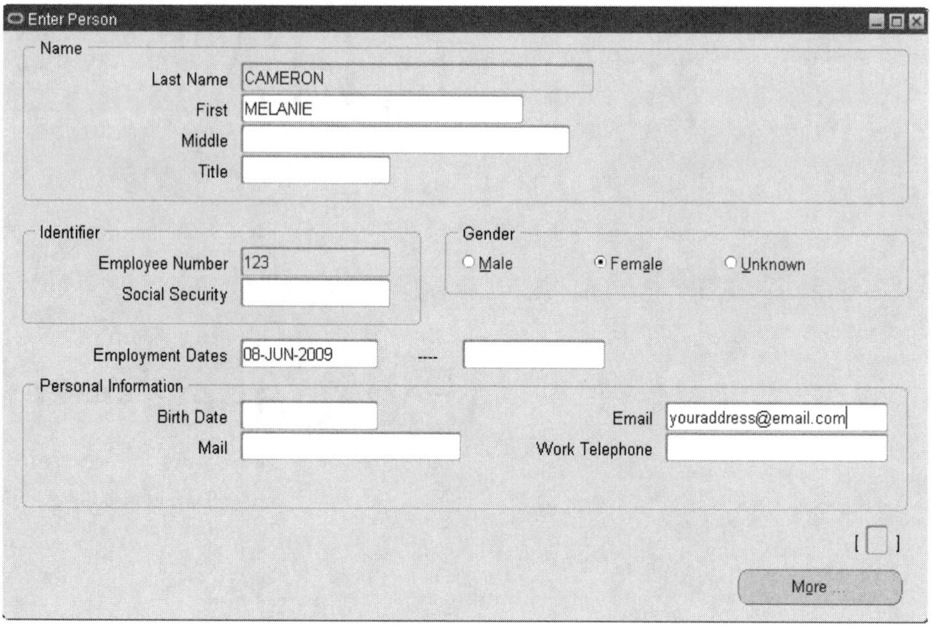

Payables | Employees | Enter Employees

FIGURE 7-1. *Entering employees under a shared HR install*

install. If not, you will receive an error message stating that HR is fully installed and that you must use the Persons form instead. While there are many ways to change the out-of-the-box installation status of HR from shared to fully installed, there is only one way to change it back, and that is with SQL. Work with your DBA to run the following script, ensuring you test it first in a test instance:

```
update fnd_product_installations
set status = 'S'
where application_id = 800
```

On the employee form, in addition to setting up Employee—Supervisor relationships, used during expense report approvals, the employee address and the default expense account are also assigned to the employee. When creating an employee only for expense processing, you must enter the employee LAST NAME and FIRST, and an EMPLOYMENT begin DATE. No other information is required on the first page. However, when an EMAIL address is entered here, it will default onto the employee's associated user record, and it is where any notifications are sent when the work flow mailer is being used. After saving the record, click More to get to the Address tab, shown in Figure 7-2. This represents to the address associated with the supplier record for the employee and will print on the reimbursement for the expense report. This address can be identified as a specific address TYPE, such as the primary home address or work location.

The ACCOUNTING INFORMATION, as seen in Figure 7-3, is important for expense report processing. Assign a LEDGER, which is where the accounting associated with this employee's expense reports will be recorded, while the DEFAULT EXPENSE ACCOUNT is used to populate certain segments of the account number, such as department, depending on how the Expense Report Template is set up.

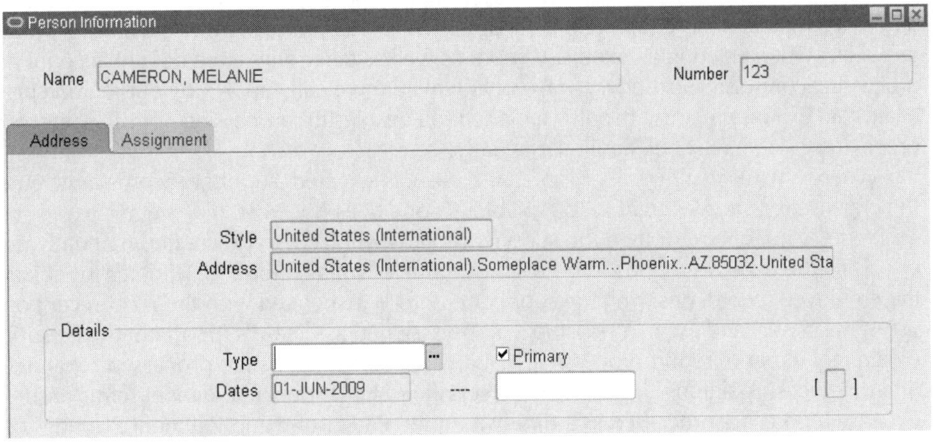

Payables | Employees | Enter Employees | More button

FIGURE 7-2. *Adding an address to the Employee record*

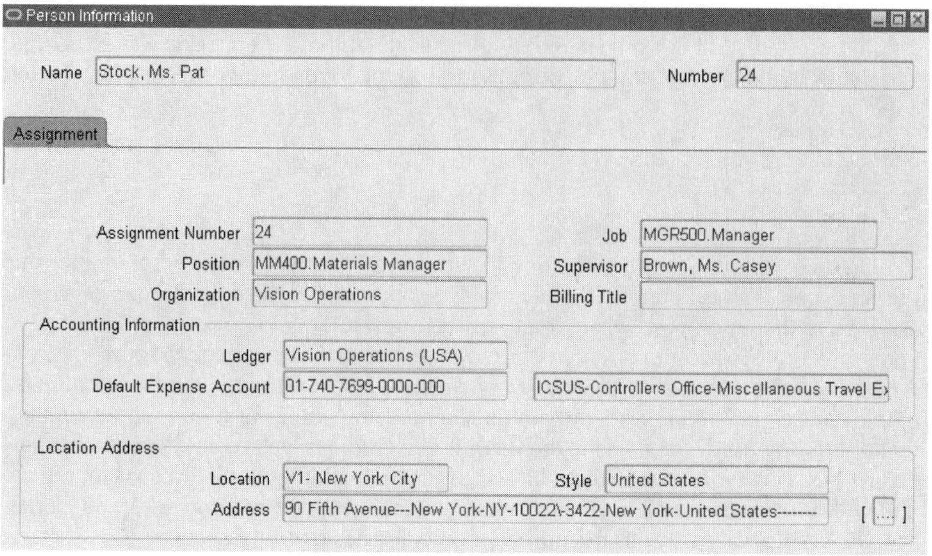

Payables | Employees | Enter Employees | More button | Assignment tab

FIGURE 7-3. *Additional Accounting defaults for the Employee*

Payables Options for Expense Report

Information set up on the Payables Options directly affects the way an expense report is processed when it is exported to Payables (see Figure 7-4). Assign a DEFAULT TEMPLATE, which will default the EXPENSE TEMPLATE when creating an expense report, but the employee will have the ability to select a different template if more than one is set up. Expense Templates identify the category an employee can select when entering an expense report, as well as determining the default account number and processing controls. Selecting APPLY ADVANCES will automatically apply any outstanding prepayments against an expense report when it is exported to Payables for processing. If this is not selected, the prepayment will have to be applied manually.

When AUTOMATICALLY CREATE EMPLOYEE AS SUPPLIER is selected, supplier records are created when the expense report is brought in to Payables, if one does not exist. If AUTOMATICALLY CREATE EMPLOYEE AS SUPPLIER is not checked, then the supplier records will have to be created manually prior to exporting the expense reports into Payables. Oracle will also look for updates to the address on the employee record, ensuring the supplier record is associated with the most recent one. PAYMENT TERMS, PAY GROUP, and PAYMENT PRIORITIES will be assigned as defaults for all employee suppliers created for expense report processing. Usually, expense reports are processed separately from other invoices. Assigning the employee's supplier record specific payment terms ensures that expense reports are processed in a timely manner. Pay Group and Payment Priorities are both used to group payments, either as high priorities, or to group them all together on a check run. The final option, HOLD UNMATCHED EXPENSE REPORTS, will ensure that this option is checked on the supplier record and that any invoices, including expense reports, will be placed on hold when they are not matched to a purchase order or receipt. Note that iExpense does not allow you to assign a purchase order number to an expense report, so this would cause all invoices for expense reports to be placed on hold.

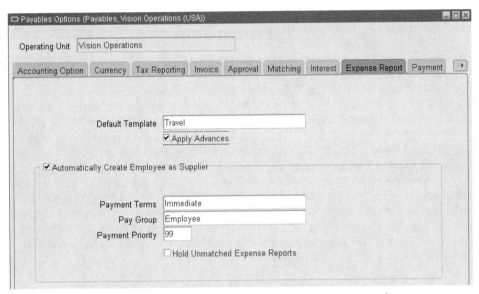

Payables I Setup I Options I Payables Options I Expense Report tab

FIGURE 7-4.   *Expense report processing options*

Viewing or Manually Entering Employees as Suppliers

If you do not have suppliers being created from employees automatically when expense reports
are brought into Payables for payment, you will have to create them manually. As mentioned
earlier, this is slightly different than entering suppliers, because you will need to ensure that the
employee record is linked to the supplier. While this is done in the same place as regular suppliers
(Payables I Suppliers I Entry I Create Supplier), the SUPPLIER TYPE will need to be set to Supplier Used
To Process Expense Payments To Internal Employees, as seen in Figure 7-5. If you are unable to

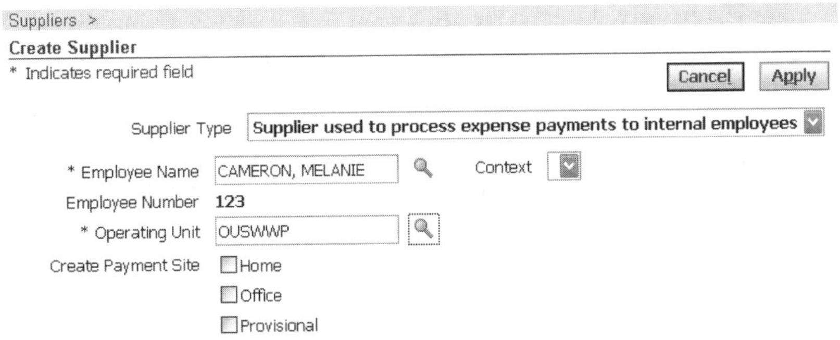

Payables I Suppliers I Entry I Create a new Supplier

FIGURE 7-5.   *Manually entering employees as suppliers*

update the supplier type, ensure the responsibility you are using has access to the function called Create/Update employee supplier details (System Administrator | Application | Menu, select the menu being used by the Responsibility).

Select the EMPLOYEE NAME from the list of values, and the EMPLOYEE NUMBER will default in. This is the link between the supplier and the employee record that is required when processing expense reports. Once an employee has been associated with a supplier, a second supplier cannot be created for the same employee. Select the OPERATING UNIT this supplier record is for, and then determine if the payment site is created from the home address associated to the employee record or from the office address associated with the location assigned to the employee. Provisional addresses are also allowed when HR is fully installed, and reflects a temporary work address on the employee record (Human Resources | People | Enter and Maintain | Office Details tab, MAIL TO set to Provisional). Once the record is saved, additional information can be added, same as any supplier, with one exception: The Address Book will not allow viewing or updating the address. This is because the address is coming from the employee record and must be maintained there. (This is new in R12—in prior releases, the address could be viewed and updated on the supplier record, which caused mismatched information between the employee and supplier records.) To see the EMPLOYEE NUMBER associated with an existing supplier record, it can be found on the Organization page of the supplier record.

Creating Expenditure Policies

Three major decisions come into play with any expense report processing system: What are your expense policies? How do expense reports get coded for accounting in the General Ledger, and who can approve expense reports? Expenditure policies are Oracle's solution to the first decision. Once your policies are defined, Oracle allows you to add these policies to the system and associate them with the expense report templates. Policies determine such things as the currencies an expense report can be created in, as well as setting daily limits and tolerances for the expense type. These can also be assigned to specific locations and roles.

Policies are set up by specific expense categories, which are Accommodations, Airfare, Car Rental, Meals, Mileage, Miscellaneous, and Per Diem. These Payables Lookup Codes cannot be modified or added to (Payables | Setup | Lookups | Payables | Type = OIE_EXPENSE_CATEGORY). The schedules available for each category have different features.

Creating Internet Expense Locations to Associate with a Policy

Locations that are associated with policies are not the same locations that are used by Purchasing to identify deliver-to addresses. Expense locations refer to areas or regions within the CONtinental United States (CONUS), as well as other countries, or OCONUS (Outside CONtinental United States), as opposed to a physical address. For example, the Phoenix, Arizona, location in iExpense refers to the greater Phoenix area, which includes Phoenix, Scottsdale, Fountain Hills, Mesa, Tempe, Glendale, and other cities in Maricopa County.

The setups are broken into Country and City Locations. When creating a country, the LOCATION name and DESCRIPTION are added. Both countries and cities have two statuses: saved and active. The status depends on which button is selected when exiting the Locations screen (see Figure 7-6), and only activated locations can be used in iExpense. A location that has a STATUS of saved can be REMOVED, while locations that have been activated can only be END DATED. Enter a LOCATION name and a

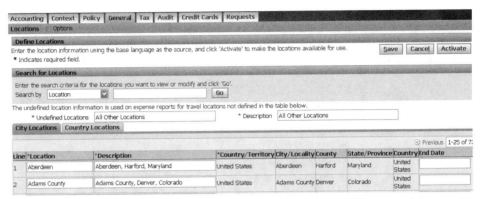

Internet Expenses Setup And Administration I Internet Expenses Setup I General I Locations I City Locations

FIGURE 7-6. *Adding locations in iExpense*

DESCRIPTION, and select the COUNTRY/TERRITORY from the list of values. The countries that appear here are not the same countries that were just entered under Country Locations, but are the countries set up in Payables (Setup I Countries). The next fields are only used when a CONUS file is uploaded; they display the CITY/LOCALITY, COUNTY, STATE/PROVINCE, and COUNTRY information for this location from the file. Both CONUS and OCONUS files provided from the U.S. Government can be uploaded into iExpense to not only create the locations but also maintain the rate schedules for per diems for meals and accommodations. This file contains the maximum rate that can be charged by both government employees and their customers working on government contracts; it can be uploaded directly into iExpense under Internet Expenses Setup And Administration I Internet Expenses Setup I Requests I Upload Rates. The layout for the file is well described in the Oracle Internet Expense Implementation and Administration Guide, Chapter 3, which can be downloaded from My Oracle Support.

Defining Accommodation Policies

Accommodation policies determine the daily limits that can be spent on hotels. Referring to Figure 7-7, add a SCHEDULE NAME and DESCRIPTION. Users will not see these names, but they are used when associating a policy schedule to an expense template. The START DATE determines the first day that this schedule is used, while the END DATE is the last day it is in effect. Oracle recommends setting the START DATE at least one day prior to the system date (usually today's date). Currency Rules can be added to determine the currencies that this expense category can be created in. Selecting SINGLE REIMBURSEMENT CURRENCY limits the expense report to a single currency, and on the next page you can then restrict the currency that is used. MULTIPLE REIMBURSEMENT CURRENCIES allows the employees to enter expense reports in different currencies; it is often used when the same policy or template is going to be used for multiple companies in different countries. The final option, LOCATION CURRENCY RATES, is used when the expense reports will need to be restricted to the currency for the location the employee traveled to, such as Peso when traveling to Mexico.

When currency rules are added, additional setups are required on the next window. For SINGLE REIMBURSEMENT CURRENCY, select the actual CURRENCY the employees are allowed to use to submit an expense report, and then select if you are going to ALLOW RATE CONVERSION or NO RATE CONVERSION. These two settings determine the actual currency that is allowed. For example, when ALLOW RATE

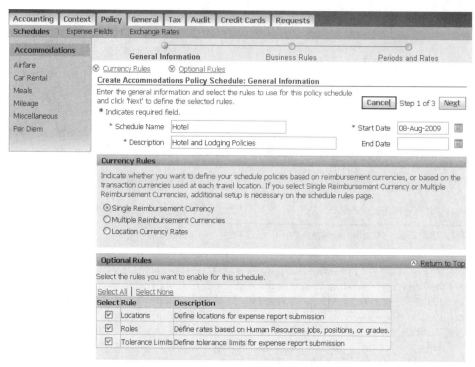

FIGURE 7-7.   *Defining accommodation policies*

CONVERSION is selected, then the expenses can be entered in foreign currencies, which are then converted to the single currency assigned to this policy. The conversion rate that is used is the rate defined in Payables. The default exchange rate type is assigned on the Payables Options window (Setup I Options I Payables Options I Currency tab), while the rate for this type is set up under Setup I Currency I Rates I Daily. When NO RATE CONVERSION is selected, then the employee must enter all expenses in the currency assigned in the CURRENCY field.

MULTIPLE REIMBURSEMENT CURRENCIES allows you to select more than one currency to associate with the schedule. The final option, LOCATION CURRENCY RATES, allows you to select an expense location that is set up in the system (Internet Expenses Setup And Administration I Internet Expenses Setup I General I Locations), and associate specific currencies to that location. Once the location is selected, details can be added on the next page, and the currency is assigned to the location. When selecting the location, Oracle will default in All Other Locations, which will also need to be associated with a currency. This allows expense reports for locations not specifically defined to be entered.

Optional Rules can also be added, which will restrict this accommodation policy to LOCATIONS or ROLES. TOLERANCE LIMITS can be added to allow overages to the limits for this policy; they allow expense reports to be entered for a set amount over the policy but track the overages for both auditing and policy violations. To add location restrictions, select location and click Next. Referring to Figure 7-8,

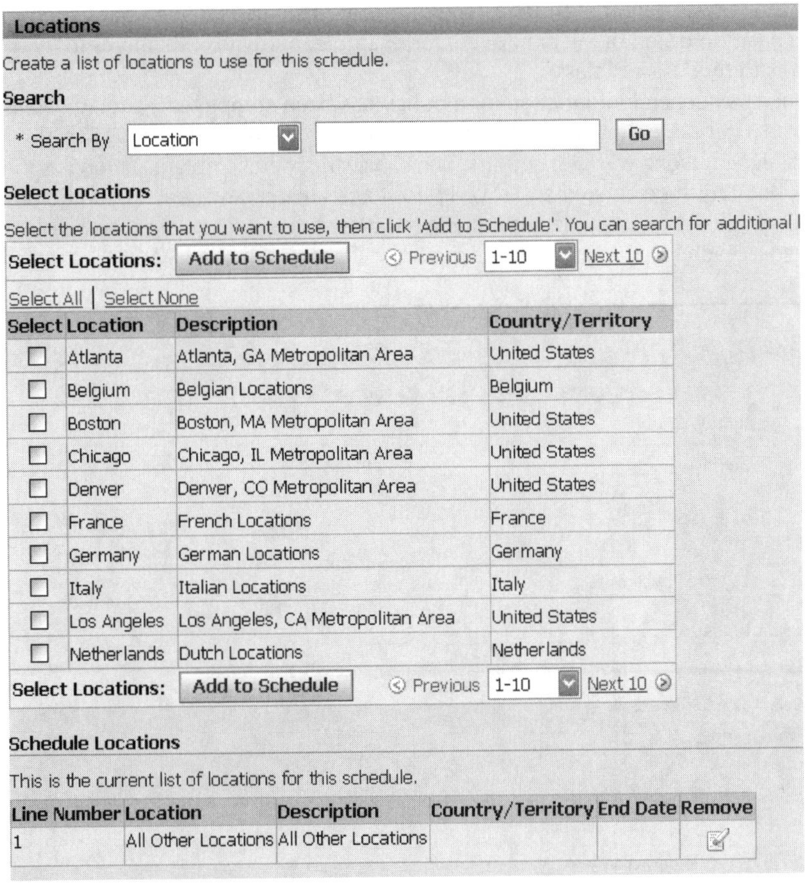

Internet Expenses Setup And Administration | Internet Expenses Setup | Policy | Schedules | Accommodations, page 2

FIGURE 7-8.   *Adding location restrictions to a policy schedule*

you can search for a location by the location name, description, or country. Check the box in the select column, and then click Add To Schedule.

Tolerance limits are based either on an expense report's INDIVIDUAL LINES or on the cumulative amount for a SINGLE PERIOD. Periods do not equate to calendar or general ledger periods but are a specific time frame for tracking information for expense report policy totals or infractions. For example, a period can be an entire year for expense limits related to an annual budget, a few months for limits that are set according to seasonal fluctuations, or no end date, making it valid until a new one is created. When you are using tolerance limits, there is a profile that controls how they are applied to expense reports. OIE: Enable Policy can be set to Prevent Submission when the expense report is over the tolerances set, or to only Warn Users or Inform Approver Only, which will allow the expense reports to be submitted.

Rules can be assigned to a specific Job, Position, or Grade (usually only used when HR is fully installed; see Figure 7-9). This type of restriction is used when your expense policy depends on the position or job of the employee, for example, allowing executives to fly first class, and directors to fly business class.

Once the General Information for a policy has been completed, specific details are added, based on a period, or time frame that this policy is effective (see Figure 7-10). The PERIOD NAME needs to be assigned, along with a START DATE. The END DATE can be left blank as long as this schedule is active, but it must be entered and saved prior to creating a new period. Additional Details are added by clicking the icon. These details include the daily limits and, if using them, tolerances that are assigned to each location and role, as shown in Figure 7-11. Click Mass Updates to update all the

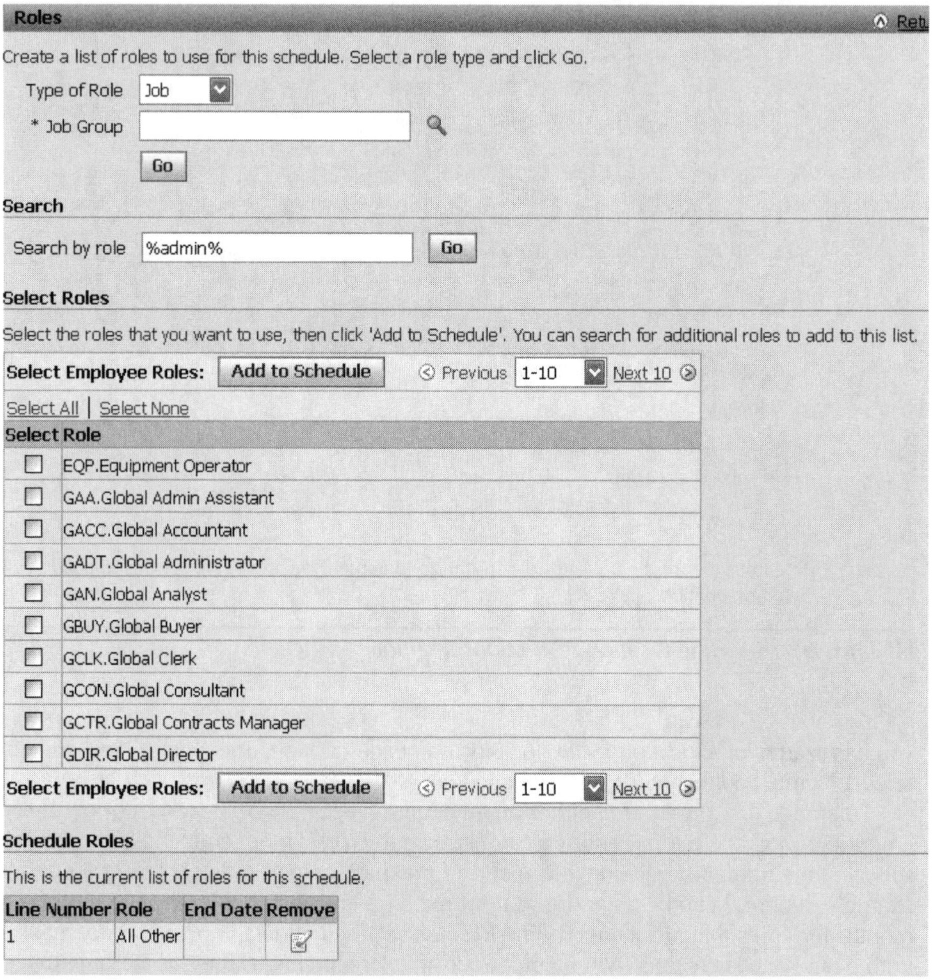

Roles ⟳ Ret

Create a list of roles to use for this schedule. Select a role type and click Go.

Type of Role Job

* Job Group [ ] 🔍

[Go]

Search

Search by role %admin% [Go]

Select Roles

Select the roles that you want to use, then click 'Add to Schedule'. You can search for additional roles to add to this list.

Select Employee Roles: [Add to Schedule] ◁ Previous 1-10 Next 10 ▷

Select All | Select None

Select	Role
☐	EQP.Equipment Operator
☐	GAA.Global Admin Assistant
☐	GACC.Global Accountant
☐	GADT.Global Administrator
☐	GAN.Global Analyst
☐	GBUY.Global Buyer
☐	GCLK.Global Clerk
☐	GCON.Global Consultant
☐	GCTR.Global Contracts Manager
☐	GDIR.Global Director

Select Employee Roles: [Add to Schedule] ◁ Previous 1-10 Next 10 ▷

Schedule Roles

This is the current list of roles for this schedule.

Line Number	Role	End Date	Remove
1	All Other		📝

Internet Expenses Setup And Administration | Internet Expenses Setup | Policy | Schedules | Accommodations, page 2

FIGURE 7-9. *Adding role limitations to an expense policy*

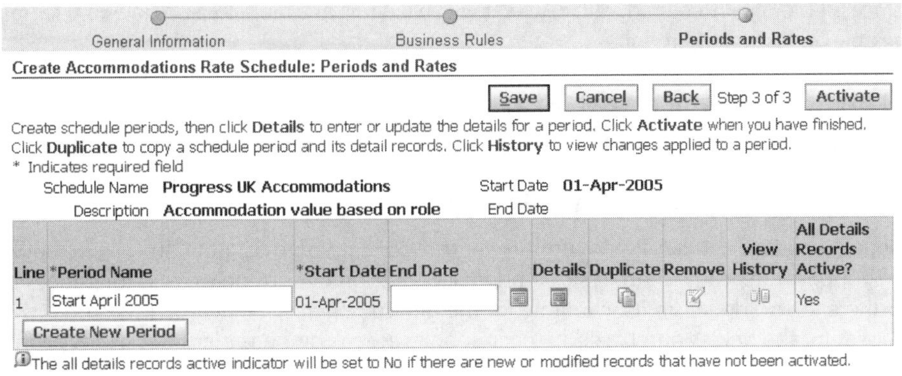

Create Accommodations Rate Schedule: Periods and Rates

| | General Information | Business Rules | Periods and Rates |

Save | Cancel | Back | Step 3 of 3 | Activate

Create schedule periods, then click **Details** to enter or update the details for a period. Click **Activate** when you have finished. Click **Duplicate** to copy a schedule period and its detail records. Click **History** to view changes applied to a period.
* Indicates required field

Schedule Name **Progress UK Accommodations**   Start Date **01-Apr-2005**
Description **Accommodation value based on role**   End Date

Line	*Period Name	*Start Date	End Date	Details	Duplicate	Remove	View History	All Details Records Active?
1	Start April 2005	01-Apr-2005		▦	▦	▯	☑	▯▯	Yes

Create New Period

The all details records active indicator will be set to No if there are new or modified records that have not been activated.

Internet Expenses Setup And Administration | Internet Expenses Setup | Policy | Schedules | Accommodations, page 3

FIGURE 7-10. *Creating a period for the policy schedule*

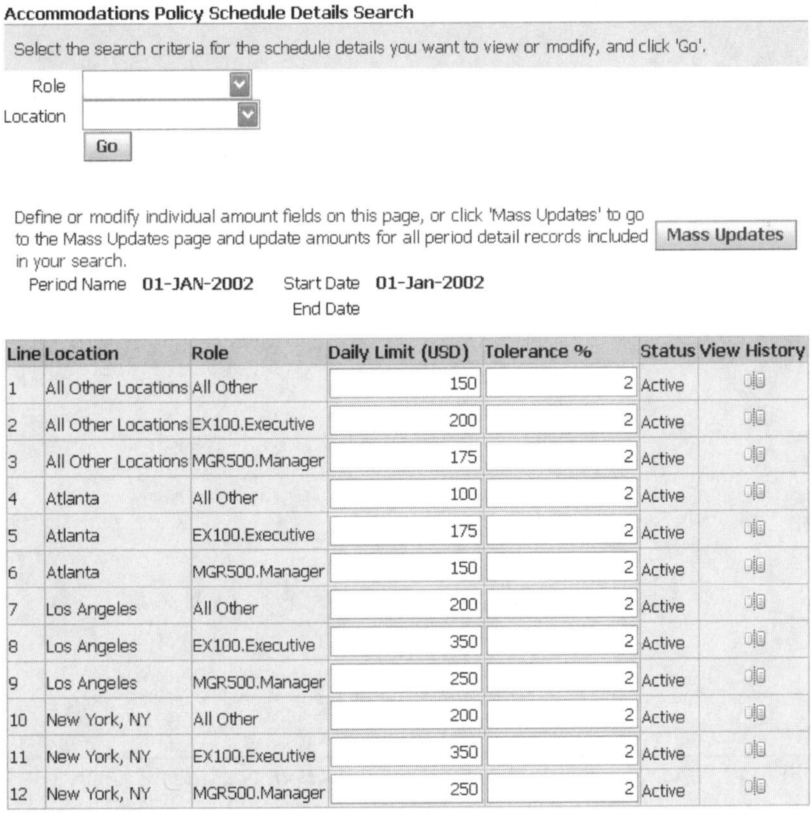

Accommodations Policy Schedule Details Search

Select the search criteria for the schedule details you want to view or modify, and click 'Go'.

Role
Location
Go

Define or modify individual amount fields on this page, or click 'Mass Updates' to go to the Mass Updates page and update amounts for all period detail records included in your search.   **Mass Updates**

Period Name **01-JAN-2002**   Start Date **01-Jan-2002**
End Date

Line	Location	Role	Daily Limit (USD)	Tolerance %	Status	View History
1	All Other Locations	All Other	150	2	Active	▯▯
2	All Other Locations	EX100.Executive	200	2	Active	▯▯
3	All Other Locations	MGR500.Manager	175	2	Active	▯▯
4	Atlanta	All Other	100	2	Active	▯▯
5	Atlanta	EX100.Executive	175	2	Active	▯▯
6	Atlanta	MGR500.Manager	150	2	Active	▯▯
7	Los Angeles	All Other	200	2	Active	▯▯
8	Los Angeles	EX100.Executive	350	2	Active	▯▯
9	Los Angeles	MGR500.Manager	250	2	Active	▯▯
10	New York, NY	All Other	200	2	Active	▯▯
11	New York, NY	EX100.Executive	350	2	Active	▯▯
12	New York, NY	MGR500.Manager	250	2	Active	▯▯

FIGURE 7-11. *Adding details to a policy schedule*

locations and roles at the same time by a specific percentage, as well as setting a NEW TOLERANCE. Once all the data is entered, click Activate to make this available to associate to a template and to be applied to expense reports.

Defining Car Rental and Miscellaneous Policies

Car Rentals and Miscellaneous categories are set up exactly like Accommodations.

Defining Airfare Policies

Defining Airfare Policies work very similar to Accommodations, but can only be applied to a role, job, or position. You cannot restrict airfare by location or currencies, and tolerances do not apply, as there are no dollar limits available for the airfare policies. You can add restrictions on the classes for the tickets purchased by each job, role, or position under the Details page, as shown in Figure 7-12.

Defining Meal Policies

Meal policies allow you to add daily limits, which apply to either an individual meal, a daily sum, or both. Select DAILY LIMITS under the Optional Rules section on the first page, and on page 2, you can select INDIVIDUAL MEAL, DAILY SUM, or BOTH. When you click Details on the Periods page, limits can be set for the options you selected (see Figure 7-13).

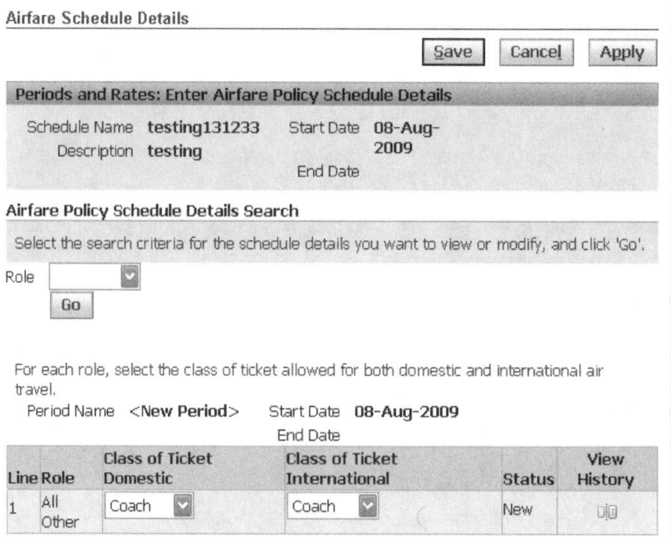

FIGURE 7-12. *Adding class of ticket to a role, position, or grade for airfare*

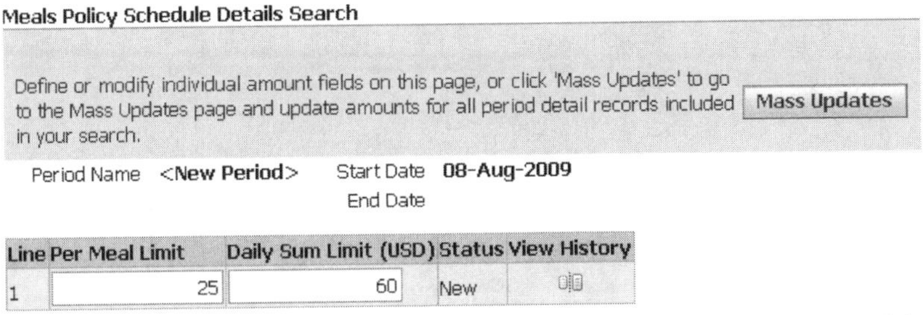

Meals Policy Schedule Details Search

Define or modify individual amount fields on this page, or click 'Mass Updates' to go to the Mass Updates page and update amounts for all period detail records included in your search. | Mass Updates |

Period Name <New Period>   Start Date 08-Aug-2009
                             End Date

Line	Per Meal Limit	Daily Sum Limit (USD)	Status	View History
1	25	60	New	

Internet Expenses Setup And Administration | Internet Expenses Setup | Policy | Schedules | Meals, Details

FIGURE 7-13. *Adding daily limits on meals for both an individual meal and the total for the day*

Defining Mileage Reimbursement Policies

Mileage policies include several options that do not appear anyplace else. First, you can select a DISTANCE UNIT OF MEASURE, selecting from Kilometers, Miles, or Swedish Miles, which are equivalent to 10 kilometers. Currency rules only allow SINGLE REIMBURSEMENT CURRENCY and MULTIPLE REIMBURSEMENT CURRENCIES. Under Optional Rules, there are several new options available (see Figure 7-14). These

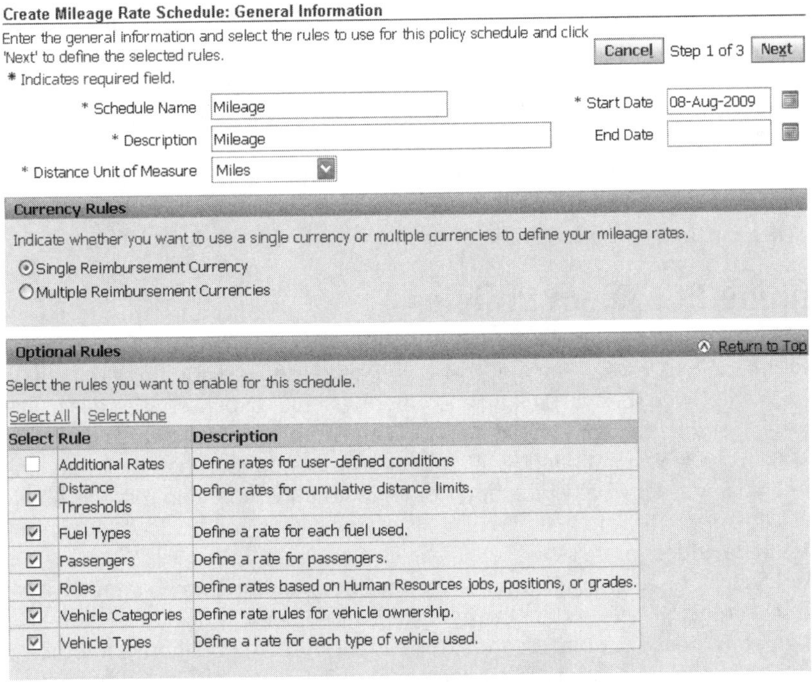

Create Mileage Rate Schedule: General Information

Enter the general information and select the rules to use for this policy schedule and click 'Next' to define the selected rules. | Cancel | Step 1 of 3 | Next |
* Indicates required field.

* Schedule Name Mileage   * Start Date 08-Aug-2009
* Description Mileage   End Date
* Distance Unit of Measure Miles

Currency Rules

Indicate whether you want to use a single currency or multiple currencies to define your mileage rates.

⊙ Single Reimbursement Currency
○ Multiple Reimbursement Currencies

Optional Rules   ⊗ Return to Top

Select the rules you want to enable for this schedule.

Select All | Select None

Select	Rule	Description
☐	Additional Rates	Define rates for user-defined conditions
☑	Distance Thresholds	Define rates for cumulative distance limits.
☑	Fuel Types	Define a rate for each fuel used.
☑	Passengers	Define a rate for passengers.
☑	Roles	Define rates based on Human Resources jobs, positions, or grades.
☑	Vehicle Categories	Define rate rules for vehicle ownership.
☑	Vehicle Types	Define a rate for each type of vehicle used.

Internet Expenses Setup And Administration | Internet Expenses Setup | Policy | Schedules | Mileage

FIGURE 7-14. *Creating a policy for mileage*

Mileage Rates

Line	Role	Vehicle Category	Vehicle Type	Fuel Type	Distance Intervals (MILES)	Mileage Rate (USD)	Passenger Rate Type	Rate per Passenger (USD)	Status	View History
1		Company	Motorcycle	Liquid Petroleum Gas	Between 0 and 10	.25	Amount	.25	New	
2		Company	Motorcycle	Liquid Petroleum Gas	Between 10.1 and 20	.35	Amount	.30	New	
3		Company	Motorcycle	Liquid Petroleum Gas	Greater Than 20	.40	Amount	.35	New	
4		Company	Motorcycle	Petrol	Between 0 and 10		Amount		New	

Internet Expenses Setup And Administration | Internet Expenses Setup | Policy | Schedules | Mileage | page 3, Details

FIGURE 7-15. *Adding rates for mileage*

can be assigned to roles on the next page, again, selecting from jobs, positions, or grade, along with additional details.

DISTANCE THRESHOLDS, applied to either a period of time or a single trip, determines the distances that can be tied to rates. Number of passengers can also be tied to rates, where the rates can include MULTIPLE RATES PER PERIOD, or only ONE RATE PER PERIOD. VEHICLE CATEGORIES are predefined as Company, Private, Rental, or All Other and can require a Vehicle Type and Fuel Type to be entered on the expense report; then the Vehicle Type of Car, Motorcycle, Van, or All Other. Fuel Types include Bi-Fuel, Conversion, Diesel, Electricity Only, Hybrid Electric, Liquid Petroleum Gas, and Petrol. The details page is where you can then add the actual rates for each vehicle (see Figure 7-15). Notice that the DISTANCE INTERVALS value, defined on page 2 under the DISTANCE THRESHOLDS, allows you to enter different rates for each distance defined, and one final rate for anything above the largest distance. The PASSENGER RATE TYPE can be set to either an Amount or a Percentage of the total rate. The rest of the options that were selected on the prior page affect the information the employee is required to enter when creating an expense report (such as Vehicle Type and Fuel Type).

Defining Per Diem Policies

Per diems are used to reimburse expenses based on a fixed amount, as opposed to the actual amounts of the expenses. Using per diems will decrease both auditing time and the amount of time each employee spends tracking and entering actual expenses. There is usually a give and take when using Per Diem reimbursements: some employees will watch their expenses and spend far less than the amount allotted, while others will spend more than the allotment; the net effect to the company usually balancing out. Coming into play more and more as hotels and restaurants offer loyalty programs is how the free meals or night stays will be accounted for. Oracle allows policies to be added for these as well.

Per Diems are set up as either an allowance per meal or a daily amount. This is determined by the schedule type selected on the policy. You also need to decide what the RATE INCLUDES, selecting from Meals, Accommodations, Meals and Accommodations, or Others. These selections will determine the rates that can be added on the Details page. The Currency Rules available are the same options as are available for Accommodations, but different Optional Rules apply. When the Schedule Type was set up as Allowance, you can only require Locations and Roles, but for

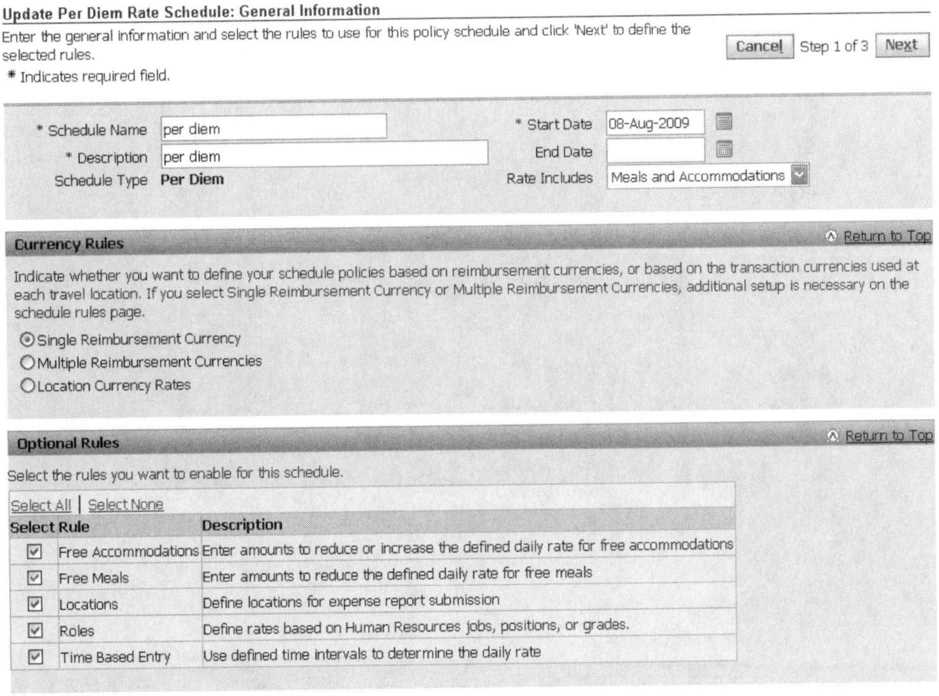

FIGURE 7-16. *Creating per diem policies*

Per Diem schedules, you have a few more options. FREE ACCOMMODATIONS and FREE MEALS can have special policies, and the daily rate can be prorated by requiring TIME BASED ENTRY for the first and last days of a trip. Usually, these days of a trip are not spent entirely on the road and are reimbursed at different rates. For example, when a trip ends by 6 P.M., your company may decide to reduce the amount of the reimbursement by the evening meal (see Figure 7-16). The next page will be different, depending on whether you selected Per Diem or Allowance.

Adding Per Diem Information

When requiring time-based entry, you first have to determine whether the Time Period for a day is MIDNIGHT TO MIDNIGHT or START TIME PLUS 24 HOURS (see Figure 7-17). This is used when prorating the per diems. When you select MIDNIGHT TO MIDNIGHT, then any time spent on the road between these times is considered a full day, and the first day and last day are prorated from midnight. There are a few options to consider under the Rate Periods, besides the Time Thresholds used to assign the Per Diem rates. For example, you can require a MINIMUM TRIP DURATION FOR PER DIEM ELIGIBILITY. By adding the hours or minutes, it will require an employee's trip to be longer than this time period to be eligible for a per diem. Next, decide if a standard rate is applied based on a time period or select STANDARD RATES PLUS FIRST AND LAST PERIOD RATES to define specific time periods and rates for the first and last days, as well as full days in between. The last option under time is

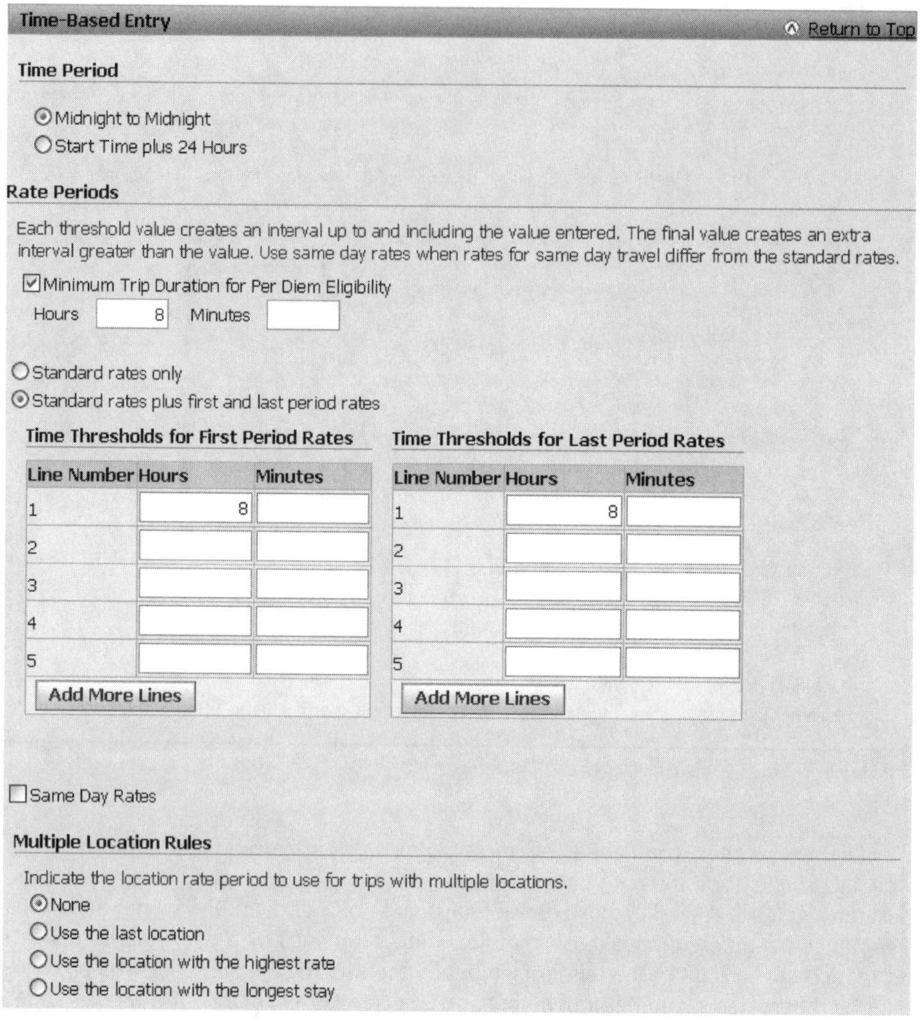

FIGURE 7-17. *Time-based entry options for a per diem*

SAME DAY RATES. When this is selected, it allows you to enter a rate for trips that are less than a day, but over the minimum trip duration.

Next, determine if the above time-based entries affect trips that take the employee to multiple locations. Selecting NONE will allow only one location per expense report, or select USE THE LAST LOCATION to use the rate for the last location the employee stayed in (based on date and time). The other two options include using the location with the highest rate, or using the location with the longest stay to determine the rates.

More and more, company travel policies are taking into consideration the free meals and free accommodations that are received as promotions. Many years ago, these benefits became small bonuses for employees and could be used to either collect a larger per diem (for example, collect an accommodation per diem for a free night); these days are in the past, as companies watch more closely the expenses incurred during business trips. Now, free meals can be deducted from the meal per diem based on the meal that was received for free, by a single set value, or by the number of meals that were given for free. Free accommodations are either added or deducted from the reimbursement amount for that day.

In Figure 7-18, you can see how this allows the rates to be entered. First, Standard Rates are set up for the time periods. Assign a rate for each specific location that will be used to reimburse each 24-hour time period, and determine what amount or percentage will be deducted for each free meal. The Free Accommodations calculation is either a deduction or an increase, again based on an amount or percentage. The same information can be added for the first and last periods, and more than one amount can be entered, which in effect pro-rates the reimbursement. A minimum reimbursement amount can also be set here.

Standard Rates

Line	Location	Role	Time Thresholds	Rate (USD)	Free Meals Deductions Calculation Method	Free Meals Deduction	Free Accommodations Deduction Calculation Method	Deduction	Status	View History
1	All Other Locations	All Other	Greater Than 23:59	50	Amount	10	Amount	10	New	
2	Atlanta	All Other	Greater Than 23:59	45		5	Amount	10	New	

First Period Rates

Line	Location	Role	Time Intervals	Rate (USD)	Free Meals Deductions Calculation Method	Free Meals Deduction	Free Accommodations Deduction Calculation Method	Deduction	Status	View History
1	All Other Locations	All Other	Between 0 and 08:00	10					New	
2	All Other Locations	All Other	Greater Than 08:00	25					New	
3	Atlanta	All Other	Between 0 and 08:00						New	
4	Atlanta	All Other	Greater Than 08:00						New	

Last Period Rates

Line	Location	Role	Time Intervals	Rate (USD)	Free Meals Deductions Calculation Method	Free Meals Deduction	Free Accommodations Deduction Calculation Method	Deduction	Status	View History
1	All Other Locations	All Other	Between 0 and 08:00	10					New	
2	All Other Locations	All Other	Greater Than 08:00	25					New	
3	Atlanta	All Other	Between 0 and 08:00						New	
4	Atlanta	All Other	Greater Than 08:00						New	

Deduction Exceptions

Minimum Reimbursement   10   USD

Internet Expenses Setup And Administration | Internet Expenses Setup | Policy | Schedules | Per Diem | Details for Per Diem

FIGURE 7-18. *Adding per diem details*

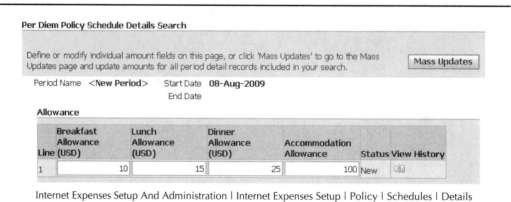

Internet Expenses Setup And Administration | Internet Expenses Setup | Policy | Schedules | page 2, Allowances

FIGURE 7-19. *Allowance rules*

Adding Schedule Information for Per Diems

As mentioned earlier, when using a SCHEDULE TYPE of Allowance, the Currency Rules available are the same, but the only Optional Rules are Location and Roles. Page 2 of the setups, however, provide options that can be made for the Allowance Rules (see Figure 7-19). Accommodation Allowances and Meal Allowance will be checked based on the selection you made on the prior window for Rate Includes (you could select Meals, Accommodations, or Meals and Accommodations). For Meals, next decide if the Allowance Method is based on the number of meals or the meal type. Then decide the Time Period, selecting from Day and Time thresholds for number of meals, while Meal Type also allows you to add daily start and end dates.

On the Details window, add the actual allowances. The fields that appear on this page will change depending on the prior selections. If Meal Type was selected, the Breakfast, Lunch, and Dinner will appear, but if number of meals was chosen, then the options are one meal, two meals, and three meals. Using this option pays by the number of meals away from home, not the actual meal that was eaten (see Figure 7-20 for an example).

Per Diem Policy Schedule Details Search

Define or modify individual amount fields on this page, or click 'Mass Updates' to go to the Mass Updates page and update amounts for all period detail records included in your search.   **Mass Updates**

Period Name   \<New Period\>   Start Date   08-Aug-2009
End Date

Allowance

Line	Breakfast Allowance (USD)	Lunch Allowance (USD)	Dinner Allowance (USD)	Accommodation Allowance	Status	View History
1	10	15	25	100	New	

Internet Expenses Setup And Administration | Internet Expenses Setup | Policy | Schedules | Details

FIGURE 7-20. *Allowance rate details*

Capturing Additional Expense Report Information

Oracle allows predefined additional information to be captured when an employee enters an expense report. These fields can be enabled, required, or disabled (see Figure 7-21). When entering Accommodations, the option to add an END DATE for the stay and a MERCHANT are available. Airfare additional information includes MERCHANT, CLASS OF TICKET, TICKET NUMBER, and FROM and TO LOCATIONS, while Car Rental only allows MERCHANT information. Meals expenditures can require the NUMBER OF ATTENDEES and the ATTENDEE name, and Mileage has the DISTANCE UNIT OF MEASURE, DAILY OR TRIP DISTANCE, LOCATION FIELDS, and VEHICLE LICENSE PLATE NUMBER available. Notice that many of these fields, which are tied to an Expense Category, tie into fields that can be used when creating rules for your Policy Schedules.

In addition to using the seeded rules, a new rule can be defined for a specific expense type (refer to Figure 7-22). After assigning the RULE NAME and DESCRIPTION, select whether the ATTENDEES OR RECIPIENTS of this expense are Employees, Non-Employees, or both Employees and Non-Employees. The Employees choice consists only of people who are set up as employees in Oracle; it does not include non-employees that are in HR, such as contingent workers. Selecting EMPLOYEE IS A REQUIRED ATTENDEE OR RECIPIENT will include the employee that submitted the expense report as an attendee. Additional fields can be required, such as name, title, tax identification number, and employer. When using the field ATTENDEE OR RECIPIENT TYPE, you can select from the list that appears to the right of it, allowing you to select which attendee types appear. Additional Attendee or Recipient Types can be set up in Payables under Setup | Lookups | Payables, where the TYPE is OIE_ATTENDEE_TYPE.

The main difference between these two types of data capture is that the first one, Expense Category, is associated with a specific expense category and will appear on all expense reports where the template line has this category on it. It is global to the expense category. But Expense Types are assigned to a specific line on an expense template and are limited to only the lines to which they are assigned. Depending on how the template is set up, expense fields for both an expense category and an expense type may appear on the same line.

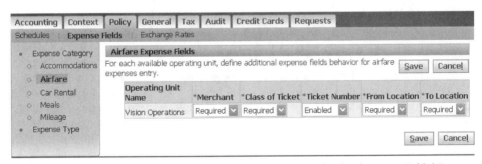

Internet Expenses Setup And Administration | Internet Expenses Setup | Policy | Expense Fields | Expense Category

FIGURE 7-21. *Enabling expense fields*

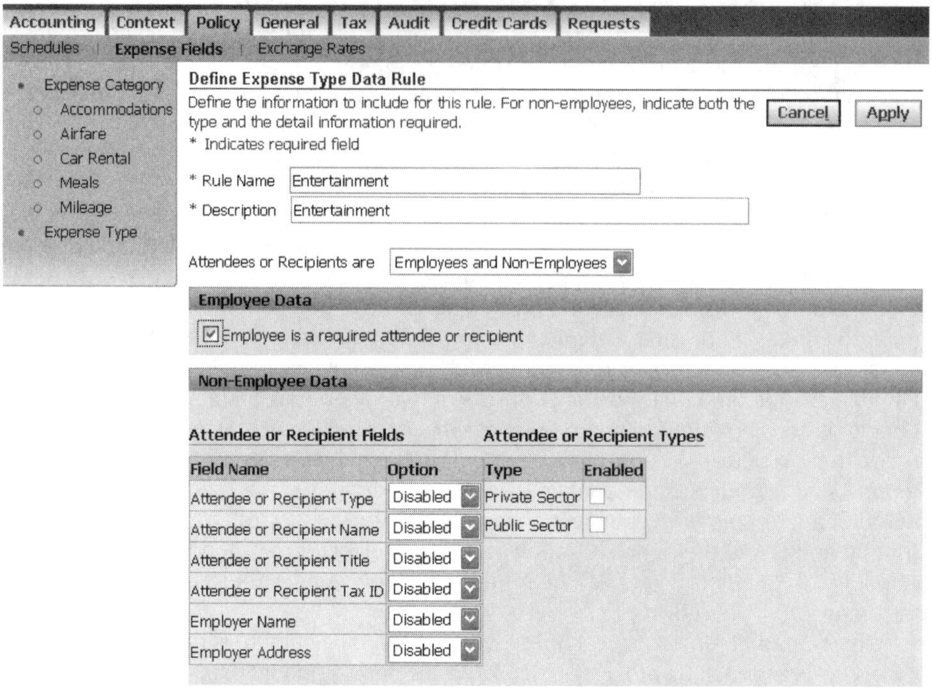

Internet Expenses Setup And Administration | Internet Expenses Setup | Policy | Expense Fields | Expense Type

FIGURE 7-22.   *Creating an expense type field to add additional data to an expense report*

Setting Up Expense Report Templates

Expense report templates are exactly what they sound like: templates that default specific information when entering expense reports, such as expense items and all or part of the general ledger account number. Since expense reports are going to be processed in Payables, they have to be associated to an OPERATING UNIT, as do the templates when they are created (see Figure 7-23). Before setting up templates, you will want to determine the types of expenses employees submit on an expense report, and then decide if it will be easier to enter one template or multiple templates that group like expenses together. For example, you can set up one template for *travel* and a second one for *client entertainment,* or you can include both types on one template.

The TEMPLATE NAME is used by the employees to select which template they will use to enter their expenses, so it should be descriptive to them. Adding an INACTIVE ON date will make this template no longer available for use after this date. Selecting ENABLE FOR INTERNET EXPENSES will allow this template to be used in iExpense as opposed to only in Payables on the expense report form (Payables | Invoices | Entry | Expense Reports). Clicking Assign Card Expense Type works with the integration of employee credit cards and iExpense, creating a cross-reference between the credit card expenses and the template expense items. This allows you to link the expense types associated to a credit

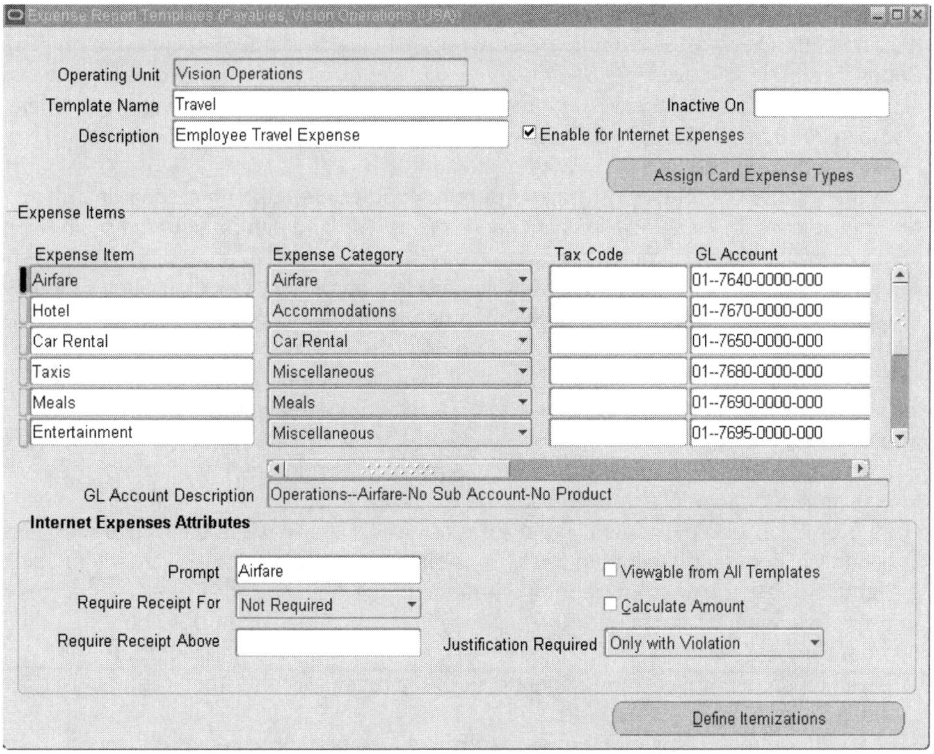

Payables | Setup | Invoice | Expense Report Templates

FIGURE 7-23. *Creating templates for expense report entry*

card to the expense item set up on an expense report template (see the later section "Credit Card Processing" for more information). Since the template and items need to exist to be linked, this needs to be completed after the template is entered and saved.

Enter a meaningful name for the EXPENSE ITEM, which is selected by the employee when entering an expense report. You want to ensure that your template(s) have enough expense items for both accurate accounting and expense tracking. Adding a Miscellaneous EXPENSE ITEM ensures that the employee has someplace to classify items that do not all fit into a specific category, but it can also become a catch-all, reducing the reportability and possibly the accuracy of the accounting on expense reports. EXPENSE CATEGORY allows additional fields for information to be added, such as Airline when Airfare is selected. Expense categories can also be used as a condition if Approval Management (AME) is being used for expense report approvals.

If taxes are required to be calculated on expense reports, add a TAX CODE to default in for all transactions entered against this expense item. The tax codes will need to be set up in Oracle's R12 tax engine called eTax. The GL ACCOUNT determines how the account number is built for the expense report; it uses the client extension called AP_WEB_ACCTG_PKG.Build Account. Out of the box, the account number on an expense report uses the general ledger account assigned to an EXPENSE ITEM, combined with the DEFAULT EXPENSE ACCOUNT assigned on the employee record under Assignments. The way the default engine works is that any segment assigned on the Expense Report Template will override the employee account number. So, if the employee is assigned Company 01 Department 500 Account 7710 (01.500.7710), and the template has defaults for Company of 02 and Account of 7520 (02.(null).7520), then the account number assigned to the expense report will be 02.500.7520.

When Oracle's Project Costing and Billing modules are implemented, a default PROJECT EXPENDITURE TYPE can be associated with each line as well and can be updated by the employees when entering expense reports. A POLICY SCHEDULE, when added to an expense type, restricts the limits, currencies, locations, and roles that each line applies to. Once a policy schedule is added to a line and saved, neither the policy schedule nor the category can be updated. Next, add a DATA CAPTURE RULE, selecting from the expense fields that were set up for an expense type (Internet Expenses Setup And Administration | Internet Expenses Setup | Policy | Expense Fields | Expense Type). The last field on the lines is an END DATE, which will make this expense item no longer appear when entering expense reports.

For each line, additional information can be added under the Internet Expenses Attributes. This section is only for use in iExpense, and can only be updated when the ENABLE FOR INTERNET EXPENSES box is checked. PROMPT is what the employee will see when entering the expense report. When this is not completed, then the Expense Item will display. The advantage to using the prompt field is that it does not require a bounce of the Apache server to have changes take effect in iExpenses, whereas changes to the expense items do. Since auditing is built into the iExpense functionality, REQUIRE RECEIPT FOR can be set to Cash Only, Cash and Credit Card, or Not Required. This will let the employee know when to submit a receipt for this line; it is also used as part of the auditing function.

In addition to the type of expense requiring a receipt, a limit can also be set by adding a dollar amount in the REQUIRE RECEIPT ABOVE field. VIEWABLE FROM ALL TEMPLATES will allow this item to be seen on all expense report templates that are ENABLED FOR INTERNET EXPENSES. This feature allows you to create a template line only once that will appear on every expense report, no matter which template is being used. I like to set up one Global template where the lines all have this box checked for items that are common to all expense reports, then individual templates for specific types of expenses, such as travel or gifts.

CALCULATE AMOUNT should be checked for all Mileage and Per Diem categories that have an associated policy schedule. This will allow Oracle to calculate the reimbursable amounts for these categories. Without this check box, you are relying on the employee to calculate the mileage and per diem reimbursements. This calculation can also be customized for more complex reimbursement policies. When this box is selected, a procedure called CustomCalculateAmount is used to calculate the reimbursement, and it can be modified to perform your company's specific calculations. The final field, JUSTIFICATION REQUIRED, determines if the employee has to complete the justification field when entering this line on an expense report. The options are Only With Violation, which means that a justification must be provided when this item is in violation of the policy assigned to it as a Policy Schedule, or Always.

Expense Itemizations can be added to any line, which will require the employee to add detailed, itemized information when entering this line. This information is entered by the employee on the details page of the expense report. This is useful when a bill (either as a receipt being entered on an expense report or as a credit card charge) contains more than one item on an expense template. An example would be a hotel bill that included lodging, meals, phone calls, Internet service, and movie rentals. To allow the employee to break this information out without creating multiple lines on the expense report (and making receipt-based auditing harder because now one line does not equal one receipt), click Define Itemizations. From here, select ITEMIZATION REQUIRED if you want to force the employee to itemize the bill, and select the expense items associated either with this template or with another template where VIEWABLE FROM ALL TEMPLATES was checked. There is also an option, INCLUDE ALL EXPENSE ITEMS, if you want them all to appear.

Approval Options

Expense reports all require approval before final processing and settlement, and there are two approval options available. The first is to assign employee's signing limits, which uses the employee-supervisor hierarchy along with the cost center associated with the expense report to assign approval limits, or AME (Approvals Management). When using the Signing Limits functionality, you assign an employee a specific limit for a specific cost center (more than one cost center and limit can be set up for each employee). When processing an approval on an expense report, Oracle will compare the cost center and approver on the expense report to the amounts set up in the Signing Limits form, and use the employee-supervisor relationships to move up the chain until the person with the proper limits is found.

AME, on the other hand, offers much more flexibility. Rules can be created for approvals based on a wide verity of data available on both the employee record and the expense report, to route the expense report for approval. For example, the owning manager of the department may have first approval on an expense report, but if the expenditure item was Computers, it may also require the IT Director's approval. While signing limits are fairly inflexible, AME can be set up to accommodate almost any approval hierarchy. To use AME, the profile AME: Installed will need to be set at either the Application or Responsibility level (System Administrator | Profile | System). See the Appendix for more information on setting up AME.

To create signing limits, refer to Figure 7-24. Select the OPERATING UNIT, then the DOCUMENT TYPE of AP Expense Report. Select the NAME of the employee you are granting signing limits to, and the COST CENTER, and then enter the SIGNING LIMIT amount.

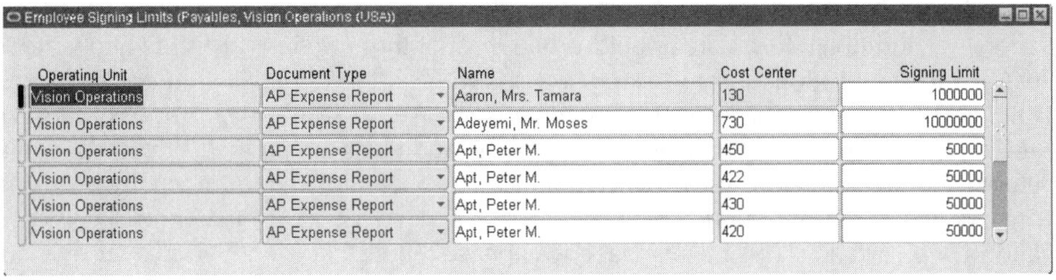

Operating Unit	Document Type	Name	Cost Center	Signing Limit
Vision Operations	AP Expense Report	Aaron, Mrs. Tamara	130	1000000
Vision Operations	AP Expense Report	Adeyemi, Mr. Moses	730	10000000
Vision Operations	AP Expense Report	Apt, Peter M.	450	50000
Vision Operations	AP Expense Report	Apt, Peter M.	422	50000
Vision Operations	AP Expense Report	Apt, Peter M.	430	50000
Vision Operations	AP Expense Report	Apt, Peter M.	420	50000

Payables | Employees | Signing Limits

FIGURE 7-24.   *Creating signing limits*

Enabling Expense Report Auditing

Companies usually have two concerns related to expense reports: Are the policies being followed, and is fraud being committed when submitting an expense report? iExpense can assist with both of these concerns. By defining rules right in Oracle that are used to create and approve expense reports, you can ensure that the policies are being followed. And by adding audit rules, you can limit the risk and exposure to fraud.

Your auditing policies need to be defined before you can create the audit rules in Oracle. These usually consist of Who gets audited, What is audited, and When is it audited. For example, you will audit a random sample of 25 percent of the expense reports submitted, all expense reports over $250, and all expense reports that required justifications. Auditing setups include rules, lists, notifications, and holds.

Oracle considers there to be two different types of audits that can be performed: paperless and receipt based. *Receipt-based* audits are achieved by comparing the receipts submitted with an expense report to the actual amounts and categories on the expense report. This type of audit is fairly manual, usually catching input errors on the expense report (either for amount or category) or perhaps the location where the expense was incurred is not supported. *Paperless* auditing, on the other hand, uses criteria set up in the system to select expense reports for auditing. These criteria in Oracle include missing receipt packages, total amount of submitted expense reports, and number of times a policy is violated. Expense reports are also randomly selected for audit above and beyond this. When you combine these criteria with comprehensive policies that are set up in Oracle, paperless auditing can be used to monitor expense reports while keeping your processing costs down. There are several steps required to setting up paperless auditing, explained next.

Audit Rules

Audit rules are set up to determine when an expense report requires auditing (see Figure 7-25). After assigning a RULE SET NAME and DESCRIPTION, determine how expense reports are selected for audit. A random rule can be set up by selecting AUDIT THE SPECIFIED PERCENTAGE OF ALL EXPENSE REPORTS. Once this is checked, the AUDIT PERCENTAGE box appears, allowing you to enter the percentage of approved expense reports that will be selected by Oracle for auditing. Reports that meet specific criteria can be excluded from this random sample by setting Oracle up to ignore specific types of expense reports. By selecting CONTAIN CREDIT LINES ONLY, any expense report uploaded from a credit card statement will be excluded from the random audits, while selecting CONTAIN ONLY EXPENSE TYPES WHERE RECEIPT AND JUSTIFICATION ARE NOT REQUIRED will exclude any expense report that does not have a receipt or a justification from the random selection for auditing.

Next, Additional Rules are added. While most of these options are straightforward, some can use a little explanation. AUDIT ALL EXPENSE REPORTS WITH POLICY VIOLATIONS is an option when the profile OIE: Enable Policy is *not* set to Prevent Submission. AUDIT EXPENSE REPORTS FOR INDIVIDUALS ON THE AUDIT LIST ensures that all employees listed on the audit lists are audited. Audit lists contain employees added by the system when a policy has been violated, or manually by an auditor for any number of reasons. Notice that AUDIT ALL EXPENSE REPORTS GREATER THAN A SPECIFIC AMOUNT only allows one currency. This means that any expense report that is entered in a currency other than the one defined here will be converted into this currency based on the exchange rate defined in Payables | Setup | Currency | Rates | Daily for the date the expense report was submitted. There is a problem, though, when Oracle does not find a conversion rate, and the rule is ignored. Because of this, you will want to carefully review how rates were set up on your policy schedules.

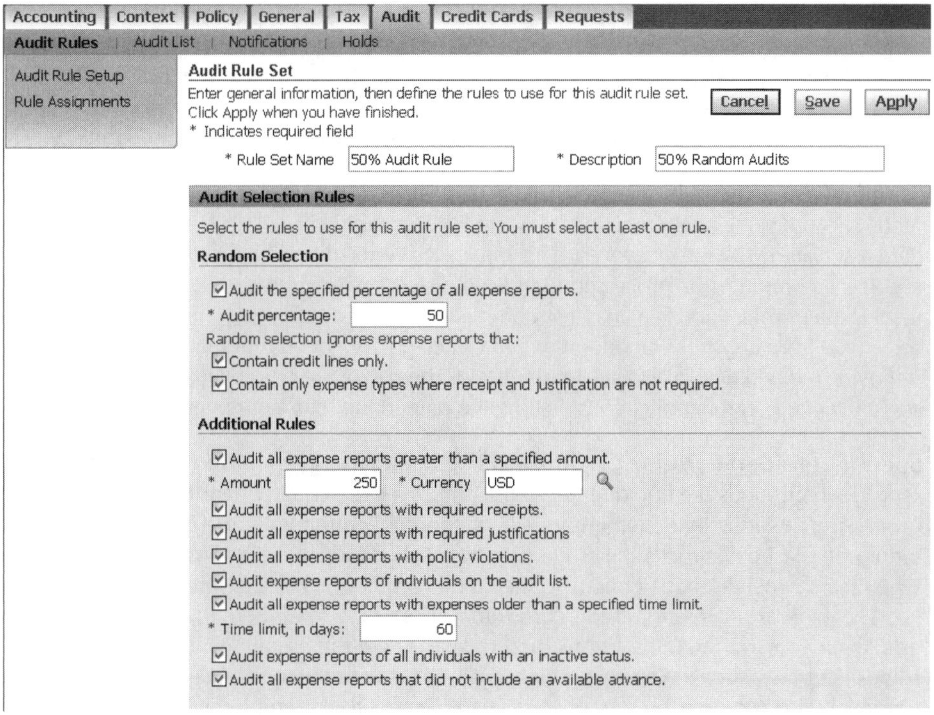

Internet Expenses Setup And Administration | Internet Expenses Setup | Audit | Audit Rules | Audit Rule Setup

FIGURE 7-25. *Creating audit rules*

Oracle has the ability to create advances, called Prepayments, in Payables. These advances can be automatically applied to an expense report when the APPLY ADVANCE check box is selected on the Payables Options (Payables | Setup | Options | Payables Options | Expense Report tab). If this check box is not checked and an advance existed that was not manually applied to an expense report, then the expense report would be selected for audit if AUDIT ALL EXPENSE REPORTS THAT DID NOT INCLUDE AN AVAILABLE ADVANCE is checked.

The final option, AUDIT EXPENSE REPORTS OF ALL INDIVIDUALS WITH AN INACTIVE STATUS, pertains to terminated employees. When this option is selected, any expense report processed for a terminated employee will require an audit. Terminated employees require special handling in Oracle; because not only do you need the ability to pay an expense report for a terminated employee, you also need the ability to prevent fraud from taking place. For this, you need to understand how Oracle handles employee terminations.

Terminations When Human Resources Is Fully Installed   When HR is a full install, there are two dates associated with a terminated employee: Actual Date and Final Process Date. The actual date reflects the last day the employee was employed with your company, but Oracle recognizes that there are transactions that need to happen after that date, such as processing benefits, final pay checks, and expense reports. While the employee can no longer access Oracle after the actual termination date in the system, expense reports that were entered prior to that date, or expense reports that are entered after that date by another user, can still be processed through to settlement in Payables. Once the Final Process Date passes, expense reports that are in the system are no longer considered valid and will not process. The options at this point would include updating the Final Process Date to a date in the future, or entering an invoice manually directly into Payables against a supplier record that is not associated with the employee.

Terminations When Human Resources Is a Shared Install   The end date on the employee record becomes the final process date when HR is a shared install and there is no actual termination date associated with the employee. This means that once the employee record is end dated, expense reports can no longer be processed for this employee. Setting the end date to one in the future will resolve the problem and is a little less complicated (from a business process standpoint—both are easy to do from a system standpoint) when Oracle HR is not your human resource system. While removing the end date is also an option, it runs the risk of the employee being left active and has some internal control implications. Setting the date in the future removes some of these control risks.

Special Considerations for Credit Card Processing on Terminated Employees   Expense reports where funds are due directly to the employee are usually handled as part of the termination procedure, ensuring that the company's financial obligation with an employee is settled on that employee's last day. Processing credit card transactions, since it does involve the employee indirectly when the payment is made directly to the credit card issuer, has a different process in Oracle.

The general process for credit card transactions is to load them into iExpense and have the employee approve the transactions. In the case where the employee is terminated, then Oracle routes the transactions to the supervisor associated with the terminated employee's record for approval. This requires the supervisor to have access to the employee's iExpense transactions. The Expense Report workflow (APEXP) will add the employee access to the supervisor's securing attributes (System Administrator | Security | User | Define | Securing Attributes), and the supervisor will receive a notification informing him that the credit card transactions for the terminated employee are ready for approval.

Assigning Audit Rules

Once the Audit Rule is saved, it will need to be assigned in order to be utilized by Oracle during expense report processing. Select the Rule Assignments link, find the operating unit you want to add the rule to, and click the update icon, seen in Figure 7-26. After clicking Add Another Row select the Rule Set Name, and add an EFFECTIVE START DATE, which is the first date that this rule will be in effect.

If you are not seeing all the operating units set up in Oracle, go to the Context tab (Internet Expenses Setup And Administration | Internet Expenses Setup | Context) and SELECT the operating units that are missing, then click Add To Selections. Operating units do not appear on the assign forms unless they are selected first on the Context tab. When an operating unit does not have an audit rule assigned to it, then no expense reports are selected for auditing for that operating unit.

Audit Lists

Oracle creates and maintains a list of users who are considered at risk for committing expense report fraud, ensuring that all expense reports for these employees are routed for auditing. The list includes users who meet specific criteria and may also be manually maintained by the auditors. To create the Audit List Criteria, see Figure 7-27. After assigning a RULE SET NAME and a DESCRIPTION,

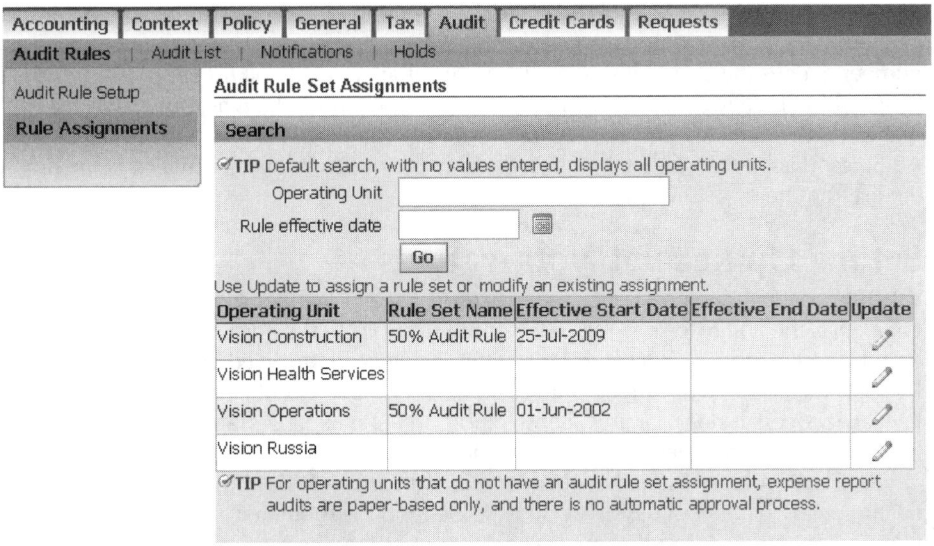

Accounting	Context	Policy	General	Tax	Audit	Credit Cards	Requests	

Audit Rules | Audit List | Notifications | Holds

Audit Rule Setup

Rule Assignments

Audit Rule Set Assignments

Search

☞TIP Default search, with no values entered, displays all operating units.

Operating Unit [   ]

Rule effective date [   ] 🗓

[Go]

Use Update to assign a rule set or modify an existing assignment.

Operating Unit	Rule Set Name	Effective Start Date	Effective End Date	Update
Vision Construction	50% Audit Rule	25-Jul-2009		✎
Vision Health Services				✎
Vision Operations	50% Audit Rule	01-Jun-2002		✎
Vision Russia				✎

☞TIP For operating units that do not have an audit rule set assignment, expense report audits are paper-based only, and there is no automatic approval process.

Internet Expenses Setup And Administration | Internet Expenses Setup | Audit | Audit Rules | Rule Assignments

FIGURE 7-26. *Assigning audit rules to operating units*

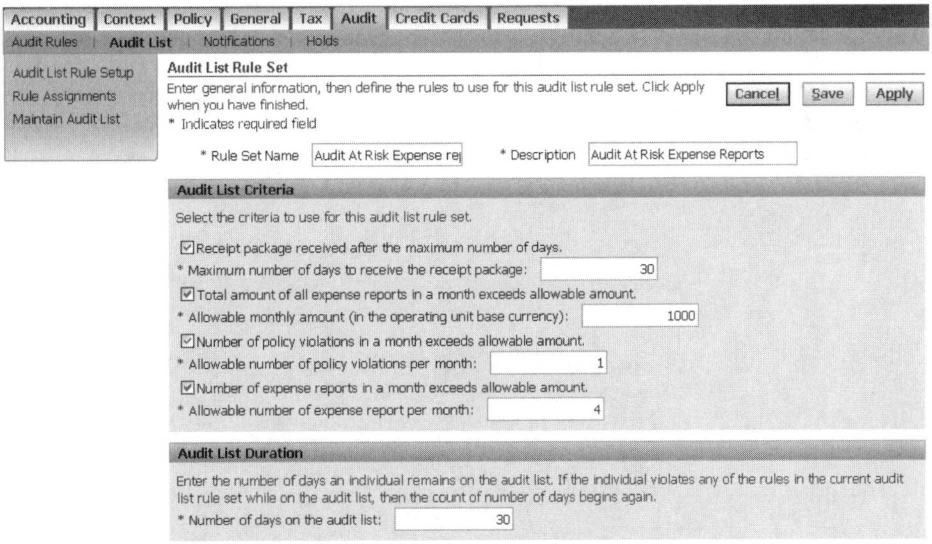

Accounting	Context	Policy	General	Tax	Audit	Credit Cards	Requests	

Audit Rules | **Audit List** | Notifications | Holds

Audit List Rule Setup

Rule Assignments

Maintain Audit List

Audit List Rule Set

Enter general information, then define the rules to use for this audit list rule set. Click Apply when you have finished.   [Cancel] [Save] [Apply]
* Indicates required field

* Rule Set Name [Audit At Risk Expense re]   * Description [Audit At Risk Expense Reports]

Audit List Criteria

Select the criteria to use for this audit list rule set.

☑ Receipt package received after the maximum number of days.
* Maximum number of days to receive the receipt package: [30]
☑ Total amount of all expense reports in a month exceeds allowable amount.
* Allowable monthly amount (in the operating unit base currency): [1000]
☑ Number of policy violations in a month exceeds allowable amount.
* Allowable number of policy violations per month: [1]
☑ Number of expense reports in a month exceeds allowable amount.
* Allowable number of expense report per month: [4]

Audit List Duration

Enter the number of days an individual remains on the audit list. If the individual violates any of the rules in the current audit list rule set while on the audit list, then the count of number of days begins again.
* Number of days on the audit list: [30]

Internet Expenses Setup And Administration | Internet Expenses Setup | Audit | Audit List | Audit List Rule Setup

FIGURE 7-27. *Creating criteria to add users to an audit list*

select the Criteria for when a user is added to the audit list. The audit list is created when an employee violates specific rules, such as not submitting receipts in a predefined number of days or submitting expense reports that violated a policy. Under the Audit List Duration section, set the number of days the user will stay on the audit list after each violation. Once the rule is saved, it is assigned to operating units by using the Rule Assignments link. When an employee has been placed on the audit list, the auditors can view and maintain the lists under the Internet Expense Audit responsibility in the Maintain Audit List window. Employees can also be manually added to the list from here.

Setting Up Receipt Notifications

When your expense report policy requires users to send in all or some receipts prior to processing, Oracle has the ability to send out different notifications to the person who submitted the expense report. The first notification can be sent when receipts are received by accounting; this is called the Receipts Received Notification. Oracle can also send out a notification when the Receive Receipt Package process is done for an expense report (Internet Expenses Auditor | Expenses Audit | Receive Receipt Package), and can be restricted to only when a delinquent receipt is received.

After that, rules are added about when to notify individuals about Overdue Receipts. First, determine the number of days after an expense report is submitted the receipts are considered overdue. Then decide how often to send a reminder that the receipts are still missing. When users receive either of these notifications, they have the ability to respond to the auditor. The next notification that goes out would be after the response is received. In the example in Figure 7-28, users are reminded after 25 days if the receipts are not received, and then every 7 days after that. If the user responds to any of the notifications, Oracle will wait an additional 7 days before sending the next notification. The last option, RECEIPT DOCUMENTATION REQUIRED IF USER INDICATES RECEIPTS ARE MISSING, determines if the user must provide alternate documentation for missing receipts, such as a letter of explanation.

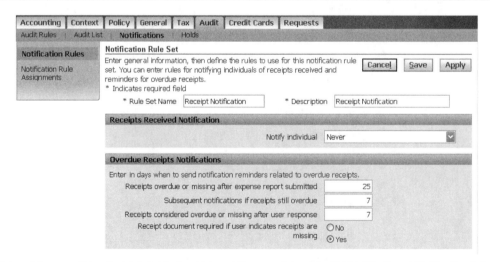

Internet Expenses Setup And Administration | Internet Expenses Setup | Audit | Notifications | Notification Rules

FIGURE 7-28. *Setting up receipt reminders for expense reports*

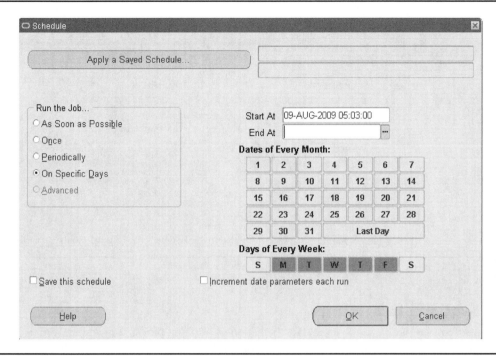

FIGURE 7-29.   *Creating a schedule for a concurrent request*

After the Notification Rules are assigned using the Notification Rule Assignment link, a concurrent request called Expenses Overdue Receipts Tracking needs to be run to send out the notifications. This request should be scheduled for each operating unit whenever you want an expense report to be evaluated for a receipt notification. Usually, once a business day works well for this request. To schedule a request, click Schedule when submitting the request for the first time. Figure 7-29 shows a schedule created to run at 5 A.M. Monday–Friday. Selecting SAVE THIS SCHEDULE will make it available to assign to future requests, but you will want to make sure that you do not schedule *all* your scheduled requests to run at exactly the same time every day, or your DBA may be calling you.

Audit Holds

Holds can be applied on all expense reports under certain conditions. Reviewing Figure 7-30, note that Individual Payment Holds can be applied across the board until the receipts are received, or only when receipts are overdue, in which case the OVERDUE DAYS will need to be specified. Normally, you would set this to be the same number of days as on your notifications, if you are using them, but Oracle allows them to be set to different numbers. This process is used when expense reports that require receipts are not audited; it can create invoices ready for payment after the expense report is approved. This will apply a payment hold (as opposed to an invoice hold) on the expense report. While many invoice holds also prevent payments, they are created for many reasons and are associated with the invoice itself; a payment hold, on the other hand, has the sole purpose of preventing a payment and is associated with the payment schedule as opposed to the invoice itself.

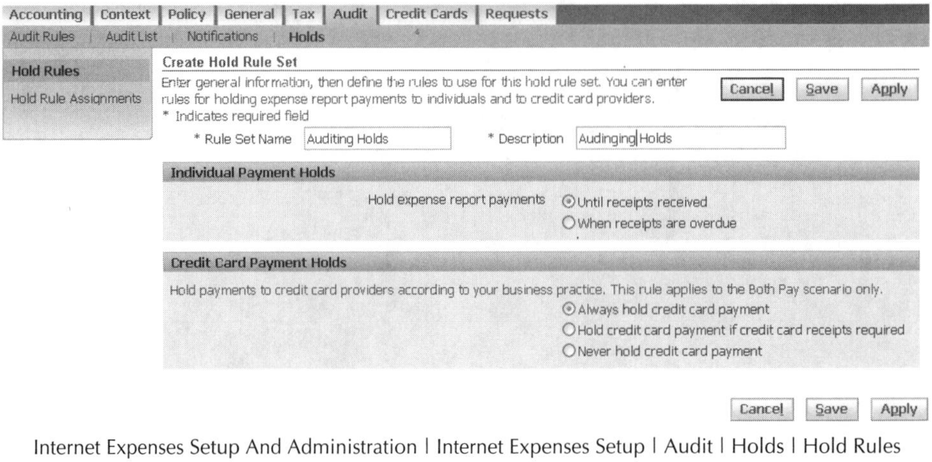

FIGURE 7-30. *Creating hold rules*

Setting Up Auditors

Auditors are set up to accommodate the paperless auditing process, assigning workload queues and the operating units each auditor is eligible to audit. Before setting up auditors, you need to first create an Audit Hierarchy and assign it to a security profile. This will assign specific (or all) operating units that the audit can have access to.

Creating an Audit Hierarchy

Oracle uses hierarchies in several places in E-Business Suite. A *hierarchy* is exactly what it sounds like: it allows parents to be created with subordinates, similar in concept to an organization chart. This was mentioned in Chapter 3, under "Creating the Position Hierarchy." At that time, a hierarchy was created for each position in the system. This time, the hierarchy is for the operating units that will be submitting expense reports; it determines which auditor(s) will be responsible for auditing the information. It is important to understand how your company plans on doing this review before creating the hierarchy, and to ensure that the hierarchy is maintained over time; any organization that submits an expense report that is *not* assigned in the audit hierarchy will be assigned to a default auditor called the *fall-back auditor.* These setups are done in Human Resources, even when HR is not fully installed.

To create the hierarchy, refer to Figure 7-31. Enter a NAME for the hierarchy, ensuring that the name identifies it in some way to be used for the audit hierarchy, mainly for clarity. After saving your work, under Version, enter **1** for the NUMBER, and select the begin date, ensuring it is some time prior to your first expense report if this is a new implementation of iExpense. At this point, you will need to save again and then requery up the hierarchy you just saved. Now the Organizations will be populated based on what is set up in your system. You will need a top-level organization that has at least one subordinate. You can either use an organization that already exists for the top level, or create a new one specifically for Auditing. I usually recommend creating a new one that keeps this hierarchy separate from all others, allowing updates to be made to it independently in the future. If your organization structures are simple, though, this may be overkill.

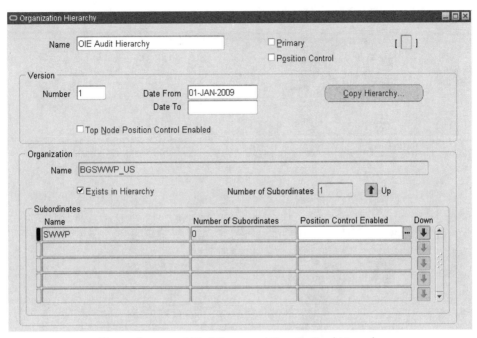

Human Resources I Work Structures I Organization I Hierarchy

FIGURE 7-31. *Creating an audit hierarchy*

To create a new organization, go to Payables I Setup I Organization and create a new organization with a classification of Operating Unit. Once it is set up, you can use F11, or find, to query it up in the Organization NAME field, and then enter the organizations as part of this hierarchy under subordinates. Once this is saved, the EXISTS IN HIERARCHY box will be checked. You can create as many hierarchies as you need to meet your organization's needs. Each hierarchy will map to a security profile, described next, and then be assigned to each auditor, determining which operating units they are responsible for auditing.

A security profile is created next for the hierarchies (Human Resources I Security I Profile). Assign the profile a NAME, and select the BUSINESS GROUP from the list of values that the organizations belong to. Select Secure Organizations by Organization Hierarchy and/or Organization List as the SECURITY TYPE, and select the ORGANIZATION HIERARCHY that you just set up. Ensure INCLUDE TOP ORGANIZATION is checked, and save your work. Next, you need to populate the hierarchy by running the concurrent request called Security List Maintenance. To ensure you do not update any other security list, select One Name Security Profile as the GENERATE LIST PROFILE, and select your list under the SECURITY PROFILE parameter. The Security Profile can now be assigned to the profile option called MO: Security Profile for the Audit responsibility, and assigned to the Auditors.

If you are updating the list after auditing has been implemented, there is one more process you will need to run, called Reassign Inaccessible Expense Reports from the Payables responsibility. This will reassign any expense reports using the new security.

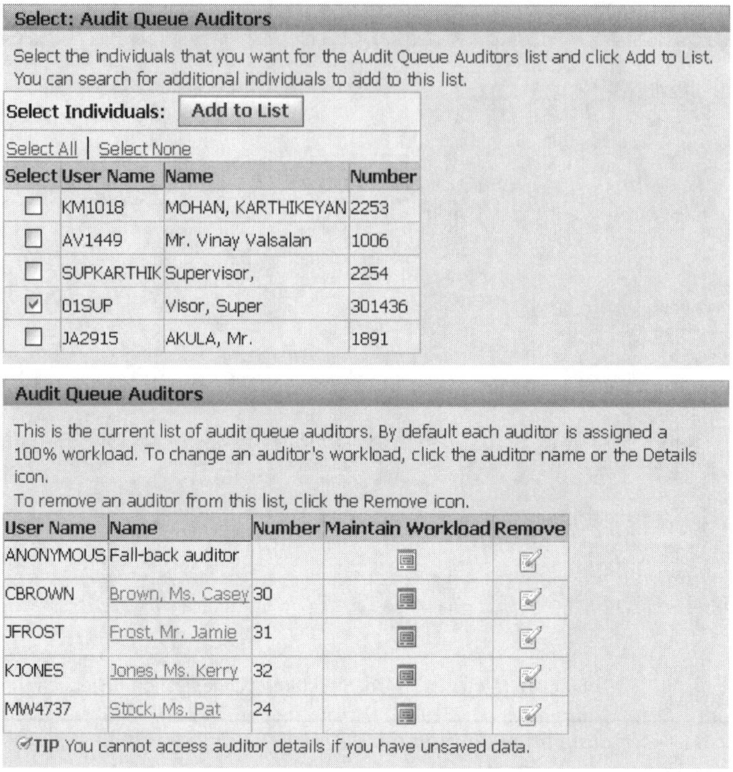

Select: Audit Queue Auditors

Select the individuals that you want for the Audit Queue Auditors list and click Add to List. You can search for additional individuals to add to this list.

Select Individuals: [Add to List]

Select All | Select None

Select	User Name	Name	Number
☐	KM1018	MOHAN, KARTHIKEYAN	2253
☐	AV1449	Mr. Vinay Valsalan	1006
☐	SUPKARTHIK	Supervisor,	2254
☑	01SUP	Visor, Super	301436
☐	JA2915	AKULA, Mr.	1891

Audit Queue Auditors

This is the current list of audit queue auditors. By default each auditor is assigned a 100% workload. To change an auditor's workload, click the auditor name or the Details icon.

To remove an auditor from this list, click the Remove icon.

User Name	Name	Number	Maintain Workload	Remove
ANONYMOUS	Fall-back auditor		▤	✎
CBROWN	Brown, Ms. Casey	30	▤	✎
JFROST	Frost, Mr. Jamie	31	▤	✎
KJONES	Jones, Ms. Kerry	32	▤	✎
MW4737	Stock, Ms. Pat	24	▤	✎

☑TIP You cannot access auditor details if you have unsaved data.

Internet Expenses Audit Manager I Expenses Audit I Auditor Setup I Define Auditor

FIGURE 7-32. *Defining an auditor*

Setting Up Auditors

Auditors need to be set up next, before the audit function can be used. On the Auditor Setup page, click Define Auditor, as shown in Figure 7-32. Under the Select: Audit Queue Auditors section, SELECT the user you want to add as an auditor and then click Add To List. The name will now appear on the lower section of the form under Audit Queue Auditors. From here, click Details next to the name and update the workload information for this auditor. The defaults will be today's date for the START DATE and 100% for WORKLOAD. After saving, the main auditor setup page will display, where you can add a SECURITY PROFILE for each auditor. This is the security profile set up in the previous step. Oracle has an engine that will assign the expense reports to auditors, based on the workload percentage and number of expense reports in their queue.

Profiles

As with all modules, many features and options in Oracle are controlled with profile options that can be set at different levels. Table 7-1 describes the iExpense-specific profile options.

Name	Default Setting	Description
AME: Installed	No	Determines if AME is used for expense report approvals.
ICX: Date Format Mask		When set, overrides the default date format of DD-MMM-YYYY.
ICX: Numeric Characters	Null will result in 1,000.00	Determines the display format for currency.
ICX: Session Timeout	30	Determines the period of time before the Internet session will time out for the user, requiring that user to sign back in.
OIE: Enable Approver	Yes	Determines if the approver field is visible in iExpense. No hides the field from the user and requires that OIE: Approver Required to be set to Yes with Default. When a valid approver does not default in, this will result in an approval workflow error, requiring the default supervisor to be resolved prior to processing.
OIE: Allow Credit Lines	Yes	Credit Lines are used for Negative Receipts, in effect creating a receivable for your organization from the employee, as opposed to a payable to them. This is for entered expense reports only and is not considered for credit card transactions, which will reflect returns as a reduction to the amount due the credit card company.
OIE: Allow Non-Base Pay	No	Determines if the users can select the currency used to reimburse an expense report. When it is not enabled, the expense reports will be reimbursed in the functional currency for the Ledger.
OIE: Approver Required	No	Approvers for expense reports can either come from the supervisor-associated employee record or be entered when the expense report is entered. When this profile is set to No, the approver is not required and does not populate on the expense report, preventing it from being routed for approval. When it is set to Yes, an approver must be entered, while with Yes with Default, the employee's supervisor will default in as the approver, but the employee can update the field.
OIE: Carry Advances Forward	Yes	Determines if an advance can be applied to more than one expense report. When this is set to No, employees must reimburse your company for any remaining prepayments after they submit an expense report.

TABLE 7-1. *Profile Options That Control iExpense Functionality* (continued)

Name	Default Setting	Description
OIE: CC Approver Req	No	Expense reports are normally charged against the cost center associated with the employee, but sometimes one needs to be charged to a different department, potentially causing a problem during the approval process, as the employee's supervisor hierarchy may not have approval rights for the different department. Setting this profile to Yes forces the employee to enter an approver when the cost center is changed.
OIE: CC Payment Notify	No	Determines if employees receive a notification when an invoice is created in Payables for expense reports, or an expense report for a credit card transaction is paid.
OIE: Enable Advances	Payables	Determines if the person submitting an expense report can decide if an advance is applied against it. Options include No, which prevents both the person submitting the expense report and Payables from selecting the advance; End User; Payables; or Both, which allows either the person submitting the expense report or Payables to apply the advance.
OIE: Enable Bar Code	No	Determines if Bar Codes are printed on the expense report confirmation page, which can then be used to retrieve an expense report during the receipt audit process.
OIE: Enable Cost Center	Yes	The cost center an expense report is charged against defaults in from the employee record. When this is set to Yes, the person submitting the expense report can update the cost center, while Read-Only will display the cost center and not allow the employee to update it. No will not display the field at all in iExpense.
OIE: Enable Credit Card	No	Enables the credit card functionality in iExpense (see "Credit Card Processing").
OIE: Enable DescFlex	Lines Only	Determines if the Header and Line Level descriptive flexfield (or configurable field) is visible in iExpense. You must also set up the descriptive flexfield if this option is enabled.
OIE: Enable Expense Allocation Splitting	No	Allows an expense line to be distributed to both a project and a non-project distribution.
OIE: Enable Expense Allocations	No	Determines if expenses can be allocated by the users, allowing them to update the allocations when expense reports are entered. This can be set to No, which prevents all users from allocating expenses; enabled by the user; and automatically enabled for all users. The option also includes whether the accounting combinations are validated or not (usually a good idea to do). When this is enabled, it is controlled by each user's iExpense Preferences (see Chapter 8).

TABLE 7-1.   *Profile Options That Control iExpense Functionality* (continued)

Name	Default Setting	Description
OIE: Enable Policy	Warn Users	Determines how Audit Policies affect if an expense report that violates a policy is handled. Options include Prevent Submission, Warn Users, and Inform Approvers.
OIE: Enable Project Allocations	No	Determines if project information is allowed on expense reports.
OIE: Enable Project Expenditure Organization	No	Used with Oracle Project Costing and Billing, determines if the employee can update the default expenditure organization on a project-related expense.
OIE: Enable Tax	No	Determines if tax-related elements are available on expense reports, which requires eTax to also be set up.
OIE: Grace Period	30	Determines the number of days *after* the end date on a rate schedule, location, expense template, or expense type that it can still be used. Specifically for Location, which affects other areas in Oracle, this allows expense reports, which are usually submitted after the fact, to be entered using information that was valid at the time of the expense.
OIE: Purpose Required	No	Determines if users must add a Purpose for expense report lines.
OIE: Report Number Prefix	No	Allows the system to add a prefix to the number assigned to any expense reports created in iExpense. This is particularly useful when expense reports are entered in iExpense as well as using the expense report form in Accounting.
PA: Allow Project-Related Entry in Oracle Internet Expenses	No	Used with Project Costing and Billing, determines if users can create an expense report against a project.
PA: AutoApprove Expense Reports		Used with Project Costing and Billing, determines if any project-related expense report requires an approval prior to processing.
WF: Notification Reassign Mode	Reassign	Determines how users can add vacation rules to any workflow that requires an approval while they are out of the office. Transfer sends all future approvals to a designated approver but uses that person's approval limits when evaluating if they can approve the notification. Delegate, on the other hand, grants that person the same approval limits that you have. Reassign will allow the user to select either Transfer or Delegate. Ensure that you set this properly to comply with any Sarbanes-Oxley rules your organization has.

TABLE 7-1. *Profile Options That Control iExpense Functionality* (continued)

User Account Securing Attributes

Each employee will have access to only his or her expense reports, as determined by the Securing Attributes associated with their user record (see Figure 7-33). The attribute ICX_HR_PERSON_ID controls the expense report that a user has access to. Users will receive an error message when signing into iExpense if this is not set. The VALUE represents the unique identification for the employee record; use the list of values to select the employee by name, and Oracle will populate the value for you. You can assign access to more than one employee in iExpense by assigning the attribute more then one time to a user. This is particularly useful when an administrative assistant is completing expense reports for executives, or if you are supporting iExpense and need to re-create an error for troubleshooting in a test environment. Just as in iProcurement, this Securing Attribute will also need to be assigned to the iExpense responsibility (System Administrator | Security | Responsibility | Define | Securing Attributes tab). Users can authorize other users to access their expense reports as well under iExpense | Access Authorization. Note that allowing someone to enter an expense report for you does not bypass any approval rules or policies set up in iExpense, as it is related to the employee the expense report is for, not the person entering the expense report.

Credit Card Processing

Credit card–related information from your provider can be uploaded into Oracle for employee review and approval, and then imported into Payables for settlement. Settlement can be made to either the credit card provider, for credit cards where your company is responsible, or to the employee when they are responsible for paying the credit card company directly. Oracle also allows for both reimbursable expenses and personal ones, where the employee is responsible for the expense.

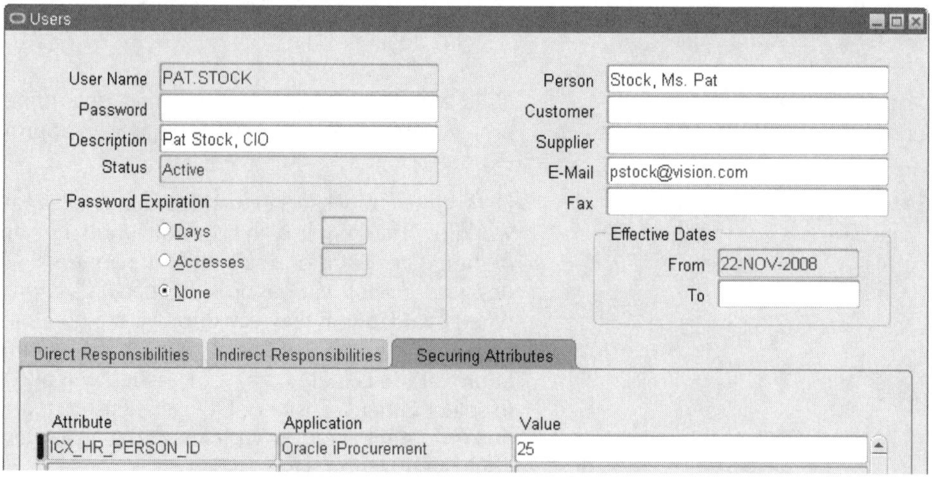

System Administrator | Security | User | Define |Securing Attributes

FIGURE 7-33. *Restricting the expense reports a user has access to*

Setting Up iExpense for Credit Card Integration

Corporate credit cards are used in many companies for travel, with the main advantage of the employee's personal credit card limit not being tied up for business expenses. There are three basic types of credit card scenarios that most companies follow. The credit cards are obtained by the company, but each employee is responsible for paying the balance due each month. These behave very similar to personal credit cards, and the company would reimburse the employee for any business expenses. Oracle calls this process Individual Pay.

Businesses can also provide credit cards where the company will pay the total amount due directly to the credit card, requiring the employees to approve the business expenses incurred, as well as identify any personal expenses that need to be reimbursed to the company by the employee. This is called Company Pay credit card processing.

The final scenario is a combination of the first two processes, where the company will pay only corporate expenses, while the employee is responsible for paying the credit card provider for any personal expenses. This is perhaps the most complicated and least common, referred to as Both Pay in iExpense. While the setups and specific processing for each of these three scenarios are unique, the basic concept is the same. Credit card transactions are received from your company's credit card provider and uploaded into iExpense. Employees then approve the expenses, providing accounting information and justification as needed, as well as identifying the expenses as either business or personal. Once the expense report is approved and, if required, audited, a settlement is created to either the individual employee, the credit card company, or a combination of both.

Defining Credit Card Policies

Credit card policies control two aspects of processing credit card transactions: the age of the transaction, and if certain types of expense transactions can be paid with cash, and if so, up to what amount.

When it comes to expense reports, some employees will play the *float* game, submitting their expenses as soon as possible so that the reimbursements can be used for either investments or paying other expenses, while others dread submitting expense reports and hold off till the very last moment possible. Either way, it can be a challenge to get some users to complete and submit expense reports on a timely basis, and when the expenses are related to a corporate credit card and are not going to be reimbursed to the employee, it can be even more challenging. Oracle allows you to set up a Transaction Submission policy that restricts when an employee can submit expense reports for direct reimbursement to the employee if they have outstanding expense reports for credit card transactions waiting for submission.

Referring to Figure 7-34, next to the OPERATING UNIT NAME you want to add a Transaction Policy for, enter a TRANSACTION AGE LIMIT. Remember, if you do not see the Operating Unit, go to the Context tab in Internet Expenses Setup And Administration and select it prior to proceeding. When the AGE LIMIT is left blank, there are no limitations on whether employees can submit an expense report for reimbursement when they have outstanding credit card expense reports waiting for approval. When it is set to 0, then all credit card expense reports must be submitted before the cash expense report. Any number higher than 0 means to look for expense reports where the transaction dates are older than today's date minus the transaction age limit, and if any are found, at least one credit card expense report must be submitted prior to submitting the cash expense report. When users must send in the credit card expense reports before they can get reimbursed, they are more apt to respond in a timely manner.

Card usage policies help to encourage employees, when submitting a cash expense report, to use their credit card. While this policy does not restrict expense reports from being submitted, it

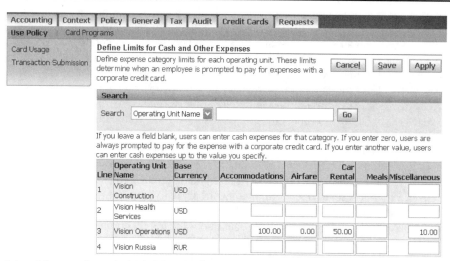

FIGURE 7-34. *Adding submission policies for credit cards*

does remind the user, as well as inform the expense report auditor and the employee's manager of a policy violation. Referring to Figure 7-35, set the usage limits for the operating unit and each category. When a category is left blank, there are no limits on the cash submitted on the expense report, while setting it to 0 reminds users to use their credit card every time they submit an expense report for cash. Any other amount will trigger a reminder only when they exceed the amount.

Accounting	Context	Policy	General	Tax	Audit	Credit Cards	Requests

Use Policy | Card Programs

Card Usage
Transaction Submission

Define Limits for Cash and Other Expenses

Define expense category limits for each operating unit. These limits determine when an employee is prompted to pay for expenses with a corporate credit card.

Cancel   Save   Apply

Search

Search [Operating Unit Name ▼] [   ] Go

If you leave a field blank, users can enter cash expenses for that category. If you enter zero, users are always prompted to pay for the expense with a corporate credit card. If you enter another value, users can enter cash expenses up to the value you specify.

Line	Operating Unit Name	Base Currency	Accommodations	Airfare	Car Rental	Meals	Miscellaneous
1	Vision Construction	USD					
2	Vision Health Services	USD					
3	Vision Operations	USD	100.00	0.00	50.00		10.00
4	Vision Russia	RUR					

Internet Expenses Setup And Administration | Internet Expenses Setup | Credit Cards | Use Policy | Card Usage

FIGURE 7-35. *Credit card usage policies*

Mapping Credit Card Transactions

Mappings between codes assigned by your credit card provider and the codes you have set up for expense types can be created so that the expenses are accounted for correctly when they are imported into Oracle. Credit card providers usually use standard codes, such as Major Industry Codes (MIC) or Standard Industry Codes (SIC) when sending a file, which can be mapped on expense report templates to specific expense items on the template. The mapping is a two-step process. First, you need to map the codes from the credit card company to a list of expense types, which are in turn mapped to specific expense items on templates.

Creating Mapping Values

Before you can begin the mapping process, you have to first define the values used by your credit card provider to classify transactions in Oracle. This is done with a *lookup*. A lookup is really just a list of values stored in the database. Oracle uses these in many processes, forms, and windows and also allows you to create lookups custom to your company for use during reporting, processing, or importing data. It is a good solution for preventing this information from having to be hard-coded into the programs. Remember when creating lookups that they can be shared for multiple purposes within Oracle. So if you already have a lookup in your system for SIC or MIC values, you do not have to create a new one but can use the one that exists. To create a lookup, refer to Figure 7-36. Assign your lookup a TYPE, which is the internal name for this lookup and should not contain spaces, and a MEANING for the codes. The APPLICATION should be Payables, and the Access Level, which decides how this lookup is maintained, is set to USER. SYSTEM is reserved for lookups used exclusively by Oracle, which cannot be updated except via a Patch, while EXTENSIBLE means Lookups provided by Oracle where you can add additional codes. Adding a DESCRIPTION of what these codes are for is always a good idea. CODE and MEANING are the only required fields and can be the same value or two different values. CODE is the value that will be sent to you by the credit card provider and is the value that is being mapped. FROM is the earliest date this code can be used, while TO is the last date.

On the same screen, review the expense types that Oracle comes with and add any additional types your company may need. These are found under the lookup type CARD_EXPENSE_TYPE and can be modified to meet your company's needs.

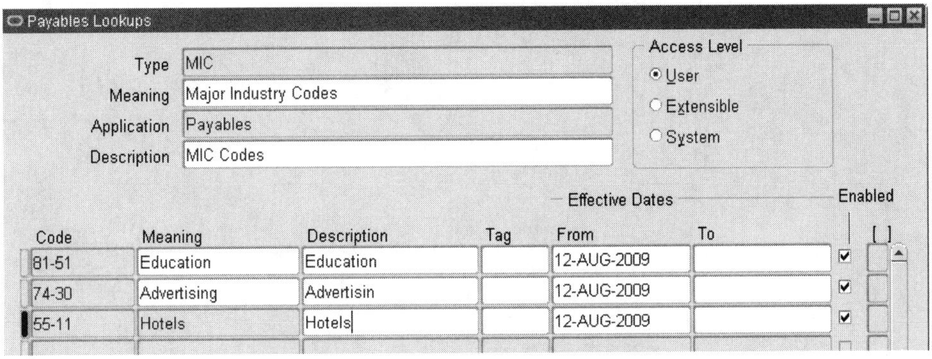

Payables | Setup | Lookups | Payables

FIGURE 7-36.   *Creating a lookup for your credit card classifications*

Creating the Mapping

These two lookups then need to be mapped to each other, creating the link between the credit card company codes and internal codes to Oracle. First, assign a MAPPING RULE name as well as its MEANING, and then select the LOOKUP TYPE that you set up for the credit card codes from the list of values (see Figure 7-37). Then select a default card expense type. This will be used for all codes loaded from the credit card provider that are not mapped. Using the SOURCE LOOKUP CODE, select the code from the provider, then map it to a CARD EXPENSE TYPE and select Add. As a reminder, SOURCE

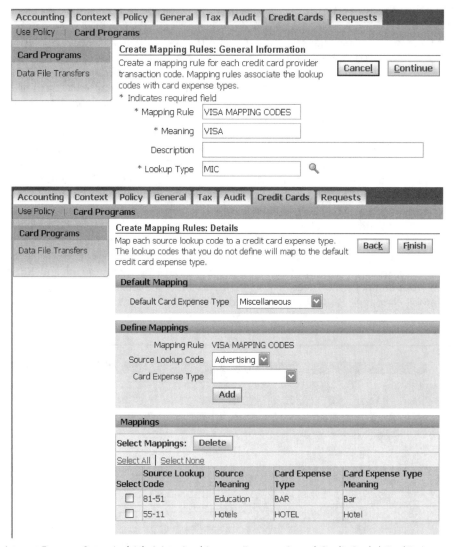

Internet Expenses Setup And Administration I Internet Expenses Setup I Credit Cards I Card Programs

FIGURE 7-37. *Creating mapping rules*

LOOKUP CODE is the lookup codes where you stored the codes from the credit card company, while CARD EXPENSE TYPE is the seeded lookup called CARD_EXPENSE_TYPE.

Assigning Your Card Expense Types to the Templates

The final step is to assign these card expense types to each item on your expense report templates (Payables | Setup | Invoice | Expense Report Templates). By mapping to internal codes, which are global, and then assigning the codes to specific expense types, you assure your mappings can be reused. Click Assign Card Expense Type, and assign each expense type in the Card Expense Type column to one of the Expense Items. While this button is on the top region of the template page, you cannot complete the assignments until your expense items are all entered and saved. Expense items that are set up as VIEWABLE FROM ALL TEMPLATES can also be selected here. If there are card expense types that you do not map, you can add a default Expense Item that will prevent the credit card transaction load from failing.

Loading Credit Card Transactions

The final setup step for processing credit cards is to create the interfaces to load the data from your credit card company. As a Functional Expert, I know all the DBAs and Developers out there will breathe a sigh of relief when I say that advising how to create these interfaces is a little outside the scope of my area of expertise. But I will give you a strong pointer in the right direction: refer to My Oracle Support Note 297919.1, which gives a very good overview of the process. Once these interfaces are created, there are concurrent requests that are run to import the transactions.

Additional Miscellaneous Setups

There are a few additional setups to help make iExpense meet your company's policies and to make it more usable for the employees.

Future-Dated Expenses

In general, expense reports are entered for expenditures that already happened, and not for future expenditures. However, there are exceptions to this rule. For example, an employee who receives a set car allowance that is reimbursed by expense report is requesting a known expense for reimbursement that can be entered ahead of time. Controlling the number of days ahead of the actual expense date can also help prevent duplicate expenses. Tolerances can be added, which control the number of days in advance expense reports can be entered. Both a WARNING and an ERROR TOLERANCE can be set, determining the number of days in advance a user can submit an expense report and receive a warning, or have the system not allow the report to be submitted. These tolerances are set by operating unit. Remember that if you cannot see the operating unit that you want to set, you must activate it in iExpense on the Context tab. These tolerances can be set under Internet Expenses Setup And Administration | Internet Expenses Setup | General | Options | Future Expenses.

Languages for Approval Notes

When your Oracle system is set up to use more than one language (MLS, or Multiple Language Support, as opposed to NLS, or National Language Support, or only one language), then you can select the language that you want the seeded messages to appear in. When this is not set for an operating unit, then the base language for your system is used. The languages are assigned under Internet Expenses Setup And Administration | Internet Expenses Setup | General | Options | Approval Notes Languages.

Setting Up Contact Links

iExpense tends to be rolled out to a large number of employees in an organization, and most of them will probably be casual users, entering expense reports on only a few occasions each year. Providing them with a way to ask questions—not only about how to enter an expense report but also on the company policies for expense reporting—can help streamline the process. There are several flows these questions can follow that come seeded with Oracle. When you are using iSupport, Oracle's support solution for both internal employees and external customers, selecting Contract Us will take the user to the service request flow you have set up. The contact link can also be set up to e-mail your help desk or some other person, or take the users to your help desk web site. This feature can be disabled, and rules can be added to route different organizations, responsibilities, session languages, and users to different email addresses. As this many options can get complicated, Oracle provides the ability to test these rules to ensure users are routed to the right location to get their questions answered.

This feature is not the only way to assist employees in entering their expense reports, and is probably more of a last resort than a first resort for them. As with any self-service application that is going to be rolled out to a large number of casual, or infrequent, users, the more help and tips you can give them, the more self-sufficient they will be. iExpense uses the technology called Oracle Application Framework, or OA Framework, and it allows specific personalizations to be made to the appearance of the system. These company-specific settings usually include such things as hiding fields, making fields that Oracle does not require be required for your instance, and adding tips for the users to follow and to anticipate questions they may have. For more details on setting up OA Framework personalizations, see Chapter 2.

CHAPTER
8

Expense Report Processing

xpense report processing is broken down into four main steps: entering expense reports, management approval, auditing, and exporting to Payables for payment.

High-Level Overview of Expense Report Processing

Before providing the details of how to process expense reports, it is good to understand the high-level steps that take place, as shown in the following illustration. After the employee submits the expense report, it is routed for approval and for auditing at the same time. If it meets the auditing criteria, it must be audited as well as approved prior to being eligible to be exported to Payables. During the export process, Oracle will check if a supplier record is already created for this employee, and if not, it will create one. Then the expense report is created as an invoice, which can be settled with any payment method that is set up in Payables, just like any other invoice.

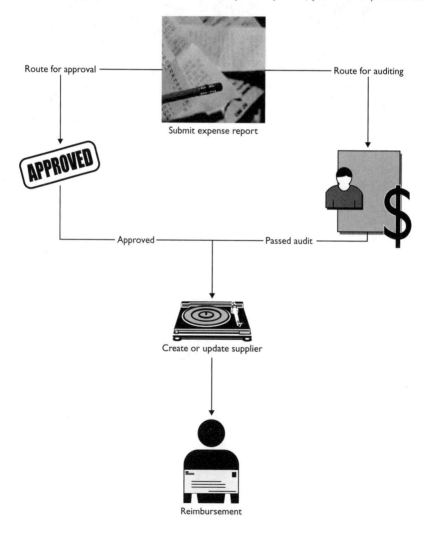

Route for approval ———————— Route for auditing

Submit expense report

APPROVED

——— Approved ——— ——— Passed audit ———

Create or update supplier

Reimbursement

Options for Entering Expense Reports

Expense reports can be created directly in iExpense, entered into a spreadsheet offline and then uploaded, or created from transactions that have been imported for credit card charges.

Access to Create Expense Reports

As a rule, each employee will have access to create his or her own expense reports, but there are times when someone will need access to enter expense reports or approve credit card transactions for another employee. Access is determined by the Securing Attribute ICX_HR_PERSON_ID assigned to a user (System Administrator | Security | User | Define | Securing Attributes tab). This is populated when a PERSON is added to the user record, but additional access can be manually added on the Securing Attribute tab. While the system administrator can grant access by adding this attribute to the user record, it can also be granted from the Access Authorizations page in iExpense, shown in Figure 8-1. Here, you can see who can enter expense reports on your behalf, grant access for someone to enter expense reports for you, and see whom you can enter expense reports for.

This access is only for entering expense reports and monitoring their status; it does not grant access for another user to approve expense reports on your behalf; this can only be done with a Vacation Rule, explained later in the section titled "Vacation Rules and Worklist Access." While you can only remove someone you can enter expense reports for, you can both add and remove users who can enter expense reports on your behalf. Users cannot grant themselves access to enter expense reports for any other users, as they must grant you the access. The NAME that appears on this window is the employee that is associated with a user, not the actual user name. While this should rarely or never happen in a production environment, if an employee is associated to more than one user record, the NAME will appear on the Access Authorization more than one time as well (one for each user it is associated with). The one restriction to adding an Expenses Entry Delegations is that the employee you are adding must be assigned to the same business group as you are. This securing attribute can also be populated by the expense report workflow automatically for credit card transactions, granting access to a supervisor to approve an employee's credit card transaction.

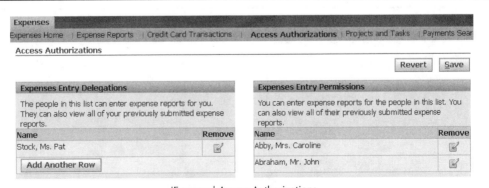

iExpense | Access Authorizations

FIGURE 8-1. *Granting access to enter expense reports*

Direct Entry

Perhaps the most common way to enter an expense report is directly into iExpense. From the Expenses Home, select Create Expense Report to get to the first page of entering expense reports, shown in Figure 8-2. Your NAME will default in, but you have the option of selecting any employee who you have Expenses Entry Permissions for. The person entered here is the employee the reimbursement will be paid or credited to. The DEPARTMENT defaults in from the default expense account associated with the employee record (Payables | Employees | Enter Employees). This field is updatable only when the profile OIE: Enable Cost Center is set to Yes. When this profile is set to No, the field is not visible at all, while Read-Only will allow the person to see the cost center but not update it.

The reimbursement currency is defaulted in from the supplier record that was created the first time an expense report was paid for this employee; and if one does not exist yet, then it will be the functional currency associated with the operating unit on the expense report template. Once a supplier record exists, then the default currency can be updated on the supplier record on the Invoice Management window (Payables | Suppliers | Entry). When Payables is set up to process multiple currencies (Payables | Setup | Options | Payables Options | Currency tab | Use Multiple Currencies), then the employee entering the expense report can select any currency enabled in Oracle to submit the expense report in.

The EXPENSE TEMPLATE will default in from the Payables Options as well, but this time on the Expense Report tab. You can select a different template if more than one is active. This template determines the expense items allowed on an expense report, and the accounting associated with each item, among other things. The PURPOSE can be entered, before selecting an APPROVER for this expense report. While approvers are always required before submitting the expense report, this field will only be populated if the profile OIE: Approver Required is set to Yes With Default; otherwise, you have to select an approver from the list if values before the expense report can be submitted.

Entering Receipt-Based Expenses

Entering the actual expenses is next. Notice that in Figure 8-3, there is more than one tab to enter expense information on; these are based on the Policy Schedules associated with the expense template. When a Policy Schedule includes predefined rates, such as per diems for meals or hotels,

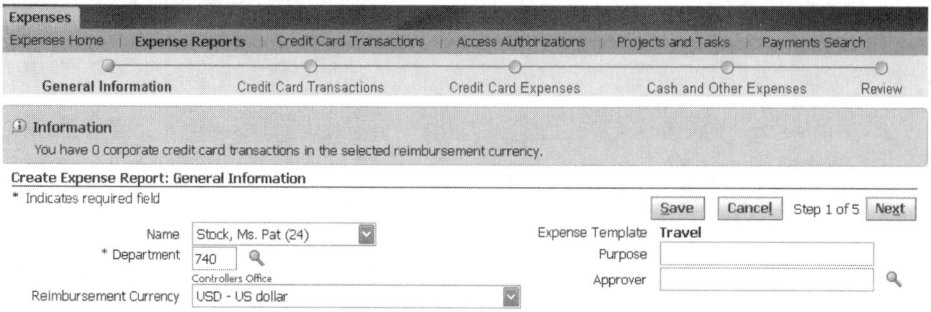

FIGURE 8-2. *Entering expense reports directly into iExpense*

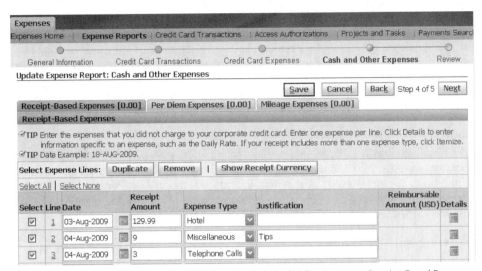

iExpense | Expense Reports | Create Expense Report: Cash And Other Expenses, Receipt-Based Expenses

FIGURE 8-3.   *Entering receipt-based expense items*

or a set amount per mile for mileage, then they will be broken out onto separate tabs for entering expenses. Policy Schedules that do not have rates associated with them, such as Airfare where the airline and flight number are required, will appear on the Receipt-Based tab.

Most of the fields on this screen are self-explanatory, so only a high-level review will be given. The DATE does not determine the accounting date, which is driven by the open periods when the expense report is exported to Payables, and should be the actual date of the expenditure. This date is used to determine if the expense report requires auditing, based on how old the expenses are, as defined in your audit rules (Internet Expenses Setup And Administration | Internet Expenses Setup | Audit), as well as to prevent future-dated expenses, based on the tolerances set (Internet Expenses Setup And Administration | Internet Expenses Setup | General | Options | Future Expenses). The EXPENSE TYPES that are available will correspond to the template that was selected on the prior window, as well as any expense types that were set up as VIEWABLE FROM ALL TEMPLATES. The Details button contains different information for each EXPENSE TYPE, based on the POLICY SCHEDULE that is associated with it on the expense template (Payables | Setup | Invoice | Expense Report Templates—policy schedules are set up in Internet Expenses Setup And Administration | Internet Expenses Setup | Policy | Schedules). Additional information that can be added on the details page includes RECEIPT CURRENCY, EXPENSE LOCATIONS, MERCHANT NAME, ORIGINAL RECEIPT MISSING, as well as ATTACHMENTS.

Many screens in Oracle allow attachments, such as files or additional information, to be added to the data saved on a page. These attachments are available for the auditors to review. After adding a TITLE and DESCRIPTION, enter the CATEGORY of Miscellaneous, Missing Receipts Declaration, Receipts, or Travel Itinerary. Additional categories can be added by the system administrator using the OA Framework personalization feature. Next, select the type of attachment. FILE allows you to use the Browse button to upload a file, such as scanned copy of a receipt, to the expense report. URL allows you to put a web address on this expense report, while TEXT can add more information when the justification field does not provide enough room.

Back on the Details screen, you can add additional lines by clicking New. The line can also be Removed from the expense report, or Duplicated to a new line. The final option available before returning to the expense page is to itemize your expenses. When a policy schedule is created, Itemization Required is one of the options, and when selected, will make this section required when entering expense reports and cause the itemization page to automatically display. If it is not required, the employee still has the option of itemizing an expense by clicking Itemization. Itemization allows you to enter multiple expenditure types for one line item on an expense report, and is most helpful when a receipt includes multiple types of expenses, such as a hotel bill that includes meals.

Entering Per Diem Expenses

Per diem expenses are added on the next tab and are classified where a flat rate is paid for a specific expense type, as opposed to being reimbursed for the actual out-of-pocket expenses. After the START DATE, EXPENSE TYPE, DESTINATION, and NUMBER OF DAYS are entered, click Calculate to determine the REIMBURSABLE AMOUNT for the line, shown in Figure 8-4. On the Details page, the per diem is calculated with the Generate Per Diem button instead.

Entering Mileage Expenses

Mileage reimbursement works very similarly to the per diem expenses, where the reimbursable amount is calculated off of the unit of measure and trip distance, as well as type of vehicle and number of passengers, if this option was selected on the policy schedule.

Once the expense items are added, a summary page is provided to review prior to submitting the expense report. The Printable Page that is generated after the expense report is submitted can include a bar code when the profile OIE: Enable Bar Code is set to Yes. When this is printed and included with the receipts when they are sent to accounting, the auditors can find the expense report with this bar code and a scanner, as opposed to the expense report number.

Uploading Expense Reports from a Spreadsheet

The upload feature allows an expense report to be created in a spreadsheet, offline from Oracle, and then uploaded at a later date. "Upload" is a bit of a confusing term here, because unlike other areas of Oracle where an upload is done either via an interface table, such as Journal Entries

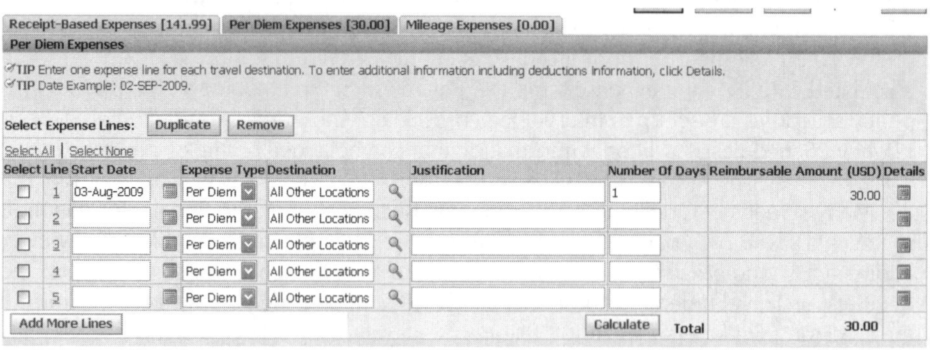

iExpense | Expense Reports | Create Expense Report: Cash And Other Expenses, Per Diem Expenses

FIGURE 8-4. *Entering per diem expenses*

created via ADI (Application Desktop Integrator), or by using the Browse button to find a file to load directly to the database, expense reports are entered into the spreadsheet and then copied and pasted directly into iExpense, where the data will populate the proper fields. There are several steps to using the spreadsheet feature. First, you must *export* the spreadsheet, which you can then open in Excel and complete the expense report. After copying the complete expense report in Excel, it is *imported,* where you can review the data prior to *submitting* the expense report for approval, auditing, and processing. Before using this feature, be sure you modify the spreadsheet to match your company's templates, otherwise errors will occur when uploading an expense report.

Configuring the Spreadsheet

In order to configure the spreadsheet, find the file in the Oracle directory $AP_TOP/html/US called apwexpmc.xls. Once you have this file, you can make the changes that are needed, such as adding the expense template name, or making a field required, or removing fields you do not need. You want to make sure that the spreadsheet is as easy for the users to follow as entering an expense report directly in Oracle. After it is modified, save the spreadsheet back to the same directory, but use a different name.

Next, you need to create a new function to include on the iExpense menu that will call your new spreadsheet. This is done in System Administrator (Application I Function). The seeded function that comes with Oracle for the seeded spreadsheet is called AP_WEB_DOWNLOAD. While you should not modify this one, you can use it as a guide, using all the same fields, but updating the HTML Call to call your modified spreadsheet instead of the seeded one. This new function then needs to be linked to the iExpense menu that you are using. On the seeded expense report menus, the menu that needs to be modified is OIE_SHORTCUTS, where you want to replace the function Download Expense Spreadsheet with the one you just created. If you want to add more than one expense report spreadsheet, then you will need to first add additional buttons using the OA Framework Personalizations feature. Once the new function is added to the menu, ensure you bounce the Apache server to make it available in iExpense.

Exporting the Spreadsheet and Completing the Expense Report

Exporting the spreadsheet is simple—click the Export Spreadsheet button on the home page of iExpense, and save the file on your computer. Once it is dowloaded, it can be opened in Excel and your specific expenses can be added. Figure 8-5 shows the seeded expense report spreadsheet.

Expense Report

Expense Cost Center	740
Reimbursement Currency	USD - US dollar
Purpose	Training
Expense Template	Travel
Approver	A Bakker
Total	100.00

Line	Start Date	Days	Daily Rate	Receipt Amount	Receipt Currency	Exchange Rate	Reimbursable Amount	Expense Type	Project Number	Task Number	Award Number	Receipt Missing	Expen Group
1	31-Aug-2009	1		100.00	USD - US dollar	1.	100.00	Car Rental					
2		0		0.00	USD - US dollar	1.	0.00						
3		0		0.00	USD - US dollar	1.	0.00						
4		0		0.00	USD - US dollar	1.	0.00						
5		0		0.00	USD - US dollar	1.	0.00						
6		0		0.00	USD - US dollar	1.	0.00						

FIGURE 8-5. *Seeded expense report spreadsheet*

The information entered here will have to comply with your template and any policies that are associated with it. For example, if a justification is required for a specific expense type on your template, then you must enter it on the spreadsheet prior to uploading it; otherwise, you will receive an error message when it is uploaded. The good news is that the error messages are very clear and will make sense to most users. While you may want to save the spreadsheet file for future reference, it is not required to upload the data into Oracle. That is done by copying and pasting the information.

Importing Expense Reports

Back in iExpense, click Import Spreadsheet to open up the Import window. Again, this is more of a copy and paste than an actual import. The way it works is that you copy the entire colored portion of the spreadsheet and then paste (Edit | Paste in Oracle) it into the SPREADSHEET IMPORT AREA, as shown in Figure 8-6. Once it is pasted, click Continue if you want to make any changes, or Skip To Review to see a recap of the expense report prior to submitting it for approval. If there are any problems with the data, such as a justification missing, an error message will inform you of the problem, which will need to be fixed on the spreadsheet, which then must be recopied into Oracle to proceed. To recopy a spreadsheet, ensure you use the Clear button before pasting the new data into Oracle.

Importing and Approving Credit Card Transactions

iExpense can be set up to import transactions from your credit card company so that the employees can approve them for payment. Transactions are imported into Oracle by running a concurrent request. Oracle comes seeded with several predefined loads programs, or your company may write a custom one, depending on who your credit card provider is. The predefined processes all contain Transaction Loader and Validation Program as part of the concurrent request name. The way this process works is that the transaction file, in the proper format, is saved in the Oracle database, where the loader and validation programs will process the data and make it available in iExpense for the employees to approve the transactions. These concurrent requests are request sets assigned to Payables; they are called American Express Transaction Load and Validate; Bank of America Visa

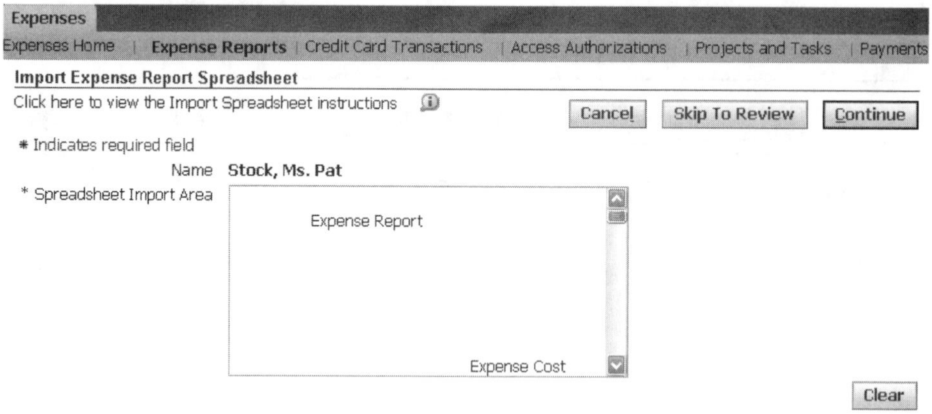

FIGURE 8-6. *Importing an expense report spreadsheet*

Transaction Preformat, Load, and Validate; Diner's Club Transaction Load and Validate; MasterCard CDF Transaction Load and Validate; MasterCard Transaction Preformat, Load, and Validate; and US Bank Visa Transaction Preformat, Load, and Validate.

Administering Credit Card Transactions

You can view the credit card transactions that have been uploaded into iExpense from the Internet Expenses Setup And Administration responsibility by using the Internet Expenses Administration link. On the Transactions window, search and review transactions that have been uploaded. This is not how users approve the expenses for payment, which is done in iExpense by submitting an expense report that includes the credit card transactions, covered in the next section, "Submitting Credit Card Transactions on an Expense Report." This allows the credit card administrator to see the credit cards that have been uploaded, and if the transactions were invalid or if they need additional information. The usual problems during an upload are an unmapped category or an employee / employee card that is not mapped properly.

When a credit card transaction is uploaded and the employee mapping did not exist, Oracle creates one for you that is then reviewed and approved by the credit card administrator. This is done under the New Accounts window. Here, you will see the card name, the employee it was mapped to, and the status. The administrator will need to be either activated or deleted and set up correctly to process the credit card transactions for this employee.

When an employee has left the company but still has outstanding credit card transactions, you can run the concurrent request Credit Card Transactions Inactive Employees process, which will send the credit card transactions to the employee's supervisor for review and approval. Running this process actually adds the employee to the supervisor's user account under the Securing Attribute ICX_HR_PERSON_ID (System Administrator | Security | User | Define).

At times, credit card lines are never submitted by employees on expense reports. This is most common when employees are responsible for at least part of the credit card payment, where they do not submit personal expenses. These transactions can be removed so that the employee is no longer prompted to submit an expense report for them using the concurrent request called Credit Card Historical Transactions Management. This will deactivate all transactions that are older than the Posted End Date entered when the request is submitted. This process can be reversed by running the same process and activating the transactions again.

Submitting Credit Card Transactions on an Expense Report

When you first click Create Expense Report, Oracle will inform you if you have any outstanding credit card transactions pending submission (see Figure 8-7). The next window will display the

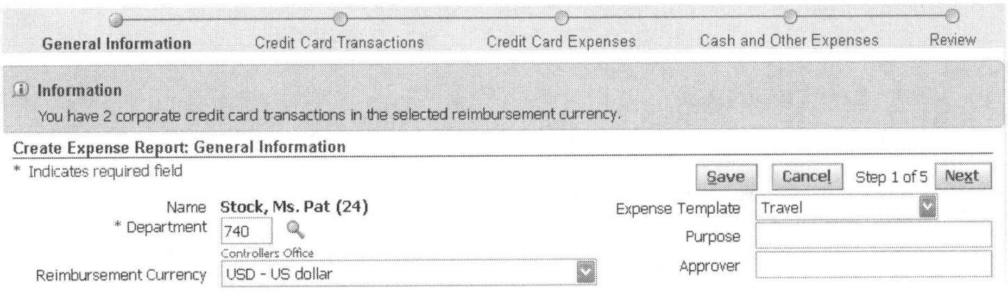

FIGURE 8-7. *Credit card transactions notification on expense report*

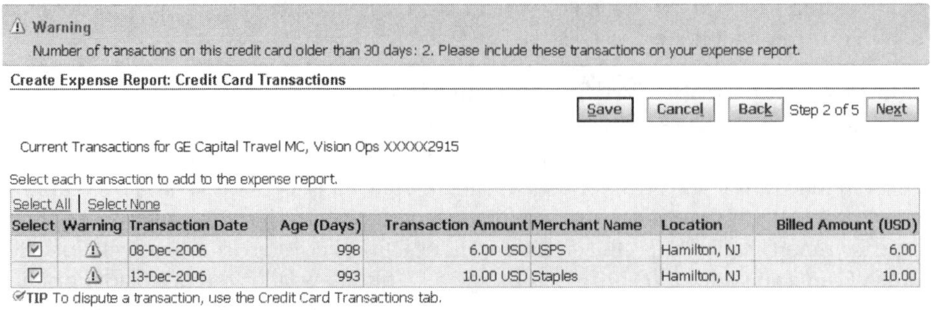

FIGURE 8-8. *Credit card transactions to include on expense report*

actual credit card transactions, allowing the user to select them for inclusion on the expense report. Depending on how your credit card use policies were set up (Internet Expenses Setup And Administration | Internet Expenses Setup | Credit Cards | Use Policy | Transaction Submission), you may be restricted from submitting an expense report without the credit card transactions being included on it. This is the message that appears in Figure 8-8.

Then you are able to add an EXPENSE TYPE and JUSTIFICATION to each line, as well as any details that need to be added. Sometimes, a corporate credit card is used for a personal expense, or non-reimbursable expense, during business travel. Select that line and Categorize As Personal, as shown in Figure 8-9. How Oracle processes these personal transactions will depend on what type of credit card program the card is set up as. When the credit card is set up as a Company Pay program, where your company pays the credit card directly for all expenses, Oracle will ensure the credit card company is paid in full for both the personal and business expenses, but will

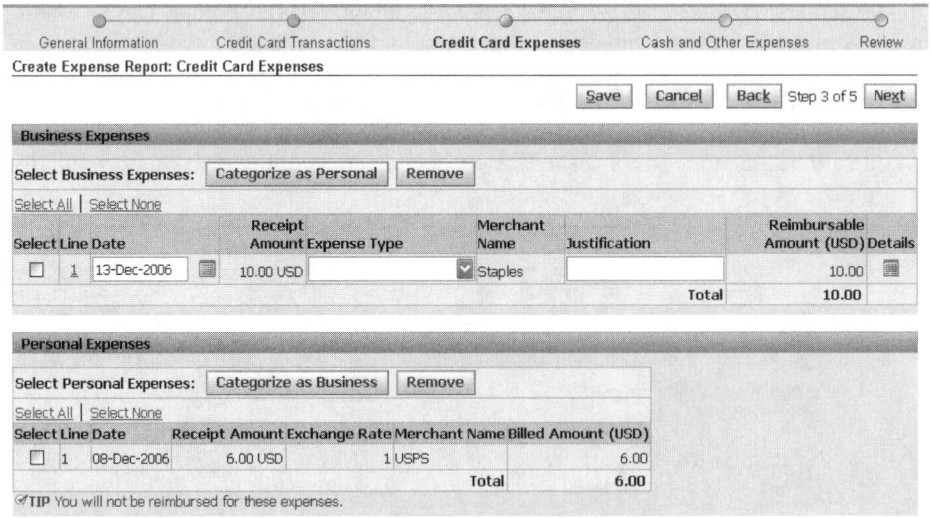

FIGURE 8-9. *Classifying credit card transactions as Personal or Business*

reduce any funds owed to the employee by the amount of the personal expenses; if no funds are due to the employee on this expense report, then a credit memo is created in accounts payables and reduced from the next cash expense report submitted.

If the credit card is set up to be paid by each employee individually, Oracle generates a check to the employee for the amount of the credit card transactions, as opposed to the credit card company. Under this scenario, the amount reimbursed to the employee will only be for business expenses and will not include any credit card transactions classified as personal. The final option is where both the employee and the company pay the credit card company, depending on if it is a personal or business expense. In this option, the invoice that is generated for the credit card company is only for the amount of the business expenses, and there are no payables transactions generated for the personal expenses; it is up to the individual employee to pay the credit card company for this amount. By default, all expenses are classified as Business. At this point, you can add non–credit card expenses before submitting the expense report for approval.

Disputing Credit Card Transactions

There are times when an expense is double-charged on the credit card, or perhaps the product or services were defective, and the credit card transaction needs to be disputed. This can be done using the Credit Card Transactions window, Disputed Transactions. A dispute can only be logged against a transaction that has not been selected on an expense report, even if the expense report is only saved and not yet submitted. When you click the Dispute link next to the transaction, you can provide a REASON before saving it. This feature does not actually submit any information to the credit card company, but it will allow the user to submit an expense report without including the disputed item. In order to file the actual dispute with the credit card company, you must contact them directly. The item can remain in dispute indefinitely, or it can be ended and submitted for payment by clicking the Update link next to the disputed item, on the same page.

Approving Expense Reports

How your company's system is set up will determine not only the path an expense report will follow for approval, but also if an expense report must be approved at all. Oracle evaluates the approval rules and will forward the expense report to the appropriate approver in the form of a notification that can be responded to in Oracle or from e-mail. Besides reviewing the information on the expense report with the link at the bottom of the page, as well as any receipts that were attached to the expense report, approvers have the option to Approve, Reject, Reassign, or Request Information. When an expense report is rejected, it is returned to the person who owns it, and can be either modified and resubmitted or deleted from the system. Reassign allows the approver to either Delegate or Transfer the expense report to another person, the same as a vacation rule would (see the later section "Vacation Rules and Worklist Access"). These options are also controlled by the profile WF: Notification Reassign Mode, same as vacation rules. Request Information will send a notification to the employee the expense report is for or to any user in the system, allowing you to answer any questions you may have on this expense report. This expense report will remain on your notification list until you approve or reject it.

Approving Executive Expense Reports

Every organization has one person who is usually the ultimate approver for all transactions. This is usually the CEO or President of the company. Oracle has a problem determining who approves the person at the top when approvals are set up as hierarchical. Most corporate policies will have someone, such as the Vice President of Human Resources, designated as the CEO's approver for expenses. When you are using AME to determine the approver for an expense report (or any other document), this is not a problem, because non-hierarchical rules can be created. When you are using the standard supervisor hierarchy, it is a problem, because the Vice President of Human Resources will ultimately report to the CEO, and having the CEO report to him or her will cause the equivalent of a Circular Reference in Oracle and the Approval Workflow will error out because it cannot find an approver. Since the CEO, or other top-level position, often has the largest expense reports, and the least amount of tolerance for not getting them paid, you need to ensure Oracle is set up to accommodate these situations.

In this case, I usually set up an employee called Top-Level Approver, and have the CEO report to it. Ensure this "employee" is set up with the proper department and dollar value for expense report approvals (Payables Manager | Employees | Signing Limits). Then set up a vacation rule for this employee and have all notifications go to the person who should be approving their expense report, in the case of my example, the VP of Human Resources. The approver will appear as Top-Level Approver, but I can demonstrate, with the vacation rule, that this person is really the VP of Human Resources by showing the auditors the vacation rule. Ensure before using this option that the CEO has unlimited approval in all areas, and that the approval workflows do not time out for the CEO and move on up the chain; this will prevent other workflows from forwarding to the Top Level Approver, such as purchase orders.

Vacation Rules and Worklist Access

In all organizations, approvers are out of the office from time to time, whether it be for personal time off or on business travel to some exotic place where Internet access is not as readily available, and their absence may interfere with expense report approvals. Oracle allows two different features to assist when this situation arises: Vacation Rules and Worklist Access. Vacation Rules allows users to temporarily *delegate* or *transfer* ownership of specific types of notifications to other users, while Worklist Access determines if other users can see and respond to items outstanding on your worklist, and *delegates* your authority for responding to these items. From an Oracle standpoint, there is a major difference between *delegating* your authority, either with a vacation rule or a worklist, and *transferring* a notification, only available with vacation rules.

Delegation literally means to assign the authority and responsibility to act upon on your behalf, and it means the same thing in Oracle. When you delegate your notification, you are also delegating the authority to act on your behalf of these notifications, including any approval authority you may have. Oracle considers any delegated notification to still be owned by you, and it will record your name and are subject to your approval limits on any actions taken against the notification on your behalf. Transfer, on the other hand, literally transfers not only the notification but also the authority to act upon it to another person, and it is that other person's approval authority and position in the hierarchy that are considered when they respond to a notification. Because of these differences, there are both pros and cons to each feature.

Delegation will allow someone who, based on a company's policy, may not have the authority to approve a transaction to be able to decide and act upon the approval. And it will record the name of a person who did not physically approve it on the transaction. This may cause some audit or legal problems.

The good news is there is a profile to control access to how vacations rules can assign access: WF: Notification Reassign Mode. This can be set to allow Transfers only, Delegate only, or Reassign, which allows the user to decide whether to delegate or transfer authority.

Transfer, on the other hand, requires that not only the person to whom the transactions were transferred, but potentially that person's supervisors as well, have the ability to approve expenses for a specific department. Once the notification is transferred to the new person, it will follow that person's supervisor or position hierarchy until the final approver is found. In order for this feature to work, additional setups may need to be turned on and off during vacations for approval limits, but the benefit to doing this is that the person who actually approved the transaction is recorded in the system. Since both users can see these notifications, some companies use this feature during peak activities, in essence having two users monitoring the notifications and responding to them. This can only be controlled by using the OA Framework Personalization to remove access to this feature.

To set up a vacation rule, see the section in Chapter 4 called "Vacation Rules." Note that both Vacation Rules and Worklist Access can be maintained by the workflow administrator, as well as the user who wants to delegate or transfer the notifications. They cannot be set up by the person who is getting the access.

Granting Worklist Access

Worklist Access is granted by using the Worklist Access link on the bottom of the iExpense home page. When granting access, you will need to enter the employee's NAME, and you can assign a START DATE and an END DATE to the access. Then decide to GRANT ACCESS TO All Item Types, or only Selected Item Types. The items that are available to you under the Selected Item Types are any workflow items that you have previously received a notification for. The option to select All Item Types is controlled by the profile option WF: Vacation Rules – Allow All. When this is set to Enable, you can grant access to All Item Types. When this is set to Disable, you must select the specific item types you want to grant access to.

Once you have granted someone access to your notifications, the Switch User button will appear in the Notifications region of the iExpense home page. You will need to click this and select the user you want to see the notifications for. This is different than a vacation rule, where the notifications will appear on your notification list; you can only view the notifications for one user at a time. This also means that if you are receiving your notifications via e-mail, the owner of the notification will still receive the e-mail, and not the person who has been granted access to your worklist.

Auditing

Oracle's auditing feature allows you to review expense reports for policy compliance, for receipts, and for any suspicious reimbursement requests. This feature works hand in hand with the policy schedules that you have defined in your system (Internet Expenses Setup And Administration | Internet Expenses Setup | Policy and Audit windows). Using the Oracle auditing features, expense reports are selected for audit when receipts are required, when a policy is violated, by a random selection, and according to an audit list, which can be maintained either by Oracle, based on policy violations, or by the auditors for the employees in question.

Maintaining the Audit List

Audit lists are stored in Oracle and determine employees whose expense reports require additional auditing either because of policy violations, or when an auditor adds the employee manually to the list. Oracle will automatically add employees to the audit list based on the Audit Rules that are set up (Internet Expenses Setup And Administration | Internet Expenses Setup |

Audit | Audit Rules | Audit Rule Setup). When an expense report meets one of the rules, then it will require auditing prior to being processed through to Payables for Payment. Audit rules select expense reports for auditing based on random selection, credit transactions, dollar limits, when a receipt or justification is required, when a policy is violated, the age of the expenses, and when an employee is inactive, or end dated, in the system or does not include an advance. The audit list is maintained by Oracle when receipts are delinquent, when the expense report exceeds a specific dollar amount, when a policy is violated, or when more than a certain number of expense reports are submitted for a given month. You can also set the time period an employee will stay on the audit list. Employees on the audit list can be viewed in the Maintain Audit List window (Internet Expenses Auditor | Expenses Audit | Maintain Audit List). From here, you can view who is currently or was in the past on the audit list, the reason, and when the audit period started and ended. You can also add someone to the audit list manually.

When an expense report has a policy violation for a dollar amount, Oracle allows the policy schedules to be set up with both a limit and a tolerance. A policy violation occurs when the amount exceeds the limits set up, but will still process the expense report if it is within the tolerance. There is also a profile that controls how violations are processed, called OIE: Enable Policy. This can be set to prevent expense reports with violations from being submitted, to warn the user that there was a violation but allow submission, or to inform the approver of the violation and allow submission.

Auditing Expense Reports

There are two main aspects to auditing expense reports: for receipts, and a general review to all other types of violations. Auditing receipts has two parts, and companies will often set different policies for each part. Part one is receiving the actual receipt package, and the second part involves verifying the receipts to the expense report. To receive an expense package, as shown in Figure 8-10, use the Receive Receipt Package window (Internet Expenses Auditor | Expenses

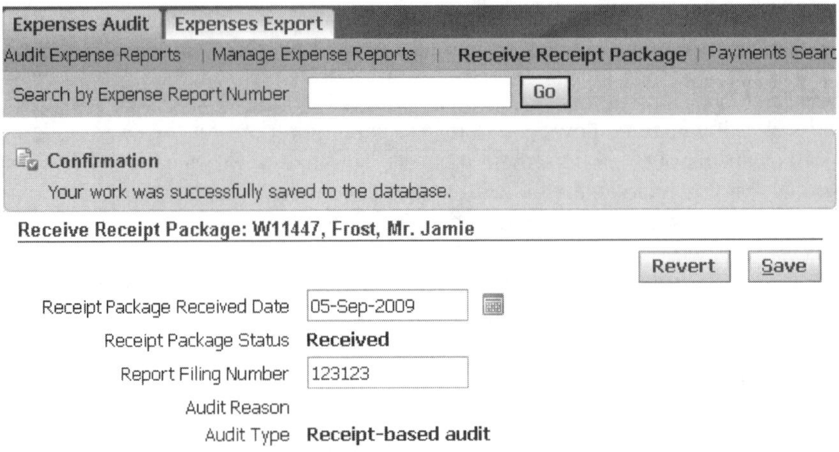

Internet Expenses Auditor | Expenses Audit | Receive Receipt Package

FIGURE 8-10. *Receiving receipt packages*

Audit | Receive Receipt Package). Add the REPORT FILING NUMBER, and click Save. This will update the RECEIPT PACKAGE STATUS to Received.

The second part, validating the receipts to the expense report, is a manual verification where an employee matches the actual receipts to the amounts submitted on the expense report. Once each line is verified, the auditor checks the box Receipt Verified, on the Audit Expense Report window.

Oracle tracks several different statuses on expense reports, including both who has reviewed the expenses report and the status of the expense report in Payables. Table 8-1 shows the different approval statuses and their meaning, while Table 8-2 explains the actual expense report statuses. These statuses are important for auditors, iExpense administrators, and the employees processing expense reports.

Figure 8-11 shows the auditors' view of an expense report with a policy violation. From here, the auditors can review the violation and any justification provided by the employee, and either approve the expense report as is or change the actual amount that is going to be reimbursed. When this is done, the employee receives a notification of the change, as well as the AUDIT ISSUE added by the auditor. Auditors can also verify the receipts and add the date the receipt package was received before marking the EXPENSE REPORT ACTION as Complete Audit, allowing it to be processed to the next step. Auditors have the ability to reject expense reports or request more information. On the Auditor Only Notes tab, additional notes can be added to the expense report for future reference.

The auditor responsibility is also a good starting point for troubleshooting expense reports that will not process to Payables, by reviewing the status of the approvals.

Status	Meaning
AP Status, Hold	The expense report is on payment hold.
AP Status, Invoice Created	Expense report has been exported into Payables.
AP Status, Paid	Expense report has been settled, either with the application of an advance or an actual payment.
AP Status, Partially Paid	Only a portion of the expense report has been settled, either with an advance or an actual payment.
Reviewed By Autoapproved	Autoapproved is checked when no auditing was required for this expense report.
Reviewed By Management	Marked by Oracle when a manager with the appropriate approval limits approves an expense report.
Reviewed by Payables	Payables reviews all expense reports that required either receipts or justification. This can either be checked manually by the payables expense administrator, or by Oracle when a receipt packages is received for an expense report.

TABLE 8-1. *Expense Approval Statuses*

Expense Report Status	Meaning
Cancelled	Cancelled by user.
Hold Pending Receipts	Expense report is on hold and waiting for receipts to be received by Payables.
In Progress	Expense reports were not saved or submitted by the person entering it, and the Cancel button was used to exit the expense report during entry.
Paid	Expense report is settled by either an advance application or an actual payment.
Partially Paid	Expense report is only partially settled by either an advance application or an actual payment.
Payables Approved	Expense report has been approved by Payables for receipts, justification, and auditing.
Pending Individual's Approval	This status is used when an expense report was submitted by one person on behalf of another employee; when this process is done, the employee whose name is on the expense report must approve it for submission before it is routed for management approval.
Pending Manager Approval	Waiting for a manager with the proper approval limits to approve the expense report.
Pending Payables Approval	Expense report is approved by a manager but is waiting for Payables approval for receipts, justification, or auditing for other reasons.
Pending Payment	Selected for payment, but the payment batch is not yet completed.
Pending System Administrator Action	Indicates that there is a problem with the information on the expense report and the workflow cannot determine how to proceed. The two most common problems are that there is no manager with the proper authority to approve the expense report, or the General Ledger account number that was generated is no longer valid.
Pending your Resolution	Expense report requires action from the person who submitted it for various reasons, including policy violations or audit questions.
Ready for Invoicing	Expense report has been approved and is ready to be exported to Payables.
Ready for Payment	Expense report is exported to Payables and ready to be paid.
Rejected	Expense report has been rejected by the auditor and is sent back to the employee for revision or cancellation.
Returned	Returned by the system administrator to correct information that prevented the expense report from being processed, such as approvers or account numbers.
Saved	User saved expense report but has not yet submitted it for approval and payment.
Submitted	Expense report has been submitted and is waiting for workflow to start the approval process.
Unused	Credit card transactions that are deactivated will be marked as unused.
Withdrawn	Expense reports that are still in the approval and audit process can be withdrawn, causing them not to be processed unless they are resubmitted. Once an expense report is exported to Payables, it can no longer be withdrawn.

TABLE 8-2. *Expense Report Statuses*

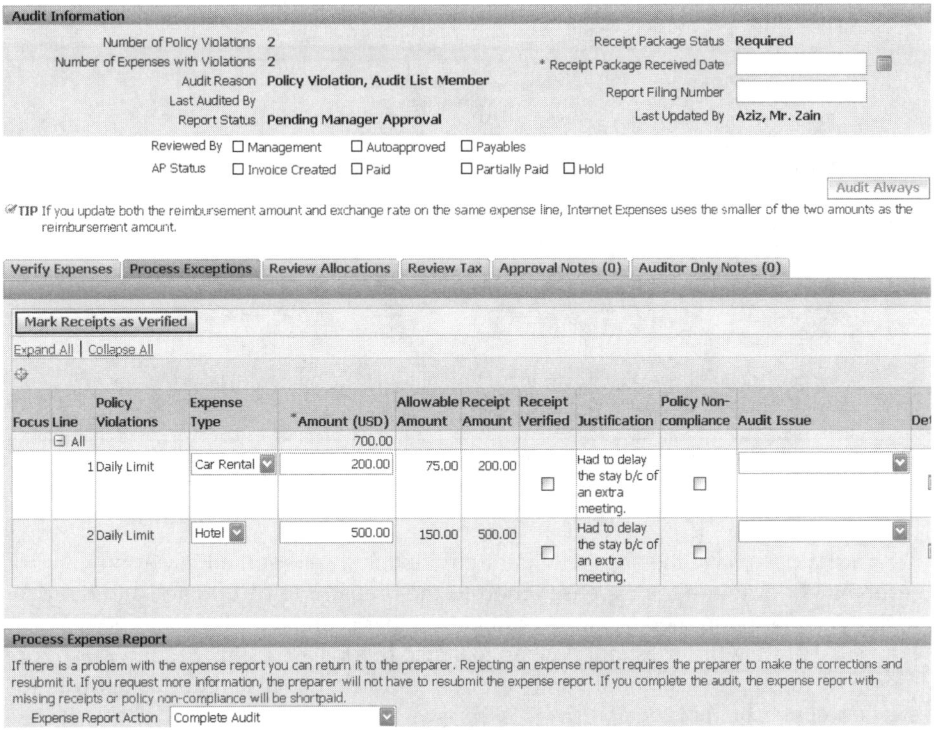

Audit Information

Number of Policy Violations	2	Receipt Package Status	**Required**
Number of Expenses with Violations	2	* Receipt Package Received Date	
Audit Reason	**Policy Violation, Audit List Member**	Report Filing Number	
Last Audited By		Last Updated By	**Aziz, Mr. Zain**
Report Status	**Pending Manager Approval**		

Reviewed By ☐ Management ☐ Autoapproved ☐ Payables
AP Status ☐ Invoice Created ☐ Paid ☐ Partially Paid ☐ Hold

Audit Always

☞**TIP** If you update both the reimbursement amount and exchange rate on the same expense line, Internet Expenses uses the smaller of the two amounts as the reimbursement amount.

Verify Expenses | **Process Exceptions** | Review Allocations | Review Tax | Approval Notes (0) | Auditor Only Notes (0)

Mark Receipts as Verified

Expand All | Collapse All

Focus Line		Policy Violations	Expense Type	*Amount (USD)	Allowable Amount	Receipt Amount	Receipt Verified	Justification	Policy Non-compliance	Audit Issue	Det
	☐ All			700.00							
1		Daily Limit	Car Rental	200.00	75.00	200.00	☐	Had to delay the stay b/c of an extra meeting.	☐		
2		Daily Limit	Hotel	500.00	150.00	500.00	☐	Had to delay the stay b/c of an extra meeting.	☐		

Process Expense Report

If there is a problem with the expense report you can return it to the preparer. Rejecting an expense report requires the preparer to make the corrections and resubmit it. If you request more information, the preparer will not have to resubmit the expense report. If you complete the audit, the expense report with missing receipts or policy non-compliance will be shortpaid.
Expense Report Action Complete Audit

Internet Expenses Auditor | Expenses Audit | Audit Expense Reports

FIGURE 8-11. *Auditors' view of an expense report with a policy violation*

Exporting to Payables

Once an expense report has been approved and audited, it needs to be exported to Payables, where it is processed the same as any other invoice. This can be done by using the expense report auditor responsibility, using the Expense Export window, or submitting a concurrent request in Payables called Expense Report Export. The invoices created in Payables will have an Invoice Type of Expense Report and are visible from the Invoice Workbench (Payables | Invoices | Entry | Invoices) and Payables Expense Report (Payables | Invoices | Entry | Expense Reports) screens. If you do not have Oracle set up to automatically create suppliers for employees when expense reports are exported to Payables (Payables | Setup | Options | Payables Options | Expense Report tab | Automatically Create Employee As Supplier), you will need to create any missing suppliers prior to running this process.

Common Expense Report Workflow Errors

The most common expense report workflow error is that the system cannot find a supervisor for an employee and therefore cannot forward the expense report for approval. This will cause the workflow to inform the administrator that there was no approver found, and allow the

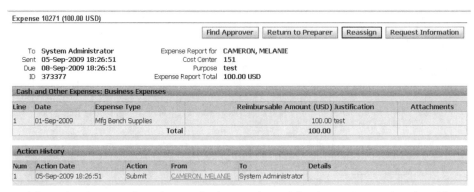

Workflow Administrator Web Applications | Administrator Workflow | Status Monitor | Find workflow and click Notifications link

FIGURE 8-12. *Expense report without a valid approver*

administrator to have the approval hierarchy updated so that the Find Approver process can be resubmitted, or return the expense report to the preparer to be updated and reprocessed. These actions can be performed from the notification that is created from the workflow, shown in Figure 8-12. I see this most often when expense reports are using a supervisor or position hierarchy for approvals, and the person submitting the expense report is allowed to change the cost center but not the approver.

iExpense Preferences

Preferences are user-specific settings that users can update, which will control specific default information on expense reports. These are broken down into two sections: general preferences, and My Allocations. These are all accessed from the Preferences link at the top of the window.

General iExpense Preferences

General preferences control the TEMPLATE, APPROVER, PURPOSE, LOCATION, and VEHICLE TYPE that will default on the expense report. You can either set up defaults that are used every time as EXPENSES PREFERENCES or use the information entered on the PRIOR EXPENSE REPORT. Note that approver is an option only if the profile OIE: Enable Approver is *not* set to No (see Figure 8-13).

There are two additional Data Entry Preferences. First is to ENABLE ACCOUNT ALLOCATIONS. This option is visible only when the profile OIE: Enable Expense Allocations is set to User-Enabled or User-Enabled, with Online Validation; it will be set at the user level when it is selected either automatically or by the user. The option to ENFORCE REQUIRED FIELDS ON DETAILS PAGE works with any personalizations your company has made to make a non-required field required in your instance. This flag ensures that it is required prior to submitting the expense report.

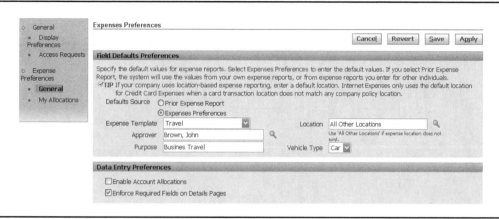

FIGURE 8-13. *Setting a user's general expense preferences*

Allocation Expense Preferences

Using the My Allocations link, users can add either Project or Account allocations for assignment to expense report lines. Project allocations are allowed only when the profile OIE: Enable Project Allocations is enabled, and account allocations when OIE: Enable Expense Allocations is not set to No, and the General Preference ENABLE ACCOUNT ALLOCATIONS is selected.

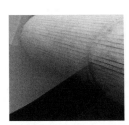

CHAPTER
9

iReceivables Setup

Receivables is a web-based application that provides customers information related to Accounts Receivable and allows payments to be submitted as well as credit requests. Like iSupplier, it includes both internal and external views, but unlike the Order Information Portal, the data is restricted to invoiced transactions and contains no order or delivery information. At the very minimum, iReceivables requires that Oracle Receivables be set up. Bill Presentment Architecture, an interface to the BI (Business Intelligence, formally known as XML) Publisher, must also be set up to design the invoices that are available in iReceivables to view and print. Additional setups include deciding how credit requests are approved, and processing for credit card and wire payment submitted via iReceivables.

Setting Up Internal Users

iReceivables is a great inquiry-only way to roll out receivables information to non-accounting personnel, such as Sales and Customer Service representatives. With the iReceivables Internal responsibility, employees can quickly access customer information, such as invoice and payment history, as well as reprint invoices or statements. Other than assigning the responsibility to the users, there are no additional steps required to using iReceivables internally.

Setting Up External Users and TCA Overview

Before an external user can be granted access to iReceivables, that user must first be entered as a contact for a customer that is classified as an *Organization,* or an actual customer that is classified as a *Person*. When you add a contact to the Customer, ensure you classify the contact as a Self Service User, under the Contact Roles (see Figure 9-1).

Unlike Payables self-service modules, iReceivables does not use any securing attributes to restrict data for external users; instead it uses a customer contact that is associated with both the customer and the user. A customer contact in Oracle is defined as either a customer that is classified as a Person, a Contact added to a customer, or a Relationship set up between a contact that is already set up in Oracle and the customer.

In order to create the external user, you will need to know the contact name that is associated with or related to the customer. While this sounds quite simple, both customers and contacts are part of Oracle's Trading Community Architecture (TCA), which is a complex series of relationships

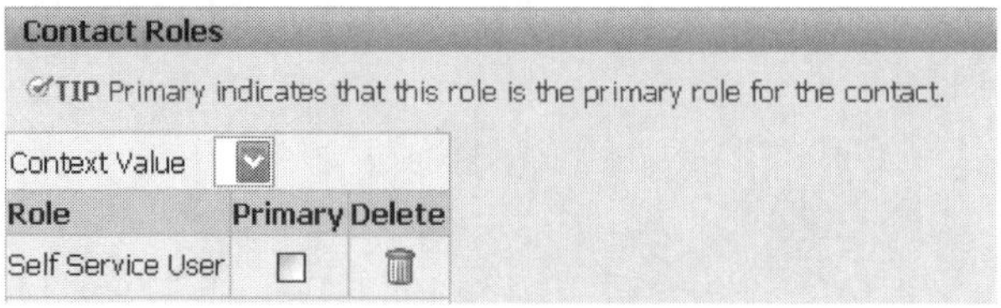

Contact Roles

☑**TIP** Primary indicates that this role is the primary role for the contact.

Context Value ▼

Role	Primary	Delete
Self Service User	☐	🗑

Receivables | Customers | Customers | Account Details |
Communication | Details | Contact Roles

FIGURE 9-1. *Adding a role to a customer contact for iReceivables*

between Organizations (customers, suppliers, and banks) and Persons (customer contacts, supplier contacts, bank contacts, and customers that are not actual entities but individuals, and employees). While understanding TCA and how it works is a book all by itself, understanding this at a 90,000-foot view is important when selecting the contacts to associate with customers.

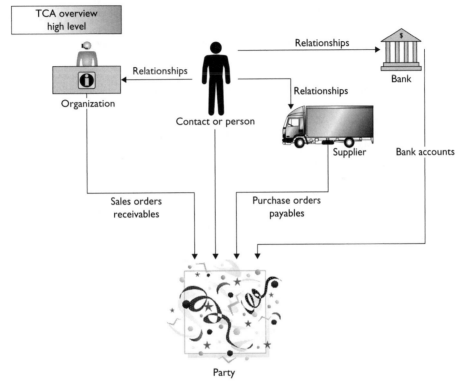

TCA overview, 90,000-foot view

TCA is a hierarchical organization of the community that your company does business with, where Party is at the highest level. Basically, every entry made for customers, contacts, relationships, banks, and suppliers will create a Party within TCA. All Parties are designated as an Organization, usually representing a legal business entity, or a Person, representing an individual as opposed to a business. When a Party is assigned an Account, it is classified as a customer and can have transactions associated with it in both Receivables and Order Management; a Party without an account cannot. It is important to understand that customers have Accounts while contacts do not. Customers and contacts can both be related to each other, building a network of interrelated parties. This association is created in the Relationship window on the customer. When a contact is not a customer and therefore does not have an account, it is added to the customer in the Communication window and no relationship is needed to associate the customer and the contact. It is these relationships that decide what customers each user will have access to in iReceivables.

Both Contacts and Customers that are classified as a Person when they are set up can be selected to associate with a User in System Administrator, which will restrict the data that the external user has access to in iReceivables. Customers that are set up as Organizations and without a relationship with a customer that is a Person or have a contact assigned to them cannot be assigned to a user and therefore cannot have access to iReceivables.

When you have a contact that is associated with multiple customers via a relationship, and you want them to have access to multiple customers in iReceivables, it is important to add the same contact (as opposed to creating a new one) to each customer. This is done with a *Relationship* as opposed to creating a *Contact*.

Relationships in TCA will also allow transactions across Accounts in Receivables. When two customers are related to each other, it allows them to have access to pay each other's transactions as well as access to transactions on both Accounts in iReceivables. When a contact is added to a customer, a new party is always created. See Figure 9-2 to see a person added as a relationship to another customer.

The next step is to set up a new user, as shown in Figure 9-3 using the contact Carlo Kim. After entering a USER NAME and the PASSWORD, the contact needs to be associated with this user, which is done in the CUSTOMER field. When searching on this field, any customer or supplier set up as a Person, and all contacts and employees will appear. For Carlo Kim, there are four entries: two contacts and two relationships for these contacts with customers. You will need to select the "customer name" (that is, the *contact*) that is associated with the customer A. C. Networks. The problem is that numbers you see next to the contact (Party Number, Contact Number, and Customer ID) were not displayed on the customer screen when you set up this contact. When the CONTACT? field is Yes, which helps when selecting a contact and not a related person. After you make a selection, save the user, and then requery the user, and you will see the customer name that this contact is associated to (see the CUSTOMER field in Figure 9-3). If you select the wrong contact, the user will not have access to the correct customer data (or any data at all if a contact that is not related to a customer is selected).

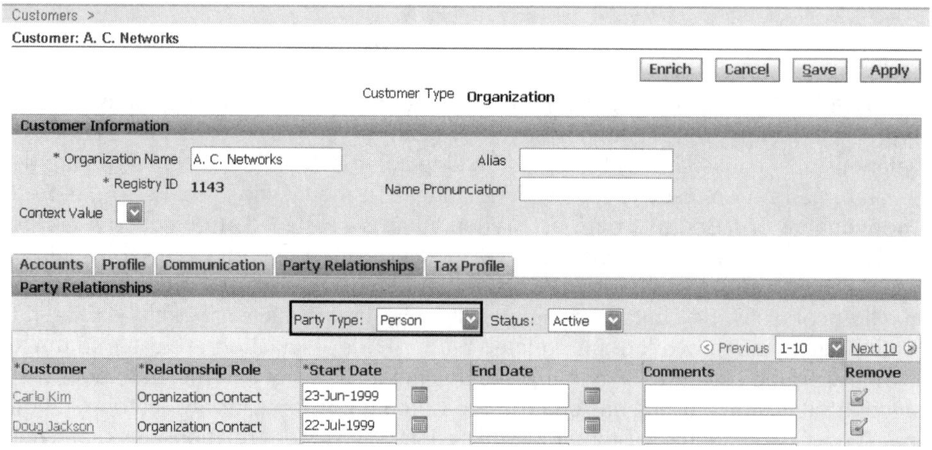

Customers >

Customer: A. C. Networks

| Enrich | Cancel | Save | Apply |

Customer Type **Organization**

Customer Information

* Organization Name	A. C. Networks	Alias	
* Registry ID	1143	Name Pronunciation	
Context Value			

| Accounts | Profile | Communication | **Party Relationships** | Tax Profile |

Party Relationships

Party Type: Person Status: Active

⊙ Previous 1-10 Next 10 ⊙

*Customer	*Relationship Role	*Start Date	End Date	Comments	Remove
Carlo Kim	Organization Contact	23-Jun-1999			
Doug Jackson	Organization Contact	22-Jul-1999			

Receivables | Customers | Customers | Party Relationships | Party Type = Person

FIGURE 9-2. *Adding a person as a relationship to a customer*

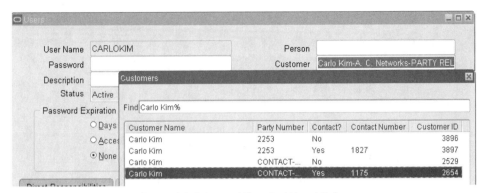

FIGURE 9-3. *Creating an external user for iReceivables*

Setting Up Self-Registration for iReceivables

While external users can always be set up from the System Administration responsibility, this is usually a secure feature in Oracle that most companies do not allow access to outside of the administrator. Oracle provides a self-registration page where the customers can register for access, creating the user automatically. This page would appear as a link from your Oracle Login home page. By default, the link is already available from the login page but does not appear until all the setups are complete for this process. Controlling which links are available on the login page has changed in R12, and the Oracle user manuals still refer to the old process, which uses the profile called Local Login Mask. This profile, while still available in R12, is ignored by the application and no longer works.

To ensure the link is active, you now need to use the Functional Administrator responsibility. On the Personalization I Application Catalog window, enter the DOCUMENT PATH /oracle/apps/fnd/ sso/login/webui/ and select Go. This will bring up the four documents that make up the login page. The second one, /oracle/apps/fnd/sso/login/webui/MainLoginPG, is where the registration link resides. Click the Pencil under Personalize Page, which opens up the Context page, and then select Apply. Here you can see all the links that are available from the home page. Ensure the Message Styled Text: Register Here is shown (see Figure 9-4). If it is not, click the PERSONALIZE link and change Rendered to True. All options are set to be shown unless they have been updated, but some, like the registration link, will not actually appear on the login page until the rest of the setups are completed.

Next, you need to set the profile called UMX: Register Here Link – Default Registration Process. This profile needs to be set to iReceivables Self Registration at the Server level. This is the only level the profile can be set at. Next, ensure that the Oracle Guest user has access to specific iReceivables responsibilities. Oracle comes with a user already called Guest, and it is the account that is used for certain types of access, such as requesting a user account. In the System Administrator responsibility, ensure that the responsibilities iReceivables Registration and iReceivables Account Management are assigned to the Guest user (System Administrator I Security I User I Define). At this point, the Register here link should now appear on your login page, as seen in Figure 9-5.

Focus	Name	User Shown	Personalizable	Personalize
	⊟ Page Layout	Yes		🖉
✛	⊞ Corporate Branding			
	Image	Yes		🖉
	Image: people image	Yes		🖉
	Spacer: (LoginRN.item6)	Yes		🖉
	Image: globalTop image	Yes		🖉
✛	⊞ Row Layout: (LoginRN.MainLoginRN.region152)	Yes		🖉
	Spacer: (LoginRN.MainLoginRN.item12)	Yes		🖉
✛	⊞ Row Layout: (LoginRN.MainLoginRN.region15)	Yes		🖉
✛	⊞ Row Layout: (LoginRN.MainLoginRN.region41)	Yes		🖉
✛	⊞ Row Layout: (LoginRN.MainLoginRN.region132)	Yes		🖉
	Spacer: (LoginRN.MainLoginRN.spacer114)	Yes		🖉
✛	⊞ Row Layout: (LoginRN.MainLoginRN.ForgotPasswordUrlRowLayoutRN1)	Yes		🖉
✛	⊟ Row Layout: (LoginRN.MainLoginRN.RegisterHereUrlRowLayoutRN1)	Yes		🖉
	Cell Format: (LoginRN.MainLoginRN.region142)	Yes		🖉
	Cell Format: (LoginRN.MainLoginRN.region143)	Yes		🖉
	Message Styled Text: Register Here	Yes		🖉
	Spacer: (LoginRN.MainLoginRN.spacer1131)	Yes		🖉

Functional Administrator | Personalization | Application Catalog

FIGURE 9-4. *Ensuring the Register Here link is displayed*

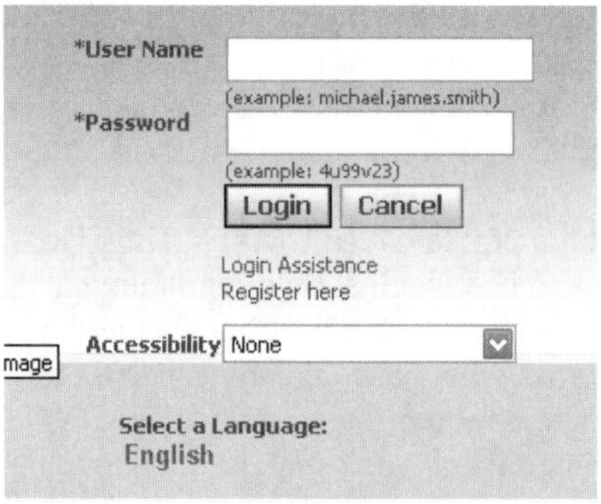

FIGURE 9-5. *Register Here link on the Login page*

The customers will be asked for specific information to ensure they are actual customers. First, they must include identifying information, such as a Customer Number, a Credit Memo, a Debit Memo or Invoice Number, or a Deposit or Payment number. Customer or Contact names are not accepted on this page, and the requestor must enter a valid value for the field selected. This will display the customer name and any addresses that exist in Oracle associated with that identifying information provided (remember: relationships grant access to more than one customer, and therefore allowing multiple customers to be displayed here). The customer can select one or all of the locations. They are then prompted to complete some personal information, such as e-mail address, name, and password. This request will be processed by two workflows: UMX Registration Workflow, which creates the user account, and iReceivables Notification Workflow, which sends an e-mail to the user that their account is ready for use. Both of these can be customized to meet your company's need, such as adding logos or an approval being required before the account is created.

Additional challenge questions can be added during the registration process that are generic or customer specific. This will add security during the login request process. To set up a security rule, use the Rules window, shown in Figure 9-6. You can set up a default challenge question, as well as specific questions that can be assigned to a specific customer.

In the Default Result section, select Customer Verification Question for the field ENTER THE QUESTION AND ANSWER. This will cause the QUESTION and ANSWER fields to display and allow you to add a generic, default challenge question. This question will display for any user requesting access who does not meet any rules that are assigned to a specific customer, shown on the bottom of the window under the Rules List. To add a customer-specific rule, click Create Rule, assign it a RULE NAME, and again, add the challenge question for this rule. This can be a different question than the one above it. Then decide which customers this rule will pertain to by adding a criteria parameter, and decide if the customer needs to meet all or any of the parameters.

Parameters can only be added for a specific customer. Select Customer from the PARAMETER list of values, and then click Add Values to select a customer from the list. This find screen gives you

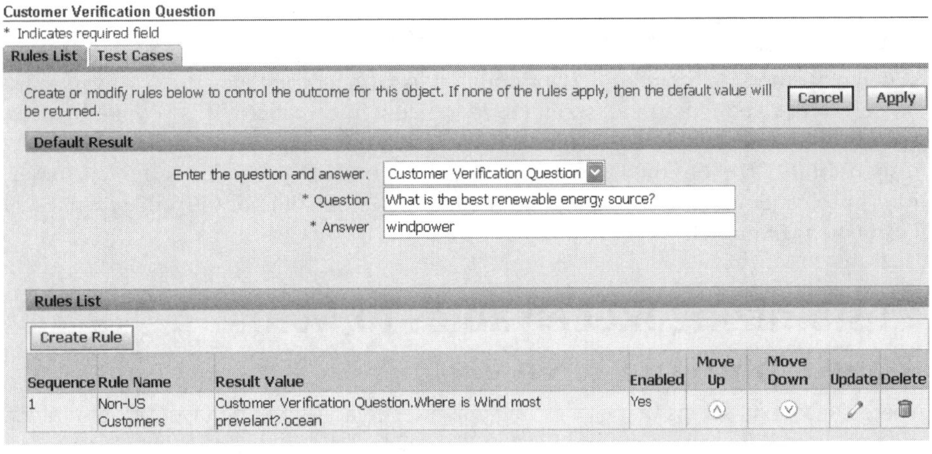

Customer Verification Question
* Indicates required field

Rules List   **Test Cases**

Create or modify rules below to control the outcome for this object. If none of the rules apply, then the default value will be returned. | Cancel | | Apply |

Default Result

Enter the question and answer.   [Customer Verification Question ▾]

* Question   [What is the best renewable energy source?]

* Answer   [windpower]

Rules List

| Create Rule |

Sequence	Rule Name	Result Value	Enabled	Move Up	Move Down	Update	Delete
1	Non-US Customers	Customer Verification Question.Where is Wind most prevelant?.ocean	Yes	⌃	⌄	✎	🗑

iReceivables Setup | Rules | Customer Verification Question

FIGURE 9-6.   *Creating challenge rules for new users requesting access* the option to search by Customer or Description. Customer is actually the account number, while Description is the account description on the account; there is no way to search on customer name. Also add a CONDITION, selecting from Not In, to exclude this customer(s), or In to include this customer(s) for this rule. Note that when using In, it is all-inclusive, which can be a problem if you assign more than one customer to this rule; no customer signing in will meet the inclusive criteria of more than one customer name. Once it is saved, any customer that meets this rule will have a different challenge question. This is an especially good idea to set up if you have intercompany receivables, ensuring that no one can access this data without the proper challenge question.

Anonymous Login

Another option to allowing customers to self-register is to create an anonymous login, where customers can access their account without a user name or a password. This process differs from the Customer Registration process, where the customers are assigned specific user accounts with passwords. Using the anonymous login, customers access their accounts directly and a user name and password is not assigned nor tracked in Oracle. While this may be a valid option when customers are just reviewing account information, the security offered with user names and passwords is more commonly used when the ability to process payments and request credit is implemented. Anonymous login is achieved using Oracle's *guest* access.

In System Administrator, find the user called Guest, and assign it the responsibility called iReceivables 2.0 Anonymous. The URL customers will use to access Oracle is http://*server:port/*OA_HTML/AnonymousLogin.jsp (case sensitive). This will direct customers to enter their account number to access iReceivables. If your instance of Oracle has been upgraded from an earlier release, you may need to modify the anonymous login .htm files to contain the proper versions of the signin pages; the filenames are ARIANLGN.htm and ARIANERR.htm.

There has been a change in release 12.1.1 with the storage of the Guest user password. In prior releases, this was stored as a profile option, but it is now part of Oracle's security vault. If you are being redirected to enter a user name and password after entering a customer number when you sign in anonymously, then the function to get the Guest password is still looking in the wrong place. You will need to update it to look at FND_WEB_SEC.GET_GUEST_USER_PWD.

Building the Search Criteria for Customers

When customers are entered new or updated in Oracle, the fields that you can search on in iReceivables need to be rebuilt to include the new information. This is done by running a concurrent request called Customer text data creation and indexing from the Receivables responsibility. Without this program, you will not be able to search on the customer name in iReceivables. Since this program will create indexes on some of the tables, work with your DBA when running it.

Customizing iReceivables to Meet Your Company's Needs

There are several setups that control the way iReceivables will behave for both internal and external users. These are set up as System Parameters, Profiles, and Rules, and many of these setups work together. For example, a System Parameter, two Profiles, and two Rules all need to be set up in order for the Service Charges feature to be enabled. Unlike most modules, Profiles can be set in System Administrator (Profile I System) as well as in the iReceivables Setup responsibility (under Profiles). The navigation paths given in this section are for the iReceivables window, but either one can be used. This section will outline the setups based upon functionality, as opposed to type of setup.

Setting Up Service Charges for Payments Made in iReceivables

iReceivables can automatically charge customers a service charge for paying with either a credit card or a wire. For example, if your bank charges you a $15 fee for incoming wires, you can set up iReceivables to apply this service charge to the customer account. This is done by having Oracle create an Adjustment in Receivables when the payment is made. If your company uses option, make sure your customer is aware of your policy and knows to increase the payment by the amount of the charge; this will avoid additional collection calls as well as dissatisfied customers. To charge service charges, first set up a Receivables Activity for the adjustment, and assign it to the Service Charge Activity parameter. To create the activity, go to Receivables I Setup I Receipts I Receivable Activities. Ensure the TYPE is Adjustment and that it is ACTIVE. The GL ACCOUNT SOURCE should be Activity GL Account, which allows you to assign the general ledger account combination that you want the services charges to be booked against in the ACTIVITY GL ACCOUNT field. After saving, this new activity can then be assigned to the iReceivables system parameter for SERVICE CHARGE ACTIVITY, seen in Figure 9-7.

Setting iReceivables Profiles

Next, the same activity needs to be assigned to the Profile OIR: Service Charge Activity ID, but you will need to know the system identification number as opposed to the actual name of the adjustment. You can get the Activity ID using the Examine feature in Oracle, which requires either the APPS password or the profile FND: Diagnostics to be set to Yes for your user. Since this feature is usually secured and not all users have access to it, you may need the assistance of your DBA or system administrator if you do not have the proper access. While in the same form where you set the activity (Receivables I Setup I Receipts I Receivables Activities) and with the Service Charge activity called up, go to the menu Help I Diagnostics I Examine. In the window that opens up, use the list of values to select RECEIVABLES_TRX_ID in the FIELD. The number that appears is the Activity ID. This is shown in Figure 9-8.

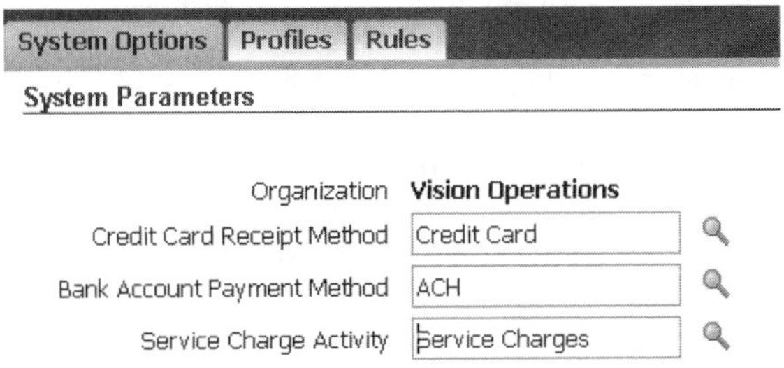

FIGURE 9-7.   *Adding the service charge activity to the system parameters*

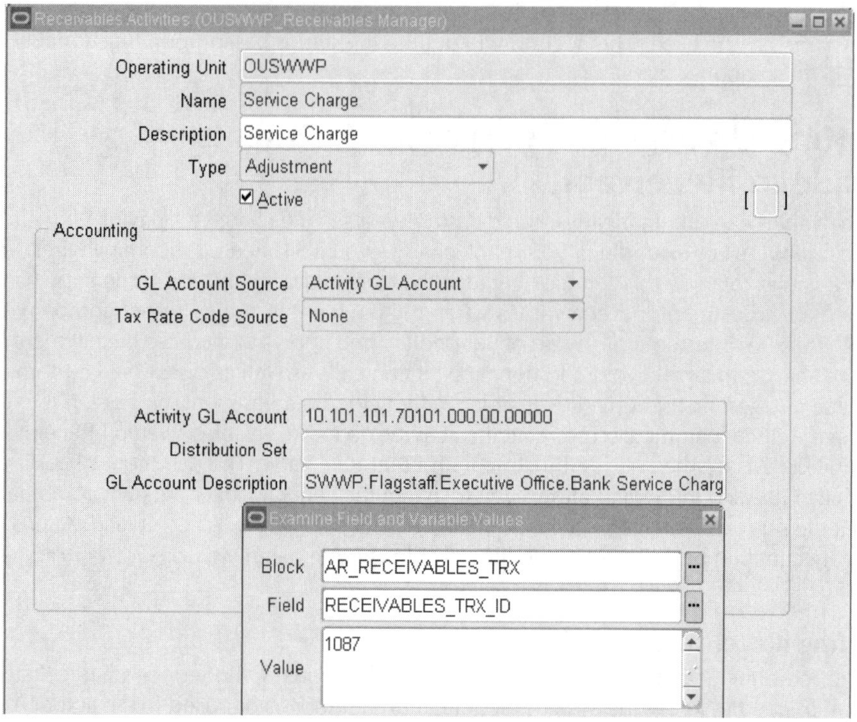

Receivables | Setup | Receipts | Receivable Activities | Help | Diagnostics | Examine

FIGURE 9-8. *Getting the Activity ID for service charges*

This ID is then populated in the Profile OIR: Service Charge Activity ID. It can be populated at different levels: Site, Application, Responsibility, or User. Where it is populated will determine who this profile pertains to. When it is set at the Site level, all users will be affected. Application will only affect the users who are assigned a Responsibility associated with this application (System Administrator | Security | Responsibility | Define | Application field), while Responsibility will only affect users that are assigned this specific responsibility. The lowest level, User, will need to be set up for each user that you want to be affected by this profile.

These levels are used by all the profiles in iReceivables, which allows you to turn on or off features at different levels. For example, if you want to charge wire fees to all the users in a specific country, then you could set this profile at the Responsibility level and assign that responsibility to all users who are located in that country. While profiles can be set for multiple applications, responsibilities, and users, they cannot be set for a specific operating unit. If your company is set up for Multi-Org Access Control (MOAC) and you want to set a profile for one operating unit and not another, you will need to either restrict your responsibilities by operating unit or set up multiple responsibilities. This is a little bit out of line with Oracle's new MOAC direction. Rules can then be set up to limit who is affected by these profiles, described in the next section, "Adding Rules to Each Profile."

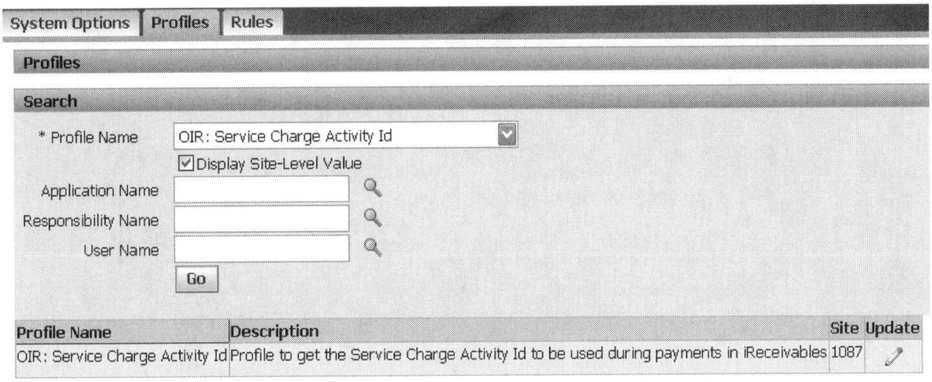

iReceivables Setup | Profiles

FIGURE 9-9.   *Setting a profile in iReceivables*

To set the profile, select the PROFILE NAME from the list of values (see Figure 9-9). You will then need to select one of the levels, such as site or application, to see the profile, and click Go. From the Update link, you can update this profile for all levels. For the site, just add the Activity ID in the SITE VALUE field. For the other levels, use the Add Another Row button to select the Application, Responsibility, or User, and enter the value as well.

There is another profile that affects service charges, and it tells Oracle if service charges are allowed in your system or not. It is called OIR: Enable Service Charge. If this is *not* set to Yes, the Activity ID that is populated will not be used and service charges will not be applied. The default for this profile is Null, which is the same as No. Setting the Activity ID at the highest level (Site) and Enable Service Charge at a lower level will offer control to use the feature at different levels.

Adding Rules to Each Profile

Once the profiles are set, there are rules that can also control when the profiles are used. These rules are assigned to either a customer or the customer's site and can set a different value for the customer or their sites that it is assigned to. The assignments are either inclusive or exclusive, meaning that you either set this profile for all the customers who *are* associated with the rule (inclusive) or for all the customers who are *not* associated with the rule (exclusive). This is controlled by the CONDITION field, where In is inclusive, and Not In is exclusive.

To create a rule, find the rule you want to update, and select the Setup Rules link. From here, the default for the rule is displayed in the DEFAULT VALUE field and can be updated. The value here will override the value set on the corresponding system profile. For Service Charges, there are two rules that can be set; one for each profile. After clicking Create Rule, enter a unique RULE NAME, and ensure the ENABLED box is checked (see Figure 9-10). This box can be unchecked when you no longer want to use this rule. In the Result VALUE, enter the value for this rule and profile.

For example, in the Service Charge Enabled rule, you would select either Yes or No, but for the Service Charge Activity ID, you would enter the Activity ID this rule pertains to. You then have the ability to add criteria for the rule, which allows you to determine when this rule is used. First, decide if all or any of your criteria will need to be matched. If you have more than one condition, and All is selected, all of the conditions will have to be met for the rule to be used. Since these rules are set at the Customer or Site level, this option does not make a lot of

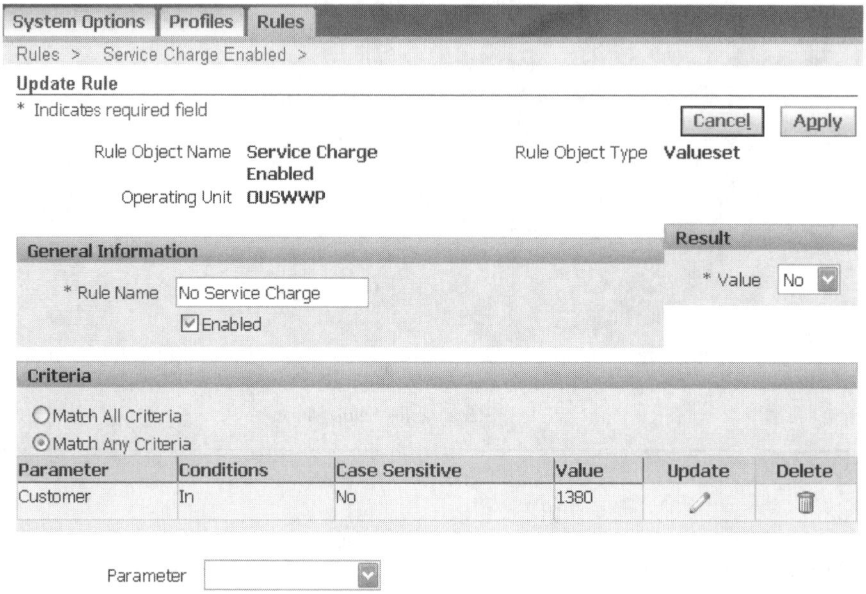

FIGURE 9-10. *Creating a rule for profiles*

sense unless you are setting it for only one customer and site; as soon as you set it for more than one customer, or a site that belongs to a different customer, the rule can never be met when MATCH ALL CRITERIA is enabled.

Next, the conditions for this rule need to be enabled. Select either Customer or Customer Site Use in the PARAMETER field, which will open up the CONDITION field. This is where you determine if this condition is inclusive, by selecting In, or exclusive, by selecting Not In. Then click Add Values and select the customer or customer site you want to add. This find screen gives you the option to search by Customer or Description. Customer is actually the account number, while Description is the account description on the account; there is no way to search on customer name. Once you are done adding customers or sites, click Add Criteria, and then Apply to save the record.

For each rule that is created, Oracle allows you to test the rules to ensure you get the expected results. The tests can be either for a specific customer or customer site, or for all customers that do not fall under a rule. To test a rule, click the Test Cases tab (iReceivables Setup | Rules | Setup Rules | Test Cases) and select Create Test. Enter a customer or a customer site, or else leave both fields blank to test the default, and select Get Results.

Adding Document Sequences
The final step to setting up service charges is to create a sequence for the adjustments. Sequences are used to assign document numbers to transactions in different areas of Oracle. While some sequences have to be set up manually, others are maintained in the background by Oracle and

the users never see the setups. For example, Oracle maintains the party numbers in TCA in the background and a sequence does not need to be set up separately. To set up sequential numbering for the service charge adjustment, use the System Administrator responsibility.

First, sequential numbering needs to be turned on for receivables. This profile only affects sequences that are set up manually, not the ones that are maintained by the system, like the standard transaction numbers. There are two choices for sequential numbering: Partially Used and Always Used. Partially Used means that you are using this feature for only some of the transactions, while Always Used means that you need to set up sequential numbering for all the transactions. This is a profile option and can be set at different levels. In this case, we want to set the profile called Sequential Numbering (System Administrator | Profile | System) at the Application level to either Partially Used, if you are only using this for service charges, or Always Used if you want to add sequential numbers to all transactions in Receivables.

Previously, it was mentioned that some numeric sequences were controlled by Oracle, such as standard transaction numbers. These transactions can also have a separate sequence of numbers assigned to them, usually used for government reporting in countries where VAT (value-added tax) is required. VAT is comparable to sales and use tax here in the United States but has more stringent reporting requirements associated with it. When this profile is set to Always Used, Oracle will assign a second number to invoices, which is then used for reporting VAT transactions. When it is Partially Used, only the transactions that are set up in the next step will have sequential numbers assigned to them.

Creating Document Sequencing

Next, a document sequence needs to be set up. This will determine the starting value for the sequence, and the type of sequence that it is. There are three different types: Automatic, Gapless, and Manual. Manual is when the number is assigned by the user manually and cannot be used for service charges, since the adjustment is being automatically created by the workflow. Automatic is when the numbers are assigned by Oracle, sequentially. It sounds like this process would result in sequential numbering without any missing numbers in it, but by nature, Oracle does not assign numbers without gaps.

In order to speed up processing, Oracle will sometimes cache numbers or issue a group of numbers to memory, which, if not used, are actually lost. For example, if you are running autoinvoice to bring transactions into Receivables, Oracle will cache 20 transaction numbers to its memory so that it does not need to read the hard drive for every transaction to assign a number. While this results in autoinvoice running faster, it also causes any unused numbers that were cached to be lost, or discarded. So by nature of the Oracle processing, Automatic numbering is not Gapless numbering. Oracle recognizes that in some cases, the need for gapless numbering outweighs the need for speed, and it allows the users to determine which they would prefer. Speed usually comes into play when thousands of transactions are being processed in a single batch, which will not be the case with iReceivables service charges, so setting this sequence to Gapless will not result in any noticeable degradation of speed, but it will assign numbers that are sequential and have no gaps. The instructions given here can be used to set up document sequences for any transaction in Oracle.

To create a document sequence, referring to Figure 9-11, assign the sequence a NAME, which will usually relate in some way to the transaction this sequence will pertain to. Next, select the APPLICATION as Receivables, and add the EFFECTIVE dates. While the FROM, or start, date is mandatory, the TO, or end, date can be left blank until this sequence is no longer used. Select either Automatic or Gapless as the TYPE, and set an INITIAL VALUE for this sequence. The final check box, MESSAGE, is used to inform any users of the sequence name and number being assigned. While this is a great troubleshooting feature, most users do not need this information. Once the record is saved, it

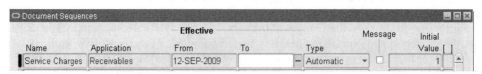

System Administrator | Application | Sequential Numbering | Define

FIGURE 9-11. *Creating a document sequence*

cannot be updated with the exception of the end date. If any changes are needed to the sequence, a new one will need to be set up.

Next, this sequence will have to be assigned to the transaction, or category of document that will use it. Note that a single sequence can be assigned to multiple transactions. Doing so will result in sequential numbering across all the transactions but will result in gaps within each individual transaction type. Referring to Figure 9-12, first select the APPLICATION the transaction exists in, in this case, Receivables. Then select the CATEGORY, or transaction, from the list. The LEDGER and METHOD are assigned next. Ledger is the ledger this sequence applies to, and allows you to have different sequences for each ledger. Method refers to how the transaction this sequence applies to is created. Transactions that are created from a concurrent request use sequences that are set with an Automatic method, while transactions that are entered directly into an Oracle form are Manual methods. Credit memos that are generated from iReceivables are considered Automatic, while creating a credit memo in Receivables are manual.

On the Assignment tab, enter the effective dates for this sequence, and select the sequence name. Once saved, END DATE and SEQUENCE are the only fields that can be updated. If you do update the sequence, you will want to ensure that the next number in the sequence you are changing it to is higher than the last number used for this transaction with the current sequence. If not, it may result in errors during processing when Oracle attempts to assign a number that already exists.

Printing Limits
On both the internal and external views, customers or employees have the option to print invoices. Oracle will print the *selected* transactions, and the users can select either individual transactions, all transactions on a page, or all transactions for the customer. Since this can be a large number of transactions, Oracle allows you to limit the number of transactions that can be printed with the profile OIR: Multi Print Limit. Rules can also be added for this profile, for either customers or their sites. The default for this profile is 25.

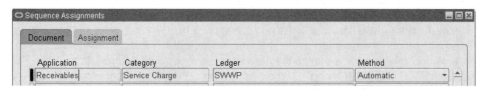

System Administrator | Application | Sequential Numbering | Assign

FIGURE 9-12. *Assigning sequences to transactions*

iReceivables Payment Processing

Besides the obvious benefit of reducing phone calls from customers about their outstanding balances and avoiding the need to resend invoices, iReceivables also allows customers to make payments online, reducing the time it takes for you to both receive and process the payments. There are several setups required for this process to work. Customers have two options for making payments: Credit Card or Bank Transfers, including wired, direct account transfers and ACH (Automated Clearing House). All of these use the new Payments module in R12, which replaces iPayments in prior releases. The Payments module allows you to interface credit card transactions with your credit card processor, validating and processing the account number, expiration date, and dollar amount of the transaction. It also can interface to either your bank or a clearing house to process account transfers, moving the funds from your customer's bank account and into yours. Once the payment is settled, Oracle will then create a receipt in Receivables and apply it against the designated transactions.

Setting Up Payments for iReceivables

The first step to set up receipt processing is to allow Payments to send outbound transactions to your credit card processor or bank. This includes several setup steps.

Creating Formats   In Oracle, formats determine the layout your data will take when it is sent to your payment processor. Oracle comes with many predefined formats, or you can create your own to comply with your processor's requirements. The formats for capturing funds, or receipts, Oracle comes with include:

- Citi Merchant Services, both Batch and Online
- Concord EFSNet Web Payment Services, Credit and Debit Cards, and Telecheck
- Electronic Bank Remittances format
- First Data North
- Paymentech
- Several country-specific formats, including Italy, Germany, Spain, and France

Other processors provide their own formats that are Oracle-compatible, such as PayPal, but are not delivered with EBS.

You can use these formats as is, create new formats from scratch, or modify one of these formats to meet the requirements of your processor. To add a new or modified format to the system, SELECT TYPE of Funds Capture Settlement Batch and then click Create (refer to Figure 9-13). What this setup actually does is associate a data definition to a template, and assign it to a specific type of process. That is because the formats use BI Publisher. BI Publisher, formerly known as XML Publisher, is a tool provided by Oracle that uses the programming language XML (Extensible Markup Language), to easily marry data with different output formats. A data definition, or DATA EXTRACT as it is called on this window, is really a program, usually written in PL/SQL or SQL, that provides the actual fields and data. Oracle then uses a built-in XML engine to convert this into XML, which can then be assigned to a template, or format. Templates use different output options, including eText, PDF, RTF, and a few different varieties of XSL. Table 9-1 explains all the output options and their common uses.

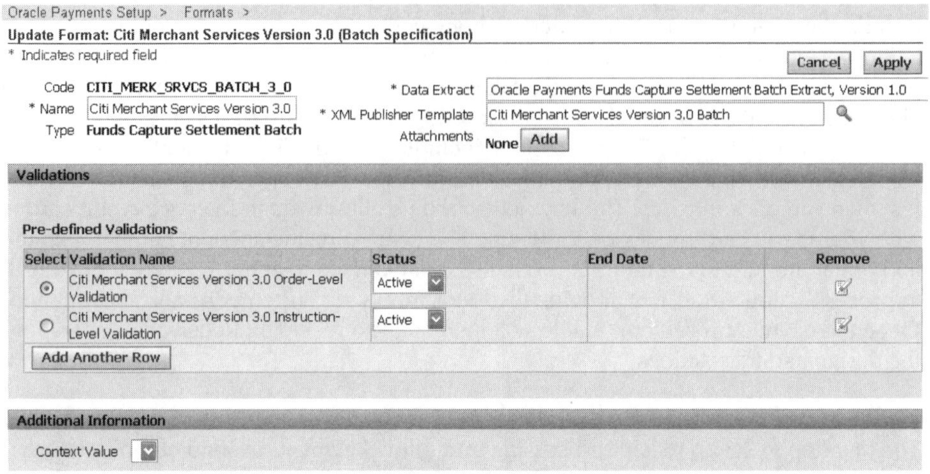

Payments Setup Administrator | Payments Setup | Shared Setup | Formats | Formats

FIGURE 9-13. *Creating a new funds capture settlement batch format*

Output Type	Description	Common Use
eText	Table-based output.	EDI (Electronic Data Interchange) or EFT (Electronic Funds Transfer)
PDF (Portable Document Format)	Report that cannot be updated.	Purchase Orders or Sales Orders
RTF (Rich Text Format)	Documents created using word processing programs.	Internal and external reports
XSL	XSL (eXtensible Stylesheet Language) is a programming language used to create formatted documents. It includes: FO (Formatting Objects) HTML (Hypertext Markup Language) Text XML	All reports, but you must know XSL programming to create this output type.

TABLE 9-1. *BI Publisher Output Options*

Oracle comes seeded with a Data Extract for Funds Capture, called Oracle Payments Funds Capture Settlement Batch Extract, Version 1.0. Since Oracle internally calls this program during the funds capture process, it needs to be used as the source of your template. In the XML Publisher Administrator, the corresponding Data Definition is iPayment Funds Capture Instruction Extract 1.0, which is a Java program. The templates that come with Oracle use RTF, eText-Outbound, and XSL-XML as the types, depending on the receiving institution's requirements.

To create a format, assign it a CODE, which is the internal name used by Oracle and should contain no spaces. Next, give it a user-friendly NAME. Usually, I like to have the CODE and NAME be the same with the exception that the NAME has spaces, whereas the CODE uses an underscore (_) instead. The TYPE will default in from the prior window and cannot be updated. If you selected the wrong TYPE, go back and select the correct one before proceeding. Then select the DATA EXTRACT and XML PUBLISHER TEMPLATE that were already uploaded into Oracle using the XML Publisher Administrator responsibility (Home | Templates).

Validations can also be added, which will validate data prior to processing to ensure it meets the requirements of the receiving processor or passes any internal validations you may want to perform. For example, you can validate that the receipt is over or under a certain amount before processing. Validations are set up under Payments Setup Administrator | Setup | Shared Setup | Validations. Oracle comes with three settlement validations: Citi Merchant Services, First Data North, and Paymentech.

Setting Up Protocols and External Relationships   Protocols, set up as transmission configurations, enable EBS to have electronic connectivity with settlement systems. Simply stated, they are a set of rules used when the two systems are talking to each other, much in the same way rules are established when two people communicate, such as the language and tools (phone, e-mail, instant messaging) being used. Protocols that are supported by Oracle are listed next. The setups are unique for each payment system and should be coordinated with your payment processing company.

- HTTP(s) POST Request
- Oracle Payments Tunneling Protocol
- Paymentech Online Spec 7.2 Socket
- Paymentech Batch Specification 2.1.0 Acknowledgement FTP Get
- First Data North Authorization Spec 10/24/02 Socket
- First Data North Magnetic Media Specification 2003.1 Settlement Batch FTP Put
- First Data North Magnetic Media Specification 2003.1 Acknowledgement FTP Get
- Citi Merchant Services 3.0 Online Socket
- Citi Merchant Services Version 3.0 Batch Settlement FTP Put
- Citi Merchant Services Version 3.0 Batch Acknowledgement Get
- Citibank Direct Debit Message FTP Put
- File Transfer Protocol for Static File Names
- Secure File Transfer Protocol for Static File Names
- AS2 Send
- Local File System Delivery

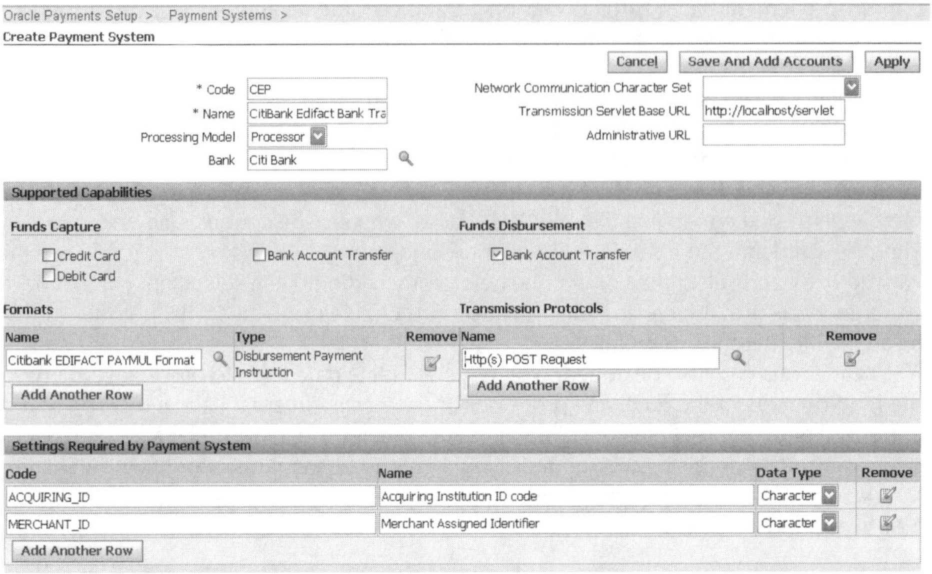

Oracle Payments Setup >   Payment Systems >
Create Payment System

Cancel	Save And Add Accounts	Apply

* Code	CEP	Network Communication Character Set	
* Name	CitiBank Edifact Bank Tra	Transmission Servlet Base URL	http://localhost/servlet
Processing Model	Processor	Administrative URL	
Bank	Citi Bank		

Supported Capabilities

Funds Capture

☐ Credit Card   ☐ Bank Account Transfer
☐ Debit Card

Funds Disbursement

☑ Bank Account Transfer

Formats

Name	Type	Remove
Citibank EDIFACT PAYMUL Format	Disbursement Payment Instruction	

Add Another Row

Transmission Protocols

Name		Remove
Http(s) POST Request		

Add Another Row

Settings Required by Payment System

Code	Name	Data Type	Remove
ACQUIRING_ID	Acquiring Institution ID code	Character	
MERCHANT_ID	Merchant Assigned Identifier	Character	

Add Another Row

Payments Setup Administrator | Payments Setup | Shared Setup | Payment Systems | Payment Systems

FIGURE 9-14.   *Payment system setups to send settlement transmissions to banks or third parties*

Adding Payment Systems   Payment systems, where the external relationships with a bank or third-party settlement company are stored, identify not only the type of settlements, but also how EBS will communicate with this bank using the transmission protocols set up in the preceding step. You need to set up one payment system for each processor that you use. Referring to Figure 9-14, first add a system CODE and a NAME for the system, and then identify the type of PROCESSING MODEL this will be used for. GATEWAY is used for debit or credit card settlements, while PROCESSOR is used for Bank Transfers. Associate a BANK with this system. Banks need to be set up first in Receivables (Setup | Receipts | Banks), then optionally add a NETWORK COMMUNICATION CHARACTER SET to identify what alphabet/language the transmission will be performed in. If this is left blank, the default language for the system will be used. While the ADMINISTRATIVE URL is not required, it can be added for a reference, but the TRANSMISSION SERVLET BASE URL is required and is for transfers, directing EBS where to send the transmission.

Under Funds Capture, select if this payment system will be used for CREDIT CARD, DEBIT CARD, or BANK ACCOUNT TRANSFER. Then add the Formats that will be used by the payment system. These formats are the XML templates you added earlier and are used to format the data to the bank or settlement processor. Settings Required by Payment System include any required fields for processing this transmission and will be populated when the Accounts are added in the next step. When utilizing Oracle's Treasury modules for cash forecasting, the BANK ACCOUNT LEAD DAYS will determine when these funds will appear in the cash balances. Once the payment system is set up, accounts are added to provide values to the parameters added in the Settings Required by Payment Systems section. These parameters and values relate to general processing information as opposed to specific payment information unique to each payment.

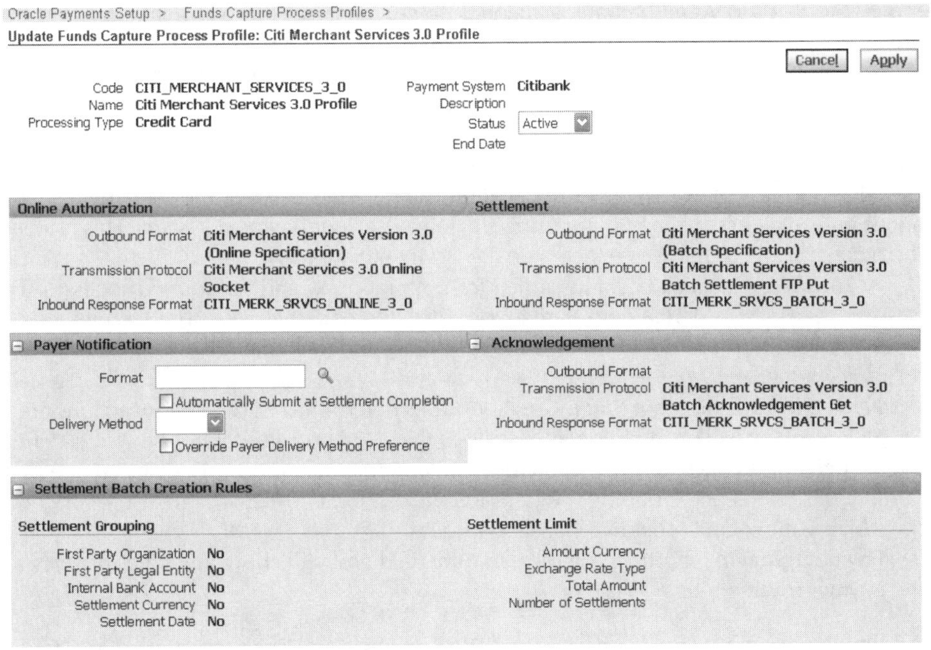

Payments Setup Administrator | Payments Setup | Funds Capture Setup | Funds Capture Process Profiles

FIGURE 9-15. *Funds capture process profiles*

Funds Capture Process Profiles Next you set up a Processing Profile for each Payment System. This setup has both required fields, denoted with an asterisk (*), and fields that are not required. To set up a profile, select the payment system from the list of values (these are the systems that were set up in the last step) and then the Create button. Figure 9-15 shows the setups. As with many setups, the CODE is internally used by Oracle, and the NAME is a user-friendly name that is seen by the users. The PROCESSING TYPE will need to be set to Bank Account, Debit Card, or Credit Card, depending on the type of transaction you want to capture with this profile. If you are using the same payment system for more than one processing type, you will need to set up one profile for each type. The PAYMENT SYSTEM will default in from the selection you made on the prior window and cannot be updated. An optional DESCRIPTION can also be added.

The next section, Online Authorization, assigns the format, the protocol, and an INBOUND RESPONSE FORMAT. Inbound responses would include the approval or declined information from the processor. These formats are set up the same place as the outbound formats (Payments Setup | Shared Setup | Formats | Formats) and use the same data definition (Oracle Payments Funds Capture Settlement Extract, Version 1.0), with a template that includes the fields the processor is sending back to you.

Settlement information can also be added, again for the same three fields, OUTBOUND FORMAT, TRANSMISSION PROTOCOL, and INBOUND RESPONSE FORMAT. Verification and Settlement are two separate processes when using credit cards. Verification ensures that the card number, expiration date, and other optional information, such as name and billing address, are accurate, and that there is enough credit on the card to cover the transaction, while settlement closes the transaction and moves the funds to your company's account. In certain cases these will take place at the same time, while in other scenarios, they will happen at different times. For example, if you order a book from Amazon, the verification happens when you place the order, but the settlement does not happen until the order is actually shipped.

Payer Notifications can also be added, where the customer is notified via e-mail, by Fax, or with a printed notification of the result of the transaction. The FORMAT is selected for the notification, as well as the DELIVERY METHOD. This notification can be sent out when the settlement is completed, and is only available when you are using a gateway as your payment system. This is identified by the PROCESSING MODEL that was selected on the Payment System.

Acknowledgments can also be added for both inbound and outbound processes. The INBOUND RESPONSE FORMAT tells Oracle how to read, or parse, the data that is returned, while the OUTBOUND FORMAT TRANSMISSION PROTOCOL contains the rules, or protocols, that tell Oracle how to go get the acknowledgments.

Next, adding Settlement Batch Creation Rules determines how the transactions are grouped for settlement, as well as defining any limits. If there are no Settlement Groupings defined, then each individual transaction will create one settlement. Since most processes charge by the number of settlements, grouping the transactions can be a cost-saving measure for companies that have high volume and repetitive transactions.

Payment System Accounts is a display-only field and will show any data that was set up on the payment system.

Adding Payees   A Payee for the funds capture process identifies the company that is sending out the settlement requests from Oracle to the processing company. Figure 9-16 shows a Payee. A MERCHANT CATEGORY CODE can be added to identify the industry your company operates in; it can used by the credit card processing company to classify the transaction on the credit card statements for your customers.

To limit this payee to specific payment systems or their associated accounts, complete the Payment System Accounts section. You can either select a specific PAYMENT SYSTEM, which will allow processing for all the accounts that are associated with the payment system, or a specific PAYMENT SYSTEM ACCOUNT, which will populate the payment system field for you. Remember from the previous setups that Payment System Accounts are added to a Payment System after clicking the Save And Add Accounts button. The accounts allow you to add unique identification information for each processor, such as Merchant ID or Passwords. Operating Units can also be assigned to limit this payee to transactions originated from a specific operating unit, or left blank to process all operating units.

Risk Formulas can be created for transactions to allow your company to evaluate the risk of a particular transaction. The risk formulas are unique for each company because of the weightings assigned to a group of common risk elements. For example, you can either increase or decrease a transaction's risk to correspond to the frequency with which the customer purchases from you. Risk Formulas usually come into play when credit cards are accepted for orders where there is a delay between the verification and settlement, as opposed to processing credit card transactions through iReceivables, where both happen within a very short time period.

Next, select which processing types will be supported by this payee.

Additional PAYMENT SYSTEM ACCOUNTS can be set up for each Payment Method you are processing transactions for. If additional payment methods are needed for your company, other than the seeded methods that come with Oracle, they can be set up in Payments Setup Administrator | Payments

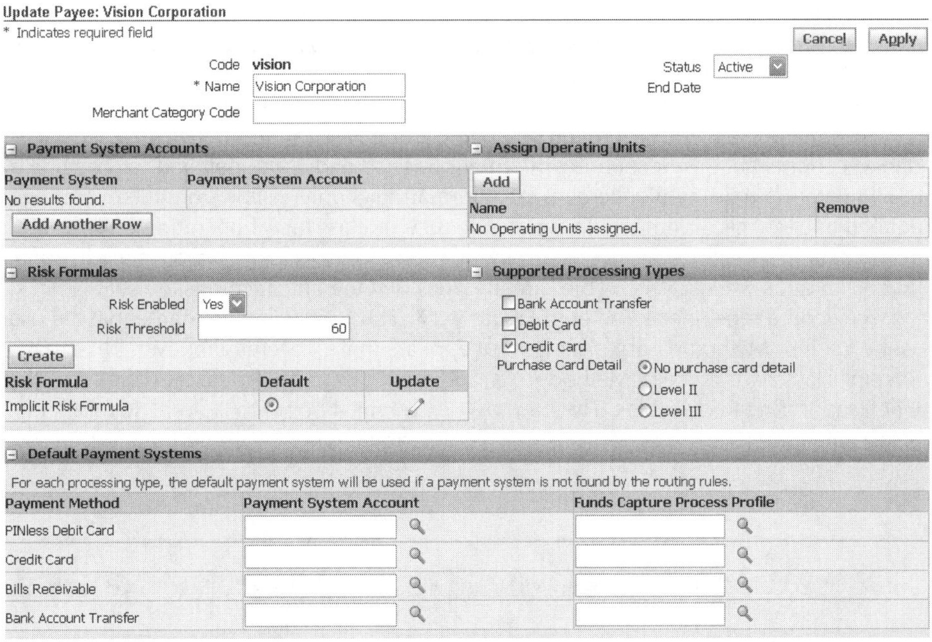

Payments Setup Administrator | Payments Setup | Funds Capture Setup | Payees

FIGURE 9-16. *Payees for the funds capture process*

Setup | Funds Capture Setup | Payment Methods. The setups include a unique NAME and PAYMENT TYPE CODE, and a FORMAT VALUE MAPPING, if one is passed in the payment file.

Finally, Routing Rules can be added, which add rules as to when a specific payment system is used. These can only be added after the Payment System Account section is saved for the Payee. Rules can be added for Amount, AR Receipt Methods, Currency, Factored Receipts, Operating Unit, Payee Bank, Bank Account, Bank Country, or Bank Routing Number; they allow you to determine when a specific Payment System Account is used. The only accounts available from the list of values to assign to a rule are ones that are saved in the Payment System Account section on the payee.

Enabling Credit Card Brands Credit card brands come seeded with Oracle, but you can determine if your company will accept them, and assign an Authorization Validity Period. This is the period of time your credit card processor will hold funds for a preauthorization, which comes into play when cards are authorized before they are settled. These are controlled in Payments Setup Administrator | Payments Setup | Funds Capture Setup | Credit Card Brands. To update a seeded credit card, click Update. Here you can determine if it is ACCEPTED or not, and select the AUTHORIZATION VALIDITY PERIOD. New brands can also be added with the Add Another Row button.

Adding Receipt Classes and Methods

The final step in setting up both credit card processing and bank transfers is to create Receipt Methods in Receivables. *Receipt methods,* also called *classes,* are used to determine not only how transactions are applied to the customer accounts, but also the banking and accounting information for the transactions. While the payment information set up in the preceding section is external facing, interacting with external parties, such as banks and credit card processors, receipt methods are the internal-facing part of the transaction, dealing with the application of the receipt on the customer's account as well as the accounting in the General Ledger.

The receipt class form is broken down into three parts: Heading, Details, and by using the Bank Accounts button, Accounting Information. The header and detailed information are visible to all operating units, while the banking information is only visible from the operating unit it is defined under. This allows you to set up one receipt class for all operating units, with different accounting information. From a user standpoint, the only receipt classes that will appear in iReceivables as well as Receivables are the ones where bank accounts are set up.

To set up a receipt class, refer to Figure 9-17. The NAME is not the name that the users will see, as the Receipt Method PRINTED NAME is what appears in the receipt windows. I like to make the Receipt Class NAME, Receipt Method NAME, and PRINTED NAME all the same, which makes it easier when supporting Receivables. The CREATION METHOD must be set to Automatic for iReceivables processing. The REMITTANCE METHOD is used to determine which account numbers are going to be

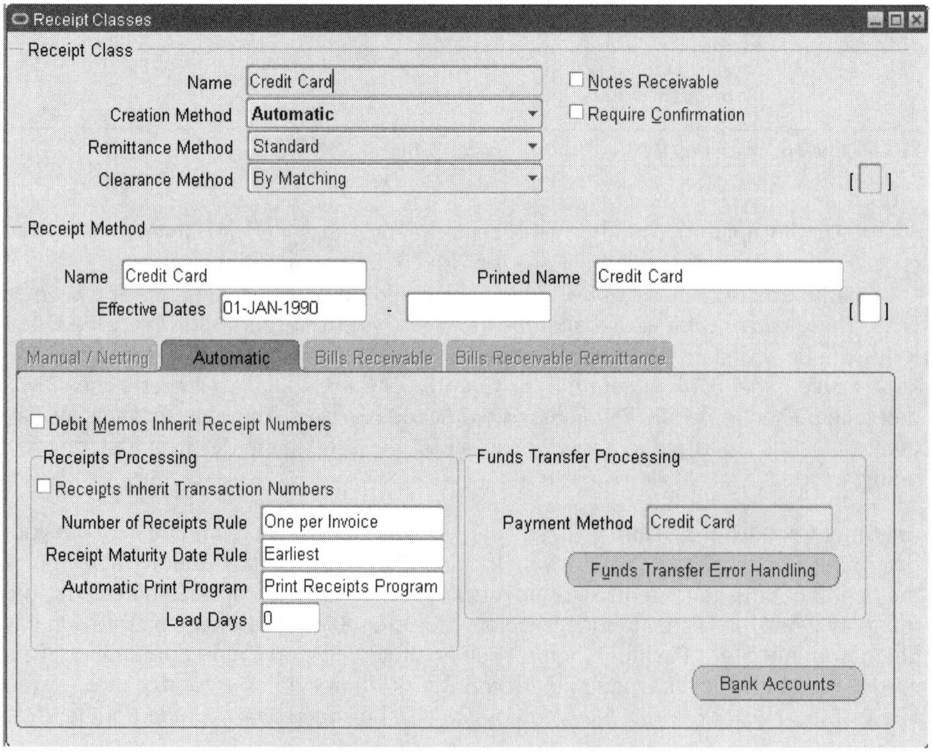

Receivables | Setup | Receipts | Receipt Classes

FIGURE 9-17. *Creating receipt classes*

used when the receipt is created. Standard will use the Remittance account, while Factoring will use the account number in the Factoring field. These accounts are assigned when you click the Bank Accounts button. If you select Standard and Factoring, then Oracle will use whichever is assigned to the receipt batch when it is created. The final option, No Remittance, is not available when the creation method is set to Automatic.

CLEARANCE METHOD determines how receipts are cleared and posted to the bank account. The clearing account, defined as Remittance or Factor accounts under the Bank Accounts button, allow receipts to be posted to separate accounts until the funds have cleared the bank. When the CLEARANCE METHOD is set to Directly, then these clearing accounts are not used and the receipt is posted directly to the cash account. By Matching and By Automatic Clearing will both post to the clearing account first, and then to the bank account when the receipt is cleared in Cash Management. In the case of By Automatic Clearing, you can also use the concurrent program called Automatic Clearing for Receipts to clear the transactions. This program uses the BANK ACCOUNT LEAD DAYS that were set up on your Payment Systems (Payments Setup Administrator | Payments Setup | Payment Systems), and moves the funds from either the Remittance or the Factor account to the actual Cash Account.

The NOTES RECEIVABLE check box will identify this receipt as a notes receivable, which is defined in Oracle as a future-dated payment or a promissory note. This should be checked for the receipt method if you are going to allow future-dated ACH payments in iReceivables. The final check box on the header, REQUIRE CONFIRMATION, can only be used with credit card receipts. This feature allows you to send a confirmation to the customer for approval prior to processing the receipt.

In the Receipt Method section, assign a NAME and a PRINTED NAME to the receipt, as well as EFFECTIVE DATES. As mentioned earlier, this form is broken down into a header section and details. Since this is a details section, you can add multiple receipt methods to one receipt class, with different options and bank accounts. All the Receipt Methods assigned to the same Receipt Class will have the same creation, remittance, and clearance methods.

There are additional options that can be selected on the Automatic tab. First, decide if DEBIT MEMOS INHERIT RECEIPT NUMBERS. When this is checked, any debit memos generated for receipt reversals, such as a credit card refund, will have the same number as the receipt that was reversed. When RECEIPTS INHERIT TRANSACTION NUMBERS, the receipt number assigned by Oracle will be the same as the transaction it is applied to, allowing you to track the receipts more easily. NUMBER OF RECEIPTS RULE determines how receipts are grouped when more than one exists in each batch. For example, you can group all the receipts to create only one receipt transaction per customer per batch, or one per invoice.

Maturity dates, or the date that a future-dated payment is settled at the bank, can be derived from the actual invoice due date. When the receipt is applied to multiple invoices, with different maturity dates, the RECEIPT MATURITY DATE RULE determines if the receipt dates agree to the earliest or latest maturity date. The AUTOMATIC PRINT PROGRAM tells Oracle the format you want to use when sending the customer either a notification that the receipt has been created or a request for confirmation before creating the receipt. These notifications are sent out only when the Format Automatic Remittances Program concurrent request is run. If you are not using this feature, you still need to select one of the seeded programs, but do not run the report. The final option in this section, LEAD DAYS, tells Oracle which invoices can be considered for automatic receipt application. Since receipts coming from iReceivables will already be associated with specific invoices, identified by the customer when the receipt was created, this field is not used.

Under the Funds Transfer Processing section, ensure the PAYMENT METHOD is Credit Card or Bank Account Transfer.

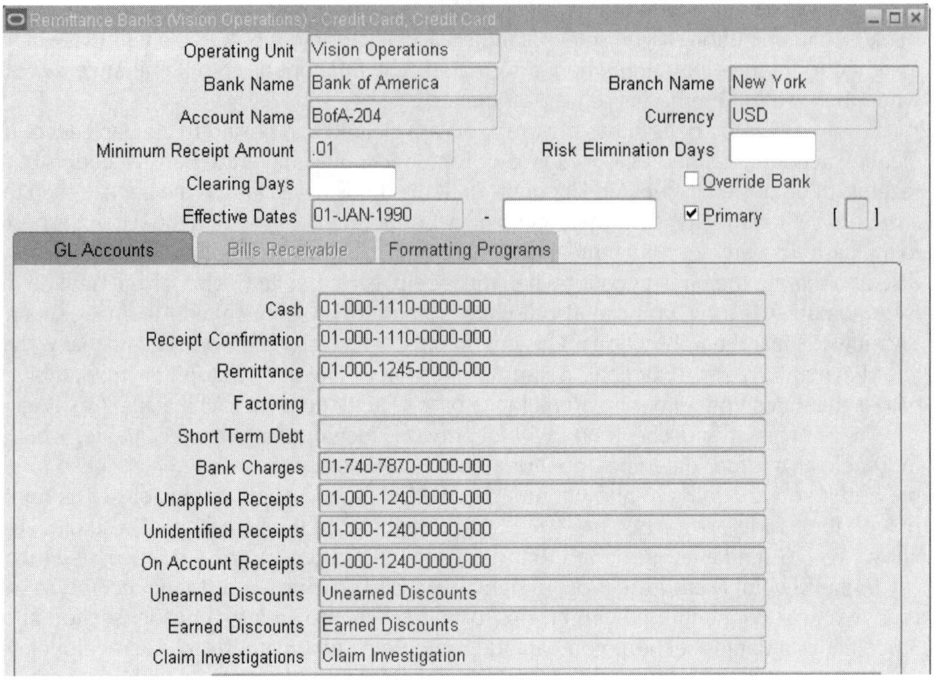

Receivables | Setup | Receipts | Receipt Classes | Bank Account button

FIGURE 9-18.   *Adding banks to receipt classes*

Bank Accounts are then added, which identify the actual bank account associated with the transaction, as well as other rules and defaults. For example, you can assign a MINIMUM RECEIPT AMOUNT, which will cause any receipts for less than this amount to be rejected. While multiple bank accounts can be associated with each receipt method, one can be selected as the PRIMARY account and will be the default that appears when no account is selected on the transaction. The primary account will be used for receipts created in iReceivables. Finally, GL Accounts can be assigned for this transaction. Refer to Figure 9-18 to see all the accounts that are available for each bank. Once this is complete, the receipt classes can be assigned in iReceivables.

Assigning Receipt Classes to iReceivables

Receipt classes are assigned in the System Parameters window (iReceivables Setup | System Parameters). You can assign one receipt method for credit cards, and one for bank account payments. Remember, each field will only show the receipt methods that are identified as the proper Payment Methods (either Credit Card or Bank Account Transfer) and that have an active bank account associated with them in the operating unit you are setting up iReceivables for. This information can also be set in the AR System Parameters (Receivables | Setup | System | System Options).

Deciding How Payments Are Handled

There are several profiles and rules that need to be set up to determine how Oracle will handle payments. Both profiles and rules are set in the iReceivables Setup responsibility; they follow the same setup steps described earlier in this chapter, in the sections titled "Setting iReceivables Profiles" and "Adding Rules to Each Profile."

The first option decides if customers can make a single payment for transactions that are associated with more than one customer. This is controlled with the profile OIR: Cross Customer Payments. When this is set to No, customers will have to submit separate payments for each customer. The next option deals with how discounts can be taken, and is controlled with both a profile and a rule. The profile OIR: Enable Discount Grace Days decides if a customer can take a discount, based on the terms associated with the transaction, after the discount period is expired. Once the profile is set, a rule can be added to override the profile for specific customers or customer sites. When this option is set to Yes, the DISCOUNT GRACE DAYS that are associated to the profile class assigned to the customer will be considered when determining if a discount can be applied. Profile Classes are created in Receivables | Customers | Profile Classes, and assigned to each account or site on the Account Profile window (Customers | Customers | Account Details).

The last profile that controls the creation of receipts is OIR: Maximum Future Payment Days Allowed, which is only applicable to ACH receipts. ACH transactions can be entered with a settlement date in the future and will be processed on that date. This profile controls the number of days in the future a customer can request an ACH receipt. When this is set to 0, then future-dated payments are not allowed. This profile is controlled with the rule Future Dated Payments, allowing different customers to have a different number of days assigned to them.

Determining How Payment Information Is Stored

When a customer submits banking information in iReceivables, Oracle gives the option of saving this information and allowing the customer to reuse it, or requiring the customer to reenter it for each transaction. The profile OIR: Save Payment Instrument Information controls this feature. When it is set to No, the information is not stored, requiring the customer to reenter it for each payment. The rule Last Used Payment Instrument is used to determine when the rule is used. Note that if you set the default for the rule to No, or the profile, when there is no rule, to No, the Pay button will not appear in the external view for the customers to make credit card payments unless you have the credit cards set up to process as a single step, as opposed to the two-step Verification and Settlement.

Setting Up Payment Approval Options

The profile OIR: Payment Approver Status controls the approval status of the transaction in iReceivables that can be selected for payment. When this is not set, or set to Disabled, then a transaction that has not been approved in iReceivables can be paid. All other settings require the iReceivables Approval Status (seen on the Account Details page in the Approval Status column) to be Approved prior to allowing the invoice to be paid in iReceivables.

Disputing Items and Creating Credit Memo Requests

Both customers and internal users can dispute any transaction that is outstanding in Receivables, which will trigger a request for a credit memo. There are several setups to enable this process, including controls that require disputes to have the proper internal approvals before they are processed into credit memos. The required setup steps mainly relate to these approvals.

Credit Memo Approval Limits

Approval limits can be set up in Receivables for four document types: Credit Memo, Adjustments, Refunds, and Receipt Write-offs. They control the limits and circumstances under which users can approve each document. The credit memo approval feature can only be used when credit memo requests are generated from iReceivables or Oracle Collections; it is not available for credits created directly in Receivables (there is no approval process available for credit memos in Receivables). In reality, the approval is for the dispute, and once a dispute is approved, then the credit memo is created; the credit memo itself is never actually approved.

Approval limits can be controlled in one of two places for credit memos. You can either use the approval limit window in Receivables to assign dollar limits (upper and lower limits) to specific currencies and transactions, or you can set up Approvals Management (AME) for your approvals, which allows much more flexibility in the approval hierarchy. Which process is used is controlled by the profile AR: Use Oracle Approvals Management in Credit Memo Workflow. When this is set to Yes, the AME will be used for your approval hierarchy for credit memos.

Setting Credit Memo Approval Limits in Receivables

Receivables approval limits create an approval hierarchy by assigning currency-specific limits as well as a credit memo reason to each user in the hierarchy. One user is set up as the primary approver for each combination. Only one person can be set up as the primary approver for each dollar range, reason, and currency combination. If a primary approver is not found, then Oracle uses the supervisor hierarchy set up on the employee record (Payables | Employees | Enter Employees when HR is not fully installed) to find the next approver with the proper authority. This functionality is not only limited, it also can become cumbersome to maintain for larger organizations using multiple currencies and reason codes.

To set up approval limits in Receivables, refer to Figure 9-19. Select the USER NAME from the list of values. Ensure that the users you select are associated with employees (System Administrator | Security | User | Define, employee field) when you are using this feature; otherwise, Oracle will not be able to route approvals where no primary approver is set up. Select the DOCUMENT TYPE of Credit Memo, which will open up the REASON field to be entered. When a credit memo is requested, the requestor is required to select a reason for the dispute, which becomes the credit memo reason.

When setting up the approval limits, note that each line is limited to a distinct reason. Next, select the CURRENCY that this approval is for; it relates to the transaction currency for each credit memo. Each user can be set up with more than one currency. Then enter the FROM AMOUNT and the TO AMOUNT. This is the actual range, in the transactional currency, that the approver can approve. If your Credit Memo transaction types are set up to only allow credit memos to be created with a negative sign (Receivables | Setup | Transactions | Transaction Types, creation sign), there is no need to set up the limits to be higher than zero. The final field, PRIMARY, can only be set for one person for each reason, currency, and amount.

Approval Management (AME)

As you can see from the setups in the preceding section, the approval options are fairly limited in Receivables, which is where AME can help. AME is a free approval engine that comes with EBS and can be set up and used for approving a large number of transactions in Oracle. Designed originally for Human Resources, it has grown and expanded over the years. AME is a very diverse application that can be set up to accommodate a large number of approval rules. Oracle markets this tool as an engine for developing both simple and complex approval rules that can be implemented by business

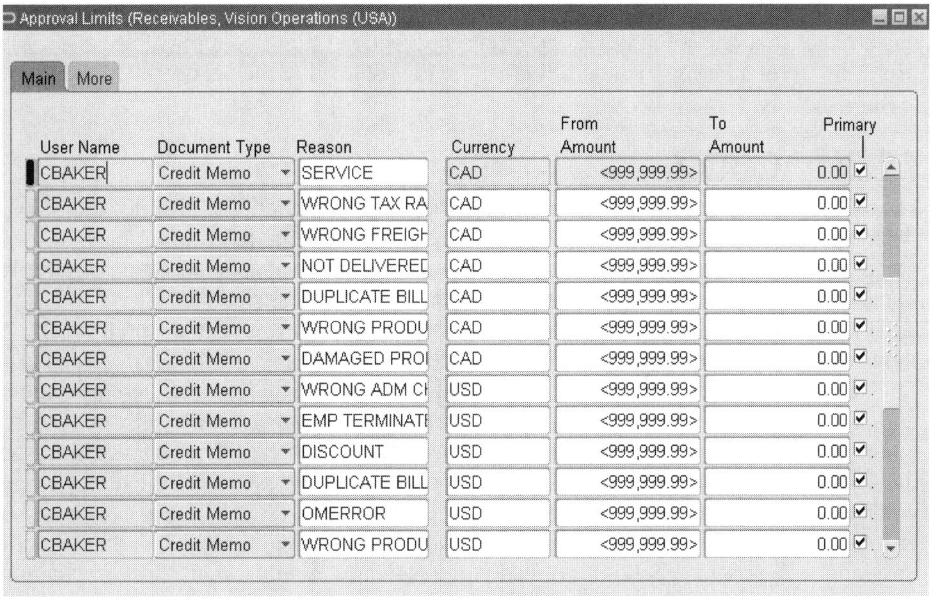

User Name	Document Type	Reason	Currency	From Amount	To Amount	Primary
CBAKER	Credit Memo ▼	SERVICE	CAD	<999,999.99>	0.00	✔
CBAKER	Credit Memo ▼	WRONG TAX RA	CAD	<999,999.99>	0.00	✔
CBAKER	Credit Memo ▼	WRONG FREIGH	CAD	<999,999.99>	0.00	✔
CBAKER	Credit Memo ▼	NOT DELIVEREC	CAD	<999,999.99>	0.00	✔
CBAKER	Credit Memo ▼	DUPLICATE BILL	CAD	<999,999.99>	0.00	✔
CBAKER	Credit Memo ▼	WRONG PRODU	CAD	<999,999.99>	0.00	✔
CBAKER	Credit Memo ▼	DAMAGED PROI	CAD	<999,999.99>	0.00	✔
CBAKER	Credit Memo ▼	WRONG ADM CI	USD	<999,999.99>	0.00	✔
CBAKER	Credit Memo ▼	EMP TERMINATI	USD	<999,999.99>	0.00	✔
CBAKER	Credit Memo ▼	DISCOUNT	USD	<999,999.99>	0.00	✔
CBAKER	Credit Memo ▼	DUPLICATE BILL	USD	<999,999.99>	0.00	✔
CBAKER	Credit Memo ▼	OMERROR	USD	<999,999.99>	0.00	✔
CBAKER	Credit Memo ▼	WRONG PRODU	USD	<999,999.99>	0.00	✔

Receivables | Setup | Transactions | Approval Limits

FIGURE 9-19. *Creating approval limits in Receivables*

analysts "without resorting to writing code." I disagree with this statement. While the AME module does remove the syntax (or specific language used when programming), it is still programming, just within a GUI environment. Without having some background or understanding of how to program, it is a difficult and confusing process to follow. Not only because of the nature of how AME works, but also because of the fact that many areas of AME require knowledge of the tables where data is stored, the AME setups are included in the Appendix of this book, where step-by-step instructions are provided. More detailed information about setting up AME can be found in the Appendix.

Credit Memo Transaction Types and Batch Sources
The last step to creating credit memos in Oracle is to ensure EBS can determine what transaction type is used when creating the credits. Typically, when you set up a transaction type for your invoices, you need to associate a credit memo type with it for this process to work (Receivables | Setup | Transaction | Transaction Types). This is the seeded path Oracle follows to find the transaction type it will use when creating the credit memo. Oracle also takes the Source from the original transaction. Both of these can be set up to use a different transaction type or source by modifying the Credit Memo Request Workflow.

Allowing iReceivables to Apply Open Credit Memos to Unpaid Invoices
Whether you allow the users of iReceivables to dispute an invoice or not, you can allow the customers or internal users (such as customer service) to apply open credit memos to open

balances on invoices. This feature is controlled with the profile OIR: Apply Credits. If this is set to No, then the button to apply credits will not be available on the Activities window. This setting has no rules that control it, but it can be set differently at the site, application, responsibility, or user level, remembering that the setting at the lowest level (which is user) will override any setting at higher levels.

Display Options

Oracle has several settings that allow you to control the way an iReceivables user can see the data. Both the contacts and aging buckets are controlled with profiles and rules.

OIR: Aging Buckets assigns the Aging that is used to display aged transactions on the iReceivables home page. The buckets available here are set up in Receivables (Setup I Collections I Aging Buckets and Interest Tiers). Rules can be added to determine which aging is used by modifying the rule called Aging Buckets. Remember, when a default is added to the rule, it will always override the profile.

Each iReceivables page has a Contact Us link at the top of the page, and default e-mail addresses can be added with rules as to when they are displayed. OIR: Active Contacts Display Limit determines the number of e-mail addresses that can be displayed on any given page, and the Contact Information rule assigns a default e-mail address as well as the ability to create rules when it is used. When adding the DEFAULT VALUE for the rule, as well as the VALUE on a specific rule, ensure you precede the e-mail address with "mailto:". This will ensure that the default e-mail program on the user's machine is opened up to send the actual e-mail. Besides creating rules for a particular customer or customer site, you can also create contact rules based on the default language for the user. The default language is defined on the Preferences window. Or you can direct users to different contacts depending on the actual iReceivables window they are on. Ensuring this is set up correctly can greatly streamline customer response.

Customizing Invoices

Invoices are the forward face of any company to their customers and can say a lot about an organization. Oracle allows invoices to be modified using BI Publisher or Oracle Reports, but neither of these can be called by iReceivables or the Order Information Portal; they both use the invoice created in Bill Presentment Architecture, or BPA. This feature has been around for quite some time but appears to be little known. From a technology standpoint, BPA is really just a GUI (graphical user interface), used to create an XML template for a data definition. Using it (as opposed to BI Publisher) has both benefits and drawbacks.

First, the drawbacks. BPA is limited to the tools and features you can find in the interface, and therefore it cannot create as complicated formats as you could using RTF (Rich Text Format) or XSL-FO (eXtensible Stylesheet Language–Formatting Objects) to create BI Publisher templates.

And the benefits? First, it took me less than 30 minutes to modify my first invoice and move it to production. If someone out there modified their first BI Publisher template in that amount of time, having never used it or a similar tool before, I would like to meet you (and you should be giving yourself a pat on the back and writing a book for the rest of us!). Second, BPA allows you to assign different invoice formats to different customers or groupings of customers. This feature is available for printed invoices that use a BI Publisher template, but since BI Publisher cannot create an HTML format, it cannot be used to create formats for viewing invoices online. Third, it is the BPA format that is used in iReceivables, in Order Information Portal, and when you view the invoice on the transactions screen in Receivables by using the icon next to the transaction number. (The profile AR: BPA Detail Access Enabled needs to be set to Yes for the icon to appear.) For these reasons, I'll give up a little on the formatting features and use BPA to customize all Receivables invoices.

Using Bill Presentment Architecture to Customize Your Invoices

Oracle comes seeded with some basic formats, or templates, and these are a good place to start. Oracle will not let you update the seeded templates, but it does allow you to copy them. A template has to be inactive in order for you to modify them. Since Oracle will always display the seeded invoice template, which uses a logo that states "Your Company Logo Here," when it cannot find an active template for your invoice, ensure you copy your production templates before making modifications, and then reassign it to the customers to use the new template once it is completed. Whether you are creating and testing the invoice in production or migrating it from a test environment, this is how it is done. (I am not promoting either way of making changes—that is for the change control folks at your company to decide—but rather giving you the options. Note that currently there is no migration tool to move BPA formats from instance to instance, but there is an enhancement request open with Oracle to provide one.) What will need to be tested in a test instance first is the template assignments to ensure that the customers are getting the right invoice, as well as any supplemental data you add to the invoice.

Technical Overview

Before I cover the functional features of BPA, let me get the technical overview out of the way. This becomes important if the fields you want to appear on your invoices are not available. BPA uses two seeded views to provide the data for the invoices. These views are called ARBPA_CUSTOMER_TRX_HEADER and ARBPA_CUSTOMER_TRX_LINE. Additional views can be created and used as supplemental data fields, but the name must begin with the prefix ARBPA_ because BPA only recognizes views that begin with this. An example of why you would want to create a supplemental view would be to add item numbers to your invoice. While this is part of the seeded line view, the join between RA_CUSTOMER_TRX_LINES_ALL and MTL_SYSTEM_ITEMS is the ORG_ID on the transaction and the ORGANIZATION_ID of your item master (I warned you this was technical!). If your system is not set up so that these organizations have the same ID, which most do not because Oracle itself recommends that the master item organization not be the same as the organization where inventory transactions are performed, then the view will never return the item number.

Oracle comes seeded with several data sources already, found in Bill Presentment Superuser | Bill Management | Configuration | Data Sources. To use any of the seeded supplemental data sources, they will first need to be enabled by checking the SELECT box next to the data source and then Go next to the MARK AS ENABLED drop-down box.

The easiest way to create a supplemental view is to take one of the existing views, modify it, create it in the database, and then register it in BPA. Make sure you test your modified view to ensure it is returning the proper data. I have run into instances where the seeded view works fine, but the supplemental view would not return data for any transaction without a tax line, and I had to delete the where condition for the supplemental view to work. Why the seeded view works with the where clause and the exact same view registered as a supplemental view does not is much deeper into the bowels Oracle than I have traveled to date, so I just accept that it does and modify my supplemental view accordingly.

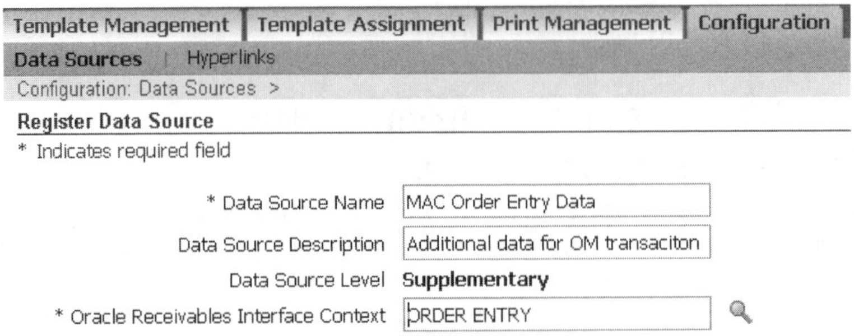

Bill Presentment Superuser | Configuration | Data Sources | Register button

FIGURE 9-20. *Registering a supplemental view in BPA*

Once the view has been created in the database, it needs to be registered in BPA before it can be used. This is done on the Configuration window, shown in Figure 9-20, using the Register button. Assign a unique DATA SOURCE NAME and a description, and then select the INTERFACE CONTEXT it will be used with. Interface context is a required field and will limit the invoices that will find data when using this view. Each context can only have one supplemental view registered against it, so you will need to plan your views carefully, making modifications to existing ones when you need to add additional fields.

ORACLE RECEIVABLES INTERFACE CONTEXT relates to the information that is found in the INTERFACE_HEADER_CONTEXT field on the Receivables transaction (RA_CUSTOMER_TRX_ALL), and comes from the data populated by Oracle in the autoinvoice interface tables. This field is *not* populated for manual transactions created directly in receivables, but *is* populated for all transactions imported from another EBS module, such as Order Management (Context = ORDER ENTRY) or Oracle Claims (Context = CLAIMS). If you are using autoinvoice to import transactions from someplace other than EBS, then you can populate this field with a unique value. This is important, because there are additional steps, described next, that need to be taken to ensure that you can use this data source for both imported and manually created invoices. This context value needs to be set up before you can use it, which is done by adding additional CODES to the Invoice Transaction Flexfield. This is a descriptive flexfield in Oracle, which used to store company-specific data on transactions (refer to Figure 9-21).

To create a new context code, first unfreeze the flexfield by unchecking FREEZE FLEXFIELD DEFINITION. Then add a CODE, which is used by Oracle internally, MEANING, which the users see, and a DESCRIPTION. Click segments, and set up the meaning for one or more of the columns INTERFACE_LINE_ATTTIBUTE 1–15. This will represent the data that you populate in this field in the autoinvoice interface table (RA_INTERFACE_LINES_ALL). For example, you can populate a legacy order reference number to provide users and Oracle with a link between the legacy transaction and the Oracle transaction. Once you have made your updates, ensure you select FREEZE FLEXFIELD DEFINITION and that the flexfield compiles normally. The flexfield is automatically compiled when you save the record.

Adding a Context to a Manually Created Invoice As mentioned earlier, this will then populate the INTERFACE_HEADER_CONTEXT field on transactions when Autoinvoice is run and the transaction is created, and all manual transactions do not have this data. If you want to use the same data source

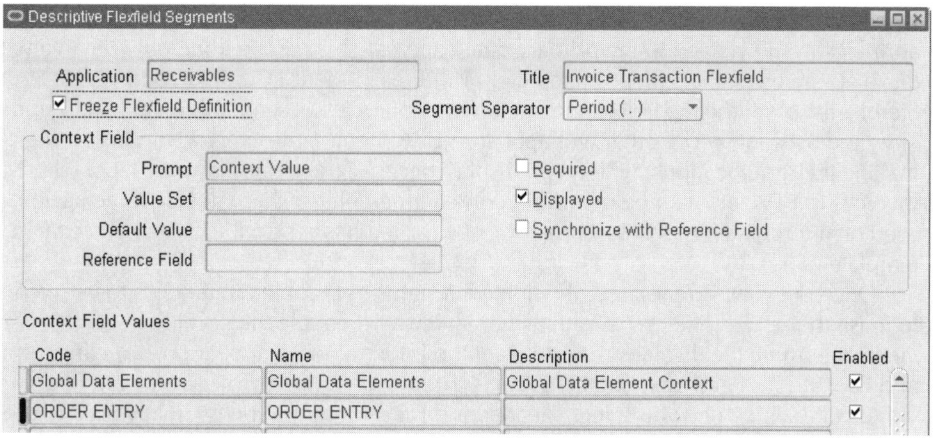

Receivables | Setup | Financials | Flexfields | Descriptive | Segments

FIGURE 9-21.   *Adding additional context values for transactions*

for transactions that are created manually in Receivables as ones that are created via the autoinvoice interface, you will need to modify the descriptive flexfield called Invoice Transaction Flexfield.

In this example, we are going to add Order Entry to manual transactions so that invoices from Order Management and those created manually can use the same supplemental data source to get the item numbers. The CODE, MEANING, and DESCRIPTION were all set up as ORDER ENTRY. Ensure that DISPLAY is checked in the Context Field area, and that the flexfield is enabled, and refreeze your flexfield, ensuring it compiles successfully. This will open up the Transaction flexfield on manual transactions, allowing you to select ORDER ENTRY. See Figure 9-22 for an example of an invoice using this context. Now, both invoices imported from Order Management via Autoinvoice and transactions entered directly into Receivables can use the same supplemental data view.

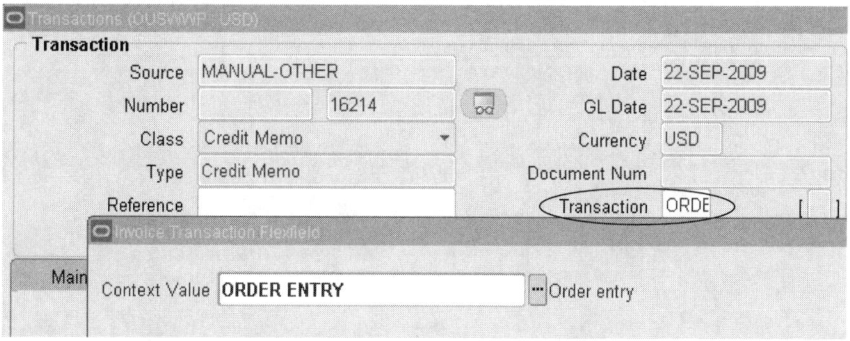

Receivables | Transactions | Transactions

FIGURE 9-22.   *Transaction with the Invoice Transaction flexfield populated*

Finalizing the View for Use

Depending on the context assigned to a supplemental view, you may need to synchronize the attributes in the view with the primary data sources. This can be done only on a view that is disabled, by using the Synchronize link in Bill Presentment I(Configuration I Data Sources). Here, a list of all the flexfields associated with your view is seen, allowing you to update the ITEM NAME and ITEM DISPLAY LABEL that will appear in BPA. Item names appear in BPA for the person making the modifications, while item display because the default display label when creating invoices in BPA, and can be overridden on each template. Then, decide if the attribute can be used on a template, by selecting TEMPLATE ITEM, or if a header attribute can be used to assign the template to a rule.

Once the view is registered, it will have a status of Disabled and needs to be queried back up to finish the setups. Select Views to assign a view and enable the specific fields. To assign the view, determine the display area you want the information to appear on, selecting from Header and Footer, Lines and Tax, or Details Page. The region of the invoice you want to use the data on will dictate which one you select. Header and Footer information is usually used to identify data that relates to the entire invoice, such as customer or invoice totals. Lines and Tax data is any information that pertains to a specific line that appears on the face of the invoice, while Details Page will display data when drilling down on a particular invoice line. Use the Register button to select a VIEW NAME (remember, only views that begin with ARBPA_ will appear here), and give the view a user-friendly display name. At this point, you need to create a link between this view and the seeded views, as well as determine which columns are visible to be added to an invoice.

The links between the seeded views and the view you are creating are set up as a Parameter, which is the join between the two views, telling Oracle how to find the data in the supplemental view based on the information passed from one of the seeded views. For example, you can use the transaction ID to link the two views, which allows Oracle to find the supplemental data for a specific transaction. In the Add Parameter drop-down, select Transaction Attribute, and click Go. Now you can add a column name from your supplemental view and link it to a value in the seeded views (see Figure 9-23).

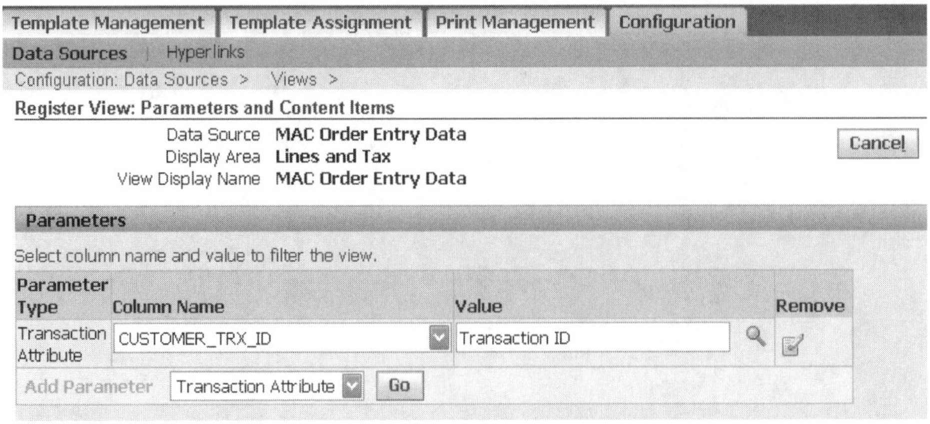

FIGURE 9-23. *Adding a parameter to link a supplemental view to one of the seeded BPA views*

Next, in the Content Item section, you can change the ITEM NAME and ITEM DISPLAY LABEL for each field on the view, and determine if it is a TEMPLATE ITEM, which allows it to be selected on a template. Once you are done, select Finish, and remember to enable the view. Note that in order to make any changes to this view, you will need to disable it again, during which time the data will not be available to print or view for any transaction; it simply disappears from the invoice, so ensure you plan your production maintenance carefully.

Modifying an Invoice

Before modifying an invoice, you will need to either copy one of the seeded invoices or copy your production invoice. Only invoices that are incomplete can be modified. While an invoice is incomplete, it is no longer available for any application to use, and the default seeded template will be used. By copying the invoice first, and modifying the copied invoice, you assure that the old format will continue to be used until your changes are complete, when you can assign the changed invoice to your rules, ensuring there is a seamless transition from the old one to the new format.

To copy an invoice, query it up and use the Duplicate link. This will open the screen shown in Figure 9-24. The only field that cannot be updated when copying a template is PRIMARY DATA SOURCE, so ensure the template you are copying is associated with the data source you want to use. Oracle comes with only two primary data sources: Oracle Receivables and Oracle Receivables Balance Forward. TRANSACTION CLASS will agree to the class assigned to the transaction you are trying to print. So if you want to use the same template for invoices, debit memos, and credit memos, you will need to create three templates, one for each transaction class. SUPPLEMENTARY DATA SOURCE can be set to any view that is registered in the Configuration window (both seeded and custom); it needs to have the same context as the transaction you are trying to print. Select Oracle Receivables Tax Printing Option for the TAX FORMAT to print the tax data in the format identified for the customer, or select Custom, which will allow you to select the fields you want to display for the tax summary. The Tax Printing Option for the customer is found on the account details in the Tax Printing field (Receivables | Customers | Customers | Account Details | Account Profile tab | Invoicing Section).

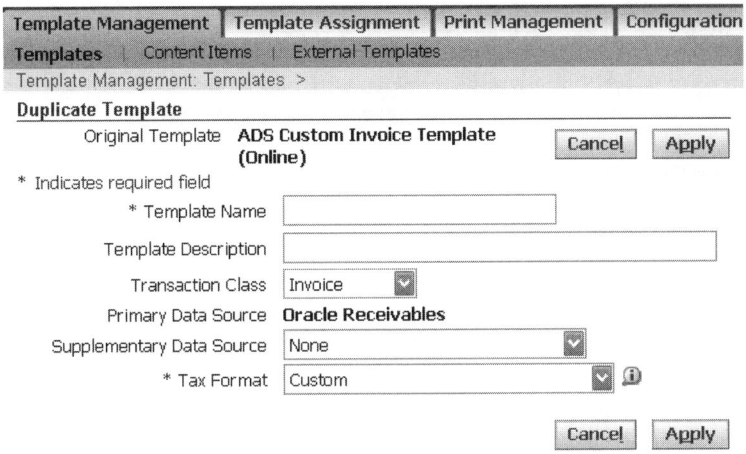

Bill Presentment Superuser | Template Management | Templates | Duplicate button

FIGURE 9-24. *Duplicating an invoice*

Once the invoice is duplicated and inactive, the Update link can be used to make modifications to the format. The same information that was available for update when the template was copied can also be updated here, before getting to the actual layout page, shown in Figure 9-25. There are a few things you *cannot* do when modifying a template, so let me cover these first. First and foremost, you cannot use the Back button on your browser. It may work for a while, but there is a bug Oracle cannot resolve that will eventually corrupt your template, which makes the template unusable, losing all your changes. Second, you cannot do a lot with fonts. You have the options to set the font and font size for the entire invoice, but the only options you have at the field level are Bold or Regular. And you have no control over the left and right alignment of the data in a field. While you can move a field from left to right, the field labels are all left justified, while the data in the field will depend on the type of data it is displaying. And you cannot add color, except by using an image, to the data or fields on the template. So you are definitely sacrificing some formatting options to use BPA. But with careful planning, you can still create some really nice-looking invoices.

The invoices are broken down into three sections: Header, Lines and Tax, and Footer. The header and footer sections can only contain data that is registered as header and footer data in the view, but they have several printing options. This data is usually non-repeating data that pertains to the entire invoice, such as customer or total invoice amount. The lines and tax data is specific to an individual line on the invoice, such as item number or quantity. The boundaries in

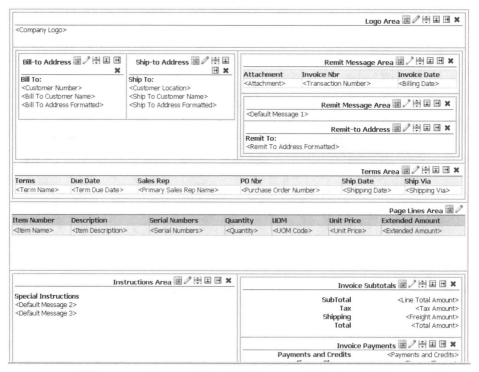

Bill Presentment Superuser | Template Management | Templates | Update

FIGURE 9-25. *Modifying the template layout*

BPA help to see the sections. In Figure 9-25, everything above and including the Terms area is header information. The section labeled Page Lines Area, which includes the item number, is lines and tax, and the box below that (Instructions Area, Invoice Subtotals, and Invoice Payments) holds footer data.

Adding Your Company's Logo and a Link to Your Web Site Oracle comes with a logo assigned to the invoice that prints "Your Company Logo." Believe it or not, I have seen implementations where the company goes live with this, sending it out to its customers this way. If no other change is made to the formats for invoice, credit memo, and debit memo, the logo must be updated. Oracle recommends that a GIF file be used to create the logo for the clearest results. Since the logo cannot be sized on the template as it can on other BI Publisher Templates, ensure you save it the size you want the logo to display on the invoice before loading it into Oracle into the OA_MEDIA directory. This will need to be done by your DBA. Ensure you have this same file, with the exact same name by which it is saved in the database, available from your PC. Once this is done, a *content item* can be created for the logo, and added to the invoice. Content items are either images or text you want to add to your invoice that does not reside within Oracle. For example, while your bill-to address does exist in Oracle, your web address does not, and you may want to add it to the bottom of your invoice—you would create a content item to do so.

To create an image content item, go to the Content Item page and select Create (see Figure 9-26). Select a unique ITEM NAME, and add an ITEM DESCRIPTION. DISPLAY LABEL only needs to be added if you want a label to display on your invoice for the image. You can add a HYPERLINK NAME if you want your customers to be able to click your logo to get to your web site. This feature is only available for soft copy invoices that are e-mailed or displayed in Oracle, such as from iReceivables, and not on printed invoices.

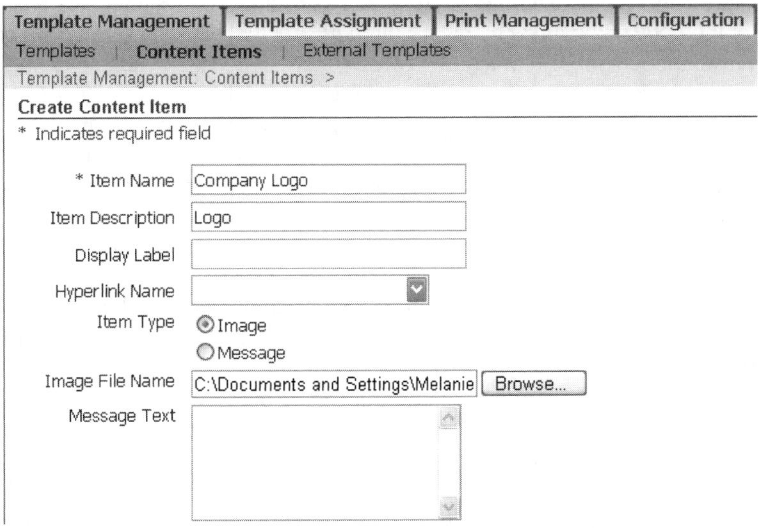

Bill Presentment Superuser | Template Management | Content Items

FIGURE 9-26. *Creating a content item for your logo*

If you decide to use a hyperlink for this or any other content item, you will need to set up the hyperlink first. This is done on the Configuration | Hyperlinks window. The only required fields are HYPERLINK NAME, which internally identifies this link in BPA, and HYPERLINK ADDRESS, which is the actual URL of the hyperlink. Additionally, you can add either a fixed value or a transaction attribute that will be included in the link. For example, if you are using an anonymous user sign-on for iReceivables, you can create a hyperlink that will open the transaction in question in iReceivables. You can review the seeded hyperlink that Oracle provides called Oracle Transaction Number Link for an example of how to do this.

Continuing with the Logo setups, add the IMAGE FILENAME by using the Browse button to find the image you have saved to either your PC or your network. This process does not actually load the image on the server but is Oracle's way of obtaining the actual filename for the image. It looks for that filename (yes, it is case sensitive) in the OA_Media directory on the Oracle database.

You can also use content items to create text, such as a contact number or legal information you are required to include on your invoice. This is done the same way as a logo is created, except the ITEM TYPE would be message. The text you want to appear is then typed in the MESSAGE TEXT field. Here is a formatting tip: since you cannot control text wrapping in BPA, and all items are either left or right justified, you may need to break the text you want to add into multiple content items. Once this is saved, it can be selected in the logo area of the invoice:

Selecting Content for Your Invoice   The icons available in each section are used to add content and format the section. To see what each icon controls, select Show Icon Legend. Content is added using the first icon in each box (the square without any arrows in it). From here, you can add fields and data from the main view, the supplemental view you selected, or any content items you have added to BPA. You can also select the way the layout will display (see Figure 9-27). First, you need to select the DATA SOURCE VIEW where you are going to get the content from. You can mix and match, taking one field from your primary data source and additional fields from your supplementary source or content items. The size of each area is dynamic as far as length goes but will wrap any items that are too wide. The main limitation in the data you can select applies if you are in a header or footer section, or the body of the invoice; this will limit the content you can select from both the primary and seeded views, though not the content items you set up, which are available on the entire invoice.

Selecting a specific DATA SOURCE VIEW and then Go will change the selections in the Available Content Items section. Oracle Receivables is the primary data source for transactions, with the only other primary data source being Oracle Receivables Balance Forward. This is used when you are using the Balance Forward feature in Receivables to roll your prior month outstanding balances into any current period activity, which works similar to Consolidated Billing in prior releases. All the other data sources that come with BPA are supplementary and have additional data for contracts, order management, finance charges on invoices, or invoices that are created from project accounting.

When you register custom data sources, they will also be supplementary. Remember when creating your company-specific data sources that you can only have one primary and one supplementary source per template. Any content items you have created, including logos, hyperlinks to allow drill-downs, and content for verbiage you want to add to your invoice, are found in the Custom: None data source view. In order to use the hyperlinks for drill-downs, which will allow online users to drill down into the details of a particular line or transaction and see additional information, ensure that the profile AR: BPA Detail Access Enabled is set to Yes.

The content items selected will display in the order they are listed, so ensure you have them set up in the correct order. The arrows to the right of the Selected Content Items box can be used to move content up and down.

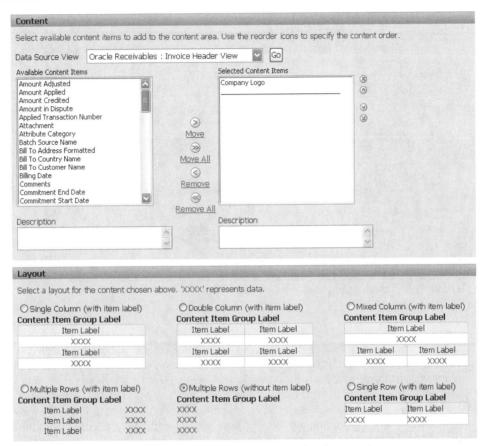

Bill Presentment Superuser | Templates | Update | Content icon

FIGURE 9-27. *Adding content and layout options to your invoice*

While working with the line and tax section of the invoice, you can modify the tax summary data that appears on the invoice if you selected the TAX FORMAT as Custom on the first page of updating a template. This will override the summary format assigned to the customer, allowing you to select the fields that will be displayed.

In the Layout section, there are six layouts to select from, and you are limited to displaying your content in one of these layouts. Once you have selected your content and layout, use the pencil link to add additional formatting. This allows you to control spacing, format labels, and decide if your data will be displayed in bold or not (see Figure 9-28). Each section on your template is assigned a name, which is not displayed on the actual invoice but is for the people who are maintaining invoices. RENAME CONTENT AREA is where this name is stored. Spaces can be added above, below, to the left, and to the right of each area, adding white space to the invoice and making it look less jumbled. The WIDTH can be adjusted as well, controlling the amount of a section each content area will take up. For example, if you split a section and now have two content areas within a border, each area will have a width of 50 percent.

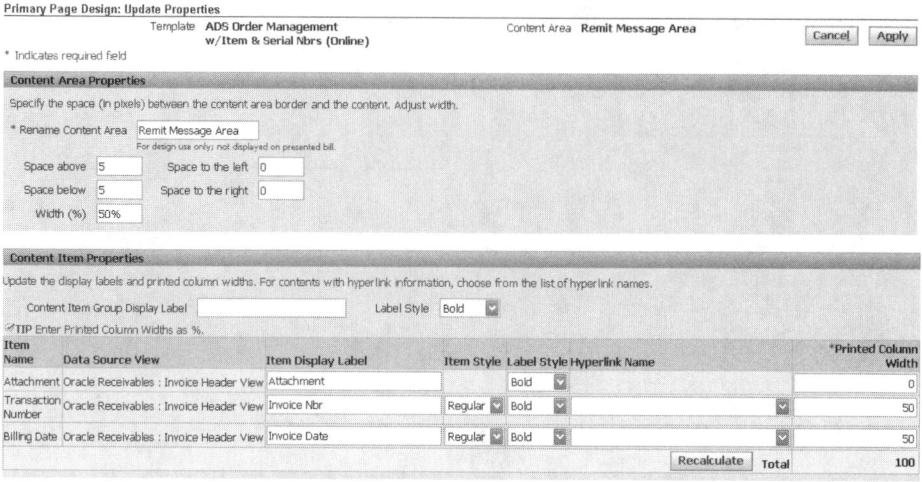

Bill Presentment Superuser | Templates | Update | Properties icon

FIGURE 9-28. *Formatting your content data*

CONTENT ITEM GROUP DISPLAY LABEL is the label that prints above all the data in a section, while ITEM DISPLAY LABEL prints either next to or above (depending on the layout you selected—not all layouts allow display labels). The CONTENT ITEM GROUP DISPLAY LABEL field is not required, and leaving it blank will display your data without any label. You can decide if a label or the item will be displayed in bold or not, but this is about the only formatting you can do for individual fields. When your layout was designated as any of the column options, or as a Single Row, then you can decide how wide each column will be. The numbers entered here are a percent of the total section, and the individual items must add up to 100 percent or less. The Recalculate button needs to be used to update the total. Note that when you add new content to a section, its width is always assigned as zero and needs to be updated in order for it to appear on a printed invoice.

If you are creating an invoice that will be printed, the only way to place the footer on the page is by adding spaces above the footer. Unfortunately, this is a fixed amount of space, and if your invoices have a dynamic number of lines, the footer will display in a different spot for each invoice. Currently, there is no work-around for this except to create an RTF or PDF template using BI Publisher, and upload this as an external template for printing only, while still using BPA to create the invoice for online viewing.

The other icons are used to split a section into two, move the content in a section, or delete a section. Splitting sections helps greatly with the formatting, and adding a section without any content can add white space and help with the formatting. Remember while working on the template that all changes are automatically saved when the section is closed, even without pressing the Save button.

The final formatting is done on the Print Setup page, after clicking Next. Here, you can select the PAGE SETUP as A4, Legal, or Letter and set the margins and paper size. Also, determine if there is a PAGE NUMBER on the printed invoice and set the FONT and FONT SIZE for the entire invoice. Header and Footer options determine how the header and footer sections appear on the printed invoices.

Using Attachments with Online Viewing   Oracle allows attachments to be added to most transactions within the core applications, including Receivables. These attachments can include web sites, text, or actual files. BPA allows these attachments to be viewed and updated. This is available from the Oracle Receivables: Invoice Header View. There are two profiles that control attachments in BPA. First, AR: BPA Attachment Update Enabled determines if an attachment can be added. This will display an Add button on the invoice, allowing the user to add attachments to the invoice. The profile AR: BPA Print Attachment Document Category controls the category that the attachments can be added under. Once saved, this attachment is also available on the transaction form in Receivables.

Previewing Your Invoices   Once you are done with the template, you can review how the invoice looks with actual data using Interactive Preview. This allows you to preview not only the HTML, or On Line, format, but also the printed format. It is important to check both if you plan on using both, as the On Line format is dynamic, while the printed PDF format is fixed and based on the paper sizes and fonts. I usually make two different templates, one that displays well in HTML, and one that prints properly on a printer. Like all responsibilities, BPA is limited to the data you can see based on the profile settings for MO: Operating Unit and MO: Security Profile. So you may need to make more than one responsibility to see transactions for a particular operating unit.

A trick when working with the On Line version is that you can leave it open on your PC while you are making modifications to a template, and use your browser's refresh button (or move from page to page on the invoice) to refresh the data instantly and see the effects of your changes. Unfortunately, this does not work with the Printed version, which is static. For this reason, I usually create the On Line template first, and then copy it once it is done to correct the spacing for the Printed version.

Once your formatting is complete, select one or more templates and use Select Template: Mark as Complete: Go to complete it and make it available to assign to a rule.

Using External Templates   I mentioned in the beginning of the BPA section that BPA makes it easier to create templates than BI Publisher but is limited in some of the formatting features. Because of this, you may decide to create an RDF or PDF template using BI Publisher and upload it into BPA. The major advantage in doing this is that you can use the Template Assignment feature to assign different template formats to different customers or transactions. The disadvantage is that you will not be able to view these templates online from Receivables, Order Information Portal, or iReceivables, as they are only available for printed invoices.

Uploading an external template first allows you to select the data sources, and then upload either a PDF or RFT file. The last step allows you to map any items on your template to the data sources that are registered in BPA, so that the tags on your template can have one name while the data sources have another.

Assigning Templates to Customers or Transactions

Oracle allows you to assign different templates to either different customers or different transactions in Receivables. For example, you can have one format for new sales, and a different format for warranty transactions. There are specific attributes associated to a transaction that you can use to assign the templates. These are listed in Table 9-2. Remember, Oracle comes seeded with one rule that uses the default templates for all transactions not assigned to a rule, so ensure your rules are all-inclusive. When printing invoices, the concurrent request will complete with a warning if a particular transaction cannot find a rule.

Attribute Name	Where Stored
Batch Source	Source associated with the transaction.
Bill To City	City on the bill-to customer on the transaction.
Bill To Country	Country on the bill-to customer on the transaction.
Bill To Customer Name	Actual bill-to customer name on the transaction.
Bill To State	State on the bill-to customer on the transaction.
Billing Date	Transaction date (not GL date).
Context Reference	Either the INTERFACE_HEADER_CONTEXT field on the Receivables transaction (RA_CUSTOMER_TRX_ALL), or the Invoice Transaction flexfield.
Legal Entity	The Legal Entity associated with the Ledger that the transaction belongs to.
Operating Unit	The Operating Unit assigned to the transaction.
Profile Class	The Profile Class assigned to the bill-to customer on the transaction.
Reverse Charge VAT Invoice	Used mainly in the United Kingdom, identifies invoices that have a tax rule that is associated with the Tax Reporting Type Code of REVERSE_CHARGE_VAT. See My Oracle Support Note 785486.1 for detailed setups.
Ship To Customer Name	Actual ship-to customer name on the transaction.
Ship Via	Freight Carrier on the transaction (using the Freight button).
Tax Printing Options	Options associated to the bill-to customer on the transaction.
Terms	Transaction terms.
Transaction Type	Type assigned to the transaction.
Unformatted Outstanding Balance	Actual balance remaining on the transaction when the invoice is generated. This allows different templates to be used for different balances.
Unformatted Total Amount	Total amount of the invoice when the invoice is generated. This means if the amount is updated, the template used may change.

TABLE 9-2.   *Available Attributes for Assigning Templates*

Templates are grouped by both primary and supplementary data sources when a rule is created, so if you have templates that have different sources, you must create different rules for them. To create a rule, see Figure 9-29. After assigning a RULE NAME, select both your PRIMARY and SUPPLEMENTARY DATA SOURCES. Next, determine what order this rule will be considered. You can set different orders for either viewing invoices online or creating a printed invoice. The only options for the Rule Order are either First, or After a specific rule. Next, add the attributes that you are going to use to select this template. You can add multiple attributes, including more than one of the same attribute. For example, you can add three different transaction types, or one transaction type with a specific source.

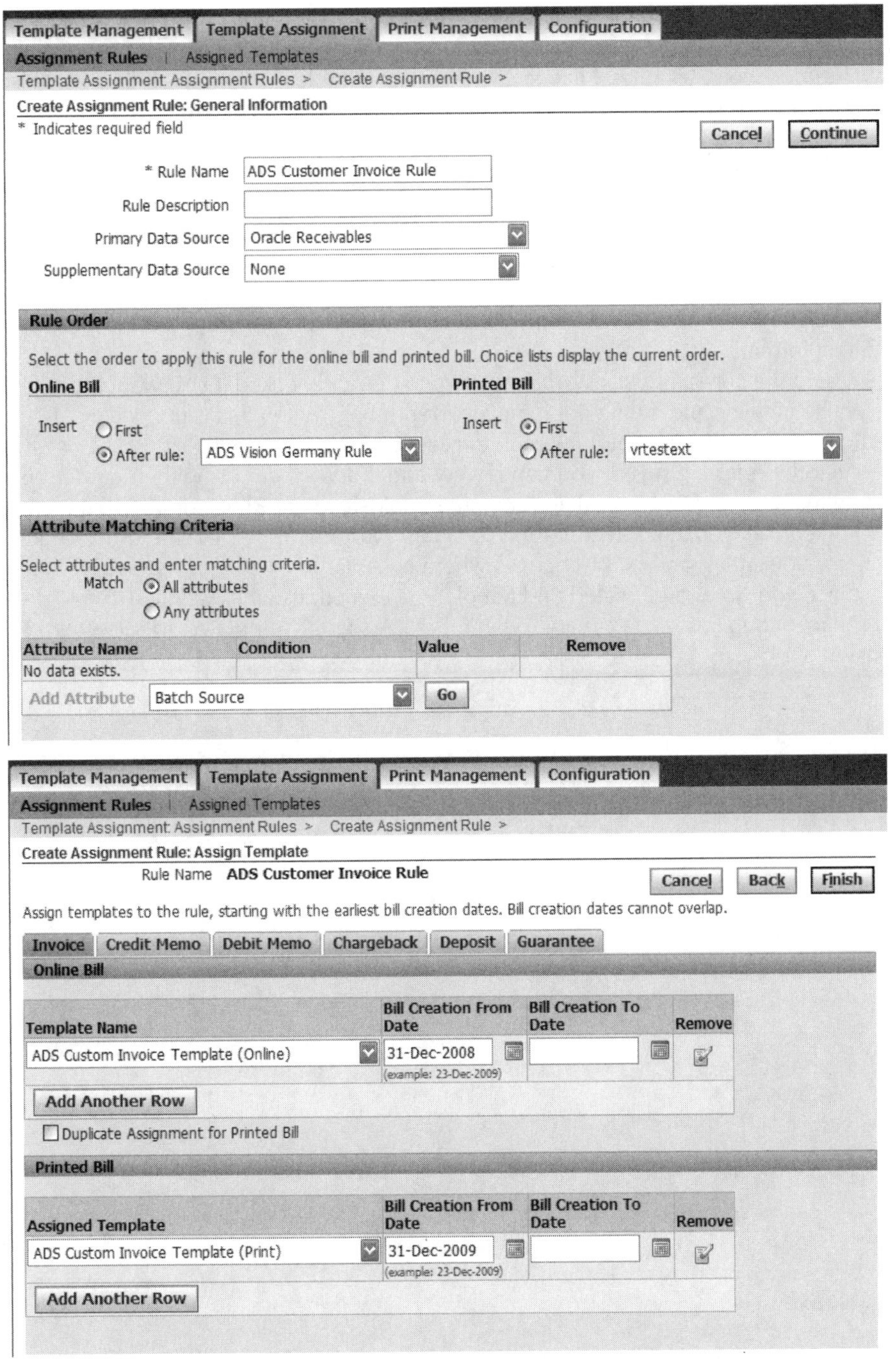

| Template Management | Template Assignment | Print Management | Configuration |

Assignment Rules | Assigned Templates

Template Assignment: Assignment Rules > Create Assignment Rule >

Create Assignment Rule: General Information

* Indicates required field

Cancel   Continue

* Rule Name	ADS Customer Invoice Rule
Rule Description	
Primary Data Source	Oracle Receivables
Supplementary Data Source	None

Rule Order

Select the order to apply this rule for the online bill and printed bill. Choice lists display the current order.

Online Bill   **Printed Bill**

Insert ○ First   Insert ⊙ First
        ⊙ After rule: ADS Vision Germany Rule   ○ After rule: vrtestext

Attribute Matching Criteria

Select attributes and enter matching criteria.
Match ⊙ All attributes
       ○ Any attributes

Attribute Name	Condition	Value	Remove
No data exists.			

Add Attribute   Batch Source   Go

| Template Management | Template Assignment | Print Management | Configuration |

Assignment Rules | Assigned Templates

Template Assignment: Assignment Rules > Create Assignment Rule >

Create Assignment Rule: Assign Template

Rule Name **ADS Customer Invoice Rule**

Cancel   Back   Finish

Assign templates to the rule, starting with the earliest bill creation dates. Bill creation dates cannot overlap.

| Invoice | Credit Memo | Debit Memo | Chargeback | Deposit | Guarantee |

Online Bill

Template Name	Bill Creation From Date	Bill Creation To Date	Remove
ADS Custom Invoice Template (Online)	31-Dec-2008 (example: 23-Dec-2009)		☑

Add Another Row

☐ Duplicate Assignment for Printed Bill

Printed Bill

Assigned Template	Bill Creation From Date	Bill Creation To Date	Remove
ADS Custom Invoice Template (Print)	31-Dec-2009 (example: 23-Dec-2009)		☑

Add Another Row

Bill Presentment Superuser | Template Assignment | Assignment Rules

FIGURE 9-29.   *Creating a template assignment rule*

Ensure you select the proper Match option (ANY or ALL ATTRIBUTES) for the data you are selecting. If you assign more than one transaction type with the Match Option of All, no transactions will ever meet the condition of the rule, because each transaction can only have one transaction type. When creating more complex rules, I like to create a catch-all rule that has no attributes that is ordered *after* the last rule. This way, any transaction that does not meet a specific rule will get a template. If your invoicing needs do not allow a generic template, set up a template that states on it "Your Invoice did not meet any rules. Please contact your Bill Presentment administrator to update the rules" instead of data, so that the users know to contact someone to correct the problem.

After the attributes are added, you can add the templates for each transaction (Invoice, Credit Memo, Debit Memo, Chargeback, Deposit, and Guarantee) in Receivables. The templates are assigned with a BILL CREATION FROM DATE and BILL CREATION TO DATE. This allows you to ensure any invoices generated prior to a specific date use one format, and those after a specific date use a different format.

Ensure the DUPLICATE ASSIGNMENT FOR PRINTED BILL is *not* checked if you want to assign one template for online viewing and a different template for printing. When this is unchecked, it opens up a section to assign the templates for each transaction for printed bills.

After the rules are saved, you can review and modify them using the Reorder button (Bill Presentment Superuser | Template Assignment | Assignment Rules). For both the Online Bill and the Printed Bill, you can select the SUPPLEMENTARY DATA SOURCE, review the order Oracle is using to evaluate your rules, and make changes where necessary.

Once your rules are created and templates assigned, use the Assigned Template window (Bill Presentment Superuser | Template Assignment | Assigned Templates) to see where each template is assigned.

CHAPTER
10

Using iReceivables

Receivables can be used both internally and externally to not only provide information, but also to request credits and submit payments. Internally, it is a nice, query-only view of a customer's account, including outstanding and delinquent balances, disputes, available discounts, and transactions. Externally, the customers have access to the same inquiry views but they also have the ability to submit a payment or request a credit memo in the form of a dispute.

Accessing Customer Data in iReceivables

iReceivables has a little more security built around it than the other self-service modules, mostly due to the fact that it includes the Anonymous Login feature. Both the external and internal views begin with a search page, which is slightly different for external customers, providing more security. The external search options include credit and debit memo numbers, credit requests, deposit, invoice, payment, (customer) purchase order, and sales order, as well as the customer number. The customer search is off the customer number, not the name. All require that an exact match be entered, and Oracle's wildcard (%) is not available. Adding a tip using Oracle's OA Framework features, outlined in Chapter 2, will help customers to sign in. Internally, users are allowed to use the wildcard in the search fields and the customer's name is available as an option, allowing greater access to the data.

Home Page

The home page shows a recap of the open transactions, payments, and credit memos, as well as the total amount due on the account (see Figure 10-1). In the Statement section, customers can download a statement of their outstanding transactions. This is an XML Publisher report

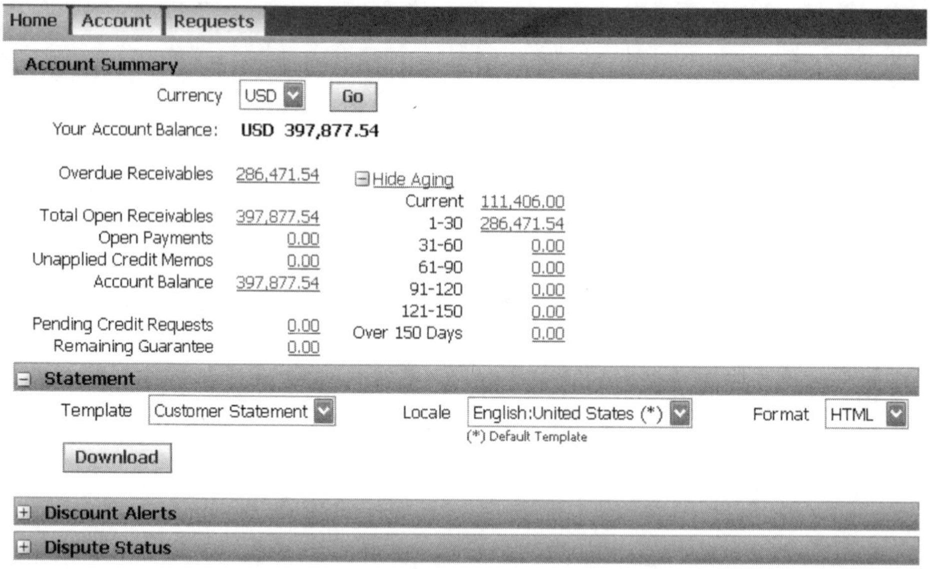

Home	Account	Requests		

Account Summary

Currency USD ▾ Go

Your Account Balance: **USD 397,877.54**

Overdue Receivables	286,471.54	⊟ Hide Aging	
		Current	111,406.00
Total Open Receivables	397,877.54	1-30	286,471.54
Open Payments	0.00	31-60	0.00
Unapplied Credit Memos	0.00	61-90	0.00
Account Balance	397,877.54	91-120	0.00
		121-150	0.00
Pending Credit Requests	0.00	Over 150 Days	0.00
Remaining Guarantee	0.00		

⊟ **Statement**

Template Customer Statement ▾   Locale English:United States (*) ▾   Format HTML ▾
(*) Default Template

Download

⊞ **Discount Alerts**

⊞ **Dispute Status**

FIGURE 10-1. *iReceivables home page*

and is not the same format as used by the Statement feature in Receivables, allowing the customers to generate up-to-date statements at any time. This report uses the data definition called iReceivables Customers Statement Data Definition, and the template is in the RTF format. This format should be modified at the very least to add your company's logo.

Requesting a Credit Memo via a Dispute

Customers can start the process of receiving a credit by disputing an entire invoice or specific information on an invoice. The way this process works out of the box is that the customer disputes an item, which is then routed to the collector associated with the customer on the transaction being disputed (Receivables I Customers I Customers I Accounts I Profile). Once the collector has approved the dispute, it is then routed to the proper person for approval, based on either the Approval Limits or AME setups. If approval is granted, a credit memo will be created for the dispute transaction based on the credit memo transaction type assigned to the disputed invoice's transaction type (Receivables I Setup I Transactions I Transaction Types).

Submitting a Dispute

When submitting a dispute, the customer has to select a reason for the dispute. These reasons not only provide some general information as to why the transaction is being disputed, they can also be used to set up approval limits. (They are required when approval limits are set up in Receivables, but optional when using AME.) Dispute Reasons can be added or disabled under the Receivables Quick Code for Credit Memo Reason (Receivables I Setup I System I QuickCodes I Receivables). Only quick codes set up with the TAG set to Y will appear in iReceivables as a Dispute reason.

Customers also need to select which section of the invoice is being disputed, with the options including Shipping, Specific Invoice Lines, Subtotal, Tax, and Total. Which they select will not only determine how the credit memo is applied to the transaction, but also the options available on the next window. Shipping, Subtotal, Tax, and Total all allow the requestor to enter either an AMOUNT or a PERCENT that they are requesting to be credited, while Line requires the quantity in dispute as well as the amount to be credited to be entered. The amount entered must equal the DISPUTED QUANTITY times the UNIT PRICE. These options are also controlled with a Quick Code, called Invoice Section. While the tag field is available with this Quick Code as it was for Credit Memo Reason, it is not used, with only the From and To dates determining if it is active. When entering the dispute information, the customer can also add a comment (see Figure 10-2).

Once the collector approves a disputed item, she must decide how the credit will be applied. This is done at the bottom of the notification, in the Response section. Here, she must select the UPDATE INSTALLMENT RULE, which decides how the credit will be applied against any installments, or split transaction terms that resulted in multiple due dates on the invoice. Update Revenue Rule is used when the invoice has invoicing and accounting rules associated with it (see Figure 10-3). These two fields are required, even if there are no rules or installments in the transaction.

For installment rules, you can select from FIFO (first in, first out), which will apply the credit memo to the first installment due before moving on to the next; LIFO (last in, first out), which applies it to the last installment first; Prorate, which will apply the credit prorated against the amount remaining on each installment; and None, which is used for transactions without installments. UPDATE REVENUE RULE allows LIFO as well, but in this case it applies the credits based upon the latest recognized revenue period. Prorate will equally apply the credit against all account assignments on the credit memo, and Unit credits the exact line for the units specified on the credit request (this is only applicable when the customer disputed a specific line). The approvers will also

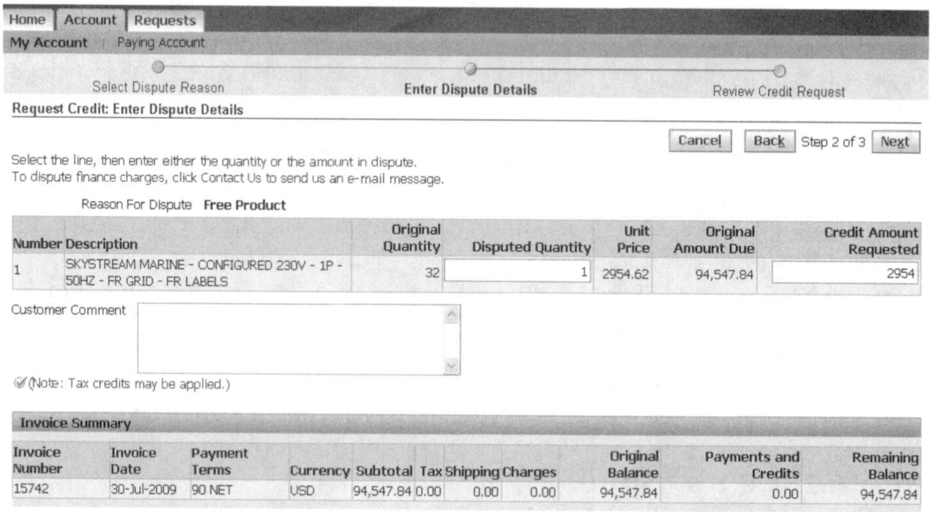

Home	Account	Requests

My Account | Paying Account

Select Dispute Reason — Enter Dispute Details — Review Credit Request

Request Credit: Enter Dispute Details

Cancel | Back | Step 2 of 3 | Next

Select the line, then enter either the quantity or the amount in dispute.
To dispute finance charges, click Contact Us to send us an e-mail message.

Reason For Dispute **Free Product**

Number	Description	Original Quantity	Disputed Quantity	Unit Price	Original Amount Due	Credit Amount Requested
1	SKYSTREAM MARINE - CONFIGURED 230V - 1P - 50HZ - FR GRID - FR LABELS	32	1	2954.62	94,547.84	2954

Customer Comment

☑ (Note: Tax credits may be applied.)

Invoice Summary

Invoice Number	Invoice Date	Payment Terms	Currency	Subtotal	Tax	Shipping	Charges	Original Balance	Payments and Credits	Remaining Balance
15742	30-Jul-2009	90 NET	USD	94,547.84	0.00	0.00	0.00	94,547.84	0.00	94,547.84

iReceivables Account Management | Account | My Account | Open A Transaction | Dispute

FIGURE 10-2.   *Disputing a specific line on an invoice*

have the option of changing these settings. In this same section, you can see whom the notification will be forwarded to. Be aware that if this field is blank, then Oracle has not found an approver.

Once the dispute is submitted, it will be routed for approval, and a credit memo will be created once the approval is given.

Making a Payment

Customers can make online payments either using a credit card or via a wire transfer. In order for this feature to be used, you must first set up Payments to process these transactions automatically, and create a link with your bank or service provider. The customer also needs to be set up with payment information (see Figure 10-4). Ensure that there is at least one RECEIPT METHOD added to the customer's account, and that it agrees to either the CREDIT CARD RECEIPT METHOD or the BANK ACCOUNT RECEIPT METHOD assigned in iReceivables Setup | Setup Checklist | System Parameters. This should also be the PRIMARY RECEIPT METHOD.

Response

Update Installment Rule	<none>
Update Revenue Rule	LIFO
Approver Notes	
Send To	Employee CAMERON, MELANIE

FIGURE 10-3.   *Response section of dispute approval notification*

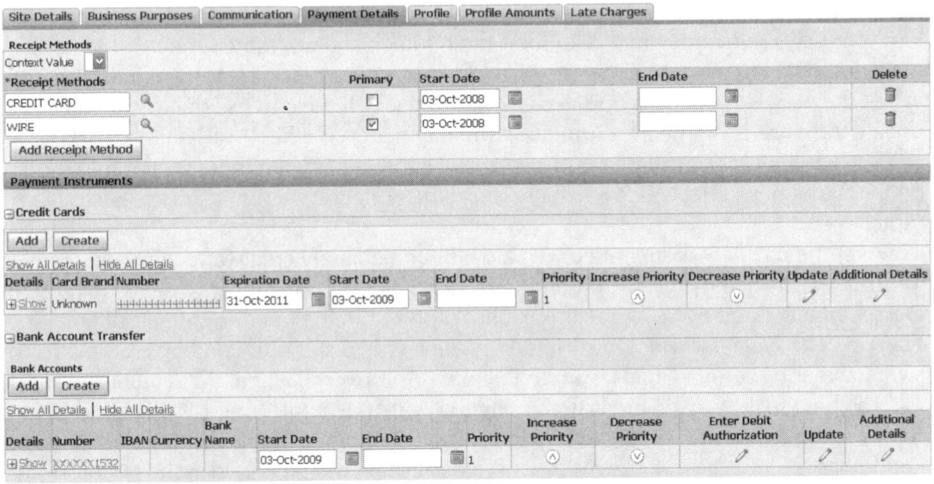

Site Details	Business Purposes	Communication	Payment Details	Profile	Profile Amounts	Late Charges

Receipt Methods

Context Value

*Receipt Methods			Primary	Start Date		End Date		Delete
CREDIT CARD	🔍	.	☐	03-Oct-2008	📅		📅	🗑
WIPE	🔍		☑	03-Oct-2008	📅		📅	🗑

Add Receipt Method

Payment Instruments

☐ **Credit Cards**

Add   Create

Show All Details | Hide All Details

Details	Card Brand	Number	Expiration Date	Start Date		End Date		Priority	Increase Priority	Decrease Priority	Update	Additional Details
⊞ Show	Unknown	‡‡‡‡‡‡‡‡‡‡‡‡‡‡	31-Oct-2011	03-Oct-2009	📅		📅	1	⌃	⌄	✎	✎

☐ **Bank Account Transfer**

Bank Accounts

Add   Create

Show All Details | Hide All Details

Details	Number	IBAN	Currency	Bank Name	Start Date	End Date	Priority	Increase Priority	Decrease Priority	Enter Debit Authorization	Update	Additional Details
⊞ Show	XXXXX1532				03-Oct-2009 📅	📅	1	⌃	⌄	✎	✎	✎

Receivables | Customers | Customers | Account (or Site) Details | Payment Details

FIGURE 10-4.   *Adding payment details to a customer account*

When the customer selects the Pay button on an open transaction, he can select from the payment methods saved on his customer account or use a new credit card or new bank account, as shown in Figure 10-5. The iReceivables profile OIR: Save Payment Instrument Information controls whether the customer can see the PAYMENT METHOD Previously Saved Bank Account. When Credit Card is selected as the payment method, the profile OIR: Verify Credit Card Details determines if the customer is prompted for information that will help to verify the credit card, such as billing address, card security code, or both.

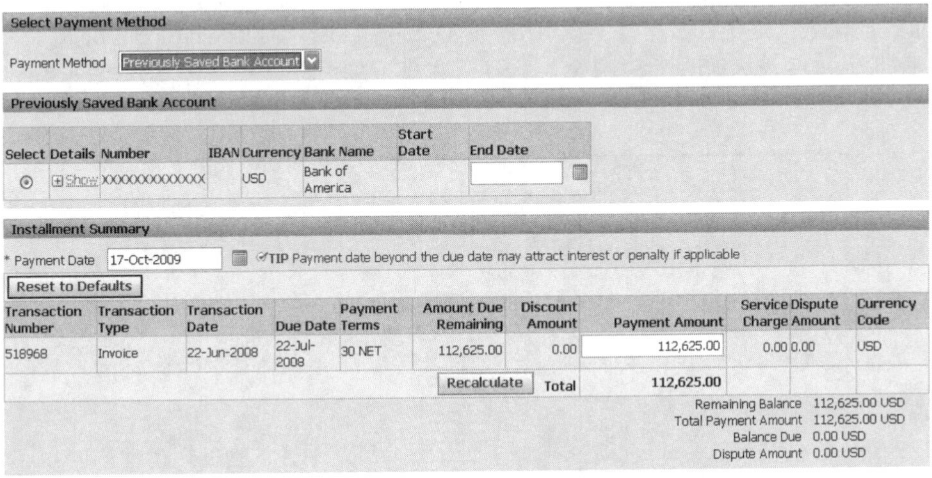

Select Payment Method

Payment Method   Previously Saved Bank Account ▾

Previously Saved Bank Account

Select	Details	Number	IBAN	Currency	Bank Name	Start Date	End Date	
◉	⊞ Show	XXXXXXXXXXXXXX		USD	Bank of America			📅

Installment Summary

* Payment Date   17-Oct-2009   📅   ✓TIP Payment date beyond the due date may attract interest or penalty if applicable

Reset to Defaults

Transaction Number	Transaction Type	Transaction Date	Due Date	Payment Terms	Amount Due Remaining	Discount Amount	Payment Amount	Service Charge Amount	Dispute Amount	Currency Code
518968	Invoice	22-Jun-2008	22-Jul-2008	30 NET	112,625.00	0.00	112,625.00	0.00	0.00	USD
					Recalculate	Total	112,625.00			

Remaining Balance 112,625.00 USD
Total Payment Amount 112,625.00 USD
Balance Due 0.00 USD
Dispute Amount 0.00 USD

FIGURE 10-5.   *Paying an open transaction in iReceivables*

The PAYMENT DATE and PAYMENT AMOUNT will default in, allowing updates to be made. Whether a future date can be added in the payment date is controlled by the profile OIR: Maximum Future Payment Days Allowed, which will limit the number of days in the future the customer can enter. Note that when making a payment, PAYMENT DATE must be on or after the actual transaction date. When the PAYMENT AMOUNT is updated, the customer will have to use the Recalculate button to update the BALANCE DUE before submitting the payment with the Apply button.

The Pay button is available in two places: when viewing an individual transaction, as well as on the Account Details window, where more than one transaction can be selected to pay at the same time.

After the payment is submitted, Oracle will immediately create a receipt and apply it to the transaction selected by the customer. iReceivable users can see the payments both on the Account Details window and by using the link Transaction List in the upper-right part of any iReceivables window. The payment will appear under this link with a status of Pending Approval if the profile OIR: Payment Approver Status is set to Payment Approver, Payer and Payment Approver, or Payer.

The final feature available is the ability to create payments for customers and parties you are related to. A customer can create payments against another customer's transactions when certain conditions are met. First, there must be a relationship created between the two customers, then the paying customer must request access to the second customer's account. Finally, the profile OIR: Cross Customer Payments must be set to Yes. For this example, the *paying* customer is A. C. Networks and the customer *owning* the transactions is United Parcel Service.

To create the relationship between the two accounts, query up the paying customer, A. C. Networks, and select the account, not the party (Receivables | Customers | Customers). This is done by selecting the Details link next to the ACCOUNT NUMBER as opposed to the NAME. Here, go to the Relationships tab and Create Account Relationship (see Figure 10-6). There are three types of relationships that can be created: Bill To, Ship To, and Reciprocal. When Bill To is selected, then the customer can have transactions created using the related party's bill-to address, while Ship To allows the same for the shipping address. Reciprocal means the relationship goes both ways. Select at least Bill To, and then decide if the relationship is Reciprocal, depending on whether the customers can pay each other's transactions, or if it is only a one-way relationship.

Once the relationship exists, then as the paying customer, you must request access to the other customer's account in iReceivables. You do this with the Manage Customer Account Access feature in iReceivables. This appears as a second function option under the seeded responsibility, iReceivables External User. When this is selected, you can see the access that you have, remove access, or request additional access, as seen in Figure 10-7. To request additional customer access, select the button and

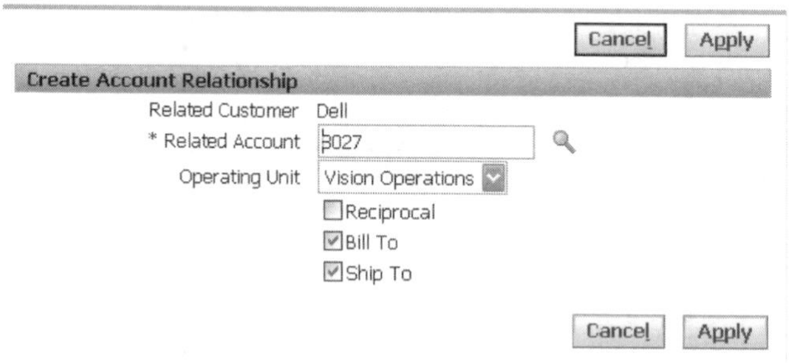

FIGURE 10-6. *Creating a customer relationship*

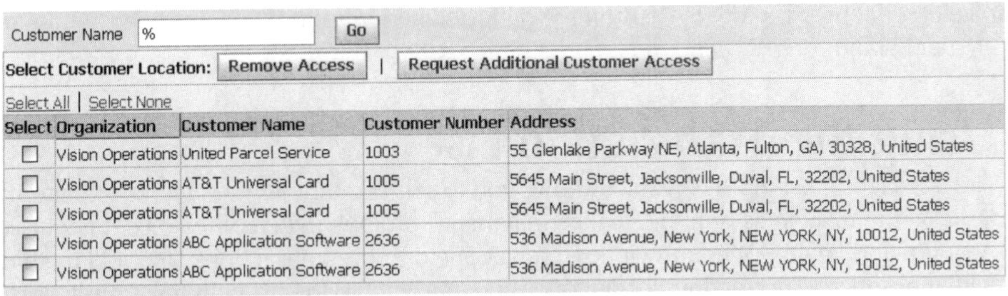

Customer Name %
Go
Select Customer Location: Remove Access | Request Additional Customer Access
Select All | Select None
Select Organization Customer Name Customer Number Address
Vision Operations United Parcel Service 1003 55 Glenlake Parkway NE, Atlanta, Fulton, GA, 30328, United States
Vision Operations AT&T Universal Card 1005 5645 Main Street, Jacksonville, Duval, FL, 32202, United States
Vision Operations AT&T Universal Card 1005 5645 Main Street, Jacksonville, Duval, FL, 32202, United States
Vision Operations ABC Application Software 2636 536 Madison Avenue, New York, NEW YORK, NY, 10012, United States
Vision Operations ABC Application Software 2636 536 Madison Avenue, New York, NEW YORK, NY, 10012, United States

iReceivables External User | Manage Customer Account Access

FIGURE 10-7. *Requesting additional access in iReceivables*

search for the customer you want access to. You can search on Credit Memo, Customer Number, Debit Memo, Deposits, Invoices, and Payments. Again, wildcards cannot be used as part of the search, and the VALUE entered must find an exact match in Oracle. If you set up a Customer Verification Question in the iReceivables Rules (iReceivables | Setup | Rules | Customer Verification Rule), it will appear now, requiring you as the user to answer properly before proceeding. After answering correctly, select the address you are requesting access to. A second challenge question, set up as the Site Verification Question rule, may appear at this point. After confirming that the Terms and Agreements of use have been read, the request is submitted, granting the customer access.

Transactions for the related customers can be seen in the Paying Account window (iReceivables | Account | Paying Account). Select the RELATED CUSTOMER and, if the relationship was set up as reciprocal, the transactions for both the customer you are signed in as (in this case, A. C. Network) and the transactions for the related customer that was selected. If there are relationships with more than one customer, only the transactions for the customer selected in the RELATED CUSTOMER field will appear, and each customer's transactions will need to be queried separately.

To pay transactions that are across customers, select the transactions here and click Add To Transaction List. From the transaction list, shown in Figure 10-8, you can pay the transactions or

ORACLE Bill Management
Vision Operations-AT&T Universal Card-12895-1005
Contact Us
Transaction List
Diagnostics Home Logout Prefer
Home
Account
Requests
Transactions
Clear All
Print
Pay
Apply Credits
Customer Name Customer Number Organization Transaction Type Status Date Due Date Purchase Order Sales Order Original Amount Remaining Amount Discount Amount Currenc
ABC Application Software 2636 Vision Operations 501216 Invoice Open 17-Oct-2009 01-Nov-2009 22,000.00 21,999.00 0.00 USD
ABC Application Software 2636 Vision Operations 518801 Invoice Overdue 31-May-2008 30-Jun-2008 304,150.00 304,150.00 0.00 USD
AT&T Universal Card 1005 Vision Operations 501217 Invoice Open 17-Oct-2009 16-Nov-2009 467.50 467.50 0.00 USD
Total 326,617.50 326,616.50 0.00

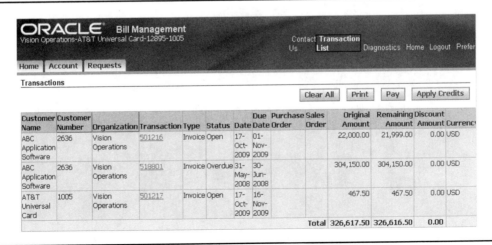

FIGURE 10-8. *Making Payments using the transaction list*

apply credit memos, detailed in the later section titled "Applying Credit Memos." Note that the receipt will appear under the customer you are signed in as, not the customers whose transactions are being paid.

Using the Transaction List

The transaction list in iReceivables allows you to select multiple transactions to perform common tasks on them, such as printing, making payments, or applying credit memos. In either the My Account and Paying Account window, select one or more transactions, and add them to the list with the Add To Transaction List button. Then, navigate to the list with the Transaction List link on the top right of the window.

Applying Credit Memos

The last feature in iReceivables is for the customers to apply credit memos to outstanding invoices. In the My Account window, select the transaction type of Credit Memos and select Go. At the top of the page, the total of all the UNAPPLIED CREDIT MEMOS will appear, while the STATUS of the transactions will let you know which one is still Open and not fully applied, as seen in Figure 10-9. After opening a credit memo that is open with a remaining balance, you can click the Apply Credits button in the upper right of the transaction list window, seen back in Figure 10-8.

Once you select Apply Credits, use the Add Invoices button to select the invoice or invoices you want to apply the credit to (see Figure 10-10). Ensure you update the amount you want to apply on both the transaction and the credit memo, as both these amounts must agree, and select Recalculate before submitting the transaction. Customers can review where a credit memo is applied using the Activities link (My Account, find credit memo | click on Transaction link | Activities). As shown in Figure 10-11, the invoices the credit memo was applied to are visible.

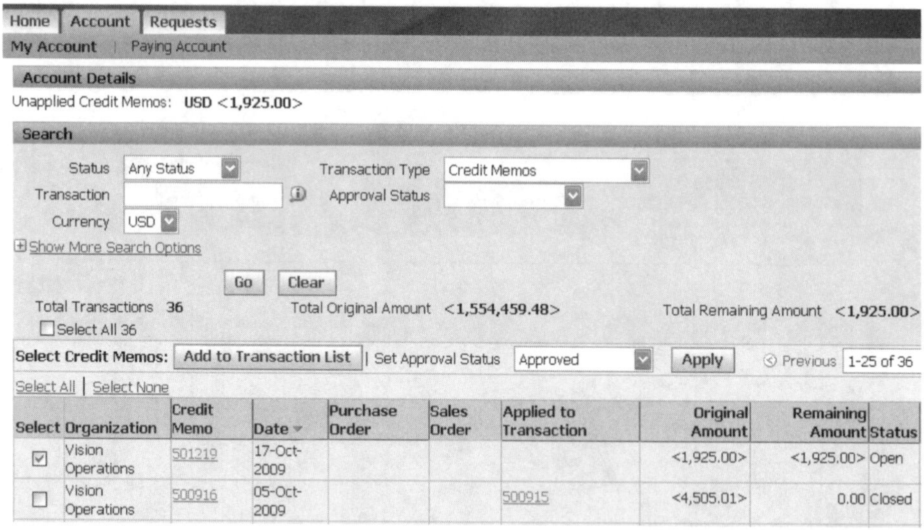

FIGURE 10-9. *Open credit memos*

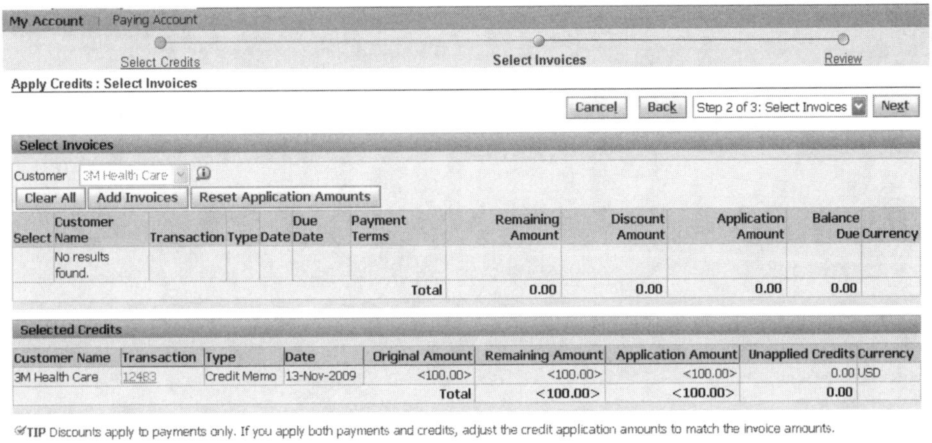

	My Account	Paying Account							

Select Credits | Select Invoices | Review

Apply Credits : Select Invoices

Cancel   Back   Step 2 of 3: Select Invoices   Next

Select Invoices

Customer 3M Health Care

Clear All   Add Invoices   Reset Application Amounts

Select	Customer Name	Transaction Type	Date	Due Date	Payment Terms	Remaining Amount	Discount Amount	Application Amount	Balance Due	Currency
	No results found.									
				Total		0.00	0.00	0.00	0.00	

Selected Credits

Customer Name	Transaction	Type	Date	Original Amount	Remaining Amount	Application Amount	Unapplied Credits	Currency
3M Health Care	12483	Credit Memo	13-Nov-2009	<100.00>	<100.00>	<100.00>	0.00	USD
			Total	<100.00>		<100.00>	0.00	

☑TIP Discounts apply to payments only. If you apply both payments and credits, adjust the credit application amounts to match the invoice amounts.

FIGURE 10-10. *Applying open credit memos to open transactions*

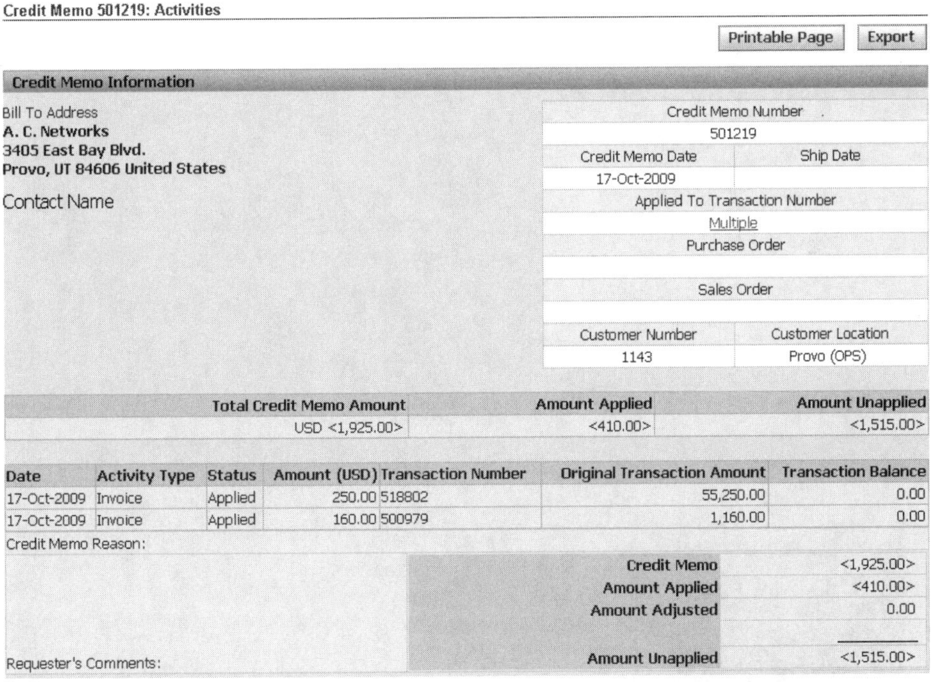

Credit Memo 501219: Activities

Printable Page   Export

Credit Memo Information

Bill To Address
A. C. Networks
3405 East Bay Blvd.
Provo, UT 84606 United States

Contact Name

Credit Memo Number	
501219	
Credit Memo Date	Ship Date
17-Oct-2009	
Applied To Transaction Number	
Multiple	
Purchase Order	
Sales Order	
Customer Number	Customer Location
1143	Provo (OPS)

	Total Credit Memo Amount	Amount Applied	Amount Unapplied
	USD <1,925.00>	<410.00>	<1,515.00>

Date	Activity Type	Status	Amount (USD)	Transaction Number	Original Transaction Amount	Transaction Balance
17-Oct-2009	Invoice	Applied	250.00	518802	55,250.00	0.00
17-Oct-2009	Invoice	Applied	160.00	500979	1,160.00	0.00

Credit Memo Reason:

Credit Memo	<1,925.00>
Amount Applied	<410.00>
Amount Adjusted	0.00
Amount Unapplied	<1,515.00>

Requester's Comments:

FIGURE 10-11. *Reviewing the transactions a credit memo is applied to*

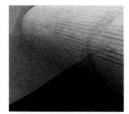

CHAPTER
11

Order Information Portal

p until now, all of the modules discussed are separately licensed modules that have their own functionality that integrates tightly with Receivables, Payables, and Purchasing. Order Information Portal is different. While adding no additional functionality to Order Management, this portal provides internal and external users the ability to view their orders and quotes, keep track of invoices and shipments, respond to any quotes that require acceptance, report a defect on a shipment, and request an RMA. The setups are minimal, and granting access is the same as creating any user within Oracle, making this an easy module to deploy.

Setups

Setting up the Order Information Portal involves only a few profile options. OM: Customer Service Feedback determines which internal user is informed when an RMA request is processed from the Portal via the Return Request link, as well as the Report Defect feature. OM: Customer Service Report Defect identifies the internal user who receives a notification when a defect is reported. And the last profile, OM: Records on Summary Page for External Users, determines the number of records that are returned on the home page for Recent Orders and Recent Delivers. When this is set to a number greater than zero, then that number of records are returned when the external user is on the home page. When this is set to N or 0, then no records will be returned.

Granting Customers Access

Unlike the other self-service modules, the Order Information Portal does not use any securing attributes to restrict data for external users; it uses a customer contact that is associated with both the customer and the user. Also, all external users will need to be set up using the System Administrator responsibility, which in most companies is a secure responsibility with limited access. A customer contact is a Person that is related to the customer. In order to create the external user, you will need to either know the contact name that is associated with the customer, or create a new contact for that customer. While this sounds quite simple, both customers and contacts are part of Oracle's Trading Community Architecture (TCA), which is a complex series of relationships between Organizations (customers, suppliers, and banks) and Persons (customer contacts, supplier contacts, bank contacts, and employees). For a high-level review of this hierarchy, see the next illustration. (TCA was explained in greater detail in Chapter 9 in the section titled "Setting up Customers and TCA Overview".)

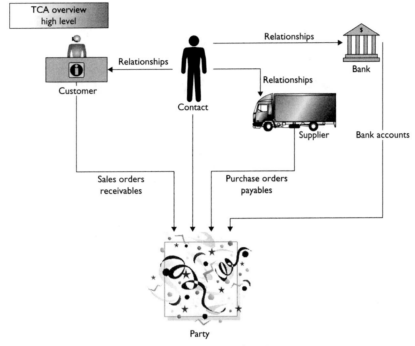

TCA overview, 90,000-foot view

Keeping this illustration in mind, let's look at customer A. C. Network. One of this customer's contacts, Carlo Kim, will be getting access to the Order Information Portal. Figure 11-1 shows that Carlo Kim has a party relationship to the customer.

Customers >
Customer: A. C. Networks

| Enrich | Cancel | Save | Apply |

Customer Type **Organization**

Customer Information

* Organization Name A. C. Networks   Alias
* Registry ID **1143**   Name Pronunciation
Context Value

Accounts | **Profile** | **Communication** | **Party Relationships** | **Tax Profile**

Party Relationships

Party Type: Person   Status: Active

Previous 1-10   Next 10

*Customer	*Relationship Role	*Start Date	End Date	Comments	Remove
Carlo Kim	Organization Contact	23-Jun-1999			
Doug Jackson	Organization Contact	22-Jul-1999			

Receivables I Customers I Customers I Party Relationships I Party Type = Person

FIGURE 11-1.   *A customer and its contact relationships*

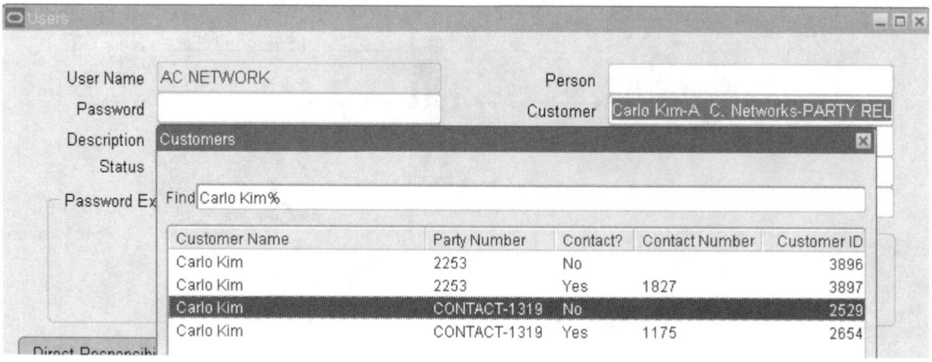

FIGURE 11-2. *Creating an external user for the Order Information Portal*

The next step is to set up a new user, using the contact Carlo Kim. Refer to Figure 11-2 for the next part. After entering a USER NAME and the PASSWORD, you will need to associate the contact with this user. This is done in the CUSTOMER field. When you search on this field, any Party that is set up as a Person will appear in the list. This will include any customer and supplier set up as a person, as well as all contacts and employees.

For Carlo Kim, there are four entries: two contacts and two relationships for these contacts with customers. You will need to select the "customer name" (that is, the *contact*) that is associated with the customer A. C. Networks. The problem is that the numbers you see next to the contact (Party Number, Contact Number, and Customer ID) were not displayed on the customer screen when you looked up this contact; they relate to the contact and not the customer they are a contact of. When the CONTACT? field is Yes, then this person is a contact of a customer, so that eliminates two of the choices. After you select one, save the user, and then re-query the user, you will see the customer name that this contact is associated to. If you select the wrong contact, the user will not have access to the correct customer data (or any data at all if a contact that is not related to a customer is selected). The seeded responsibility for the Order Information Portal is Order Information External User.

Viewing Orders

When viewing sales orders, either from the Home page or from the Order Status page, there are several links available to the viewer, displayed with underlines as in Figure 11-3. VIEW QUALITY PLAN only contains data when you have Oracle Quality installed and there is a quality plan associated with the order. VIEW DELIVERY SUMMARY displays the delivery information in a summary window, while VIEW LINE DETAILS will show the detailed information. Pricing information, available via the VIEW PRICING DETAILS link, displays the details for charges and any adjustments to the price list. A summary of the invoice can be seen under VIEW INVOICE INFORMATION, with an additional link to display the actual invoice created from Bill Presentment Architecture (BPA). See Chapter 9, "Customizing Invoices," for information on setting up BPA.

If this were a quote instead of a shipped order, the user could Accept or Reject the quote information prior to the order being booked. Additional details and delivery information are available from the links by each line, as well as a separate link to the Line Invoice Detail, which again displays the invoice created with BPA.

Sales Order 64207

Printable Page

General	Shipping	Billing
Customer Name **A. C. Networks**	Freight Terms **To Be Determined**	Bill To **Provo (OPS)**
Customer PO	Shipment Priority	**Provo, UT, 84606, US**
Order Date **28-Jul-2009 05:01:54**	Delivery Summary View Delivery Summary	Payment Terms **30 NET**
Need By Date **28-Jul-2009 05:01:54**	Delivery Line Details View Line Details	Price List **Corporate**
Booked Date **28-Jul-2009 05:04:20**		Total **<1,013.37> US dollar**
Status **Closed**		Pricing Details View Pricing Details
Quality Plan View Quality Plan		Invoice Information View Invoice Information

Lines

Select Order Lines: Actions [Accept ▾] [Go]

Select All | Select None

Select	Line Num	Item	Item Description	Ordered Quantity	UOM	Fulfilled Quantity	Unit Price	Extended Price	Expected Delivery Ship Date	Acceptance Status	Acceptance Date	Details	Return Request	Line Invoice Detail
☐	1.1	AS18947	Sentinel Deluxe Desktop	-1	Ea	-1	<1,772.10>	<1,772.10>	📅			🔲	✎	🔲
☐	2.1	CM76840	Lightning Inkjet Printer	-1	Ea	-1	<210.00>	<210.00>	📅			🔲	✎	🔲

FIGURE 11-3. *Order Information Portal, orders*

The last option is for the customer to request an RMA, or Return Request. When it is selected, an e-mail is sent to the internal user set up under the profile OM: Customer Service Feedback, requesting to return a specific order or item on the order. This does not automatically create an RMA, just the notification asking for an RMA.

Viewing Deliveries

The Delivery page displays delivery and shipping information on orders, along with review invoice information as well as means to report defects. Both of these features are only available after the order has shipped (see Figure 11-4). Clicking the Report Defect link allows an e-mail address, phone number, and description of the problem to be entered, and an e-mail is sent to the

Delivery Number: 638189

Printable Page

Shipping Information

Ship From **FLAGSTAFF**	Weight **18 LBS**		
Waybill	Freight Carrier **BEST METHOD**		
Planned Ship Date **19-May-2009 23:59:00**	Actual Ship Date		
Planned Arrival Date **19-May-2009 23:59:00**	Actual Arrival Date		
Status **Open**			

Delivery Lines

Item	Item Description	Order Number	Ship From	Ship To	Quantity	UOM	Pick Status	Tracking Number	Lot Number	Details	Report Defect	Line Invoice Detail
1-ARXM-10-12	AIR X - MARINE - 12V	90404	FLAGSTAFF	Merritt Island, FL, 32952, US	1	Ea	Staged/Pick Confirmed			🔲	✎	🔲

FIGURE 11-4. *Order Information Portal, deliveries*

person set up in the profile OM: Customer Service Report Defect. If you do not have a person identified here, this feature is not disabled, but no one will receive the e-mail. Ensure you remove the links using the OA Framework personalization feature if you do not want customers to use this process.

Personalizing Views

All search pages can be personalized for the data that is displayed, and the sort options, among other features. This is done with the Personalize button, shown in Figure 11-5. These views are unique to each user and are not shared.

To create a view, first assign a VIEW NAME, as shown in Figure 11-6, and determine the NUMBER OF ROWS DISPLAYED on each page. You can select up to 25 rows at a time. Checking SET AS DEFAULT will ensure this view is defaulted in for all queries, and a DESCRIPTION can be added.

Next, you can select the columns you want to display in this view. This is limited to the columns associated with the specific page. When the column is a number, such as shipment total, click the Rename Columns / Totaling button, and you can add a total for that field. This is only available for fields that contain amounts. You can also assign more user-friendly names than what Oracle has assigned.

Next, you can select up to three columns to sort the returned data on, as well as the order it is sorted, shown in Figure 11-7. You can also add specific criteria to filter the data that is returned. While these options are also available with the Advanced Search option, adding a view for commonly used searches can reduce the time it takes to retrieve the data.

While this module adds no major functionality, it is a good, basic interface for customers to get some of the commonly asked questions answered without taking up time from your sales team.

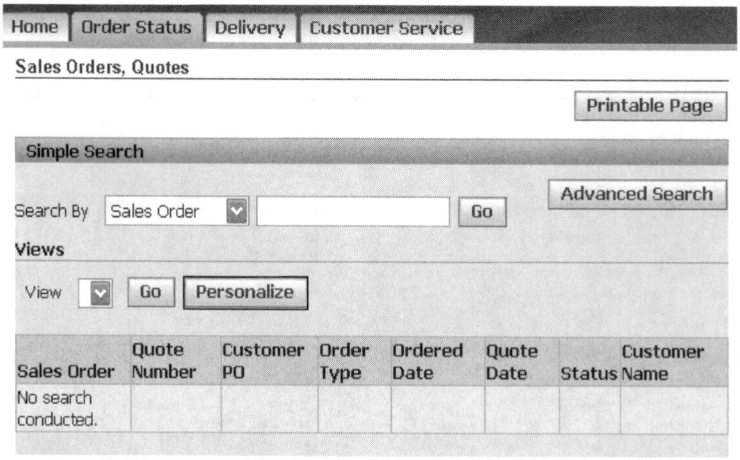

FIGURE 11-5. *Personalizing a view*

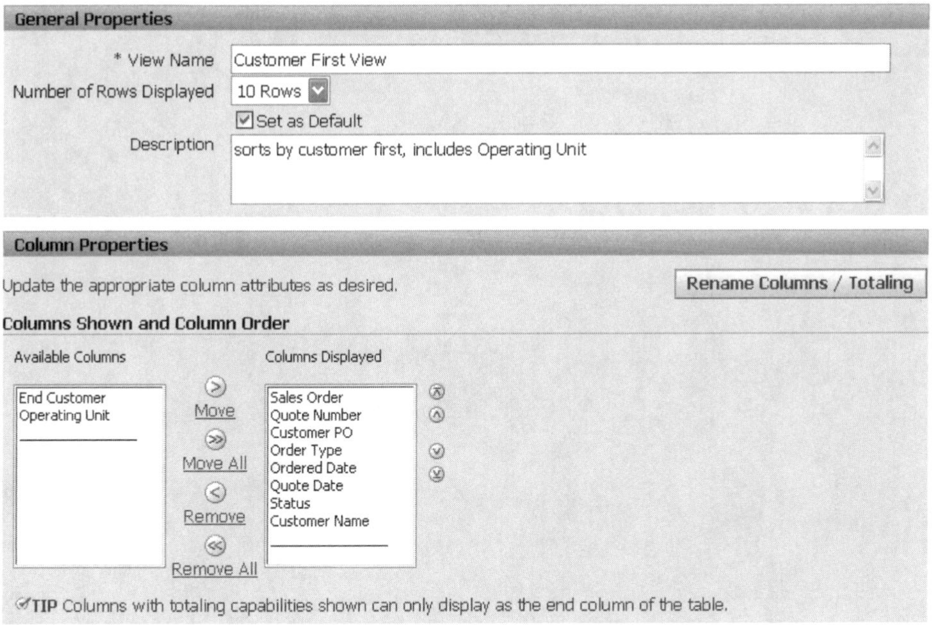

General Properties

* View Name	Customer First View
Number of Rows Displayed	10 Rows
	☑ Set as Default
Description	sorts by customer first, includes Operating Unit

Column Properties

Update the appropriate column attributes as desired.

[Rename Columns / Totaling]

Columns Shown and Column Order

Available Columns

End Customer
Operating Unit

⊘ Move
⊚ Move All
⊙ Remove
⊛ Remove All

Columns Displayed

Sales Order
Quote Number
Customer PO
Order Type
Ordered Date
Quote Date
Status
Customer Name

☑TIP Columns with totaling capabilities shown can only display as the end column of the table.

FIGURE 11-6. *Creating a personal view*

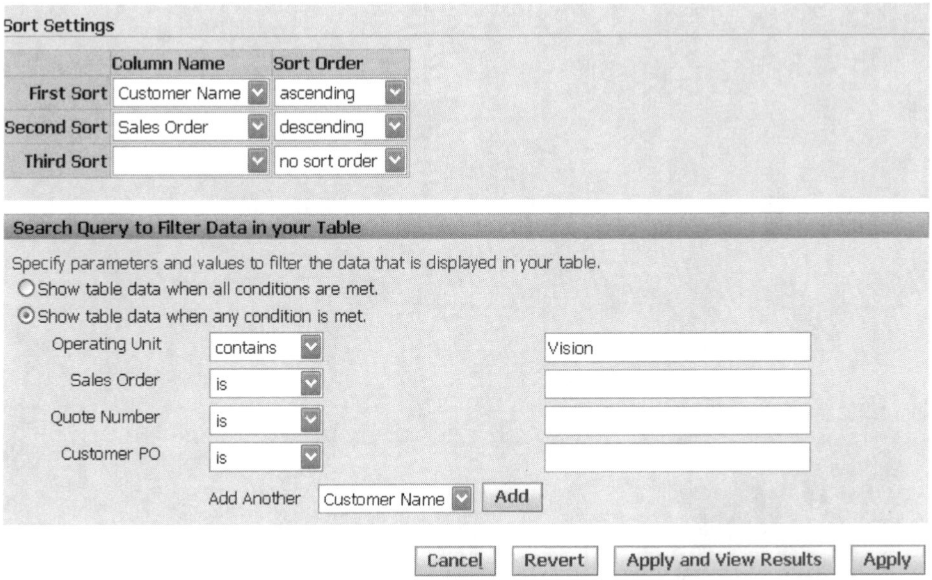

Sort Settings

	Column Name	Sort Order
First Sort	Customer Name	ascending
Second Sort	Sales Order	descending
Third Sort		no sort order

Search Query to Filter Data in your Table

Specify parameters and values to filter the data that is displayed in your table.

○ Show table data when all conditions are met.
◉ Show table data when any condition is met.

Operating Unit	contains	Vision
Sales Order	is	
Quote Number	is	
Customer PO	is	

Add Another [Customer Name] [Add]

[Cancel] [Revert] [Apply and View Results] [Apply]

FIGURE 11-7. *Adding sort and querying options*

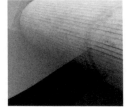

APPENDIX

Approvals Management

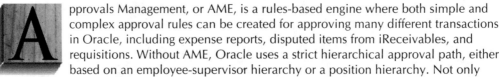

pprovals Management, or AME, is a rules-based engine where both simple and complex approval rules can be created for approving many different transactions in Oracle, including expense reports, disputed items from iReceivables, and requisitions. Without AME, Oracle uses a strict hierarchical approval path, either based on an employee-supervisor hierarchy or a position hierarchy. Not only does AME allow these hierarchies to be used, custom hierarchies can be created, along with detours from any hierarchy. An example of where AME is required would be for purchases made for computer equipment. Besides requiring the approval of the requestor's supervisor, your organization may require that information technology approve all configurations for personal computers, and that your Project Management Office, or PMO, approve all software purchases.

AME is marketed as a business analyst's tool for creating rules without having to code. While it is true that no straight development is required when using AME, an understanding of how code is written as well as at least a basic understanding of the underlying table structures of the data you want to use in your approvals is required. Analysts who write at least basic SQL statements against the data being used by AME will probably pick up AME fairly easily, but if you are purely functional and have never used SQL with an Oracle database, you will probably struggle using this tool.

General Overview

AME is really just a giant If-Then-Else statement. If a transaction meets a particular condition, then route it this way for approval, or else send it along another path. Oracle creates this statement for you, using reusable building blocks. These blocks are built separately and independently of each other, and then used over and over to create the final paths and approvals Oracle will follow for different transactions.

There are several steps involved in setting up the approval process. The first is to declare the components that will tell Oracle how to find transactions and submit them for approval. This includes Attributes, Conditions, Action Types, and Approver Groups.

Attributes not only decide how AME will behave for this approval, but also what elements of the transaction will be used to route it for approval. For example, you assign attributes to decide how rejections will be handled or if the requestor can approve their own transactions, and elements from the transaction as well as other areas in Oracle, such as amount or account number, are used to create the approval routing.

Conditions get assigned to attributes. Conditions are the rules that are going to be followed, such as Is the Purchase being charged to a Fixed Asset account?

Action Types define what will happen when an attribute and a condition are met, such as to use the supervisor approval hierarchy to approve all requisitions and use a preapproval group when certain conditions are met.

The final setup, *Approver Groups,* determines who will act upon the required actions by assigning the users who will be doing the approvals. This can use either one of the hierarchies that already exists in EBS (supervisor or position) or a person or group of people assigned in AME to the actual approval group. Each of these four components are independently created, and then they are mixed and matched to create the final approval process.

It is these components that become the building blocks for AME to generate an approval list. The best explanation I have seen for what AME really does is that it is a huge GUI (graphical user interface) that uses the components to build a giant If-Then-Else statement. As a quasi-programmer (more functional than technical, I find it impossible to do my job without looking at a PL/SQL package or data in a table almost every day, or using complex formulas in Excel), I know firsthand how complicated an If-Then-Else statement can get, even if it is used in a simple spreadsheet and not a mammoth database such as the one used by Oracle E-Business Suite. AME is no less complicated but takes some of gotchas out of the programming. It is the *Attributes* assigned to the *Conditions* that create the IF portion of the statement. And the *Action Types* and *Approver Groups* are used to create both the THEN and ELSE part of the statement. These are all then combined into a Rule that combines the components to create the statement.

Referring to the illustration, the If-Then-Else statement being built would read as follows: If the Requisition is delivered to an Expense location and it is assigned to a Fixed Asset account number, then route it to the Fixed Asset Accountant for preapproval before sending it to the person in the requestor's supervisor hierarchy with an approval level of at least 3.

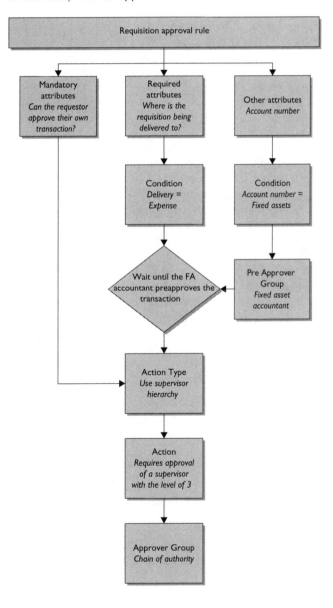

This chapter will walk you through how to set up AME for disputed items, or credit memo requests, in iReceivables.

Granting Access to AME

In Release 12, AME is controlled by Oracle's role-based access control (RBAC), and you must take a few extra steps before you can get access to it. This access is granted first by assigning users a role, then by granting users access to specific or all transaction types. This is only required for users who will be modifying or troubleshooting AME, and not for users who are submitting transactions for approval in AME. If you are unfamiliar with Oracle's User Management, it is the ability to assign access based on a role, which is then in turn assigned to users. This access controls not only the functions and reports the users have access to, but also the data they can see. The advantage of using RBAC is that if you have twenty-five sales reps who all need the exact same access, which includes seven responsibilities, you can create one role with that access, and then in turn assign the role to the twenty-five users. If that access were to change, you only need to update the role, which would in turn update all the users assigned the role. Prior to RBAC, each user would need to be assigned all seven responsibilities, and each one would then need to be updated separately if there were a change.

Out of the box, only the seeded "sysadmin" user has access to User Management, and you will need to either sign in as that user or have your system administrator assign you access to User Management. The sysadmin user is often a secure user, where only a limited number of people have the password. Note that this is not the same as the System Administrator responsibility, but actually a user that you sign into Oracle with. User Management can also be assigned to any user following the same steps outlined next, but you would perform them for the role Security Administrator instead of the roles mentioned in Table A-1.

After signing in either as the sysadmin user or a user who has already been granted access to User Management, select the User Management responsibility, which will open up the Users window. Using the search fields, find the user you want to assign the AME roles to. Select the Update link, and then Assign Roles. There are five AME roles, outlined in Table A-1. Since these roles are "cumulative," with each role having access to the lower roles, you would normally assign a user only one role. Ensure you add a Justification for each role before saving.

Role Name	Access
Approvals Management Administrator	Same access as Process Owner and System Administrator, but can also create Action Types and modify system defaults.
Approvals Management Process Owner	Views the business dashboards.
Approvals Management System Viewer	Views the Administrative dashboards.
Approvals Management Business Analyst	Business dashboard complete access.
Approvals Management System Administrator	Same as System Viewer, but can also create and maintain transaction types.

TABLE A-1. *AME Roles*

Once you assign the roles to a user, that user will automatically have access to the responsibilities called Approvals Management Administrator and Approvals Management Business Analyst. These are assigned as *indirect* responsibilities as opposed to *direct,* because they were assigned based on a role in User Management, or indirectly, as opposed to directly on the user screen. They appear on the Indirect Responsibilities tab on the user screen (System Administrator | Security | User | Define).

Next, you will need to grant the user access to the data she is going to create approval rules for, in this example, transaction types. This security allows multiple users to have access to create and maintain rules in AME, but the rules they have access to are limited. This is done using the Functional Administrator responsibility, which opens to the Security | Grants window, where the Create Grant button is used to gain the access to transaction types (see Figure A-1). Access only needs to be granted to the users who will be creating or modifying these transaction types, not users who are included in the approval hierarchies or who are submitting transactions for approval.

After assigning the grant a unique NAME, add a DESCRIPTION to help future administrators know what this grant is set up for. Select Specific User for the GRANTEE TYPE, which will open up the GRANTEE field. Here, select the user name from the list. The list will contain all the employees set up in Oracle, not the users, so you will need to ensure each of the users is assigned an employee.

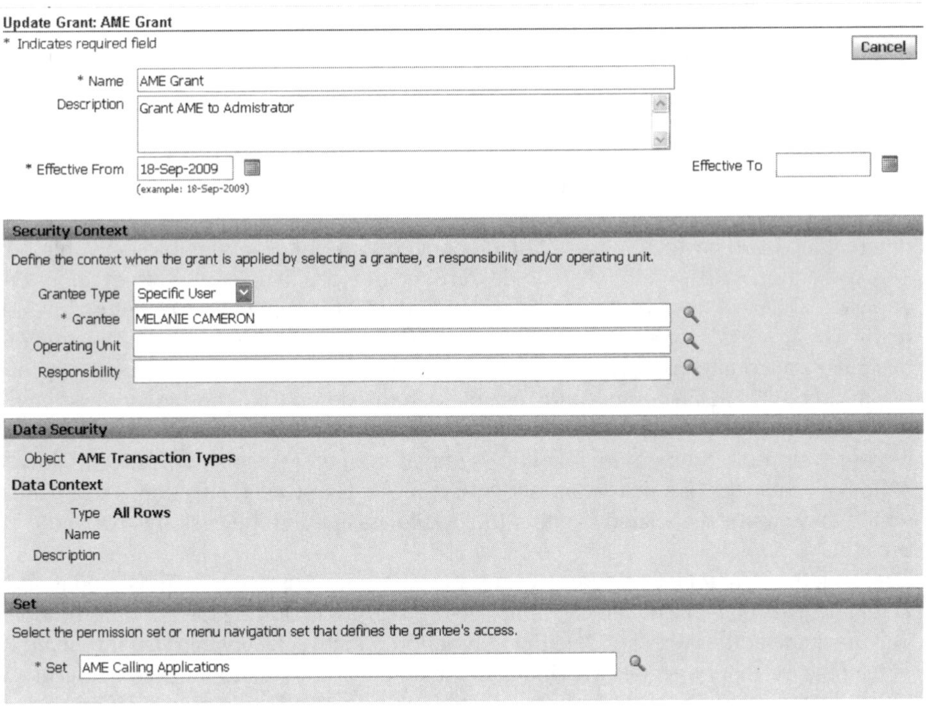

Functional Administrator | Security | Grants | Create Grant

FIGURE A-1. *Granting users access to AME transaction types*

Other grantee types include Groups of Users and All Users. When Groups of Users is selected, then the grantees that you can select are actually responsibilities. In this way, you can grant access to specific data to a responsibility, and then all users who are assigned that responsibility, both directly and indirectly, will also have access to that data.

Next, determine the Data you are adding security to by selecting the Object. For AME, the OBJECT will be AME Transaction Types. Then determine if you are going to grant access to all the transaction types in AME by selecting the Data Context Type of All Rows, or if you are going to limit the data either to a particular instance or to an instance set. When limiting the data to a particular transaction type, enter both the FND_APPLICATION_ID and the TRANSACTION_TYPE_ID. These are the unique database identifiers for each field and cannot be seen in the application. And just to be user friendly, there is no list of values on the fields, either. Both of these are stored in the table AME_CALLING_APPS. In the case of credit memos, which belongs to Receivables, the APPLICATION_ID is 222.

There are three transactions that are used for credit memo approvals: Receivables Credit Memo Approval Chain, which has the TRANSACTION_TYPE_ID of AR_CMWF_APPROVALS; Receivables Credit Memo Collector, which uses AR_CMWF_COLLECTOR; and Receivables Credit Memo Receivables, which is TRANSACTION_TYPE_ID AR_CMWF_RECEIVABLE. The TRANSACTION_TYPE_ID is also the Transaction Type Key that is assigned in AME. And yes, this is a catch-22 here: you can get the data you need to get access to AME in AME, but not until you have access to it.

The last step is to select the set you are granting permissions to. A set is equivalent to either a menu navigation or a grouping of data. In this case, it is the menu navigations we want access to by assigning the SET called AME Calling Applications. At this point, you can access AME and begin setting up the approvals.

AME Approval Setups

The approvals are set up using the Approvals Management Business Analyst responsibility. Note that the screenshots used in this section are from 12.1.1, which did include enhancements to the Dashboard, shown in Figure A-2; if you are using an earlier version, you may have a slightly different look and navigation path, but the concepts and steps remain basically the same.

As mentioned earlier, there are three transaction types that need to be set up for credit memo approvals. These follow the actual processes in the credit memo approval workflow. There are really two approvals for each credit memo request: first from the collector in charge of the customer's account, and second from the financial person with the authority to approve writing off the amount. The first process, Receivables Credit Memo Collector, identifies the collector that is assigned to the customer or bill-to site on the customer. (If you do not have collectors assigned to your customers, then ensure that you modify the Credit Memo Approval Workflow to identify a collector. Collectors are first set up under Receivables | Setup | Collections | Collectors, after which they can be associated to either the profile assigned to the customer, or to the customer directly.)

Next, the transaction type Receivables Credit Memo Approval Chain is used to identify the actual approval chains that are set up for credit memos, including the conditions under which they have the authority to approve the transaction. Finally, Receivables Credit Memo Receivable finds the customer or person who initiated the actual credit memo request, and is used as a basis for routing the request. These three transaction types pass all the required information to the credit memo approval workflow and tell Oracle how to route the transaction for approval.

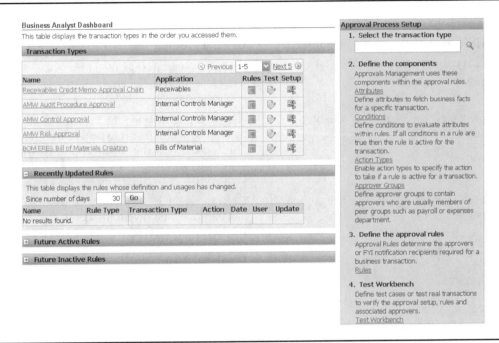

FIGURE A-2.   *Approvals Management Dashboard*

Setups for these three transaction types, as well as all transaction types, all follow the same steps in AME: select the attributes, add conditions and their Action Types, and then assign the approval groups. While it may appear that AME is a user-friendly GUI feature in Oracle, don't let the screens kid you. AME is programming, just using GUI instead of code. Most of the fields use the field names as they appear in the tables, as opposed to on the screens. No matter how you slice it, some technical understanding of the inner workings of Oracle is required.

Creating Attributes

Attributes, or the elements of the transaction used to decide the actions that will be taken by AME, have three types: Mandatory, Required, and Other. The difference between Mandatory and Required attributes is that the mandatory ones are shared by all transaction types in AME, while required ones are set specific to each transaction type. Both of these types of attributes, listed in Table A-2, can greatly affect the way AME works, and are worth understanding.

The final Attribute Category that can be set is Other. These are specific optional attributes that can be set for each transaction type. Typically, you can select any element that exists on a transaction to be used as an attribute. For example, credit memos include elements such as Bill To Customer Name, Currency, and Reasons, all of which can be selected as attributes to be used during the approval process. While Oracle comes seeded with a large number of attributes, you can also create additional attributes. When setting either an existing attribute or creating a new one, it can be set as a Static USAGE TYPE, where the value is assigned directly to the attribute, or as Dynamic, where it is determined using SQL from the transaction itself. See Figure A-3 for an example of the attributes.

Attribute Name	Mandatory or Required	Use and Meaning
Allow Deleting Rule Generated Approvers	Mandatory	When this is set to true, then Oracle will allow a module, such as Receivables, to suppress an approver that was added by a rule.
Allow Empty Approval Groups	Required	A false setting will stop the approval workflow if the approval group fails to generate any approvers. This is usually used when an approval is required at all times as opposed to only under specific conditions.
Allow Requestor Approval	Mandatory	Determines if the person requesting the transaction can approve their own transaction. This attribute works in conjunction with specific Action Types (Absolute Job Level, Final Approver Only, Manager then Final Approver, HR Position, HR Position Level, and Supervisory Level) and determines at which levels the requestor can approve his own transaction.
At Least One Rule Must Apply	Mandatory	When this is set to true, then a transaction that does not meet any of the transaction type rules will be returned to the requestor.
Effective Rule Date	Mandatory	When this is not set, then the effective dates for a rule are evaluated against the system date. This can be set to other dates, such as the transaction date itself, allowing older transactions to use older rules, and works well when a policy is changed with an effective date, such as all travel that takes place on or after January 1, 2001, will utilize the new rule.
Evaluate Priorities Per Item	Mandatory	Determines if the priorities are evaluated individually or as a group.
First and Second Starting Point Person ID	Required	Can be used to override the starting point for the approval process, which is usually the TRANSACTION_ REQUESTOR_PERSON_ID. For example, it may be appropriate to set this when iReceivables is set up for outside users, and all requests should begin with the collection manager for evaluating the approval hierarchy.
Include All Job Level Approvers	Required	Used when there is more than one person holding a particular job, and determines if all the holders will be selected for approval or only a specific holder.

TABLE A-2. *Mandatory and Required Attributes*

Attribute Name	Mandatory or Required	Use and Meaning
Rejection Response	Mandatory	Determines if additional actions can be taken on a transaction after it has been rejected. It is important to set this rule properly if you want users to be able to resubmit a rejected transaction. For example, if you are using AME to approve Payables invoices, not allowing a rejected invoice to be resubmitted for approval to another approver or with different account coding would force it to be canceled and reentered, usually not something you want to do as it can lead to duplicate payments.
Repeat Substitutions	Mandatory	Identifies if Oracle re-evaluates the approvers at the end of the approval process to accommodate changes that may have been made during the approvals. This can be set for specific transaction types.
Supervisory Non Default Starting Point Person ID	Required	Working the same as the job-level non-default starting point person ID, this setting is used when the approval hierarchy being used is the supervisor hierarchy as opposed to the position hierarchy.
Top Supervisor Person ID	Required	Identifies the top person in the supervisory hierarchy, such as the CEO or President.
Transaction Requestor Person ID	Required	Determines the person who is requesting the transaction, and if there are no overriding factors, it will be the starting point for the approval process. This person is overridden when Required or Supervisory Non Default Starting Point Person ID is set.
Workflow Item Type	Mandatory	Needs to be set when Oracle Workflow is being used (most EBS modules).

TABLE A-2. *Mandatory and Required Attributes* (continued)

Adding Conditions

Conditions, or the rules that need to be followed, are added next, and assigned to each attribute, as shown in Figure A-4. Conditions are set up as Ordinary, Exception, or List Modifier. Both the Ordinary and Exception rules are set up exactly the same but are used differently when they are assigned to the Action Types. Ordinary conditions become the main road the actions will follow, while Exceptions become the detour. Use care when setting up your Conditions—the STRING VALUE, or value passed from the transaction that determines when the condition is met, is case sensitive and does not contain a list of values. For example, if you are using the credit memo reason as your string value, make sure it is entered exactly as the reasons setup in your lookup code (Receivables | Setup |

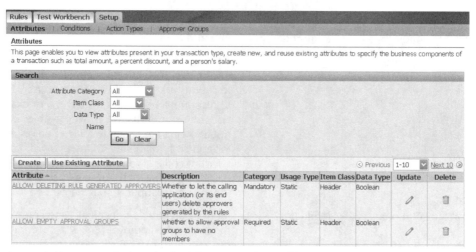

| Rules | Test Workbench | Setup |

Attributes | Conditions | Action Types | Approver Groups

Attributes

This page enables you to view attributes present in your transaction type, create new, and reuse existing attributes to specify the business components of a transaction such as total amount, a percent discount, and a person's salary.

Search

Attribute Category [All]
Item Class [All]
Data Type [All]
Name [_____]

[Go] [Clear]

[Create] [Use Existing Attribute]   ⊙ Previous [1-10] Next 10 ⊙

Attribute ⌃	Description	Category	Usage Type	Item Class	Data Type	Update	Delete
ALLOW DELETING RULE GENERATED APPROVERS	Whether to let the calling application (or its end users) delete approvers generated by the rules	Mandatory	Static	Header	Boolean	🖉	🗑
ALLOW EMPTY APPROVAL GROUPS	whether to allow approval groups to have no members	Required	Static	Header	Boolean	🖉	🗑

Approvals Management Business Analyst | Business Analyst Dashboard | Select a Transaction Type | Attributes link

FIGURE A-3. *AME attributes*

| Rules | Test Workbench | Setup |

Attributes | **Conditions** | Action Types | Approver Groups

Setup: Conditions >

Create New Condition

* Indicates required field   [Cancel] [Create Another (1)] [Apply]

Condition Type [Ordinary]
* Attribute [AR_REASON_CODE] 🔍

String Values

String Value	Delete
DEFECTIVE	🗑
FAILED QUALITY	🗑

[Add Another Row]

[Cancel] [Create Another (1)] [Apply]

Approvals Management Business Analyst | Business Analyst Dashboard | Select a Transaction Type | Conditions link

FIGURE A-4. *AME conditions*

System | Quick Codes | Receivables where the type = credit_memo_reason). To create a condition, determine if it will have a CONDITION TYPE of Ordinary or Exception, then select the ATTRIBUTE it will pertain to from the list. The STRING VALUE is the value of the attribute when the condition will be true. If you want to set up a different approval process for each credit memo reason code, you will need to set up a separate condition for each value that exists. Use the Add Another Row button to multiple values to any condition. Once the condition is set up and assigned to a rule, you can track the rules that use it in the Show Rules Using This Condition section.

Defining Any Modifiers

Modifiers are used to augment the actual approval list that is generated by Oracle. This is done by first creating a List Modifier (Approvals Management Business Analyst | Business Analyst Dashboard | Select a Transaction Type | Conditions link | List Modifiers) and then assigning it to a specific rule, where it will modify the list that is generated by Oracle. Modifiers can be created for any approver in an approval group, or for only the final approver, depending on the selection in the APPROVER ORDER. The APPROVER NAME can be selected from either the HR People or FND User, depending on what is selected in the APPROVER TYPE.

Creating the Actions

After the conditions are created and assigned to attributes, determine what approval actions will need to be taken in order for the transaction to be approved. For example, how many approvals are required for the transaction to be approved? What hierarchy will be followed to determine the approver? Are there any Exceptions to this approval action? This is accomplished by creating Action Types, and assigning them to a Rule Type and specific Actions. This gets a little confusing, so let's break it down.

Rule Types determine when the rule is called. You can select from six different Rule Types. These will determine what type of approval list you are generating. The main type, Chain of Authority, determines the approval chain that will be followed, while List Modification and Substitution are both used to change one or more approvers in the Chain of Authority. Pre and Post List Approval Groups will leave the main approval hierarchy alone but add additional approvers either before or after. The final option, Production, not available for all transactions, pertains to items that are generated by AME itself, such as a digital certificate that has an eSignature associated with it. These can be generated at a transaction, item, or approval level.

Action Types exist for each Rule Type and determine the hierarchy that will be used for the Rule Type. These hierarchies can be selected for the Oracle seeded hierarchies, such as Job or Position or Supervisory hierarchies, which are maintained within EBS itself and would require all people in the hierarchy to approve the transaction. Or you can shortcut the approval chain by only requiring the person's manager and the final approver, or just the final approver. This is also where you would decide to augment the approval hierarchy with additional users outside of the approval hierarchy, which would include the people set up in an Approval Group. It is the Rule Type that is associated with the Action Type that determines how the rule is called. The Action Types and Rule Types are used universally in AME and can be assigned to multiple transaction types. While some Rule Types can be added multiple times to a transaction and then assigned an order in which they are evaluated, each Action Type can be selected only one time for each transaction type and will appear grayed out when setting up a new Action-Rule combination.

The Rule Types and Action Types will also determine what *Actions* will need to be taken for the combination. These actions are different depending on the Rule Type and do not actually assign a specific action that will be followed; that is done when the Rule is created. Instead, it determines what actions *can* be assigned in the Rule.

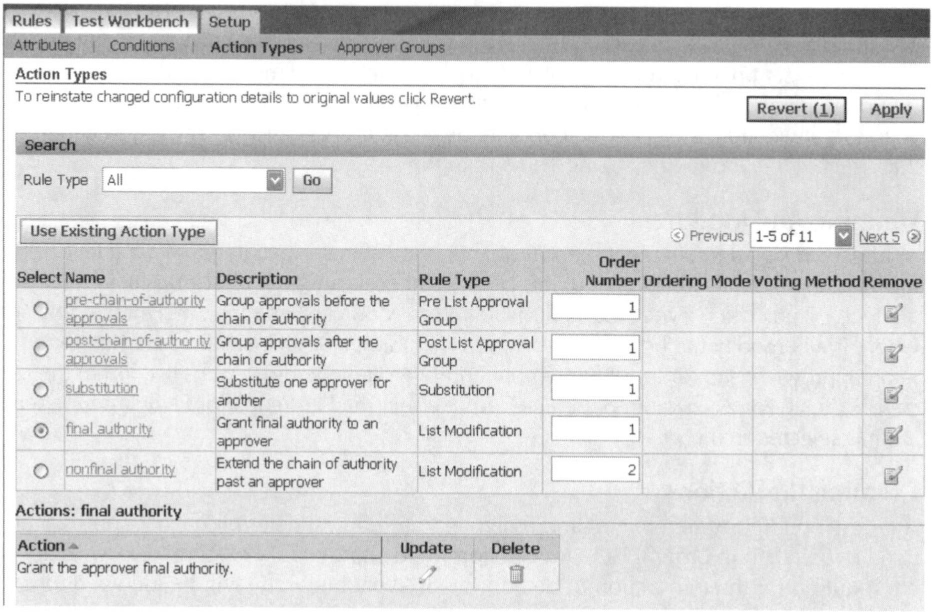

Select	Name	Description	Rule Type	Order Number	Ordering Mode	Voting Method	Remove
○	pre-chain-of-authority approvals	Group approvals before the chain of authority	Pre List Approval Group	1			☑
○	post-chain-of-authority approvals	Group approvals after the chain of authority	Post List Approval Group	1			☑
○	substitution	Substitute one approver for another	Substitution	1			☑
◉	final authority	Grant final authority to an approver	List Modification	1			☑
○	nonfinal authority	Extend the chain of authority past an approver	List Modification	2			☑

Actions: final authority

Action ▲	Update	Delete
Grant the approver final authority.	✎	🗑

Approvals Management Business Analyst | Business Analyst Dashboard | Select a Transaction Type | Action Types link

FIGURE A-5. *Associating Rule Types with Action Types, and their allowed Actions*

To create an Action Type for a specific Rule Type for your transaction, click the Use Existing Action Type button. When the new window opens up, select the Rule Type you want to create the action for, and select the Action Type you want to associate with it. Oracle will determine the Actions that can be used with this combination and will list them on the main Action Type window, seen in Figure A-5.

There are two other options that can be set, besides the ORDER NUMBER in which a rule will be considered. These options offer the final advantage to using AME. The first advantage is the ability to create a condition when a rule is followed. Second, you can create approval groups or hierarchies that are not part of Oracle's seeded hierarchy (Job, Position, and Supervisor). The third and final advantage is that you can determine the order in which approval notifications are sent out as well as when a transaction is actually approved.

The ORDER MODE can be set to Serial, where the approval requests are sent out one at a time and not advanced to the next person until the prior person has responded, while Parallel will send out all the approval requests at the same time. Sending out the approval requests at the same time has two distinct advantages. First, it can shorten the approval time. Second, it allows you to set up VOTING METHODS, which decides how responses from the users are evaluated. When the ORDERING mode is set to Serial, the VOTING METHOD should also be set to Serial. This means one approval request is sent out, and then the system waits for a response before moving on to the next approver. (Note: when you create a Rule, it is the Action you select for the Action Type that determines how many approvers are required.)

When the ORDERING MODE is parallel, however, then you can determine how the responses are going to be handled. When you select First Responder Wins for the VOTING METHOD, then the responses of the first responder(s) (how many will depend on the action selected when creating the rule) will be used to approve the transaction. Consensus, on the other hand, will wait until all the approvers have responded, and they approve or reject the transaction based on the general agreement of the approvers.

Adding Additional Approval Groups

The final step to setting up the components is to add any supplementary approval groups to your transaction. These bypass Oracle's seeded hierarchies, such as Position or Job or Supervisor, and create a group of users that can be used for approving a particular transaction. An example would be if the Collections Director needs to approve any credit memo request over $10,000, after the normal approval hierarchy has approved the request. In this case, you would create an approval group with this one person in it, and also create an Action Type for the Rule Type Post List Approval Group. There are predefined approval groups you can select from, and once an approval group is set, it is available to all transaction types. When adding an approval group, you can either select specific users in the Group Member section or use a SQL QUERY to find the approvers. The APPROVER TYPES that are available from the list are maintained in the Approvals Management Administrator under Approver Types (refer to Figure A-6).

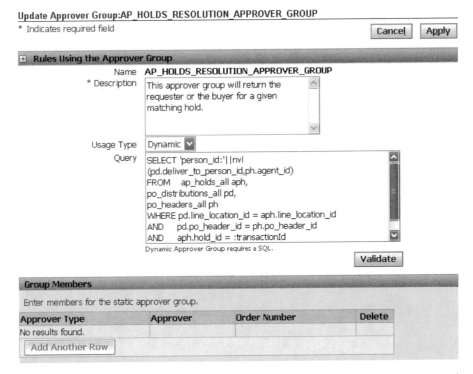

Approvals Management Business Analyst I Business Analyst Dashboard I Select a Transaction Type I Approver Groups

FIGURE A-6. *Creating a SQL Approver Group*

Combining the AME Components into a Rule

Once all the components have been set up, they are combined together to create a transaction-specific rule. Until this step is done, AME has no idea how to combine all the elements to create the If-Then-Else statement. To create a rule, assign it a unique NAME, and determine what RULE TYPE it will be. The Rule Types that are associated with a rule are the same Rule Types that are associated with each Action Type, with two additions. In addition to each individual Rule Type, you can combine different Rule Types to create a combined rule for list creation, and a separate combined rule for list modifications.

Shown in Figure A-7, this allows you to combine different actions into one rule. The PRIORITY field seen here is only available when AME has been configured to used priority modes to evaluate which rules are used when more than one rule applies to a transaction (Approvals Management Administrator | Configuration Variables | Rule Priority Modes). When any of the Rule Types has a priority DEFAULT set to either Absolute or Relative, then a priority can be added to each rule. Oracle evaluates each rule and its priority, comparing it to the value assigned to the Rule Type in the Rule Priority Mode, and determines if the rule is applicable or not. Absolute is evaluated by selecting any rule with a priority that is equal to or lower than the default assigned in the priority mode. Relative, on the other hand, is the maximum number of rules that can be considered for each Rule Type.

On the next window, select the conditions under which this rule will apply. These are the conditions that were created for your attributes. Then determine the Action Types and their associated actions you want to apply to these conditions. When you have set up a custom

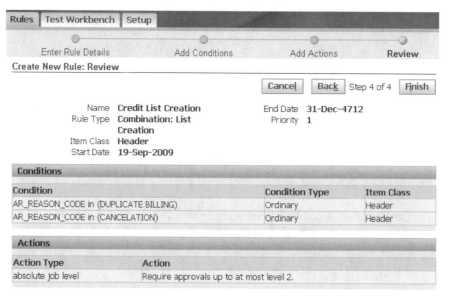

Approvals Management Business Analyst | Business Analyst Dashboard | Select a Transaction Type | Rules

FIGURE A-7. *Creating a combined rule*

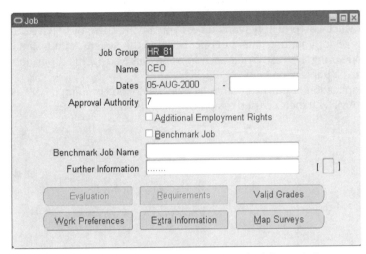

Human Resource Manager | Work Structures | Job | Description

FIGURE A-8. *Approval levels assigned to a position*

approval group, and you assign it to a rule, you are basically telling Oracle that when these conditions are met, this person is authorized to approve the transaction. What is a lot less apparent is who is authorized to approve a condition that is using one of the predefined approval hierarchies, such as Job, Position, or Supervisor. While the hierarchy path is different for each of these options, the approval limits are assigned for each person in the same place, which is on the Job that is associated with a person (Payables | Employees | Enter Employees when HR is a shared install) See Figure A-8 to add an APPROVAL AUTHORITY level. So a Job gets assigned an approval authority level, say of 1, which in turn gets associated with an employee. This means that every time a rule is set up with the Action of Requires Approvals up to at least (or most) level 1, all employees this job is associated with will be qualified to approve the transaction. The one that is selected will depend on the person who submitted the transaction that is being approved, and the hierarchy that is being followed.

Since each rule ties conditions to specific actions and Action Types, you will need to create multiple rules if you want different actions for the conditions. You will want to make sure that all transactions meet one of the rules that you have set up, especially if you determined that empty approval groups are not allowed, basically telling Oracle that all transactions must meet a condition and find an approver.

Testing Your Rules

As you can see, rules can get a little hairy, so Oracle provides two methods to test your rules. First, you can add different variables for your transaction and see which rule is selected. This is done by creating test cases. Or you can use an actual transaction from Oracle to see the path it follows by selecting the Run Real Transaction Test button. These real life tests are done by using the transaction_id you want to test. The easiest place to find this is with the Examine feature on the actual transaction (Help | Diagnostics | Examine). You will need either to have the apps password, which you probably won't unless you are the DBA, or to have the profile FND: Diagnostics set for your user; this can only be set in the System Administrator responsibility. Both tests are done using the Test Workbench in Approvals Management Business Analyst, after you have selected a transaction type.

Each application or transaction has its own way of determining if AME is used, and once it is turned on, AME will then be used to approve all those transactions.

Glossary

BS has its own set of terms and language, which I call Oracle-ese. The most commonly used terms in this text can be found here.

3-way matching   A purchase order option that allows invoices from Payables to be matched to both a purchase order and its receipts.

Advance Shipment Notice (ASN)   Notifications received electronically from a supplier when they ship an order, alerting you to the anticipated receipt date as well as the items and quantities shipped. Can be used to create receipts on the expected delivery date.

Approvals Management Engine (AME)   A module that comes delivered with EBS (it is not a separate license) and can be used to configure both hierarchical and non-hierarchical rules for approving, among other things, expense reports, credit memos initiated from iReceivables, and Requisitions.

balancing segment   A segment in the General Ledger chart of accounts where debits must always equal credits, often referred to as Company or Entity.

business group   A grouping of employees in EBS.

chart of accounts   The accounting flexfield used to track all financial transactions.

Concurrent (Processing) Manager   A method used in EBS to run reports and processes.

cross-validation rules (CVRs)   A set of defined rules in EBS that control the account combinations that can be created.

descriptive flexfields   Also called DFF, these are fields denoted with [] on different windows that can be enabled to track data specific to your company.

dynamic insertion   The ability to create flexfield value combinations on the fly in EBS, based on rules defined in the cross-validation rules.

flexfield   A definable and flexible field in the Oracle database for storing data.

General Ledger key flexfield   The EBS name for the segment definitions in a chart of accounts.

iExpense (also called Internet Expense)   A web-based interface for submitting, approving, and monitoring expense reports and settlements. Can be integrated with credit card feeds from your bank.

internal requisition   A request made to purchase an item from within your own organization, usually associated with an internal sales order from the shipping organization (also called the IR-ISO process in Oracle).

internally sourced items   Items set up and maintained within Oracle Purchasing (even if they are purchased from a supplier).

inventory organization   Groupings of locations within a warehouse for processing inventory transactions.

iProcurement   A web-based interface for buying or requesting items or receiving orders that integrates to Purchasing.

iReceivables   A web-based interface for reviewing receivables transactions, such as invoices, credit memos, and payments, which allows both credit requests and payment submissions.

iSupplier Portal   A module that integrates with Purchasing and Payables, allowing suppliers to see invoice and purchase order statuses, request updates, and see statistics about specific supplier information.

key flexfield (KFF)   A required but flexible field in EBS. Key flexfields include such things as General Ledger account numbers (Accounting flexfield), item numbers, and item categories.

Ledger   Defined by the 4 C's—Chart of accounts, Calendar, Currency, and aCcounting methods—where transactions are segregated according to this commonality.

legal entities   Literally, the entities responsible for paying obligations, including invoices and payroll, or performing any transaction.

list of values   A predefined list of fields that users can select from when entering data on a form. Fields that are associated with a list of values are identified with a small box with three dots in it (...). Lists of values are most often defined as a key flexfield, a descriptive flexfield, or a lookup code.

MOAC (Multi-Org Access Control)   Allows multiple operating units to be accessed from one responsibility.

Multi-Org   The ability to set up and use multiple operating units within Oracle. Even when only one operating unit is set up, most implementations are still Multi-Org, allowing the ability to have more than one in the future.

operating unit   Also known as an Org or Organization in EBS, segregates data in submodules like Receivables and Payables. MOAC allows operating units to be grouped for centralized access. This is not to be confused with an inventory organization, which is one level lower and only pertains to inventory transactions.

Oracle Exchange   A free hosted site provided by Oracle to enable iProcurement punchouts to supplier sites. *https://exchange.oracle.com.*

Oracle Supplier Network   A free hosted site provided to Oracle to enable electronic document exchange and supplier collaboration. Can be used with iSupplier Portal. *https://osn.oracle.com.*

Order Information Portal   A web-based interface for viewing order and shipping information.

organization   Organizations are defined at several levels in EBS. The more commonly used ones include Business Group, Legal Entity, Operating Unit, and Inventory Organization.

outside processing   Items and services sourced to a third-party supplier that are used in a manufacturing process.

party   Both customers and suppliers are part of the Trading Community Architecture (TCA) in R12, and are called parties. These parties represent entities (corporations and individuals) your organization legally does business with.

Processing (Concurrent) Manager   A method used in EBS to run reports and processes.

profile option   A variable that is set in System Administration for any of the system levels as well as the user level. The system profiles can be set for Site, Application, Responsibility, or User, controlling certain features of the system.

punchin   Allows suppliers using Oracle Supplier Network to request access to iSupplier Portal to manage and inquire on purchase orders, deliver document approvals and advanced shipment notices, and view invoice and payment information.

punchout   Allows requestors to shop suppliers' catalogs via secure and private web sites, bringing the shopping carts back into Oracle to submit for approval and processing by purchasing.

requestor   The employee, or shopper, who is requesting an item or service to be purchased, and is usually the same as the person entering in the requisition.

responsibility   A grouping of forms (functions) and reports that can be assigned to specific users or roles (which then get assigned to users). Also, many system profiles are set at the Responsibility level, controlling the data that is accessed (such as when a ledger is assigned) or how the system behaves (such as when sequential numbering is set).

return material authorization (RMA)   Items authorized for return from customers against a previously shipped order.

seeded   Data that gets installed with the base EBS database and is accessible for all companies to use is referred to as seeded. Some seed data can be disabled if it is not going to be used, while other data is required to stay active for the system to function properly.

segment qualifier   Additional attributes added to a flexfield to provide additional functionality.

Services Procurement   A licensed Oracle product used to procure and track contractor requisitions in iProcurement.

shopping cart   Items selected for purchase.

site   An address associated to a specific supplier or customer.

subledger   Subledgers refer to non–General Ledger modules that are available from EBS, such as Payables and Receivables.

Subledger Accounting (SLA)   Also known as Accounting Methods, provides rules for how subledger transactions are accounted and represented in the General Ledger.

supplier-sourced items   Items available from a transparent punchout.

transparent punchout   Allows items from a supplier's web site to be returned during searches in iProcurement. This differs from a regular punchout, where the shopper will access the supplier's web site to search for and purchase items.

Vacation Rules   A rule defined in Oracle for a particular user to transfer or delegate approval authority while that user is out of the office.

value set   Value sets are lists of data that are both used by EBS's programs and selected and entered by users. They can be as important as valid General Ledger account numbers, and as trivial as a designation for a supplier. Value sets can be added not only for custom data, like your Accounting flexfield, but also to restrict data allowed in descriptive flexfields. These are also a good way to track data that may change for custom reporting so that users, not just programmers, will have access to make updates. When multiple languages are installed, EBS also uses value sets to store translated data.

workflow   A workflow is a service used by certain EBS functions either to process a transaction, based on a set of rules, or to send a notification to a specific person or group of people for information or to request an action or approval.

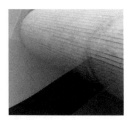

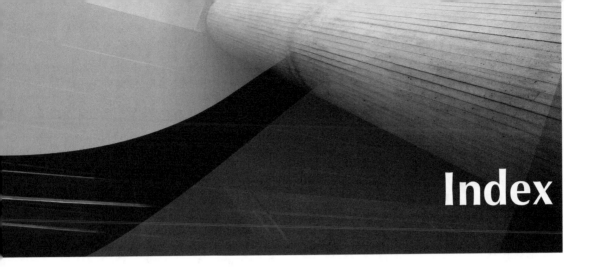

Index

References to figures and illustrations are in italics.

GET YOUR FREE SUBSCRIPTION
TO *ORACLE MAGAZINE*

Oracle Magazine is essential gear for today's information technology professionals.
Stay informed and increase your productivity with every issue of *Oracle Magazine*.
Inside each free bimonthly issue you'll get:

- Up-to-date information on Oracle Database, Oracle Application Server, Web development, enterprise grid computing, database technology, and business trends
- Third-party news and announcements
- Technical articles on Oracle and partner products, technologies, and operating environments
- Development and administration tips
- Real-world customer stories

If there are other Oracle users at your location who would like to receive their own subscription to *Oracle Magazine*, please photocopy this form and pass it along.

Three easy ways to subscribe:

① Web
Visit our Web site at **oracle.com/oraclemagazine**
You'll find a subscription form there, plus much more

② Fax
Complete the questionnaire on the back of this card
and fax the questionnaire side only to **+1.847.763.9638**

③ Mail
Complete the questionnaire on the back of this card
and mail it to **P.O. Box 1263, Skokie, IL 60076-8263**

ORACLE®

Want your own FREE subscription?

To receive a free subscription to *Oracle Magazine*, you must fill out the entire card, sign it, and date it (incomplete cards cannot be processed or acknowledged). You can also fax your application to +1.847.763.9638. **Or subscribe at our Web site at oracle.com/oraclemagazine**

O **Yes, please send me a FREE subscription *Oracle Magazine*.**   O No.

O From time to time, Oracle Publishing allows our partners exclusive access to our e-mail addresses for special promotions and announcements. To be included in this program, please check this circle. If you do not wish to be included, you will only receive notices about your subscription via e-mail.

O Oracle Publishing allows sharing of our postal mailing list with selected third parties. If you prefer your mailing address not to be included in this program, please check this circle.

If at any time you would like to be removed from either mailing list, please contact Customer Service at +1.847.763.9635 or send an e-mail to oracle@halldata.com. If you opt in to the sharing of information, Oracle may also provide you with e-mail related to Oracle products, services, and events. If you want to completely unsubscribe from any e-mail communication from Oracle, please send an e-mail to: unsubscribe@oracle-mail.com with the following in the subject line: REMOVE [your e-mail address]. For complete information on Oracle Publishing's privacy practices, please visit oracle.com/html/privacy/html

X

signature (required)   date

name   title

company   e-mail address

street/p.o. box

city/state/zip or postal code   telephone

country   fax

Would you like to receive your free subscription in digital format instead of print if it becomes available? O Yes O No

---

YOU MUST ANSWER ALL 10 QUESTIONS BELOW.

① WHAT IS THE PRIMARY BUSINESS ACTIVITY OF YOUR FIRM AT THIS LOCATION? (check one only)

- ☐ 01 Aerospace and Defense Manufacturing
- ☐ 02 Application Service Provider
- ☐ 03 Automotive Manufacturing
- ☐ 04 Chemicals
- ☐ 05 Media and Entertainment
- ☐ 06 Construction/Engineering
- ☐ 07 Consumer Sector/Consumer Packaged Goods
- ☐ 08 Education
- ☐ 09 Financial Services/Insurance
- ☐ 10 Health Care
- ☐ 11 High Technology Manufacturing, OEM
- ☐ 12 Industrial Manufacturing
- ☐ 13 Independent Software Vendor
- ☐ 14 Life Sciences (biotech, pharmaceuticals)
- ☐ 15 Natural Resources
- ☐ 16 Oil and Gas
- ☐ 17 Professional Services
- ☐ 18 Public Sector (government)
- ☐ 19 Research
- ☐ 20 Retail/Wholesale/Distribution
- ☐ 21 Systems Integrator, VAR/VAD
- ☐ 22 Telecommunications
- ☐ 23 Travel and Transportation
- ☐ 24 Utilities (electric, gas, sanitation, water)
- ☐ 98 Other Business and Services _____

② WHICH OF THE FOLLOWING BEST DESCRIBES YOUR PRIMARY JOB FUNCTION? (check one only)

CORPORATE MANAGEMENT/STAFF
- ☐ 01 Executive Management (President, Chair, CEO, CFO, Owner, Partner, Principal)
- ☐ 02 Finance/Administrative Management (VP/Director/ Manager/Controller, Purchasing, Administration)
- ☐ 03 Sales/Marketing Management (VP/Director/Manager)
- ☐ 04 Computer Systems/Operations Management (CIO/VP/Director/Manager MIS/IS/IT, Ops)

IS/IT STAFF
- ☐ 05 Application Development/Programming Management
- ☐ 06 Application Development/Programming Staff
- ☐ 07 Consulting
- ☐ 08 DBA/Systems Administrator
- ☐ 09 Education/Training
- ☐ 10 Technical Support Director/Manager
- ☐ 11 Other Technical Management/Staff
- ☐ 98 Other

③ WHAT IS YOUR CURRENT PRIMARY OPERATING PLATFORM (check all that apply)

- ☐ 01 Digital Equipment Corp UNIX/VAX/VMS
- ☐ 02 HP UNIX
- ☐ 03 IBM AIX
- ☐ 04 IBM UNIX
- ☐ 05 Linux (Red Hat)
- ☐ 06 Linux (SUSE)
- ☐ 07 Linux (Oracle Enterprise)
- ☐ 08 Linux (other)
- ☐ 09 Macintosh
- ☐ 10 MVS
- ☐ 11 Netware
- ☐ 12 Network Computing
- ☐ 13 SCO UNIX
- ☐ 14 Sun Solaris/SunOS
- ☐ 15 Windows
- ☐ 16 Other UNIX
- ☐ 98 Other
- ☐ 99 None of the Above

④ DO YOU EVALUATE, SPECIFY, RECOMMEND, OR AUTHORIZE THE PURCHASE OF ANY OF THE FOLLOWING? (check all that apply)

- ☐ 01 Hardware
- ☐ 02 Business Applications (ERP, CRM, etc.)
- ☐ 03 Application Development Tools
- ☐ 04 Database Products
- ☐ 05 Internet or Intranet Products
- ☐ 06 Other Software
- ☐ 07 Middleware Products
- ☐ 99 None of the Above

⑤ IN YOUR JOB, DO YOU USE OR PLAN TO PURCHASE ANY OF THE FOLLOWING PRODUCTS? (check all that apply)

SOFTWARE
- ☐ 01 CAD/CAE/CAM
- ☐ 02 Collaboration Software
- ☐ 03 Communications
- ☐ 04 Database Management
- ☐ 05 File Management
- ☐ 06 Finance
- ☐ 07 Java
- ☐ 08 Multimedia Authoring
- ☐ 09 Networking
- ☐ 10 Programming
- ☐ 11 Project Management
- ☐ 12 Scientific and Engineering
- ☐ 13 Systems Management
- ☐ 14 Workflow

HARDWARE
- ☐ 15 Macintosh
- ☐ 16 Mainframe
- ☐ 17 Massively Parallel Processing

- ☐ 18 Minicomputer
- ☐ 19 Intel x86(32)
- ☐ 20 Intel x86(64)
- ☐ 21 Network Computer
- ☐ 22 Symmetric Multiprocessing
- ☐ 23 Workstation Services

SERVICES
- ☐ 24 Consulting
- ☐ 25 Education/Training
- ☐ 26 Maintenance
- ☐ 27 Online Database
- ☐ 28 Support
- ☐ 29 Technology-Based Training
- ☐ 30 Other
- ☐ 99 None of the Above

⑥ WHAT IS YOUR COMPANY'S SIZE? (check one only)

- ☐ 01 More than 25,000 Employees
- ☐ 02 10,001 to 25,000 Employees
- ☐ 03 5,001 to 10,000 Employees
- ☐ 04 1,001 to 5,000 Employees
- ☐ 05 101 to 1,000 Employees
- ☐ 06 Fewer than 100 Employees

⑦ DURING THE NEXT 12 MONTHS, HOW MUCH DO YOU ANTICIPATE YOUR ORGANIZATION WILL SPEND ON COMPUTER HARDWARE, SOFTWARE, PERIPHERALS, AND SERVICES FOR YOUR LOCATION? (check one only)

- ☐ 01 Less than $10,000
- ☐ 02 $10,000 to $49,999
- ☐ 03 $50,000 to $99,999
- ☐ 04 $100,000 to $499,999
- ☐ 05 $500,000 to $999,999
- ☐ 06 $1,000,000 and Over

⑧ WHAT IS YOUR COMPANY'S YEARLY SALES REVENUE? (check one only)

- ☐ 01 $500, 000, 000 and above
- ☐ 02 $100, 000, 000 to $500, 000, 000
- ☐ 03 $50, 000, 000 to $100, 000, 000
- ☐ 04 $5, 000, 000 to $50, 000, 000
- ☐ 05 $1, 000, 000 to $5, 000, 000

⑨ WHAT LANGUAGES AND FRAMEWORKS DO YOU USE? (check all that apply)

- ☐ 01 Ajax
- ☐ 02 C
- ☐ 03 C++
- ☐ 04 C#
- ☐ 13 Python
- ☐ 14 Ruby/Rails
- ☐ 15 Spring
- ☐ 16 Struts
- ☐ 05 Hibernate
- ☐ 06 J++/J#
- ☐ 07 Java
- ☐ 08 JSP
- ☐ 09 .NET
- ☐ 10 Perl
- ☐ 11 PHP
- ☐ 12 PL/SQL
- ☐ 17 SQL
- ☐ 18 Visual Basic
- ☐ 98 Other

⑩ WHAT ORACLE PRODUCTS ARE IN USE AT YOUR SITE? (check all that apply)

ORACLE DATABASE
- ☐ 01 Oracle Database 11*g*
- ☐ 02 Oracle Database 10*g*
- ☐ 03 Oracle9*i* Database
- ☐ 04 Oracle Embedded Database (Oracle Lite, Times Ten, Berkeley DB)
- ☐ 05 Other Oracle Database Release

ORACLE FUSION MIDDLEWARE
- ☐ 06 Oracle Application Server
- ☐ 07 Oracle Portal
- ☐ 08 Oracle Enterprise Manager
- ☐ 09 Oracle BPEL Process Manager
- ☐ 10 Oracle Identity Management
- ☐ 11 Oracle SOA Suite
- ☐ 12 Oracle Data Hubs

ORACLE DEVELOPMENT TOOLS
- ☐ 13 Oracle JDeveloper
- ☐ 14 Oracle Forms
- ☐ 15 Oracle Reports
- ☐ 16 Oracle Designer
- ☐ 17 Oracle Discoverer
- ☐ 18 Oracle BI Beans
- ☐ 19 Oracle Warehouse Builder
- ☐ 20 Oracle WebCenter
- ☐ 21 Oracle Application Express

ORACLE APPLICATIONS
- ☐ 22 Oracle E-Business Suite
- ☐ 23 PeopleSoft Enterprise
- ☐ 24 JD Edwards EnterpriseOne
- ☐ 25 JD Edwards World
- ☐ 26 Oracle Fusion
- ☐ 27 Hyperion
- ☐ 28 Siebel CRM

ORACLE SERVICES
- ☐ 28 Oracle E-Business Suite On Demand
- ☐ 29 Oracle Technology On Demand
- ☐ 30 Siebel CRM On Demand
- ☐ 31 Oracle Consulting
- ☐ 32 Oracle Education
- ☐ 33 Oracle Support
- ☐ 98 Other
- ☐ 99 None of the Above